MILNER

Terence H. O'Brien

MILNER

Viscount Milner of St James's and Cape Town

1854–1925

Constable London

First published in Great Britain 1979
by Constable and Company Ltd
10 Orange Street London WC2H 7EG
Copyright © 1979 by Terence O'Brien

British Library CIP data

O'Brien, Terence
Milner.
1. Milner, Alfred, *Viscount Milner*
2. South Africa – Governors – Biography
941.083′092′4   DT776.M6

ISBN 0 09 457880 X

Set in Monotype Fournier 12pt
Printed in Great Britain by
The Anchor Press Ltd, and bound by
Wm Brendon & Son Ltd, both of
Tiptree, Essex

To Renée and Imogen with love and gratitude

For there is good news yet to hear and fine things
    to be seen,
Before we go to Paradise by way of Kensal Green.

G. K. CHESTERTON

Contents

Illustrations

For forms of government let fools contest;
Whate'er is best administered, is best:
For modes of faith let graceless zealots fight;
His can't be wrong whose life is in the right:
In faith and hope the world will disagree,
But all mankind's concern is charity:
All must be false which thwart this one great end.

Pope, *An Essay on Man*, III

Foreword

History has not dealt kindly with Alfred Milner, largely by accident and by default. He is in part to blame for not wanting his official biography to be written, for possessing a self-effacing nature and for writing private and confidential letters on his work which, even by the standards of his day, were inordinately long. It can be said that all his life these letters were Balliol essays parading the arguments against the policy he thought proper, then refuting them as a prelude to arguing in detail what ought to be done.

Fifty years after his death two biographies of him have been written and other posthumous books about him are a handful. He happened to marry late in life a lady of strong will and, for her day, unusual literary talents, who outlived him by thirty-three years. As she had every right to do Lady Milner jealously guarded his large collection of papers; and, it appears, paid almost exclusive attention to defending his controversial South African service. She employed Cecil Headlam to make a selection of Milner's South African papers. But her plan to publish material on his later career came to nothing.

The first posthumous biography, Sir Evelyn Wrench's *Alfred, Lord Milner*, was written under her eye in the last years of her life. It gives a larger selection in time of Milner's letters; but these are often too little edited and crowd out much which took place of significance in his life. Neither this book nor any other describes with much detail his second and more important public service, his work with Lloyd George in the First World War and the peacemaking which followed.

Two South African historians, J. S. Marais and G. Le May, divide between them his work in their country of which they take an unfavourable view. A. M. Gollin's *Proconsul in Politics*, concerned with his later political role, completes the handful of studies of substance on Milner. Though useful, this paints Milner, in this writer's opinion, too much as the leader of a cult and a conspiratorial figure; and it seems to misjudge his contribution to the War and his views on the Peace which came after. An attempt to present a fuller, more balanced view of Milner's work and opinions seems now to be due.

He will always be a controversial figure presenting contradictory features. He was autocratic by nature, impatient of disorder and muddle and incompetent leaders, feeling (which was probably often true) that he could do a job better himself. Yet he accepted democracy as inevitable, and worked to the limit of his strength, without arrogance and in harmony with all kinds of men, to guide it. He was an idealist with intense moral convictions on certain subjects; yet a realist with awareness of the practical limitations of his schemes for which he has seldom been given enough credit. He had powers of expression which sometimes led him to make extreme statements in public or in private letters, which were rarely reflected in his actions. He faced a real dilemma in his dedication since his undergraduate days to the State and yet uncertainty how best to serve it. His latent distrust of party politics grew stronger when, in middle age, he observed it at first hand in South Africa and later on in Britain.

His first weapon was not intrigue but persuasion. He was tireless in trying to make allies in the small ruling class of his day – the trustees, as he saw them, of an adolescent democracy – for the policies he believed in. He put much trust in administration, an activity in which he excelled but which is hard to define, as a prime means of improving society. For him this meant not government by one man but government *through* men. His patience with colleagues and subordinates less able and slower than himself was almost boundless. To study his papers is to learn that not only Milnerites but persons of many persuasions who worked with him or for him acquired admiration and affection for him as a man.

In public matters his most intense convictions were for the British race and Empire, which must be seen in the context of his times. Race did not mean for him something reactionary or exclusive. He saw the British of the Late Victorian and Edwardian eras as a creative civilizing force which, in a competitive world still dominated by Europe, alone could hold together and adapt to new conditions the Empire as it then existed. His aim has been called more spiritual than material. But his practical instinct did not envisage a united British South Africa or some kind of Imperial Council as things which could be quickly achieved.

Was he then a supporter of lost causes? And how much did what the *Oxford Magazine* called after his death a 'perceptible German tinge' influence his make-up? The reader must be left to frame answers from his frank statements, by necessity much condensed, in this story. It can be argued that he made real contributions to the progress in his lifetime of both his chief aims. South Africa never became as British as he had hoped, but he and his staff laid the foundations of a Union which under Botha and Smuts leant strongly towards the British connection. During 1916–19 the Imperial Executive he desired came, largely by his efforts, into being. It was only in his last years that, as he was aware, the centrifugal forces began to erode such close Imperial co-operation.

My first thanks must be to the Warden and Fellows of New College, Oxford, the owners of the bulk of Milner's papers, for permission to study and publish what I chose of their material. It has formed the principal source of all that follows. It is convenient to add here that in his earlier years Milner occasionally kept a diary for brief periods; from the age of nearly forty until his death he kept one daily with only rare interruptions. It is tantalizing to think what this might have revealed had he chosen, which he did not, to comment on some of the many public persons he knew. In fact it is an engagement book, highly discreet and designed it would seem as an aid to his memory. The most he allows himself is to allude to some talks and meetings, for example of the War Cabinet, as 'unsatisfactory'.

My second main obligation is to the Bodleian Library, on two counts. To the Curators for a similar permission with regard to a number of manuscript collections which are their property. Then to D. S. Porter and others of the staff of the Western Manuscripts Department for their knowledge and unfailing helpfulness with advice. Their generosity enabled me to persevere and complete what, as those who have studied Milner's papers will know, was an arduous task.

I am also grateful to the following for allowing me to make use of family and other archives: Viscount Harcourt; Mrs. Gell; the Governors of King's School, Canterbury; Sir Edward and the Hon. Lady Ford; the Director of the National Army Museum; the New Beaverbrook Foundation; the Clerk of the Records of the House of Lords and the Courtauld Institute for the use of material formerly in the Beaverbrook Library; the late Sir Walter Moberly and the Board of the British Library.

Those to whom I feel especially grateful for information and advice are: the Rev. Canon J. H. Edmonds, Headmaster of the Junior School (Milner Court), King's School, Canterbury; E. V. Quinn, Fellow and Librarian of Balliol College; the 6th Earl of Harrow by (Viscount Sandon during Milner's last period of public office); the Warden and the Librarian and his staff of Rhodes House; the staff of the Historical Manuscripts Commission; Helen, Lady Hardinge of Penshurst, and her daughter the Hon. Mrs. Johnston; and Miss Mary Potter for the map of Southern Africa.

Oxford, 1976

Part I

APPRENTICESHIP

Chapter 1

Youth

(March 1854 – December 1872)

Boyhood in Germany and England – Mary Milner's
Death – King's College, London

Alfred Milner was born on 23 March 1854 at Giessen, Hesse-Darmstadt,
a small university town some fifty miles east of the Rhine. His mother
Mary Cromie, a widow of forty-two living in Bonn, had recently engaged
Charles Milner, a medical student of twenty-three, as tutor to her two
elder boys. Mary and Charles were then married by the British chaplain
at Cologne on 9 December 1853. Alfred became their only child.

Towards the end of his life Milner said he had been born with a copper
spoon in his mouth. His boyhood did not prove easy and in adolescence
tragedy overtook him. Thereafter his progress depended much on his
own efforts.

Charles Milner came of English north-country commercial stock. His
grandfather James had founded a Manchester firm of merchants and
fustian manufacturers, and by 1795 was living in some style in a house
he had built at Patricroft outside Manchester. His eldest son, James
Richardson Milner, started a branch of the family business in 1805 in the
Rhineland engaging *inter alia* in shipping wine. In the 1820s he was
living in Düsseldorf where he married Sophia von Rappard, the daughter
of an important German official of Aachen and his wife Anna, *née* Focke,
the offspring of an ancient Dutch family. Charles, Alfred's father, was
born near Düsseldorf, the eldest of six children.

From the records which survive it seems that James Milner the Manchester merchant died in the year of Charles's birth, and that the firm he
had founded more or less died with him. Many years later one of Alfred's
few known English relatives on his father's side, writing to him about
family history, concluded that the French wars and James Richardson's
venture in Germany had been 'disastrous for the English firm' which was
certainly wound up not later than the death of its founder in 1830.[1] In any
case James Richardson stayed in the Rhineland and his sons, except
Charles, married German wives, became German subjects and begot
numerous children.

Mary Ierne Cromie had been born in 1811, the second daughter of Major-General (as he became) John Ready. Whereas the Milners, up to the time of James Richardson's emigration and marriage, were unmistakably English of the commercial class, the Readys were unmistakably English of the military class. The General's grandfather, born in the year of Queen Anne's accession, was a Captain, of East Grinstead. John Ready, born in 1774, married Susan Bramley who gave him two sons and two daughters, including Mary, and died young. He was appointed in George IV's reign Lieutenant-Governor of Prince Edward Island. The historian of this province wrote to Milner years later that he was the best Lieutenant-Governor the Island ever had; energetic, popular and much concerned with the Island's welfare.[2] Appointed in 1832 to be Lieutenant-Governor of the Isle of Man he remained there until his death thirteen years later. Four years after his arrival, at the age of 62, he married a second wife, Sarah Tobin, daughter of Sir John Tobin of Liverpool. She bore him a daughter and a son, whose descendants carried on the Readys' Army tradition. As a boy Alfred Milner formed close ties with his mother's relations and descendants, which he kept up all through his life.

In 1837, the year after her father's remarriage, Mary Ready married Captain St. George Cromie of the 34th Regiment of Foot (later the Border Regiment, 1st Bn), younger son of the Rev. John Cromie, of The Neale, Co. Mayo. Records of her girlhood and first marriage, which lasted fourteen years, are scant. Her elder sister, Susan, had died aged 18 soon after her father went to Prince Edward Island. Long afterwards Alfred Milner, when High Commissioner for South Africa, through what seems a chance association, was writing to persons in Charlottetown about Susan Ready's grave and being sent local newspaper cuttings. An elderly lady remembered Mary Ready as 'very gay and sprightly, fond of riding and often to be seen on her beautiful mare "Columbine" '. It gives a clue to Milner's affections to read that after returning to England in 1905 he asked a Ready uncle about this mare, learning that in 1826 the Governor had shipped two thoroughbreds to the Island at his own expense to improve the breed in the colony.

Odd sheets of a journal kept by Mary in her early twenties on the Isle of Man offer something more substantial. She was deeply in love with Cromie, though for reasons not apparent the path of their love was often far from smooth. In this situation, her account of their 'suffering' and advice to her lover have a ring of uncommon generosity. Some notes of books read show that her reading was unusual for a young woman of her class at the time of Queen Victoria's accession. Scott, Disraeli's *The Young Duke*, Bulwer and other novels are outnumbered by works of

English history and biography, some political economy, a little German, a history of America and lectures on St. Paul.

In a storm that blew round Milner's head long after her death Mary Ready was described as 'an Irish lady'; but no evidence exists to contradict Milner's assertion that she was 'of pure English descent for many generations'.[3] Milner's own and his father's German background were much later and especially in the Boer War and the First World War to cause him a good deal of embarrassment. St. George Cromie, however, as his name might suggest, was Anglo-Irish. His father, a parson, married a daughter of the first Lord Kilmaine, became the valued agent in Ireland of his brother-in-law the second peer and was rewarded by being housed probably free of rent in The Neale, Co. Mayo. There is proof that St. George and Mary had settled in a modest house near Hollymount not far from this place by 1840. A son, John, was born to them in 1839 and another, Charles, two years later. St. George Cromie was shot, possibly in some agrarian outrage, in 1852.[4]

It is a pity these facts cannot be supplemented, less in order to reconstruct Mary Cromie's story than to learn what effect her tragic Irish experience had upon Alfred Milner. The Neale was the place to which John Browne, an Englishman and founder of the Kilmaine family, had gone in the reign of Elizabeth I to help in the composition of Mayo. Whatever else may be said about Mayo in the 1850s it is agreed that it had ceased to be composed. Michael Davitt, for example, concludes that it 'suffered more from the manifold evils of the landlord system than any other Irish county' and adds it was 'no tame sufferer under landlordism'.[5] The horrors of the Famine were followed in 1849–51 by wholesale evictions, emigration, congested workhouses, crime. What of all this, one would like to know, did Mary talk about later to her precocious boy Alfred? Did her experiences contribute to his energetic opposition, as a young man in the mid-'80s and again before 1914, to Home Rule for Ireland?

Her second marriage failed to bring Mary Milner ease of financial circumstances or freedom from care. Charles continued his medical studies for a time at Giessen and then the family returned to Bonn, where Alfred was baptized by the British chaplain on 21 December 1854. In the autumn of the next year, when Alfred was one-and-a-half, the family moved south to the pleasant town of Tübingen in the Kingdom of Württemberg. Some difference with his Bonn professor, Tübingen's cheapness and facilities for *die Jagd*, to which Charles was very devoted, were the reasons for choice of this place, which was to remain the centre of the lives of the parents and of the boyhood of their youngest child.

They took with them as tutor to the Cromie boys a medical student, to whom Charles was much attached, Albert Günther, who had taken his *Doktorat* at Tübingen University and written a book on the fishes of the River Neckar.[6] Charles Milner took his M.D. at Tübingen in 1856.

Basil Williams charitably calls Charles Milner 'a man of brilliant parts but with interests too varied to make him a success in his chosen profession'.[7] It seems more true to conclude that he had chosen the wrong profession, or even that he found any recognized profession distasteful. Alfred Milner is alleged to have said that his father had 'thrice my brains'. If so, he always found difficulty in applying them. His efforts to get work during the next few years were unsuccessful. Two years after he had qualified Mary wrote to Günther in London that 'Milner is still without anything in the shape of employment, which is very trying to us both', but 'we all like Tübingen as much as ever'. Then later 'My dear Doctor' is still looking for an outlet though having 'continued delight in the joys of the chase'. In the meantime 'dear wee Alfred . . . a quaint little man' was growing stout, showing a keen interest in birds, fishes and Tübingen uniforms but putting up resistance (at five and a half) to being taught to read. 'I am sure,' she wrote confidently, 'the brains are there whenever they are called into action.'

In the spring of 1860 the family moved to London, probably at Mary's urging and certainly into the company of Mary's relations. General Ready's family had developed close associations through marriage and friendship with the Anglican Church. The Milners, described as very poor, lived first in lodgings off the Old Kent Road found for them by Mary's cousin Mrs. Snape, wife of the vicar of St. Mary Magdalene. After a bit they moved to the home in St. George's Square, Pimlico, of John Malcolm, son of Mary's aunt Jane Ready, a widower to whom and to whose only child Marianne she became most attached. Malcolm's sister, Mrs. Benjamin Jones, lived in some splendour in Cheyne Walk. Another of Mary's cousins had married the Rev. Gerald Blunt, just appointed Rector of St. Luke's , Chelsea, friend of Carlyle, Rossetti and other celebrities and father of seven children about Alfred Milner's age.

Dr. Charles set up his plate as a G.P. in Paulton's Square, Chelsea, in 1861. So from soon after his sixth birthday until he was twelve and a half Alfred lived, though his parents were far from affluent, in the lush, serene, Victorian world in its heyday. If employment for 'the Doctor' (as Charles was generally known) proved elusive and the Milners' income was small, hospitality and practical help never seemed lacking. The milieu was that of self-assured, middle-class Victorians, much connected with service to Church and State, much occupied with family matters, and considerate towards those inside or outside their circle whose misfortune came to their notice.

Mary and Charles were both at home in this milieu, and well liked; and their sociable natures and this environment had a lasting effect on young Alfred. 'The Doctor' was happy, gaining the special affection of the young; a figure, in the memory of one of the Blunt boys, of 'brightness and twinkling gaiety'.[8] He did much walking with the Rector, a knapsack tour of the Lake Country and long excursions during holidays at Brighton. As a first-class shot he soon became a sergeant in the Chelsea Company of the South Middlesex Rifle Volunteers. His happiness, however, was now marred by ill-health. Mary wrote in the summer of 1863 that he was 'freer from pain than he has been for a very long time'.

By then he had been practising for over a year at 23 Danvers Street, 'a little house out of the bustle and noise', five minutes from the buses of the King's Road and three from Cheyne Walk and the boats of the Thames. Alfred, nine years old, learnt Latin from his father and other subjects from Charles Cromie, and his parents were clearly exercised about his schooling. Hopes arose of some employment for 'the Doctor' at Malvern College, then being built; and Mary showed her decided preference for England by confiding to Marianne Malcolm that her present conditions

made the atmosphere of my life far other than it has been for many years . . . for me to have a first hope of holding on by old England at all will be an incalculable comfort.

Holding on for much longer to old England was not, however, to be her destiny. The Malvern job failed to materialize; and Alfred was sent to St. Peter's, Eaton Square church school in Lower Belgrave Street, which still stands on its corner site. Mary became occupied over the future of her elder sons, John eventually going to India as a railway engineer and Charles to the silk trade in China. In the summer of 1866 'the Doctor' accepted employment as a *Lektor* in English Literature in Tübingen University at a salary of £80 a year. Plans were begun for the family to return there, to be followed by various English boys who as Dr. Charles's pupils would provide an additional source of income. Before they left Alfred had justified his mother's confidence by becoming head boy of St. Peter's School.

From the autumn of 1866 until his mother's death three years later Tübingen was Alfred's home, and it seems that his holidays were confined to the Black Forest and other places within easy distance. Attending the *Gymnasium*, which he disliked, he grew tall, well grounded in the Classics and in 3 years reached the top of the school. Mary's surviving well-written letters give a picture of the Tübingen household, in which she was clearly the dominating figure. It is evident, as much from what she neglects to say as from what she says, that her rule was based on self-abnegation, and the philosophy, which she writes she has only lately acquired, that the 'doubts and dreads' of the human condition 'must be worked into our life, and accepted as something to be dealt with'.[9] Alfred later said she had splendid gaiety and a grand laugh.

Numerous though her anxieties were, life in the household was sociable and strenuous. The supply of English boys – they aimed to have 'six with Alfred' – was fairly constant; a family of Gordons related to 'Chinese Gordon' is prominent in the earlier letters and one of Bovills later. Visits from English relatives and friends, including the Malcolms, Edward Blunt and Francis Synge, curate of St. Luke's, added to the variety of their lives. Charles's father, James Milner, was sometimes their guest; and several of his brothers lived not far away in the Rhineland. 'There is such a hum all about me always you must make allowances', Mary wrote home to a Miss Gordon. They breakfasted at 6.15 and began work at 7, some at their schools in the town and others in the Doctor's schoolroom in the garden. Work continued until 4, after which bathing, boating on the Neckar and gymnastics gave them relief. Music, cards and Shakespeare readings were the pastimes of the evenings, on Saturdays Mary sending them to bed at 8.30. On holidays the Doctor's passion for *die Jagd* led them up the Neckar or further afield, especially to the Black Forest.

Her husband's continuous ailments become a familiar theme of Mary's letters, though reported in a tone of resignation not of complaint. Charles himself, still some years under 40, gives an historian little help in discovering the nature of his ailments; 'those who know me', he wrote to Günther, 'realize how I shirk writing'. Nine months after their return to Tübingen Mary reported he had fewer headaches but bad nights and trouble with his back, adding up to 'what we have learnt to look upon as well.' Poor health was accompanied by failing prospects of better-paid work, at least outside Tübingen. Mary later wrote of a chance that the University might make Charles's lectureship permanent, adding 'it is not a very handsome pittance to give altogether about £80 a year, but still it is better than nothing and a sort of calling and vocation.'

In Mary's mind Alfred's citizenship was linked with this situation as his schooling had been linked with the hoped-for job at Malvern.[10] Alfred himself figures little in this early maternal correspondence. When he does the impression conveyed is that of a studious boy, fully sharing in family loyalties and responsible beyond his years. His cousin Marianne Malcolm, almost eleven years his senior, had obtained a warm place in his affections as well as in those of his mother. Writing to her in London at the age of fifteen his schoolboy humour forecasts some of the later man's predilections. Life at Tübingen seems to him 'humdrum' even 'nonsensical', failing to offer any 'scrap of news, good or bad'. He envies her the liveliness of her existence compared with his own in 'this queer little nest'. Quoting 'Men may come and men may go . . .' he ends, 'I myself do not seem to move or ever to be going to do so.'

As he wrote, though he could not suspect it, his life was about to be radically changed. Early in 1869 Mary, in her 58th year, began to feel unwell, though during an Easter visit to London neither she nor her husband disclosed the fact. By May a swelling under her arm had caused her German doctors to advise an operation, postponed until a telegram had summoned to Tübingen from England her younger brother Colonel Charles Ready, followed by his wife Ellen.[11] The operation proved difficult, but no one felt despondent except the 'Doctor' himself who was convinced that the growth was malignant, admitting, 'I am of a very nervous temperament, always taking the most gloomy view of things', and testifying 'dear Alfred bears it bravely and shames his father who shows and has so little hope and courage'. Recovery was slow, but seemed real. In July Alfred told Marianne that things were much better; 'my poor mama's extreme fortitude . . . has till now been well rewarded . . . by her recovery so far'. His uncle reported she had left her room ('her spirits are truly wonderful'), and soon was being taken for drives. Her doctors were advising sea air. But fairly suddenly there came a turn for the worse. On 1 August, though fever continued, the doctors still held out hope; but on the following morning she died.

A few days later she was buried in Tübingen cemetery. 'She must have been greatly beloved,' Colonel Ready wrote, 'I suppose the chief part of the society here attended . . . perfect simplicity . . . the Lutheran service very affecting.' Soon afterwards the whole family left Tübingen for England and a holiday in the Isle of Man.

Alfred was exceptionally fond of his mother and old enough to appreciate much of her quality. This devotion was a major influence upon his whole adult life.

Marianne Malcolm wrote a month later from Scotland to Alfred in the Isle of Man that she couldn't have felt Mary's death more deeply 'had I been in truth her own child as I was in heart'. The relationship between the woman of 26 and the schoolboy of 15½ became that of an elder sister and brother. John Malcolm, barrister and Master of the Crown Office, had been Mary's confidant and manager or trustee of at least part of her small estate. Before anyone had envisaged Mary's death the Malcolms had asked Alfred to treat their home in St. George's Square as his 'London H.Q.' In previous discussions of Alfred's further schooling Mary showed a clear determination that this should take place in England. What appears to have been her last letter to him, written on her Easter visit to London, told him, 'Don't let [some Tübingen teacher] call you *Herr* Alfred.' After negotiations in which the Doctor proved difficult by pressing Alfred to return with him to Tübingen and Marianne used her influence with her father in a contrary sense, Alfred enrolled in October at King's College, London.

Milner was fortunate in his time of entering this institution. The Rev. Alfred Barry, son of the architect of the Houses of Parliament, had become Principal in the previous year. Still young, though with varied experience behind him, a broad churchman, he was building up a place described by its historian as 'in the awkward and unprepossessing stage of transition from the Anglican seminary to the University College.'[12] Its General Literature and Science Department, which Milner entered, 'which should have been the centre of the College . . . was languishing into insignificance' with only about 50 students. Small classes meant generous individual tuition. The Rev. J. B. Mayor, an eminent ancient philosopher, had been appointed to the College to teach Latin and Greek; Professor Brewer, who taught history and literature, was assisted by S. R. Gardiner, lately of Christ Church, who achieved high standing as an historian of the English Commonwealth.

Built forty years before by Robert Smirke, the College stood in the backyard of Somerset House, a narrow strip running south from the Strand to the river. In Milner's first year the construction of this part of the Victoria Embankment and of the Metropolitan Railway beneath it was still in progress, a fact held responsible for the collapse in December 1869 of the entire roof of the College Dining Hall under the terrace fronting the Thames 'with a loud crash, burying the kitchen in ruins'. The School, founded as the junior department of the College in 1830, was occupying some parts of the cramped range of buildings.[13] The daily scene was an active one, since besides its Theological, Literature, Applied Sciences and Medical Departments the College had a large Evening Classes Department, at that time about the only institution of its sort in London.

Not many of Milner's letters of the next three years have survived; these were written to Marianne while she was away from London or he was with his father at Tübingen. What seems to be the first of them, after saying that the work was hard and apologizing for failure to pay for some trousers, refers to Philip Lyttelton Gell among his King's College friends. Gell, the son of a Derbyshire clergyman and two years older than Milner, remained his close friend for the rest of his life, preceding him by a year to Balliol, sharing the anxieties of his early career in London, and after his marriage his host in Oxford and elsewhere. Ability was not lacking among the College's students since those more or less Milner's contemporaries included the future Mr. Justice Avory, J. W. Lowther (later the Speaker and Viscount Ullswater) and W. L. Clowes, the eminent naval historian. An historical curiosity is provided by the presence in the College during Milner's last year of the Prince Imperial, whose French tutor was struck by the fact that English students whistled incessantly in the corridors.

However absorbing Milner found his work and the society at King's, his home with the Malcolms in Pimlico and the relations and friends centred on it meant much to him. Sociable by nature, his week-ends were filled with engagements. For example, on a Sunday when Marianne was away he heard 'a very good sermon' from Dr. Barry in King's, dined with some friends and walked to Richmond to see others. The fortunes of his uncle Charles Ready, his two Cromie half-brothers and the friends of his Chelsea boyhood were to him of continuous interest. He wrote to Marianne in detail about domestic affairs in St. George's Square when he returned there from Germany in her absence.

Through affection and loyalty to his father Milner spent annual holidays at Tübingen. It was probably in October 1870 that he described how, on arriving from Germany for the new term at King's, Mayor told him, 'now you must really work earnestly for the Balliol or some good thing of the kind', adding that if he couldn't manage it this time he certainly ought to do so next. His relations with his father on this issue did not prove smooth. Suffering from increasing ill-health, reluctant to write letters, and with small financial resources, the Doctor became more difficult or irritable. He wanted Alfred to try for the Indian Civil Service and opposed with what vigour he could any other plan.

Charles Milner continued to take pupils, particularly a family of

Bovills, and to entertain English friends. In the summer of 1870 the impact of the Franco-Prussian War on the Tübingen household claims interest. Going out from London to his father in May Alfred had a 'very eventful journey . . . Prussia, indeed all Germany, is up in arms'. France's declaration of war on 19 July caused the Malcolms to telegraph Alfred, 'get your passport and await events'. His father had neglected to register his birth, and Mr. Bovill sent him a passport to help him avoid possible conscription, and drew on his sons' reports to assure an anxious Marianne that 'there must be at least as much pot valiance in Württemberg as there can possibly be elsewhere whatever *The Times* may say'.

Alfred probably reassured her more by writing that the minimum age of conscription in the Kingdom was 21; and putting forward views on tactics which, whatever their merits, gain interest from his later close association with two wars. Tübingen, he explained, was 'entirely out of any possible line of march', thousands of Prussians were already threatening Paris in the north and so on. As his father, he wrote, had no 'certificate of baptism as a British subject' it was unthinkable that he should desert him. In the event, the great German victory over MacMahon at Wörth, in which Bavarian and Württemberg troops fought, occurred on 6 August and Sedan fell on 2 September. Alfred wrote on 11 September that when ending a tour of the Black Forest he had watched Strasbourg's bombardment. A fortnight or so later he heard that Strasbourg had been taken – 'the flags are hung out here and there is vast excitement.'

The following summer Marianne's health was causing anxiety. He wrote from Tübingen that his father, though without any positive illness, had a 'constantly growing nervous complaint . . . and sleeplessness far worse than I ever imagined.'[14] He rarely complained about the fact that his ambition to enter Oxford was still being opposed by his father, firmly rejected his father's preference for Tübingen University and on one occasion at least 'abused' the Germans and 'laughed at German scholarship.' His father's circumstances, however, troubled his conscience. Parts of a letter he wrote to Marianne must be quoted at greater length since one of his lifelong dislikes was confusion:

> I am as it were living two lives alternately in two perfectly different spheres and at a given time I am pitched headlong out of one into the other . . . I do not mind all this. It is rather refreshing; it certainly produces surprising physical results; it destroys narrow-mindedness . . . but its drawback is confusion of the brain . . . Each world is pleasant enough in its way, but you know very well only one of them feels like my own world.

Soon after his return to St. George's Square and King's College his father abandoned opposition, promising John Malcolm to help Alfred with £50 a year provided he implemented his claim to be able to 'work his way to Oxford.' Alfred began strenuously to prepare to do this during twelve months which, on the small stage of his private affairs, proved eventful.

In April 1872 John Malcolm died, having mismanaged the family finances including a small legacy Alfred had inherited from his mother. Alfred's letters to Marianne during the rest of this year refer constantly to her worries and the need for them both to exercise great economy. Two months later his father, reassuring Alfred about the £50 a year if he could make his way to Oxford, added that he had not been able to 'gather courage' to speak to the mother of Miss Walz, a young Tübingen lady he now wished to marry; a postscript states he had now done this, and they all rejoiced – though the event had not helped him to sleep or cured his heart trouble. In July Alfred finished his time at King's gaining, Professor Hearnshaw writes, 'distinctions as brilliant as any that had been attained by his predecessors in the palmiest days of the Department . . . during 3 years he carried off almost every prize in classics, history and literature open to its students.'[15] Gell had left earlier with a good record.

King's had many links with the ancient universities; and it was presumably Mayor or another teacher who told Milner of people who might coach him for the Balliol scholarship exam. On a rowing trip up the Thames in July he expressed determination to try to secure for this purpose Evelyn Abbott, who had won firsts in 'Mods' and 'Greats' at Balliol a few years before and was now an assistant master at Clifton College. In making this choice, whatever help he received, Milner showed acumen. Arrangements suited to his limited means having been reached, he joined Abbott in August at Clevedon on the mouth of the Severn.

'Abbott,' he wrote, 'quite young, very good looking,' though stricken with the injury which made him a cripple for life, 'is working me very hard. Every day I see more clearly in how utterly hopeless a case I should have been had I not gone to him.' In supplying information he thought him 'not at all equal to Mayor – but he knows so well the *sort of thing* to which you ought to pay most careful attention.'[16] In rooms with a friend a hundred yards from the sea he swam, visited the Hallam memorials in the church and wrote long advice to Marianne about her 'bodily pain' and her trials with solicitors dealing with her father's estate. At the end of August he moved with Abbott to Clifton for a further very busy two weeks. He kept an account of every penny he spent, saying they would both find the next six months very hard financially.

He must have fulfilled his intention during the following two months
in London to 'utilize every moment', as he put it, 'to work out Abbott's
hints.' At the end of November he was writing from 26 St. Giles, Oxford,
where he had gone to stand for the Balliol scholarship.[17]

The five-day exam began with an English essay, 'Are wars likely to
diminish as nations become more civilized?' He felt pleased with his
performance over this and other early papers, but much cast down over
the muddle he had made of the history paper – 'it seems hard to have
thrown away one's chances.' But when the candidates assembled in
Balliol Hall on the last evening to hear the results, Mr. Milner of King's
College had achieved the considerable feat of winning the First Classical
Scholarship. He sent telegrams to Mayor and Marianne, to whom he
wrote the next day 'the good luck has come at last you see and a fine burst
of it too.'

Francis de Paravicini, one of Balliol's Classical dons, told him at
breakfast the next day that what got him the scholarship 'was undoubtedly
the essay, of which he spoke as warmly as is consistent with the character
of a don.' Milner called Oxford 'the sort of place where down-right
excellence in a few things compensates for endless blunders'. Before
leaving Oxford he called on Jowett, who 'was very kind and said he
would secure rooms in College for me by next term.' But he forecast
correctly that his breathing space would be short – 'it is very evident
that they intend to work me as hard as ever they can and I shall have a
great deal on hand till I go up.'

Oxford

(January 1873 – January 1879)

'Balliol made me, Balliol fed me' – New College Prize Fellow

Sir Geoffrey Faber concludes that Balliol's success in becoming so famous a nursery of public men after Jowett's rise to the Mastership in 1870 was 'the result of accepting Jowett's simple gospel of hard, honest, brain work.' The heart of the matter lay in 'the living tradition of strenuous work which he succeeded in communicating to generations of Balliol undergraduates and supported by his own ceaseless example.'[1] Alfred Milner as much as any man of his time accepted this gospel, and continued to apply it for the whole of his life.

Fortunately, Marianne Malcolm kept his frequent letters from Oxford to her which give an intimate picture of his life there.[2] They prove that during his four years at Balliol three things occupied much of his mind and energies: his work, in the form of the series of examinations, including University and College scholarships and prizes, in which a star performer in the Oxford Greats school was encouraged with ardour by the Balliol dons to compete; his home, represented by Marianne and her circle in London, and more remotely by his father and stepmother in Tübingen; and the Oxford Union Society, as a club, a forum of debate and an avenue to a larger world of the future.

Clearly the world of his College, from where 'the sun rises over Wadham and sets over Worcester', offered plenty to absorb his energies for some time. Balliol, as even its critics had to admit, was pre-eminent in this part of Oxford, and for some distance beyond it. Jowett, a Fellow of the College since 1838 and for some years its dominating personality, was entering on his full inheritance as the mentor of members, past and present, the friend of statesmen and men of letters, a national figure. T. H. Green, his right-hand man and Senior Dean, held a leading place in Oxford philosophy and liberal reform. Courtenay Ilbert was Senior Bursar; J. L. Strachan-Davidson, R. L. Nettleship and Paravicini were in their early years as Tutors in the small Tutorial body of this date.

The College had about 180 undergraduates, the second largest in a university of some 2,500 junior members, and was expanding. The baronial south (facing Broad Street) and east wings of the Front Quad designed by Waterhouse had only recently been completed. In Milner's first term the Master and Fellows decided to build extra rooms at the north end of the Garden Quad, and later to raise funds for a new Hall, with rooms for lectures and other activities. The existing Hall had become too small for its purpose and was later turned into what it is today, a Library and Reading Room. Jowett set about to raise the large funds required for these schemes.

Milner visited Oxford again before the end of 1872, seeing much of his future tutor 'Paravie' and his wife, consulting his scout about his 'outfit' and visiting his rooms on the same staircase as Gell, No. 5, staircase VII (now XVII). His rejoining Marianne in London coincided with their move together from her parents' home at 61 St. George's Square, Pimlico, to the cheaper accommodation of a lodging-house kept by Lizzie, a former maid of his mother's, a few streets further west, 54 Claverton Street, where they were to live for some years. 'Don't think', he wrote to Marianne, 'that I look upon coming back to see Claverton St. as anything else than going home.' In January, in the Hilary term, he began to reside at Balliol where T. H. Green, in his capacity as Dean, was very kind about his coming up in a by-term but insisted on his taking Smalls. He had already been persuaded to enter in March for the Hertford scholarship.

Herbert Warren, a Classical scholar of the previous year, recalled that when he first met Milner at the November scholarship exams he was tall, slender and wearing 'a sort of long, dark student's coat, and a tall hat, or a very foreign-looking bowler.'[3] The impression he gave of some foreign element derived not only from his dress but 'from something more pensive and serious in his mien than was usual with lads of his age.' He was nearly 19, and his experience hitherto had been markedly different from that of a normal English public schoolboy of the day. He was fortunate in his choice of a College since variety, in terms of social origins, schools and nationality, was already a feature of the Balliol undergraduate body.

Sociable by nature, he soon found his circle of acquaintances at Balliol spreading; and friends of his boyhood and King's College turned up in Oxford. A contemporary, Sir Charles Lucas, later wrote:

> there was nothing in him of the superior person. All sorts and conditions of his contemporaries regarded him with goodwill ... welcomed by the distinguished band of Balliol scholars ... but equally at home

Ruskin's Hinksey diggings, begun in 1874. Milner in dark trousers, third from left

Arnold Toynbee at Oxford

among undergraduates who were not in the least distinguished or likely to take high honours in Schools.

Early in the term he was invited to breakfast by Herbert Asquith, another Classical scholar about two years his senior and midway in his undergraduate career. Visits to St. Mary's church to hear eminent preachers and attendance at Balliol chapel were a regular feature of his Sundays. For exercise he at once adopted rowing though 'not very heavily yet, as I have a theory that very hard work and very hard exercise don't go together, though a moderate amount of exercise is the very thing to enable you to work.' He stuck to this attitude and never, it seems, figured much in College rowing crews.

He told Marianne he suspected that 'Paravie' himself had come to the conclusion 'that though it was a bold and original idea to get a fellow to do 2 years' [work for the Hertford] in 2 months, yet he slightly under-calculated the time in which the experiment could be carried into effect.' In the exam he came to grief, beaten by Herbert Warren. During the whole of it he had felt 'very much under par . . . I think it's the first time in my life that my head and my luck have failed me both together and very likely it will not happen again.' Balliol, he continued, had had a bump each night in Torpids and were 'cocky in proportion.' His 'howler' over the Hertford had the compensation that he had received 'a burst of invitations to breakfast, wines etc. of which I have accepted about half.'

After a short Easter vacation with Marianne he was back in Oxford in late April much enjoying himself and 'not doing much work, but then nobody does in the Summer Term.' He had been out with Evelyn Abbott, his coach of the previous year at Clevedon, just appointed to a Lectureship at Balliol and 'decidedly more cheerful and happy for coming up here.' A failure on his part to mention wine in a letter was not, he assured her, 'ominous'; he had not bought any at Balliol, nor did he intend to squander a recent present of £5 from one of his Ready aunts.

These assurances occasion some comment on his relationship with Marianne. It has been seen that their intimacy had its roots in their mutual love for Mary Milner, who had died four years before.[4] In what appears to have been her first letter to Alfred after this event Marianne had signed herself his 'very loving sister-cousin', and this perhaps conveys all that needs to be said. Milner's family, in the narrowest sense, was composed of her and a father in Germany who had already remarried. Marianne, an orphan, now almost 30, devoutly church-going, probably lonely, was subject to the restrictions convention imposed on women of her class in the 1870s and later. Inevitably she was continuously mothering

Alfred by writing about his health, his wardrobe and all his activities, and was alternately petulant and devoted.

Since very few of her own letters survive an historian can only see her in the mirror of Milner's affection and solicitude. The topic is important since the close relationship of the two continued, in essentials unchanged, until Marianne's death twelve years after this summer term at Oxford. A letter from Alfred to her supplies what may well be a significant fact. A Captain Armstrong with whom she had broken off an engagement two years before died of heart disease in India, and she was overwhelming herself with self-reproach. Alfred did his best to console her, pointing out that heart complaints could be fatal in England as well as in India and reminding her that in him she had 'a sincerely sympathizing heart not far from you.'

Like so many Oxford generations before and since Milner was exhilarated by his first summer term. He continued his exercise on the river, one day persuading Philip Gell to row 12 miles and on another rowing with companions the 37 miles to Reading. He had joined the Oxford Union, reporting two very uproarious meetings in one week, one of which was 'a perfect riot', with a late division at which 450 members voted. At a very festive wine in Balliol given by 'a man of the name of Raleigh . . . who had just got the Lothian Prize . . . another feather in the cap of our College' they didn't disperse until Jowett had sent his butler 'to ask whether the gentlemen hadn't better sing "God Save the Queen".'[5] Terrific excitement was caused by Balliol winning a success which had eluded it since the '50s and going Head of the River – 'is it surprising', Milner wrote, 'people here accuse us of being conceited?' He was planning that Marianne should visit Oxford in Commem. Week to see among other things the procession of boats and the more feminine attraction of the Worcester College flower show, a special event at this time.

Jowett had asked him to tutor a boy called Grenfell. He went immediately after Commem. to Tübingen for five weeks, 'which I think is the only *minimum* of a four months' holiday which is compatible with decency towards, to say nothing of affection for, one's father.' He thus met his new German stepmother, Elise Walz.[6] In August Milner was writing from Taplow Court where his pupil, 'by no means a fool and I think it will be no hard matter to get him into Balliol', was Willy Grenfell, who successfully entered Balliol the following year and became eminent as a sportsman and public servant, a lifelong friend of Milner's and eventually Lord Desborough.[7]

With his return to Oxford in October the summer river and idle days were over. Jowett at the beginning of term looked 'as fresh as a daisy'; before long Milner had breakfast with him after chapel when he was very jolly. Reporting that he and some others had founded a Balliol Shakespeare Club for which he had been writing a paper, led him to make the reflection that 'work which is done under no compulsion and with no other object than the love of the subject-matter is always the pleasantest, though the grind it entails is disagreeable, like every grind.' He makes another variation on the theme of Jowett's gospel of work in a letter which referred to Marianne's teaching at some night-school – this, he wrote, 'must be a grind, but a grind after all is good for one, as long as there is any interest in it.' Still another from a different letter must be quoted. He had begun to row in College Fours, and commented he would be glad when these were over as 'the regularity of the thing is a bore, quite apart from the grind, and it does interfere more or less with one's work.'

The Shakespeare club was composed of a few intimates, two at least of whom need mention. Leonard Montefiore had come up from University College, London to Balliol in the same term as Milner, and was the elder son of Nathaniel Montefiore and Emma Goldsmid, daughter of Sir Isaac Goldsmid.[8] With brilliant gifts he was one who, Milner later wrote, found Oxford and Balliol 'peculiarly congenial to him. The stirring intellectual life of the place absorbed without exhausting him.'[9] Another intimate, James Rendel, the son of Sir Alexander Rendel, one of a family of civil engineers, had won an Open Exhibition to Balliol from Marlborough and like Milner was reading Classical Mods. Montefiore this term won the Taylorian Exhibition for German. Soon afterwards Gell, although very seedy all the time he was taking the exam, won the Brackenbury History Scholarship putting Milner, he wrote,

> in an effervescent condition . . . how little we thought, when we left King's, that within a year and a half we should both be scholars of Balliol.

No attempt to record Milner's life at Balliol and later can fail to emphasize his concern for Marianne's fortunes and those of other relations. The scholastic successes of Milner and his friends were of course punctuated by failures. But while a graph of these would appear as a rising curve with some dramatic dips usually followed by quick recoveries, a graph of Marianne's fortunes as recorded in Alfred's letters would look quite different. Her illnesses and money worries began to form such regular themes that one must draw it as a straight sombre line. It needs emphasizing that Milner's letters are full of inquiries over her health and visits to the doctor, and admonitions not to mope or get into 'the morbid habit of thinking life is entirely in the past.'

Her dealings with solicitors over her father's estate – referred to once by Alfred as 'the unlucky estate' – dragged on. These involved the fortunes of his Cromie half-brothers, as well as the small legacy Alfred had been left by his mother. In this summer, after much thought, he resolved not to enter any personal claim against the estate. His Balliol scholarship of £80 a year did not relieve him from the need to budget carefully, and he continued to regard his own income and Marianne's as one. The extra money he sometimes won from a scholarship or prize, or from teaching, helped in such extras as holidays with Marianne at the seaside.

There are indications that in time Marianne's income somewhat improved, and Alfred's letters became increasingly full of advice about investments and simple money matters. In his second year he reported his battels for one term as 'heavy, as much as £34', and asked her if he could borrow £5 from some joint fund. Later on he had been guilty of a tremendous piece of extravagance buying 'a capital dark grey tweed suit for £4. 5s. 6d. ready money which will last for several winters.' Proposing to row down to London at the end of the summer term 'to shake off the fumes of an examination room' he assures her that the three days' journey will hardly cost more than 25–30s.

The Union Society held its jubilee celebrations in October 1873. The day after the jubilee banquet in the Corn Exchange Milner wrote that Jowett gave a great lunch to old Balliol men at which the two Archbishops Tait and Manning were present. He seems to have made his maiden Union speech a week later. Returning to Oxford after Christmas, he commented on the great excitement prevailing about Parliament's dissolution, and attended, as a supporter of the Liberal candidate George Brodrick[10], the Woodstock election ('most exciting') which first brought Lord Randolph Churchill into Parliament.

For Milner work, reading at least seven hours a day for another try for the Hertford, came before politics at the Union or elsewhere. This time he was successful, securing what was then sometimes called Oxford's 'blue riband', one of its three chief Classical awards. 'Paravie was in a state of crazy exultation,' he wrote, 'he was the first person to tell me of the result.' Characteristically, he had himself been despondent about it beforehand. Wrench prints his high moral letter expressing his innermost feelings about this success, his hope that it would produce in him a profounder feeling of duty and a continual awareness that 'these gifts are only valuable, if one uses them for some unselfish end.'[11]

It is not a coincidence that such a letter was written at about the time of his first reference to Arnold Toynbee, 'a friend of mine here – you may have heard me mention him.' The son of a successful aural surgeon, Toynbee was eighteen months older than Milner. After a school at Wimbledon for boys intending to enter the Army, attendance (probably evening classes) at King's College, and months of solitary study in remote places, he had entered Pembroke College when Milner entered Balliol. His unsuccessful attempt to win the Brackenbury History Scholarship brought an offer by Balliol to give him rooms in College, to which the Master of Pembroke took objection. Toynbee left Pembroke, but continued to live in Oxford. A year after the stage this narrative has reached, in January 1875, he entered Balliol as a Commoner. Taking a Pass Degree in *Lit.Hum.*, three years later he was elected Tutor of Balliol in charge of probationers for the Indian Civil Service, and lectured on political economy and social questions. He was made Senior Bursar in 1881 but died two years later at the early age of 30. Balliol had by this time, it seems, decided to elect him a Fellow.[12] By any standards Toynbee (the uncle of the eminent historian Arnold J. Toynbee) was a remarkable man, who exerted deep influence on many persons concerned about social and industrial issues. What matters here is the important and lifelong influence he exerted on Alfred Milner, who gave ample witness of the fact. In his much-quoted address to members of Toynbee Hall in 1894 Milner spoke of 'the extraordinary impression which Toynbee's personality made upon those with whom he came into contact'; and asserted that of all his friends Toynbee had 'exercised the most decisive influence upon him, no less after his premature death in 1883 than during the brief years of their friendship.'[13]

Milner said that in Toynbee's five years as an undergraduate his career was 'retiring and unambitious', and his influence was confined to a small circle. Fuller notice of the friendship between the two must be deferred until Milner had become a Fellow of New College and Toynbee was at his most active stage. It is more relevant here to record Milner contemplating 'a mild kind of Hertford wine', and though 'a little worked out' by the examination effort, taking heart at 'Paravie's' advice that all he need do now was to read on steadily (6 hours a day) for Mods in the summer. His Easter vacation included visits to Mrs. Synge at Norwich with whom his father was staying, and to Taplow Court to tutor a second Grenfell.

In June, with Mods 'at last over . . . on the whole I don't think I'm likely to have missed my first' (and he hadn't) he went for over three months to Tübingen. His stepmother Elise, he decided on fuller acquaintance, was a woman of high principle, though not brilliant or striking. The familiar pattern of his father's 'attacks' of some sort and depression recurred, but he noted 'the tremendous strength of his constitution.' A visit to Switzerland with him brought delight at his first sight of the snow regions of the Bernese Oberland, and two 'tolerable ascents' of up to some 11,000 feet.

Ascents of a different kind began again at Oxford, where early in the term he reported Jowett preaching the best sermon he had ever heard from him, supposedly in Balliol chapel, on 'Rejoice in thy Youth'. Later he heard Jowett's 'very remarkable sermon . . . quite a systematic outline of the new religion' to an overflowing St. Mary's, the University church. Jowett's personal interest in him, which began when he won his scholarship, had now developed further. Invitations to breakfast and week-end parties of celebrities at the Lodgings had been followed by inclusion in reading parties at the Master's establishment in West Malvern. With reference to an invitation to Scotland in the next year, 1875, he wrote:

> I don't know why it is that Jowett is so especially kind to me, but one cannot help acknowledging it now as a *fait accompli* and the most valuable of friendships if I don't do anything silly to interrupt it.

It will be seen that their friendship remained close until Jowett's death eighteen years later.

Now reading for Greats, Milner's first tutor was T. H. Green, then rising to the height of his teaching powers and influence.[14] Green belonged to that still rare species, the married don, and Milner, dining in his home, found he told amusing stories and 'appeared quite in a new light as the social man . . . Mrs. Green must at one time have been very handsome.' Though his place as a founder of 'New Liberalism' is well known, the assessment by a more modern Oxford philosopher of his significance deserves quotation.

> The school of Green sent out into public life a stream of ex-pupils who carried with them the conviction that philosophy, and in particular the philosophy they had learnt at Oxford, was an important thing, and that their vocation was to put it into practice. This conviction was common to politicians so diverse in their creeds as Asquith and Milner, churchmen like Gore and Scott Holland, social reformers like Arnold Toynbee, and a host of other public men . . . Through this effect on the minds of its pupils, the philosophy of Green's school might be found . . . penetrating and fertilizing every part of the national life.[15]

R. L. Nettleship, Green's disciple and successor, and Evelyn Abbott were Milner's other Greats tutors. Outside the walls of Balliol Ruskin was lecturing, and Milner fell under his spell to the extent of joining Toynbee, Montefiore and other friends at the celebrated amateur road called the Hinksey diggings. He told Marianne that instead of going on the river he had been digging. 'Ruskin's plan, you know! It is good exercise too, and it does not matter much what exercise you take as long as you get some.' He gave more time and enthusiasm to the task, which with another Balliol scholar Charles Vaughan and Montefiore he had undertaken at Green's request, of teaching each week a class of boys from an Oxford Dissenting School.

As his third undergraduate year began he got leave to spend some days with Marianne at Hastings. He was reading for the Ireland Scholarship, and her health – 'the one great object to me, dearer than many Irelands' – was still causing anxiety. He was not sanguine about his scholarship chances, considering that he had not read enough. The dramatic outcome was told in a letter of early March. He had torn up his last paper (Greek Verse) and walked out, to be told by Jowett the same evening that he had been 'a long way ahead' and had he handed in '*any* papers that last day' he would have won the coveted prize, 'the highest distinction Oxford can give me.' It is hardly surprising to find him soon expressing some irritation with the Balliol dons for pressing him to compete for the Jenkyns Exhibition – 'I am deadly sick of this examination business' – which, nevertheless, he won.

His distinction in another sphere, the Union, was growing. Elected to its Standing Committee before Christmas, he had just won the Treasurership by a large majority over E. B. Iwan-Müller, a Conservative of New College and a colourful character who became an influential journalist. Characteristically, he returned to Oxford in April ahead of term to make a thorough examination of the Union while the rooms were empty, as well as to get on with his Greats work.[16]

The historian of the Union in its jubilee year calls Asquith's defeat in a Presidential election of 1873 by E. Ashmead-Bartlett of Christ Church 'the first instance of anything like regular canvassing, political fashion.'[17] Milner relates with relish hot contests in which what might be termed either the 'Balliol' or the 'Liberal' party was engaged. Gladstone had been banished from Downing Street by Disraeli; Pius IX had shut himself in the Vatican; the famous Union frescoes were still decaying and the 'swells' were continuing to ignore the rule against bringing dogs on to the premises. An historian sometimes finds it hard to discern which of these issues most concerned the members; and the answer is perhaps that it did not matter. Asquith won the Presidency in 1874, with George Parkin, a Canadian schoolmaster eight years older than Milner spending a year 'unattached' to any College at Oxford, as Secretary. Milner bided his time, neither speaking often nor striving after higher office.

Asquith wrote long afterwards that the Union of his time was 'overwhelmingly Conservative in politics, with the result that active Liberals, like Milner and myself, were almost always in a small minority.'[18] It is unreal, however, to regard most active members as closely tied to any national party. Milner was certainly one of those who expressed independent judgements, though it is not possible to glean more than hints about his views.[19] Prominence must certainly be given to his support of Parkin's motion on behalf of Imperial Federation, and of a similar motion later. He joined in censure of the Government, and favoured gradual extension of the franchise. But he refused to support the House's reprobation of Disraeli, and favoured resistance to Russia's encroachments. Later, in his first term at New College, he introduced a motion for the total abolition of the Poor Law.

The biographer is on firmer ground in studying his three terms' tenure of the Treasurer's office. 'The Union', he told Marianne, 'goes on swimmingly . . . have had plenty to do in answering questions in Private Business.' The supply of square envelopes and theological journals, subscriptions, the 'dog nuisance', the use of College arms on notepaper were his responsibility before a Society which Warren, then Librarian, called 'highly critical and demonstrative'. Though the decoration of the Debating Hall roof was successfully completed at this time under William Morris's supervision, a special Committee reported the ultimate extinction of the frescoes to be 'inevitable'. The rooms had also become too overcrowded, and Milner and his colleagues on the Standing Committee were making plans for a general improvement of the buildings.

In the summer of 1875 he had gone for a shorter stay to Tübingen, burning some of his mother's papers, discovering the virtues of the University Library ('one of the largest in Europe and yet so capitally arranged') and grateful for Marianne's reliability in sending him English periodicals. In September he paid another visit to Jowett at West Malvern, and his father was again with the Synges at Norwich. Back in Oxford in October he was scotching a cold. At the Union Presidential Election in December Gell was decisively beaten; he had again been ill, and 'it was a mistake', Milner wrote, 'running him at all, he was not sufficiently well known.' Before Christmas he paid the first of many visits to the Montefiores' home, Coldeast, in Hampshire.

He began his fourth year in digs alone at 2 Ship Street, temporarily avoiding the Union and working again for the Ireland. Trouble of some sort was brewing in the Claverton Street household, and he was planning for Marianne to come to Oxford for some months. But Union business, since he was Treasurer, could not be shaken off for long. The Building Committee proposed the purchase of property from Brasenose with a view to putting up new buildings. He again made a short stay with Jowett at West Malvern, 'glad to get away from Oxford for a day or two.' On his return he was elected President of the Union without opposition. Still embroiled with the business of the Society's property purchase, he wrote:

it is something to have been rewarded with the highest prize, which like most big prizes is rather a reward for service already done than an imposition of any very onerous duties in the future.

He had missed his former chance and failed again for the Ireland, though his comment this time is lacking. A letter of condolence from Toynbee reveals the close relations between the two men, as well as a feature of the Oxford (most of all perhaps the Balliol) of the day – what Toynbee once called 'the teasing manacles and ties of prize-competition'. On top of these Milner had some more pressing problems with regard to Marianne. It seems that she came to lodgings he found for her in Beaumont Street, Oxford, for about three months of the summer. For reasons which will be explained he had later to ask her to admit that this experiment had 'conspicuously' failed.

In rooms now at 45 Broad Street[20] with Jim Rendel and Montefiore he decided to postpone taking his Finals to the Michaelmas Term. His nomination of Montefiore for President of the Union was defeated, he wrote, by a Conservative and public school 'whip' securing the return of a candidate who was 'the facile exponent of the views of the majority.' After term he went to read at Aldeburgh for two months, with Gell, Toynbee and other friends joining him for varying periods. Bathing and lawn tennis gave him exercise, but he found 7 hours' work a day 'as much as I can do. More tires me', and decided there could be 'no rest for me now till Christmas.'

Greats work absorbed him till the exam began in November. Before this he reported his first dinner in Balliol's new (and present) Hall, 'very much pleasanter than any I have been accustomed to in the old barn . . . one has some chance of a hot, as against a lukewarm, dinner.'[21] In early December he telegraphed to Marianne that both Jim Rendel and he had got Firsts. He was said to have got an alpha in every paper.

But his exit from Balliol, like his entrance to it four years before, was made with small opportunity for relaxation. In January he was sitting a five-day examination for a New College Open Fellowship. After attending a big banquet formally opening Balliol Hall he heard he had been successful; and a few nights later went to eat his first dinner in New College Senior Common Room.

Milner, though he did not of course know it, was to stay to dinner in New College for the rest of his life. His Prize Fellowship came under old statutes and would only be vacated on marriage, acceptance of a benefice worth £300, or succession to property worth £500 a year.[22] In the event he held it until his marriage forty-four years later, when the College elected him to an Honorary Fellowship.

What it gave him at this time was security, financial and otherwise, greater than any he had yet known. His Fellowship of £200 a year could be supplemented by scholarships and coaching. He at once presented Marianne with a silk dress, and took over a larger share of her expenses. On a different plane his security can best be called 'more time to think' – about politics and society, and his own future role with regard to them.

He had no wish to stay in Oxford teaching, and had decided on the alternative, chosen by many men with small resources, of the Bar as a career. His legal studies were still at the stage of 'eating his dinners', and in this first graduate year his time for reflection cannot have been ample. He successfully competed in the summer for a Craven Scholarship then worth £80 for three years, commenting before he knew the result that it 'would have needed 6 months' hard reading to make it anything like a certainty for me.' After a month's holiday in Scotland he led a reading party for some weeks at Cookham on the Thames. In the Michaelmas term he wrote that though his work was heavy he felt very well, and

I find I can do twice as much when one has not the anxiety of always thinking now how much of this shall I be able to remember and put down on such and such a day.

At the Union he had been added to the Building Committee, presided over by Alfred Robinson, the able Senior Bursar of New College; the records suggest he took a major part in the work which ended in the Society's decision to build a new (the present) Debating Hall.[23] He was taking various pupils for New College, Jowett and other people. Lastly, Toynbee and the small circle of his friends continued to engage in earnest group discussion. At the end of term he went to stay with some friends in Worcestershire whose son he was coaching, walking part of the way with his pupil to Stratford and Warwick. After Christmas he visited the Montefiores' Hampshire home for a dance.

His activities of 1878 merge with those of the three following years, when he lived with Marianne in London and read for the Bar. He added the Eldon Law Scholarship and Derby Scholarship to his list of successes; he visited Provence, Florence and Venice, partly in Gell's company, in the spring and spent some weeks in Tübingen when he shot hares and partridges with his father. In October he paid a visit with Leonard Montefiore, who was well furnished with introductions, to Berlin.

His letters give clear evidence of his capacity for friendship, often with men younger than himself. He had become on familiar terms with H. B. George, a New College Tutor and pioneer of military history at Oxford, and his wife for several years. Living on No. I staircase, Old Buildings (now rooms 4 and 5) he mixed easily with the Rev. W. A. Spooner, the Dean and later the successor of James Sewell as Warden, and his other new colleagues. His letters show him missing a Bar dinner in London in order to work all day with a pupil trembling on the verge of a plough, about whom Jowett was 'in a great state'; and taking much trouble in these two graduate years with the problems of a variety of young men on lower rungs of the ladder he had himself just ascended.

Journalism and Politics
(early 1879 – December 1886)

The Toynbee Society, and the Bar Found Wanting –
Pall Mall Gazette – A Bid for Parliament – Fighting Home
Rule – Irish Holiday

Early in 1879 Milner went to live with Marianne at 54 Claverton Street to read for the Bar. The four or five years which followed were important ones for him, most of all owing to the several careers he began to follow but then abandoned, since they failed to give him proper satisfaction. Towards the end of his life he wrote in his last book that his experience had been 'exceptionally varied.'[1]

G. M. Trevelyan has written that the last half of Victoria's reign was the period when Oxford and Cambridge were most in the public eye. Their reform, notably the abolition of religious tests, had brought the governing classes closer to the ancient Universities than to 'the declining aristocracy or the rising plutocracy . . . trained intellect was to be a young man's best passport, instead of social patronage or fashionable friends.'[2] Statements of this kind are, of course, relative. It is impossible to imagine anyone writing to Milner what St. John Brodrick wrote to George Curzon, who entered Balliol in 1878, that his stay there would be merely 'the brief interval which must intervene between Eton and the Cabinet.'

Without Curzon's schooling and aristocratic background Milner also lacked the enthusiasm for the Bar of, for example, Herbert Asquith, the son of a wool-stapler. The Bar offered, however, the most obvious career at this time for a man with political ambitions and little else except a first-class academic record. So Milner kept his terms at the Inner Temple and studied for the Bar exams in the company of Gell and other friends.

His association with Arnold Toynbee, which linked the worlds of London and Oxford, the spheres of study and action, was undoubtedly the central feature to him of these years. The two men still often met. Their intimacy, obvious in Toynbee's letter about the 'Ireland' referred to in the previous chapter,[3] is also evident in an episode at New College in 1877. Milner had dislocated his elbow in a riding accident and Toynbee was at his side writing his letters, as well as one of his own to Marianne to assure her that Milner had 'plenty of friends to do his errands for him' and to discourage her, no doubt wisely, from hastening up to Oxford.

Milner's testimony to Toynbee's influence over him must be supported by evidence of what Toynbee thought of Milner. In the letter of 1876 about the 'Ireland' Toynbee wrote that, with Greats behind him,

> You will be educating yourself for a statesman . . . in the middle of things, a leader of men. . . . May we help each other! You have splendid powers, and I don't know anyone of like ability who is more sure to use them nobly and for others.

By 1879, as Milner later said, Toynbee, in strong contrast to his undergraduate seclusion, had embarked on a 'career of intense educational and social activity.'[4] At Balliol he was in charge of the candidates for the Indian Civil Service just beginning to be admitted to the College. He had chosen political economy, historically treated, as his special study; and Sir William Ashley, one of his graduate pupils and later a leading economic historian, has written of his industry in reading the sources for this.[5] He married that year Charlotte Atwood, who shared and supported his interests. Though continuously handicapped by ill-health he began in 1880 to lecture to working-class audiences in the North and elsewhere. The next year he undertook what Jowett, in a valuable *Memoir*, describes as 'the rather difficult office of College Bursar.'

Apart from this public activity he created in the late '70s what F. C. Montague, its secretary, calls 'an informal society of several of the most studious of his younger contemporaries.'[6] His aim was 'to utilize for political reform the ferment of thought at the Universities.' He remained throughout 'the guiding and animating spirit' of this group which met, in Oxford and in London, about once a term almost until his death. Years later a member of the society, W. N. Bruce of Balliol, wrote of Milner's share in its activities as follows:

> His great Oxford reputation both academical and as a speaker at the Union, combined with his wide knowledge of political matters at home and abroad, gave him great authority amongst us. He was far from showing any consciousness of this; his way of conducting discussion, and stating his own views or questioning those of others was most winning.[7]

What can be called the Toynbee–Milner partnership bore fruit in the work which sprang from the missionary zeal of the Rev. Samuel Barnett and his wife Henrietta of St. Jude's Vicarage, Whitechapel. Mrs. Barnett's description of the visit to Oxford in Eights Week, 1875, of her husband and herself to discuss 'the mighty problems of poverty and the people . . . with that first group of "thinking men", so ready to take up enthusiasms in their boyish strength' is well known.[8] What deserve repetition are her sketches of the two men now being discussed:

> Arnold with his earnest eyes and strong face, eloquent silences, scorn of trivialities and passionate interest in war . . . Milner, tall, dignified and grave beyond his years, weighing evidence on every subject, anxious for the maintenance of absolute justice, eager to organise rather than to influence, and fearful to give generous impulses free rein.

Toynbee, Milner, Montefiore and others began regularly to visit Whitechapel to learn conditions in the East End and help the Barnetts' efforts. Montefiore, whom Mrs. Barnett called 'that man of rare gifts and fascinating personality', used to give up weeks of Long Vacations to help with the St. Jude's flower show. Of equal consequence were the efforts which centred round the Barnetts for University Extension, the experiment of 'bringing the Universities to the People'.

Cambridge had made the first move in this sphere and inspired the creation in 1875 of a London Society for Extension of University Teaching under the presidency of the Liberal statesman G. J. Goschen. Though other eminent persons lent support Goschen later stated that

> the infancy of the movement was a very troubled one. The question of funds almost drove us to despair. It was very long indeed before the movement, to use the slang of the day, 'caught on'.[9]

In the autumn of 1877 a large committee met in the Commercial Road and formed a Whitechapel branch of this society, with Barnett as its chairman. Fred Rogers, a bookbinder of Mile End, and Leonard Montefiore became its joint secretaries, and lectures began in the Medical School of the London Hospital.[10]

Milner was elected a Fellow of King's College in 1879, and Professor Hearnshaw suggests he was giving help to Mayor, his former teacher, about this time. The fact that S. R. Gardiner was one of the handful of Whitechapel lecturers strengthened his links, in any case close, with this movement. They were soon to be closer still through an event which clouded this first graduate autumn in London.

He was staying in September with his father at Tübingen when he learnt that Leonard Montefiore had died, at the age of 25, on a visit to the United States. He wrote to his younger brother Claude, then at Balliol, that

> Leonard's death is the greatest blow I have ever felt, save one, a greater loss than that of a brother was,[11] a greater, I think, than that of any relation I have living could be . . . our interests and aspirations had so much in common.

On his return to England he paid a visit to the Montefiores in Hampshire. In writing during this visit he said that Leonard's cheerfulness had been invaluable to his parents – a reflection, no doubt, of his own benefit from this friendship.

He went to stay with Rendel, the third occupant of the 'digs' of three years before in Broad Street, in a Yorkshire inn. A senior New College don, A. O. Prickard, recollected the two men

> making an intensive study of political science with many large books on law, social economics, etc. But Milner was always in fine out of door spirits, and heartily enjoyed the fine moorlands of the North Riding.

During the next two years Milner edited anonymously a volume of Montefiore's *Essays and Letters* to which he contributed a long memoir.[12] The essays this contains, some reprinted from the *Fortnightly* and other reviews, show Montefiore's large knowledge of German literature and modern history. Milner soon took his friend's place as joint secretary with Fred Rogers of the Whitechapel Extension Committee.

Milner's letters of 1877 contain references to Oscar Wilde, then in his fourth year at Magdalen, calling on him at New College to announce the illness and later the death of Miss Cromie, a mutual friend. This elderly lady was perhaps the sister of Milner's mother's first husband. Wilde, Rupert Hart-Davis's edition of his *Letters* discloses, was much attached to Leonard Montefiore, and had proposed unsuccessfully to his sister Charlotte.[13]

For the events of Milner's next two years a biographer can only rely on scraps of information. Jowett, a staunch friend, invited him for a week-end at Balliol to meet Lord Coleridge, who became Chief Justice of England in 1880. His half-brother Charles in Shanghai ran into financial and other trouble from which he helped to rescue him. He lectured in Whitechapel on 'The State and the Duties of Rulers' in company with Toynbee ('The State and Religion') and James Bryce, who had just entered Parliament for the Tower Hamlets division. Gell left his Bar studies to join a publishing firm, which led him in 1883 to become (with

Jowett's assistance) Secretary to the Delegates of the Oxford University Press.

Milner was called to the Bar by the Inner Temple in January 1881, and joined the Midland Circuit. He appears to have been sent no briefs and, doubtful about his future course, to have made no great effort to acquire them. An acquaintance wrote later that he disliked the Bar's atmosphere.

In November he started to keep a diary in a very irregular fashion. This shows that he started to work occasionally in the capacity of a 'devil' for Goschen. George Joachim Goschen, at the age of 50, had behind him a successful career in his family banking business and high office in Gladstone's first Ministry. Now M.P. for Ripon, he was critical of certain Liberal policies and was holding himself aloof from Gladstone's second Government. Besides possessing much financial ability he had inherited the literary interests of his German grandfather, a Leipzig publisher. After Rugby he had gone to Oriel College and become one of the Union's most successful Presidents. The jubilee historian of the Union states that on a visit to Oxford he 'expressed himself in glowing terms about Milner's speeches.'[14]

Milner was also engaged in freelance journalism, mainly about Germany, for the *Pall Mall Gazette* and the *Fortnightly Review*, both of which were edited at this time by John Morley. As a further occupation he was coaching and reading to the Earl of Dysart, a young man who was partly blind and physically weak, his association with whom was probably due to Jowett.

Written, of course, for his own eye alone, Milner's diary and letters reveal that Marianne Malcolm, now nearly 40 years old, had taken to the bottle. She had probably started to do so some years before, though just when one has no means of knowing. Milner's comment on her stay in Oxford several years earlier may furnish a clue to the problem.[15] *Autres temps, autres mœurs*; one must remember Victorian reticence about such a situation, and the complications of trying to keep it secret. Milner had on occasions to employ a nurse, and his comments reveal that he faced a grim state of affairs. Just before Christmas of 1881, for example, he notes that her being 'well' for four weeks was 'the longest respite I can remember having this year'. Returning in October 1882 from abroad he is hoping 'to find a better state of things at home . . . and indeed there is need, for last year was *frightful* beyond words.'

His fondness for Marianne and his strong feeling of family loyalty have already been emphasized. One can assume that the rows, tension and scenes in 54 Claverton Street imposed a severe strain on him. It is small wonder that he often felt much depressed in spirits.

He used his diary at this time and occasionally later as a vehicle to examine his future aims and to draw up a balance-sheet of his prospects.[16] This December he was approaching 28, and he notes five years had passed since he had taken his degree. He had been pondering the problem of whether to give up the Bar. He was dissatisfied with the amount and the quality of the work he was doing, and uncertain about alternative careers. Characteristically a fortnight later his mind was firmly made up, and he wrote:

Resolution fixed. Bar thrown overboard. Off I go upon the wide ocean. . . . as long as I keep my health . . . I have nothing to fear in a life, the first condition of which is celibacy. One cannot have everything. I am a poor man and must choose between public usefulness and private happiness. I choose the former, or rather I choose to strive for it.

He and Philip Gell both wrote letters to Jowett about this decision, which escaped the general holocaust of Jowett's papers and are printed in full by Sir Geoffrey Faber.[17] After acknowledging Jowett's 'incessant and valuable help of and thought for him' Milner continued:

Versatility is not my gift. If I were to stick to the Bar I should become absorbed in it, so absorbed that I could not work at anything else, but never, I am quite certain, so absorbed that I should not regret the work I had left behind me. The only subject I am deeply interested in, is literature, especially political literature, and politics . . . What alarms me is the likelihood of being entirely taken up with legal work . . . I am quite determined not to commit myself to any new career till I have looked about me. I can afford to wait, provided I continue learning – both from books and men.

Gell repeats that the Bar had never absorbed him, adding with perception

he is a man who never does anything well until he is absorbed . . . What he craves and what alone will hold him are strong human interests . . . the only barrier which would economize, accumulate and direct his energies is fixed work in which his heart can take hold. Offer him this, and you make a man of him forthwith.

This fixed work, Gell explained, could be only 'on the staff of a journal or in political life – using the latter word in a sense far wider than parliamentary life.' For example, the secretaryship to a Royal Commission, a leading politician or a political association. Milner himself, soliciting Jowett's aid more obliquely, wrote that he would 'at some future time be very glad of a private secretaryship to a really eminent politician.' What Gell adds as a secret known only to a few – and Milner does not mention – is that 'a friend' had guaranteed Milner's expenses if he would stand for Parliament at the next election, and had already lodged £1,000 for this purpose.

Sir Geoffrey Faber seems to be right in seeing Milner's decision to abandon the Bar as a victory of Toynbee's influence over that of Jowett, whose natural advice it would have been for him to stay there. Toynbee, besides infecting Milner with his idealism, acted on him as a strong intellectual spur. Milner had promised Fred Rogers to give some lectures on 'Socialism' to the Tower Hamlets University Extension Society and after a visit to Oxford in December he noted,

> My long talks with Arnold were the best part of it. What an immense task, though, I have undertaken in these lectures on 'Socialism'. It seems harder, but also greater, than ever since I have spoken to him.

And he resolves, 'those "Socialism" Lectures for the East End must be made *good*.'

Early in 1882 he gave four of these lectures, mainly concerned with the history of Socialist theories, at St. Jude's School, commenting that they were 'not so good as I could wish yet not wholly a failure.'[18] These were, however, only a first instalment. His extensive February plans included the study of political and social subjects, especially Germany and Socialism, as well as keeping his eyes awake for 'any good political opening', learning French and practising public speaking and 'one or two – but only one or two – good works in the line of social improvement.' This programme had soon to be modified by his accepting an offer to join the staff of the *Pall Mall Gazette*.

The *Pall Mall Gazette*, a 2*d*. evening paper, ranked high at this date as a daily Liberal organ. It was still, as a Radical rival scoffed on its foundation in 1865, 'professing to be conducted by scholars and gentlemen *par excellence*.' Morley's reputation and skill as its editor had lately been reinforced by the energy and journalistic flair of W. T. Stead. Milner, already an occasional contributor, became the third member of a small editorial staff, which relied much on outside contributors and the news in the morning papers. Agreeing to join, Milner wrote cautiously on 2 April to Stead,

> I don't want to give myself up to journalism . . . but I would rather do it regularly than spasmodically. I will regard attendance at 9 a.m. as imperative and get up my news beforehand.[19]

As this letter suggests he saw his job as another form of apprenticeship for what he wished to become, 'a useful politician in the best sense of the word.' In the event he stayed in it for three and a half years. He became absorbed as his diary, when he chose to keep it, proves, in the current political scene.

This scene was the troubled one of Gladstone's second Government. 1882 was the year of more obstruction by Bradlaugh and the Parnellites in the Commons, and the Phoenix Park murders. Abroad, Majuba and Transvaal independence were legacies of the previous year; Britain had evacuated Afghanistan, but in September Gladstone reluctantly occupied Egypt; Germany and Austria–Hungary were joined by Italy to form the Triple Alliance.

No attempt has yet been made to pay much attention to Milner's political standpoint since material for doing so is scarce. He had been, in the main, a man of the study; though his boyhood in Tübingen and his travels had given him, as Gell reminded Jowett, an unusual knowledge of and interest in foreign politics. The liberal causes he supported at the Oxford Union, and the faith in the Empire which Parkin reinforced in him, have been noticed. Attention has rightly been given by others to his forthright expression of views at the Palmerston Club at All Souls in January 1878. This society included statesmen, as well as aspiring statesmen, and dons as honorary members. That Milner was not overawed by Mr. Gladstone's presence on this occasion is less interesting than the fact that he was chosen to propose the toast of the Army and Navy, coupled with the health of Lord Cardwell, the Liberal reformer of the Army. He stated his view of true Liberal policy as being not swashbuckling but equally not that of

> a small but noisy section, who seek to ensure peace by a policy of consistent cowardice . . . [it consisted of] a clear statement of the rights which we will fight for and a self-restraint, which shall move no muscle until these rights are actually touched.

Also interesting on this topic is the evidence of W. N. Bruce, a fellow-member of Toynbee's discussion group who has been quoted earlier:

> What struck me most about him at first was the difference of his standpoint from that of the ordinary English politician. . . . He showed no affinity with any British political party. . . . [His combination of devotion to the Empire and semi-socialistic doctrines, and his] critical detachment from English political traditions or conventions made his conversation impressive and instructive.

Detachment, except among his intimates or on rare occasions in public, seems to have been the note of his current political standpoint. As a junior editor his function now was to observe and report events, not to propose unorthodox remedies. This kept him busy enough. He notes slow progress with Henry George's famous book *Progress and Poverty* about which Toynbee had sent him a 'portentous list of questions'.

He saw much of his half-brother Charlie, on leave from Shanghai this year, and something of his uncle John Ready, home from India.[20] The main family event of the year, however, was his father's death in Tübingen in August at the age of 52. Milner only arrived there in time for the funeral, but found this

> most touching . . . the grand old prayers . . . every one of his colleagues now in Tübingen followed the body to the grave, with the officers of the University in their robes of State and many tradesmen and poor people from the town.

Charles was buried with Mary. Milner found that his stepmother would be left comfortably off, and insisted on her keeping all his father's inheritance. He disposed of his father's beautiful dog 'Milord' to the King of Württemberg's adjutant. He visited their faithful maid Emma Eberle, and did some work on his lectures for 'my East End people'.

After a few days with his Uncle Ernst and his family at Kreuznach he spent a fortnight in Normandy with Hugh Glazebrook, the artist brother of his Balliol friend Michael Glazebrook. Hugh, who later painted his portrait which hangs in the National Portrait Gallery, remembered him arriving 'very tired and sad.' But congenial company, exercise ('he swam with great judgement in those rapid and treacherous swirls that raced round the coast') and his interest in the peasants' life soon 'made him ready for work again.'[21]

It was characteristic of him at this time that on returning to England his diary recorded intense pleasure from this Normandy visit, but despondency about his work and prospects – 'my life is passing and I have done no work of value.' What his existence with Marianne in Claverton Street had become was one cause for depression. He gave more lectures on 'Socialism' in Whitechapel before Christmas, which Fred Rogers describes as having

> certainly laid the foundations of a scheme of scientific Socialism, but the men who talked Socialism at workmen's clubs did not come to University Extension classes, and the excellent lectures were condemned to be delivered largely to a middle-class audience.[22]

In spite of periods of depression the daily grind on the *Pall Mall Gazette* was congenial. Milner's scraps of diary for 1883 are mainly notes of events at home and abroad among which major Parliamentary debates and speeches by party leaders 'outside' are prominent. Comment and records of personal doings are few. This year two more major events took place in his personal life, and one of significance in his professional life. The most important was the death of Arnold Toynbee.

Toynbee had been wearing himself out. His lectures on the 'Industrial Revolution' at Oxford had been followed by an important summer conference there of Co-operators, and a mission of inquiry to Ireland. For months past, Montague states, he had been growing 'pale and haggard'; the death of T. H. Green had 'deepened his depression. Yet he sought no rest.' He had written to Michael Davitt after his Irish visit of his intention to criticize Henry George 'from the point of view of a Social Democrat' and, as has been seen, enlisted Milner's help. He gave two lectures in Oxford on *Progress and Poverty* and repeated these in January to a London working-class audience, going home to Wimbledon for his last illness.

Charlotte sent proofs of these lectures to Milner to edit, asking him to arrange with Kegan Paul for their publication.[23] Since the Barnetts' activities in Whitechapel meant much to both men, it is suitable to include an occasion in February recorded by Mrs. Barnett.

> Milner brought his cousin to the party . . . a capital one; about 80 real students came and we formed a Students' Union. Milner made one of the merriest of speeches. The people enjoyed him.

Toynbee died on 9 March. Jowett, who had known many young men in his fifty-odd years at Balliol, must be given the last word. The secret of Toynbee's influence he found to be 'his transparent sincerity . . . there was nothing in that *schöne Seele* which might not have been seen and known to all men.'[24]

The second personal event was Milner's ceasing to live with Marianne in Claverton Street, their home for eleven years, and going into bachelor quarters. He went in October this year for a fortnight's holiday abroad, and from Strasbourg wrote her a fourteen-page letter announcing his resolution in which he said,

> from the point of view of my work the thing does not answer. And I have reached a point in my life so intensely critical that for the sake of everyone who belongs to me or cares about me . . . it is not only a duty, it is a necessity, to arrange my life [more suitably] . . . I am determined never to do or say anything to weaken the tie between us . . . My love for you is unaltered.

He hoped still to be 'very much with her'; and would continue to supplement her income and, if she wished, manage her money affairs.[25]

He took temporary rooms near the *Pall Mall Gazette* office, which was a 'little old house' at 2 Northumberland Street, Strand. Before long he moved to live with a friend, Henry Birchenough, a product of University College, London, to rooms in 8 York Street, St. James's. In August 1883 Morley left the *Pall Mall Gazette* to enter Parliament as Liberal M.P. for Newcastle-on-Tyne. Milner became Stead's No. 2 in what was to prove some adventurous and, in terms of the time, sensational journalism.

Milner's telling Marianne he had reached an 'intensely critical' point in his life referred to his promotion on the *Pall Mall Gazette* and probably to his aim to try to enter Parliament if a favourable opening arose. His letter again reflected his absorption in his job and anxiety, a strong part of his make-up, over adequate preparation beforehand.

His work for Goschen also began to increase and a close relationship, professional and personal, began with him which lasted many years. Their association in Oxford and in London University Extension has been noted, and it is possible that Jowett had again put in an oar in Milner's favour. The experienced Liberal statesman and the young journalist with political ambitions had obvious interests in common:[26] German ancestry (in Milner's case one German–Dutch grandparent only) and knowledge of German, especial skill in finance, real concern for social reform and – of significance at this date – the detachment which Goschen had now developed from party ties and labels.

Defending Gladstone and other Peelites at the Oxford Union in the '50s, Goschen had declared for principles as against party attachments, and thirty years later he was putting this profession into fuller practice. Refusing Gladstone's offer of the Secretaryship for War and of nomination as the Speaker, he found himself in 1884 (he wrote later) at the opening of a new chapter in his career. His official biographer, Arthur Elliot, writes 'his position of independence became more accentuated'.[27] He opposed the Government's franchise scheme while, he told the Commons, refusing 'to give a political blank cheque to Lord Salisbury'. Distrustful both of Randolph Churchill's skirmishes on the Right and Chamberlain's on the Left he had almost decided by the end of this year that the Liberal Party was about to break up.

Milner's work for his two masters, Goschen and Stead, seems for a time to have dovetailed well. He had joined the New University Club.[28] His work at the *Pall Mall Gazette* office was mainly confined to the mornings, leaving him the rest of the day to read, write letters and fulfil social engagements.

Letter-writing and social intercourse were always forms of work for him as well as of pleasure. Politics, though a career more easily entered by University and professional men in the '80s than formerly, was still a ladder with well-spaced social rungs. The majority of Gladstone's Cabinet colleagues were Whigs; and Ensor has written that of the five 'new men of genius' rising into the front political rank in the mid-'80s all but one (Chamberlain) were 'scions of the landowning oligarchy which had ruled Great Britain and Ireland for two centuries.'[29] Two of them, Churchill and Parnell, were in a few years' time to fall by the wayside. With the others, Rosebery, Balfour and Chamberlain, Milner was in time to become closely associated.

He was making his way among the intellectual not the landowning aristocracy, though these were far from mutually exclusive. For example, his diary of 1883 sometimes became 'notes of what I hear and see of interesting people.' He noted a Sunday at Jowett's lodgings in Balliol where Henry Fawcett, the blind economist and Postmaster-General, 'did most of the talking'; a dinner at which Frederic Harrison, the Positivist, gave first-hand impressions of Turgenev and Garibaldi; a dinner when he met Edmund Gosse whose 'talk, though clever, sickened me', and a visit to *Faust* with Rosalind Howard (later Lady Carlisle) who argued all the way to the Opera about Disestablishment.[30]

He quickly got on good terms with Stead, the son of a Congregational-ist Minister and a journalist in the North until Morley brought him to London in 1880. When Stead became the *Pall Mall Gazette*'s editor Milner got him to add E. T. Cook, a New College man, ex-President of the Union and another member of Toynbee's Society, to the staff. Stead has des-cribed how Milner, though a bit sedate and having what he called 'the University tip', entered with 'glee' into his brisk re-modelling of the paper. The outcome was what Matthew Arnold denounced as 'a new journalism . . . full of ability, novelty, variety, sensation, sympathy, generous instincts [but] feather-brained.'[31]

Milner's lieutenancy to Stead presents an engaging picture, and a corrective to those who think of him as a 'Don of the cold and doubtful breath'. Stead aroused his staff's devotion and was a happy family man of unfailing geniality and humour. He was also the chief exponent of his day of the use of the Press to flutter official dovecotes and champion unpopular causes. After his death in the *Titanic* disaster thirty years later Milner recalled,

> We were always in hot water with one or other large portion of the public . . . the recklessness with which the *Pall Mall* of those days urged its invariably very pronounced opinions naturally excited no little animosity . . . I do not think that within my recollection any newspaper in the country has ever exercised so much influence upon public affairs as the *P.M.* did during these first years of Stead's editor-ship.[32]

Milner added that he and Stead were agreed on certain main lines of policy; 'we were both enthusiasts about the Race and the Empire . . . shedding very fast the old tradition of the *laissez-faire* school.' Stead's biographer considers that the 'whole-hearted and joyous' cooperation of the two men was based on a shared enthusiasm over social reform and over J. R. Seeley's recent lectures on *The Expansion of England*.[33] The first of a long series of what Stead called his 'escapades', the campaign of October 1883 in support of the pamphlet *The Bitter Cry of Outcast London* championed a general cause which Milner had much at heart.

This saw the Barnetts' work for the East End poor as a positive step towards realizing Toynbee's vision. That vision had grown in conditions of which only bare mention is possible here – the advance of democracy since 1867, the economic depressions of 1876–9 and later, the feelings of uncertainty and guilt these roused in sections of the governing classes. The assurance of the Britain of Milner's boyhood was a thing of the past, and growing awareness of social evils was evoking active forms of response; for example, the Socialist societies of Morris, Hyndman and the Fabians, and new and substantial support for the Barnetts. The story of the Barnetts' fresh campaign in Oxford in the winter of 1883–4, of the formation of the Universities' Settlement Association and of Toynbee Hall is well known. The historian of Toynbee Hall writes that in grappling with the problem of poverty 'opinion at Oxford had to some extent anticipated that of the nation.'[34] Far more people in Oxford now took up this cause. Milner ventilated the Settlement plan in the *Pall Mall Gazette* and served on a committee to choose a site and a warden. A disused boys' school near St. Jude's Vicarage, and the Rev. Samuel Barnett provided the answers. The man and the place will continue in this story since Barnett was Warden until he became a Canon of Westminster in 1906; and Milner remained a life-long friend of Toynbee Hall, becoming the chairman of its council before the First World War.

Toynbee's *Lectures on the Industrial Revolution in England* and other literary remains were published in 1884 with a preface in which his widow Charlotte wrote, 'the whole has been revised by the friend who shared my husband's entire intellectual life, Mr. Alfred Milner.' Since Toynbee, as already noticed, spoke *ex tempore* or only sometimes lectured from notes the editing of this volume was a laborious task. Discussing its place in English social thought the historian Sir George Clark calls it influential from its publication until at least some point in the 1920s.[35]

Milner's work for Goschen continued from early 1884 for more than a year. It did not take long, Arthur Elliot states, for Goschen to

come to look upon Milner almost as a colleague and adviser in the political work which he had on hand. Together they studied the Blue Books, talked over every part of the political situation, and, in regard to the best use that could be made of Goschen's energies and influence, spent much time in discussing the when, the where, and how.

Goschen had an active wife and six children and lived in Portland Place and at Seacox Heath near Hawkhurst. As 1885 opened Milner was staying at Seacox discussing Egypt, South Africa and other critical issues, and Goschen noted that 'Milner and Lucy [Mrs. Goschen] are pitching into me tremendously to make a speech on foreign and colonial affairs.'

Elliot records Goschen's high qualities and achievements but pays little attention to his defects which included hesitation and some diffidence. Reading Goschen's correspondence with Milner one is inclined to think that Elliot's description of his regarding Milner as 'almost a colleague' had now become an understatement. A certain speech, for example, Milner told Goschen, had made him 'the subject of the hour . . . the spokesman of what must remain a very influential section of public opinion;' then he continued with frank remarks on the speech's defects and advice on the essential ingredients of the next one, ending with the imperative 'No Jingo'.

Once the 1884–5 Franchise Bills had been passed a general election could not long be delayed. Presumably Milner's unnamed friend was still ready to pay his election expenses since early in 1884 he began to receive invitations to stand in the Liberal interest.[36] He declined an offer from Cheltenham, and broke off approaches from Joseph Rowntree (an admirer of his views on social questions) over York on grounds of growing distrust of the Government's Egyptian policy. Declining an invitation from the Oxford Liberal Association he wrote that, though on domestic questions

> a strong and advanced Liberal, I have once again had occasion to dissent from the majority of my party on points of foreign policy, and my dissent was never stronger than it is now from the course which the Government is pursuing in Egypt. [He was no Jingo and not anxious to extend the borders of Empire. . . . But within the limited sphere Britain ought to be] more and not less vigorous, resolute and courageous . . . [to attempt escape from responsibilities once assumed would increase our difficulties, as well as bring loss of reputation and self-respect.]

The General Gordon imbroglio was then at about its half-way stage. It had been one of Stead's 'escapades' to interview Gordon at the beginning of the year; and Milner had been a friend since boyhood of members of the General's family. Perhaps these personal links explain his deep concern, including letters to Reginald Brett (later Lord Esher) and others in official positions, over Gordon's fate. When Gordon's murder became known in England in February his indignation boiled over in a letter to Goschen.[37]

In his eyes this episode was the latest betrayal of what he had called at Oxford's Palmerston Club 'true Liberal policy'. The Powers, especially Germany, were no longer confined to Europe but 'touched us at every point, in Africa, in Asia, in Australia.' Gladstone ('apparently as much as ever without any constructive policy of his own') and those who thought like him were selling the pass. Soon after his New Year visit to Seacox he had told Goschen 'all is plastic' (in Liberal Party politics) and 'this is the psychological moment.' He wrote again while visiting Rosebery at Mentmore, urging Goschen to 'make a stand now to check the stampede among moderates' which Chamberlain's speech-making was causing.

Soon he accepted another offer, this time from the Harrow Liberal Association, to step into the Parliamentary arena. He talked to Goschen and wrote regretting the 'suspension' of his work for him, adding:

> If I should succeed in getting into Parliament my great hope will be to serve in the ranks of a party of which you were one of the leaders. With you in a Liberal Government one would feel safe. Otherwise I fear the days of my Parliamentary life might be 'few and evil'. . . . I hope my work under you has only begun.

Goschen noted, a little testily, in his diary,

> Milner will leave me now . . . what with the *Pall Mall*, his electioneering work, and Society, he would not give the necessary time. He has been a capital secretary in most respects.

Gladstone resigned in June and Lord Salisbury formed a government, dependent on Parnell's support, to caretake until the General Election. Milner had been sitting loose from the start on the *Pall Mall Gazette*. In the previous summer he had mentioned to Goschen an idea of giving it up and combining work for him with 'independent study', perhaps a book on Egypt. That he had now begun to nurse a constituency must have fostered this idea. What translated it into action was the death on 30 June, at the age of forty-one, of Marianne Malcolm. Writing in Cairo five years later he called this event the first of the 'great landmarks in my life' of those years. Within a few days he resigned from the *Pall Mall Gazette*.

Rather strangely, Milner's spasmodic diary and surviving letters contain no reference to Marianne in the last two years or so of her life. But a diary of her own which survives shows that he gave her his time, financial help and affection to the end. He later bought the Claverton Street house and supported 'Lizzie' as its landlady for many years.[38] Did the anxieties and drain on his energies which Marianne caused Milner at least since his undergraduate days deter him from marriage? Some, at any rate, of the various ladies who became his close friends felt little doubt that they had.

Milner had to stay at the *Pall Mall Gazette* until September. In his tribute to Stead, already referred to, he wrote that his main difference with him concerned tactics and style, and decided that 'lack of balance was Stead's Achilles' heel.' He had hardly given in his resignation when Stead launched his most colourful escapade so far, 'The Maiden Tribute of Modern Babylon', a series of articles on the white-slave traffic based on personal, elaborate, inquiries. The shock these administered to Victorian readers, though hard to appreciate today, was severe. Milner, writing to Cook while the storm blew, said:

Stead talks, writes and thinks of nothing else but his virgins past or present (the Criminal Law Amendment Bill being at present before the Commons, they are perhaps more exacting than usual).

Gell, writing from Balliol to Cook, was somewhat priggishly indignant –

We condemn the outrage of publication in this form, the brutality of detail, the beastly placards in the streets. . . . I think that in a fortnight the *P.M.G.* has perceptibly lowered the tone of sexual refinement and of modesty throughout English society.[39]

Stead, however, triumphed. Though he was convicted of criminal libel and imprisoned for two months, the Bill to which Milner referred raised the age of consent from fourteen to sixteen and in other ways gave more protection to young girls and women.

This autumn party politics grew in confusion and drama. While the Conservatives appeared to be bargaining with Parnell, who held strong cards, Gladstone remained ambiguous on a peak at Hawarden. Chamberlain's 'unauthorized programme' sowed disunion between the Radicals and the moderate Liberals led by Lord Hartington and others. Goschen, standing for East Edinburgh, can be labelled a 'detached moderate'. Though admired for his ability he appeared to many what the *Pall Mall Gazette* called 'a somewhat lethargic politician'. Milner continued respectfully to try to ginger him up, urging:

do make your speeches as constructive as possible and on the old sober lines, and only critical in the second place, I mean back Hartington rather than attack Chamberlain. Forgive my impertinence . . .

and sent him 'constructive proposals to beat Chamberlain's appeal.'

Milner began his own intensive electioneering in mid-October, with a

Conservative, W. Ambrose, Q.C., as his opponent. Harrow, a new Middlesex county division, was what the Press called 'metropolitan in character'.

Milner gave much effort to preparing his election address and his many speeches. These show him as progressive, nearer in many respects to the 'Brummagem doctrine' than to Goschen's moderation. He welcomed the recent Reform Acts as a basis for new social legislation and for the same reason wanted local government reform. He supported free elementary education, local option, House of Lords reform, taxation of ground rents and liberalization of the land laws.

Milner's only contemporary biographer must, since little comment from others is available, serve as the main authority on this campaign.[40] He writes that Milner's speaking was 'a persistent and painfully obvious struggle to be exact, intelligible, and concise', though he grew more professional as he proceeded. He concludes that Milner lost votes through dogged refusal to support disestablishment of the Anglican Church and through his association with Goschen who, disregarding his recent advice, spoke for him at Hendon attacking Chamberlain's policies.[41] He affirms that he 'stood as a party man, and identified himself naturally and thoroughly with the party.' A friend called him 'a sort of independent Gladstonian'.

Milner gave a major speech on foreign policy which he had reprinted and sent to Rosebery, Morley and other Liberal friends. This defended the late Gladstone Government's record in South Africa, Egypt and India, and argued strongly for Liberalism as a progressive force and a policy of 'concentration in developing the vast empire already ours rather than expansion.'[42]

Milner's helpers in the campaign included his Balliol friends Asquith and Michael Glazebrook, Alfred Lyttelton, Gladstone's nephew and a barrister, Haldane and G. W. E. Russell. In spite of this support and Lord Aberdeen putting his carriages at Dollis Hill at his disposal on polling day, 4 December, Milner was well beaten. Ambrose 4,214 votes, Milner 3,241, and a resulting Conservative majority of 973 were figures which broadly squared with the national outcome: London and the towns turning against Liberalism, and the rural areas giving the Liberals support. All the other Middlesex country divisions returned a Conservative after a straight fight with a Liberal. Before long the dramatic result was known of what the *Pall Mall Gazette* called 'as near a dead heat as possible in politics,' or the number of Liberals returned exactly equalling that of the Tories and the Parnellites combined.

Goschen, who easily beat his Radical opponent, wrote to condole with Milner and say he would gladly have him back as his secretary. Milner's reply has not survived, but he wrote to say there were 'great consolations' in failing to get into Parliament and that he was off on a month or two's holiday in Italy and Sicily with Philip and his brother Henry Gell. He left to the sound of the *Pall Mall Gazette* raising 'three cheers for the Grand Old Man' for reasserting his leadership and hoisting the Home Rule flag.

Milner wrote to Birchenough in January from Genoa in carefree mood. Though Philip was turning back after Naples, he hoped to have Henry's companionship in Sicily. His future plans were uncertain; he even had 'wild thoughts of becoming a vagrant for a year and seeing the States and India.' But soon a letter from Gell and urgent ones from Goschen recalled him to England. Gladstone had just formed his third Government with the aim of carrying Home Rule. Hartington, Goschen and Bright had all declined to join it.

From early March, when Milner got home, until the general election in July, party politics were tumultuous and bitter. In a passage of interest where Milner is concerned the historian J. L. Hammond compares the conditions in which Gladstone failed to give the Irish self-government in 1886 with those in which Campbell-Bannerman succeeded in giving the Boers self-government twenty years later.[43] In 1886 recent foreign disasters, he writes, had induced a mood of firmness and 'stubborn maintenance of rights and privileges', the Liberal party was splitting, the Opposition strong and the Press doubtful or hostile. The Home Rule issue, with 'race, religion, and class all blazing below the surface, lent itself easily to inflammatory management.'

Milner, though he could not enter the House of Commons, found himself a ringside seat from which he was anything but a passive specta-tor. His letters make it easier to follow his actions than to define closely his views on the central issue. 'Home Rule', of course, was a label with a variety of meanings. In speeches at Harrow and in letters to Stead he expressed sympathy towards the cause – i.e. an Irish Parliament – provided this did not 'endanger the unity of the Empire.' After the fight was over he told Goschen all his 'natural leanings were to Home Rule', which he still thought 'in the far future the best, or the only constitution for Ireland.' But he thanked Providence and Goschen, in about equal proportions, for saving him from taking the Gladstonian side.

To his distrust of Gladstone (now in his seventy-seventh year) and his faith in Goschen as a Liberal leader must be added the influence of Gell, a stout Unionist, and other close friends. Hammond in his classic account maintains that the forces arrayed against 'the People's William' 'included not only the wealth and social power, but the intellect of England'. Milner's progress up the social-political ladder, due to his brains and capacity for friendship, had been steady. His recent social engagements had included several invitations from Mary Gladstone to dine at 10 Downing Street, and one from Oscar Wilde to attend his 'private' wedding. More important to him, no doubt, than these were the close relations he had formed with, among others, Sir Robert Morier, the distinguished diplomatist and G. E. Buckle, the youthful editor of *The Times*. Thanks to the good offices of Jowett, Lord Rosebery, Gladstone's Foreign Secretary, was well disposed towards him. An account of a political dinner at Rosebery's London house was included in the first letter he wrote to Goschen after returning to England.

After a phase of uncertainty Gladstone introduced his Home Rule Bill on 8 April. Hartington's position was now clear as the leader of those Whigs and Liberals – to be distinguished from Chamberlain's small group of Radicals – who opposed the Bill, with Goschen as probably his chief runner-up. Goschen's clear aim, his biographer Elliot states, was

> the leadership by Lord Hartington of a reconstructed and steadied Liberal Party; . . . [and] Goschen himself contributed a vast proportion of the energy, the spirit and the ability with which the Liberal Unionist movement was to be conducted, and which ultimately brought it success.[44]

Elliot, it should be added, was M.P. for Roxburghshire in 1886 and an ardent Liberal Unionist from this time until the end of his career.

Though Randolph Churchill coined the phrase 'the Unionist Party' in March, this amorphous body was born at a meeting at Covent Garden Opera House on 14 April which the Lords Cowper, Salisbury and Hartington, and Goschen (but not Churchill) attended. The Liberal Unionists had no intention of giving up their independence, and soon created a small committee which opened an office of two rooms at 35 Spring Gardens, Westminster, with a secretary, F. Maude. Milner with two M.P.s, A. Craig Sellar and Albert Grey,[45] joined Maude in the task of building an organization. Milner also moved at this time with Birchenough to live in the nearby 47 Duke Street, St. James's, which remained his London home until early in the First World War.

For two and a half months he worked with zest at tasks which in later times were conducted by large public relations offices – writing and distributing literature, watching the Press, tabulating constituencies, corresponding with candidates and M.P.s. With his colleagues he at once met the difficulty, more pronounced in the 1880s than it later became, of the dislike of many of his leaders for personal publicity. Hartington, slow-moving in most matters, was reluctant for his name to be used, and Goschen disliked pressing him in the matter. At first a contribution by Goschen of £80 formed over half the committee's total funds. Milner and his associates produced 'a cloud of circulars and leaflets' but lacked a clerk, a third room and simple books of reference. His enthusiasm is shown by his writing,

> We must set the constituencies in a blaze of dissension right and left and frighten the party-men thoroughly as to the consequences of passing these measures.

He nevertheless preserved his balance and friendships with opponents. Stead, after three months in Holloway Gaol as the price of his 'Maiden Tribute' escapade, strongly backed Home Rule in the *Pall Mall Gazette* and in particular pressed Gladstone to retain Irish Members at Westminster. Milner wrote to him cheerfully,

> to lose Ireland and to keep the Irish members seems a rum ideal. . . .
> [And later when Stead's campaign began to achieve results] you are going to make the Old Parliamentary Hand [Gladstone] drop the only redeeming feature of his rotten Bill! Not approving, I cannot but admire!

Cook, Milner's friend and eventual successor as second editor, was also a Home Ruler from Imperial Federation motives. When unwittingly another Home Rule friend, Lord Dalhousie,[46] wrote to offer Milner 'a perfectly safe [Gladstonian] Liverpool seat' Milner sent on the offer to Cook suggesting he might like to enter Parliament. He himself declined a request from the Harrow Liberals to stand again, calling himself the wrong man to represent them in an election in which Gladstone's Irish policy would presumably be the main issue.

In the weeks before Gladstone moved the Bill's Second Reading on 10 May 'the most intense excitement', Elliot writes, 'prevailed all over the country.' The National Liberal Federation, 'the Birmingham Caucus', came out squarely in Gladstone's support. Speech-making by leaders including Goschen went on apace. The hard work of Milner and his colleagues bore fruit at a meeting in London on 22 May, with Hartington

(*left*) Milner at Balliol, 1873. (*right*) Milner when a Fellow of New College. Photograph taken in 1877

George Joachim Goschen, 1st Viscount Goschen, in old age

as chairman and Goschen making the main speech, which created the Liberal Unionist Association. A committee of some sixty persons was formed which included a large number of peers, sons of peers, and Liberal intellectuals.

This Association's first aim was to defeat the Second Reading – a result which Joseph Chamberlain's attitude, *inter alia*, made far from certain. Milner plied Goschen with suggestions for lobbying the wavering M.P.s and detaching the Radicals, estimating there were 'some twenty or thirty doubtfuls with whom members of our Committee have influence.'

At one critical point he was firmly against a plan that Liberal Unionists should walk out from the vital Parliamentary division rather than vote. On 8 June the Bill was defeated by thirty votes – 343 to 313.

The majority consisted of 250 Conservatives and some 93 (in Gladstone's phrase) 'dissentient Liberals'. About half of these Liberals were thought to be Chamberlainites. Gladstone dissolved Parliament and the final round of the struggle began.

Milner, suffering some ill health, stayed at a house which the Gells had bought, Langley Lodge in Headington, Oxford. He returned to his post at Spring Gardens calling himself 'a sort of general adviser', again sending Goschen material and advice for speeches, and overseeing a Liberal Unionist large-scale pamphlet war. Elliot later wrote that Milner's 'services in the early days of the Association [were] impossible to over-estimate', and described him as, though longing to be in Edinburgh with his chief, 'writing almost daily accounts to Goschen, and at the same time urging him to further efforts.'[47]

The July general election was a Unionist triumph, 78 Liberal Unionists (only twelve of whom the *Annual Register* reckoned as Chamberlainites) being returned and 316 Conservatives. Gladstonians ('separatists' to *The Times*) numbered only 191 and Parnellites 85. Goschen himself, however, was soundly defeated at Edinburgh by a Gladstonian. Gladstone resigned to be succeeded as Premier by Lord Salisbury, who first offered to serve under Hartington. With Conservative leaders of top quality notably scarce, it was reasonable to expect Goschen to find a seat and possibly an office before much time had elapsed. Milner was now, and almost always remained, self-effacing. Yet there can be small doubt that his abilities, journalistic experience, enthusiasm and close relations with Goschen made him a key man in this first stage of Liberal Unionist organization.

He was, for the time being, in the thick of party politics. The success of the Liberal Unionists at the general election, it is clear, owed much to the efforts of Lord Salisbury and the Conservative Central Office to restrain Conservatives from opposing them in the constituencies. From the start the Liberal Unionists had, however, been determined to maintain their separate organization. They had proved, from the Conservatives' point of view, uneasy allies and were to continue to do so.

Goschen went in August for a six weeks' holiday to Bad Ems, and Milner went in September on a visit to Ireland. As usual he entered on his holiday with zest, casting off the burdens of Spring Gardens. Yet his interest in political issues was such that the holiday was also a tour of inquiry into that part of Ireland, the western counties, where impoverishment and disturbance were most pronounced. He was well-furnished with introductions to Unionists and others, and the special diary he kept was a source-book of facts and impressions for use on his return.[48]

This gives a vivid picture of conditions in Ireland's West on the eve of the important Plan of Campaign. Landing at Cork, Milner at once indulged his habit of talking to fellow-guests at the hotel *table d'hôte*, car-drivers, publicans and others. Journeying north to Killarney he had talks with officials and others of the Protestant Ascendancy, including General Buller, sent by Lord Salisbury to restore law and order in Kerry, and later to be associated with Milner in the earliest, most disastrous, stage of the Boer War. He visited Lord Kenmare, whom he thought an incompetent landlord, and his Liberal Unionist friend Lord Monteagle whose house he found 'getting terribly out of hand' due to his impoverishment.

Entering County Clare he indulged his love of the sea dating from boyhood visits to the Isle of Man, seeing for the first time at Kilkee 'the unbroken Atlantic' and walking alone for miles along the Cliffs of Moher. Crossing the 'splendid bay' to Galway he visited Father Fahy, a national hero, in gaol; but his interest there was more stirred by a 'very well-dressed and exceedingly handsome' girl waiting to see her brother arrested after disturbances on the notorious Clanricarde estates. She had, he noted, 'an inward consuming fire' and seemed to him a revelation of 'the ungovernable temper of certain places and breeds of men in this moral patchwork of Ireland.'

Morals must have figured often in long talks this product of Balliol then enjoyed with a Nationalist priest, Father Conway of Carraroe – 'the "world's end" of the south-western seacoast of Connaught' – at whose cottage he stayed some days. He tramped across the hills to see evictions, spoke to the people after mass and surprised the Father by his reasonableness on burning issues.

He then joined English friends, the Henry Hobhouses, at Glendalough, Co. Galway, to go with them up the eastern shores of Lough Mask, Co. Mayo. They drove past Captain Boycott's former house and their guide pointed out two places 'of bloody memory' on the other shore, one being Maamtrasna, the scene of agrarian crime which had caused a big stir in England a few years before and led Arnold Toynbee to visit Ireland in the last autumn of his life.[49] Of larger significance to Milner must have been the fact that they passed close to 'The Neale', the place where his mother had lived with her first husband, St. George Cromie, for twelve years.

It is hardly conceivable that his mother had failed to talk to him about her life in Ireland. Yet Milner makes no mention of these associations. It was in keeping with his nature to feel too deeply about them to do so. On a visit to Tübingen as an undergraduate he had destroyed his mother's diaries of these years, commenting in a letter to Marianne,

there are some things we write for ourselves and ourselves alone, and upon that privacy not even the nearest and dearest have any right to intrude.

Milner left the Hobhouses and turned east, writing: 'the part of my tour in Ireland which deserves special record as fruitful in experiences of a political bearing' had ended and the rest, though delightful, was 'a week of ordinary touring'. He visited his uncle John Ready stationed at Athlone ('the experience of barrack-life was very interesting'), visited Clonmacnoise, had some good walks and soon returned from Dublin to New College.

Back in London he was again working for Goschen and immersed himself in political affairs. He wrote Goschen long letters the main themes of which were now the problems of finding Goschen a seat and Liberal Unionist policy towards Ireland. He pursued a probable vacancy of the combined Edinburgh and St. Andrews Universities' seat, consulting various people, paying attention to publicity and telling Goschen,

the best thing for you would be to hold yourself in readiness, should nothing offer in the meanwhile, to strike a blow for the Edinburgh [university] seat.

Goschen for his part did not forget Milner's need for advancement, and a vacancy of secretary to the committee of the proposed Imperial Institute seemed a good prospect. Milner's lack of interest in this opening sheds light on his ambitions. It was not, he thought and he believed Goschen agreed, an important undertaking 'from a national point of view.' He wanted to see his way clearly and to be able to believe

> that the work I am engaged in is a *big work* . . . my own part may be as small as it pleases. But I do ask that the cause shall be important, [as it had been during the recent election when, however humble his own share, the issue was large].

Salisbury's majority depended on Liberal Unionist support, and Milner agreed with Goschen's belief in 'the absolute necessity of keeping up the Liberal Unionist Party, for the time at least, as a separate organization.' He strove to induce him to make Liberal Unionist Irish policy more constructive. Though no one could yet foresee it, the Irish Question was to remain, as Winston Churchill has written, 'the principal theme of British and Imperial politics . . . the main process by which parties gained or lost the majorities indispensable to their power' for much of Milner's official life.[50] He was to take a significant part in another round of the struggle a quarter of a century later.

Goschen confided to his diary that at a Liberal Unionist banquet in December he received an ovation. He also expressed pessimism about Ireland, his memory, and the efforts the Conservatives might be making to find him a seat.[51] He was to be guest of honour at a banquet in Edinburgh in the New Year and Milner again pressed him to 'make a constructive speech about Ireland.' The Conservatives, he argued emphatically, had begun a period of Irish 'strong government'; in the interest of party tactics as well as humanity Liberal Unionists should emphasize Irish land purchase, industrial development and other remedial measures with enforcement of the law 'only as a means to and condition of these.' They should not make the mistake of identifying the cause of the Union more than necessary with the cause of landlordism. He correctly forecast that 'sensitive public opinion in England, which it is absolutely essential to keep on our side' would not long stomach unadulterated coercion.

When Goschen had been First Lord of the Admiralty in the '70s a tag had been in circulation, 'Goschen has no notion of the motion of the ocean.' Whatever the truth of this, he certainly had no notion that the chance of high office was suddenly to open up before him. Randolph Churchill's sudden resignation as Chancellor of the Exchequer and Leader of the Commons surprised the nation as much as Lord Salisbury's acceptance of his resignation seems to have surprised him. *The Times* announcement of this event two days before Christmas struck Milner, he wrote at once to Goschen, 'all of a heap'. The Irish and foreign countries would lose belief in the Government's stability, and Churchill's action he added was surely 'unpardonable egotism' in imperilling the prospects of his country and party 'rather than abate anything of his extreme self-will.'

This comment sheds some light on the ten days' political crisis that followed. Salisbury's position was still insecure and the Liberal Unionists, as mentioned already, were uncertain allies. What concerns this story are Goschen's hesitation to accept possible office, and Milner's pressure on him, if the chance arose, to do so. He wrote three letters urging him to accept the Chancellorship of the Exchequer if Salisbury offered it, with or without Leadership of the Commons. This was a chance for 'the more natural arrangement of parties' with moderate Liberals like him and Hartington joining the progressive Conservatives. Of the possible alternatives he preferred Goschen's joining the Government, with Hartington on the sidelines leading 'a friendly band of Unionist Liberals'. It seemed, he wrote, as if

the crisis, for which you have long been holding yourself in reserve, has actually come.

Goschen was not going to be rushed, wanting 'the very strongest call from the Conservative leaders and rank and file' as well as Hartington's full approval. The latter, recalled from Rome and unwilling to supersede or serve under Salisbury, advised Goschen to take the plunge. 'The fate of the Government', Churchill's biographer writes, 'hinged upon Goschen's decision; in a few days Salisbury was able to tell his associates "we have caught our fish".'[52] Goschen wrote from the Athenaeum to Milner asking him to come to London to help him in 'drawing up statements for the papers and in sundry other ways.'

Chapter 4

Her Majesty's Treasury
(January 1887 – November 1889)

Chancellor's Private Secretary – Social Diversions – African Prospects

Goschen appointed Milner to be his Principal Private Secretary. Approaching thirty-three, Milner thus added to his roles of academic, barrister, journalist and party organizer that of quasi-civil servant. He was to stay in this post for almost three years, and to continue for a further seven years, first in Egypt and then again in London, as an official mainly concerned with finance.

In Cairo, he wrote in retrospect of these Treasury years, 'nothing but volumes could give an adequate account of this interesting but exhausting time.' Much to his regret his diary-writing almost ceased in this phase. 'Alas! for my diary', he wrote later,

How many interesting people, and how much good talk have I failed to record during the last fifteen months. A full life is good, but a life so full, that one experience drives out another without you having enough time to weigh and compare, much less to record them, is quite a different matter.

It was his business to be always at Goschen's right hand. Judging by the relations the two men had reached, his contribution to Goschen's thinking and actions was greater than history has so far acknowledged. Goschen, of course, was occupying what was usually held to be the second office in the Government, and Milner was only a 'new boy' at the Treasury. As Elliot's biography illustrates, the time was far off when much credit was publicly given to a Minister's subordinates, his civil servants.

Goschen has been somewhat neglected by history, perhaps because he lacked the quality the man he supplanted, Lord Randolph Churchill, so conspicuously possessed – wide popular appeal. He had wide interests, and his friends and admirers included persons as different as Queen Victoria and Jowett.[1] He ranked high as a conversationalist at dinner-tables and at many of the exclusive literary and political societies of the day. But in his career of politician he was handicapped by undue caution. The Rev. Samuel Barnett of Toynbee Hall described him as 'able and halting,' assured of a prominent place in the Kingdom of Heaven 'where weeks are months'. Lady St. Helier, his warm friend and a leading hostess at this time, found that 'his great caution and his analytical mind' made him much too liable for his own political good to see two sides to every question.[2] Margot Tennant, a member of Sir Charles Tennant's large family, was also fond of him but much younger and more ruthless in her comment, writing:

> as a public man he is not attractive; he has innate suspicion and none of the courage which goes with generosity; he does not share blame or distribute praise; he is keenly alive to public and even private opinion.

As the only Liberal Unionist in Salisbury's Government Goschen was still applying, under conditions of some embarrassment, his doctrine that principles are more important than party attachments. A good many Liberal Unionists, particularly in Scotland, disliked his joining the Government and he was inclined to be distrustful both of the Tory leaders and their rank and file. At the end of this January 1887, he suffered the rebuff of defeat by a Gladstonian Liberal by seven votes for a Liverpool seat. Soon afterwards he easily turned the tables on an opponent of a similar complexion at the safe Conservative seat of St. George's, Hanover Square, which he represented until his retirement from office and elevation to the Lords in 1900.

For Milner the corridors of the Treasury must have offered a strong contrast to Stead's vivacious newspaper office, or the cramped amateur atmosphere of Spring Gardens. He had reached, if only on a temporary basis, the centre of Imperial Government, what President Lowell called 'the axle on which the machinery of State revolved'. This august institution, it must be said, was far smaller and less highly organized in the late 1880s than it later became. Its Permanent Secretary, Sir Reginald Welby, was trying on principle to resist the introduction of women typists into Government offices. A bachelor, member of a dozen clubs and a good judge of wine, he disliked hansoms and the new Americanism of 'week-ends'. He was a staunch defender of the taxpayers' interests, and the trusted adviser of the Cabinet on a wide variety of questions.

His Department was at this time also leisurely and aristocratic. Though entry to the Civil Service by open competitive examination had been introduced in 1870, there were a good many exceptions to this, especially in its upper reaches.[3] Those who profited most by the competitive method were the first-class products of the Oxford and Cambridge examination systems. During Goschen's first years as Chancellor an inquiry into the Service reaffirmed the aim of a small Upper Division composed of men of broad liberal education.

Milner, according to his habit, became absorbed in a job which interested him and which he thought worthwhile. What is notable is the speed with which he appears for the first time to have acquired special aptitude for figures and finance; also the speed with which he gained the confidence of the senior, mainly permanent, officials with whom he worked. W. B. Luke states he attacked his work with devouring energy and under the tuition of Welby and others 'soon proved himself a capable and even an enthusiastic official.' He also, this writer claims, showed 'remarkable powers of concentration.'[4]

Goschen was to prove an exacting master due to the political circumstances of these years, the fertility of his brain and his habits of work. Sir Algernon West, then Chairman of the Board of Inland Revenue, wrote that he 'loved minute criticisms, often criticizing his own criticisms, . . . and was 'fond of deferring his decisions', contrasting him with Lord Randolph Churchill who was 'sharp, short and decisive'.[5] His first Budget introduced that April gave a boost to a Government still in troubled waters. It showed technical mastery, individuality of approach and was remarkable for 'the ingenuity it displayed in distributing benefits and burdens.'[6]

The following year he improved on this record, taxing (in the figurative sense) his energies and those of his subordinates still more highly. The year 1888 was that of his best-known achievement, Conversion of the National Debt. It was also the year of the County Councils Act, which involved much readjustment between Imperial and local finances. In connection with a Budget proposal to tax bottled wines he sent Milner in the spring on a diplomatic mission to Paris and Bordeaux.

This episode is only recorded in a few notes Goschen scribbled to Milner. It is desirable to add that Milner's surviving letters to Goschen, which again become important after he had gone to Egypt, are far more numerous than Goschen's letters to him. Goschen's handwriting, in addition, was so bad that it must have caused something like havoc among the Ministers, diplomats and civil servants with whom he dealt during his thirty-five years' official life. Notably bad in his Rugby schooldays, it deteriorated steadily to the point at which, it is said, he eventually became unable to read his own notes for his speeches in Parliament.

His '88 Budget, following his successful Conversion scheme, further consolidated his position. The *Annual Register*, describing the Budget speech, noted his 'power of infusing an almost literary interest into the dull columns of figures which he had to lay before the House.' Milner may be assumed to have been a contributor to this achievement since he was soon to earn acclaim, notably with regard to his book on Egypt, for this particular art. It was part of his duty to spend many hours in the Commons in attendance on his chief. W. H. Smith had been appointed, after Churchill's resignation, First Lord of the Treasury and Leader of the Commons, though he was not yet regarded as in the heavyweight political class. Balfour wrote to Lord Salisbury that Goschen's 'fussiness', fidgeting and habit of making frequent comments on the front bench 'drove Smith mad.'[7] The famous T. P. O'Connor recorded that Goschen also had the disability of a 'raucous' voice which reminded him of the croaking of frogs he had heard in California; but added that he was 'a very great Parliamentary figure' with great debating powers and Parliamentary courage.[8]

This summer Milner received an offer from Lord Lansdowne, a Balliol man and a Liberal Unionist who had been Governor-General of Canada, to accompany him as his private secretary to India where, still in his early forties, he was about to go as Viceroy. The offer shows the reputation Milner had now acquired, but is chiefly interesting for his response. His existing post, of course, was temporary. The Private Secretaryship to the Viceroy was a plum job; his friend Alfred Robinson of New College told him it meant £2,000 a year almost free of expenses for five years and 'a splendid opportunity' to learn everything about India and then perhaps enter Parliament as an Indian expert. Milner had, as the reader knows, great interest in the Empire and, as he once rather curiously wrote, no genuine roots in England.

His refusal of the offer illustrates Sir Geoffrey Faber's conclusion that 'his mind was as realistic as it was idealistic.' It was not made before he had carefully studied accounts of the work by Lord Dufferin, the retiring Viceroy, and Sir Donald Wallace, his secretary, and had written to Lord Lansdowne four sheets of analysis. Lord Dufferin's picture of his private secretary, he argued, had described

> two men, the indefatigable worker, devouring files all day and into the small hours of the morning, and the cool-headed, clear-sighted man of the world with unimpaired tact, temper and judgement, who is able to cope with innumerable applicants and to give the most invaluable moral support to his chief.

With most men, of whom he was certainly one, he thought that the latter qualities would be bound to succumb before the amount of grind which the post now required. Goschen had said he was 'a good horse to drive hard to catch a train, but not so good for doing a steady twenty miles every day of the year.' Jowett's gospel, and his admission to Jowett about his health when he abandoned the Bar six years before, are reflected in his continuing:

I enjoy a good lot of work at all times. But it would be a fraud to pretend that I am one of the toughest of men. Habitual overwork . . . would knock me over. Quantity would kill quality, and as for tact, temper and judgement under these circumstances, I am afraid to think what would become of them. . . . I should like to go with you to India. But it would be hard on you and a disaster for me if you found, when we got there, that I was not strong enough for the job.[9]

The two men talked it over again and the proposal was dropped. Mrs. Goschen wrote to Milner saying that her husband had been almost certain he would accept so good an offer, but would certainly be pleased at the outcome.

For Milner 'a full life' had come always to embrace a sociable one. Heredity, environment and temperament seem to have combined to make him need and enjoy frequent intercourse with other persons. He was the opposite of a man, for example, like Jan Smuts who, as Sir Keith Hancock shows, shunned his fellow-undergraduates at Cambridge and later on, in First World War England at any rate, confined his private life to a few special friends.[10]

Balliol, in this as in other respects, cast a long shadow. With his growing success in the larger world his circle of friends had widened; many, though by no means all, of these were able, successful, members of the much more restricted ruling class of this late Victorian age. Lord Rosebery, a good judge in such matters, testified on a famous occasion to his charm. This was not due, in particular measure, to physical appearance. Though tall and upright, his mien was normally grave and thoughtful, and by strangers he was often thought frigid. He looked what he principally was, a serious-minded official and man of the study.

His friendships were due to his combination of intellectual power and genuine interest in what others had to say or were doing. He was not one who, as he climbed the ladder, spurned lesser mortals or knocked over the occupants of the lower rungs.

With a good salary, bachelor rooms in St. James's and two clubs he was well placed to indulge his fondness for society. His stable-companion in Duke Street, Henry Birchenough, married in '86 the Dean of Westminster's daughter and had been replaced by Clinton Dawkins, a civil servant at the India Office. At Balliol about five years later than Milner, Dawkins became a close friend, succeeding him both at the Treasury and then later on in Egypt.

Balliol, New College and Gell's Headington home were fixed points in his personal life. A senior New College colleague, A. O. Prickard, remembered him in his early days at the College as a frequent visitor to his Horspath home, 'taking an interest in all country village life, and having a flair for sermons and preachers.' The College's Senior Bursar, Alfred Robinson, sought his expert advice in these Treasury days on the College's financial affairs. A younger New College don, Percy Matheson, prominent in the work of the College and the University for many years, became another close friend.

With Goschen's family Milner was on intimate terms. Others with associations reaching further back continued close friends for the rest of his life. Claude Montefiore, younger brother of Leonard, became eminent as a Jewish Biblical scholar and leader of Liberal Judaism, and with Emma his mother was a member of Milner's inner circle. Jim Rendel was a lifelong correspondent. Milner often met Courtenay Ilbert, Balliol's Bursar in his undergraduate days, recently Law Member of the Viceroy of India's Council and later Clerk to the House of Commons. Mrs. Ilbert, with her recent Indian experience, had tried to influence Milner to accept Lord Lansdowne's offer, writing that in spite of the sacrifices of health and other things,

> the great reason for going is the charm of doing such a big bit of work. And that charm is a very potent one. I shall never regret having made Courtenay go.

Milner's numerous Ready relations formed part of his inner circle. He enjoyed visiting one Ready family who lived at Hickling in the Norfolk Broads, and was at this date helping one of their [then] less gifted sons to find a junior Civil Service post and corresponding regularly with another, Oliver, who after Cambridge was in business in Peking. Milner's close relations on his father's side were confined to several uncles who had settled permanently in Germany and had a number of children.[11] One of these, Richard, living near Berlin, wrote to him regularly about German politics ('Englishmen are very unpopular here. It is supposed they are fanning the fire' of France's aggressive intentions), gave him family news and solicited help with his son Richard's school fees. Milner responded liberally to this request; and once when thanking him his uncle added details of the past which Milner kept and labelled 'interesting'.

He had, this uncle considered, though he can hardly have known him well, 'inherited much from your grandmother and the Rappard blood', though fortunately not everything, since grandfather Milner had given all his children in varying degree some of 'the calm blood of the national Englishman'. Their grandmother Sophia von Rappard had been the child of remarkable parents who became people of consequence in Düsseldorf. Her brothers had all been

> exceptionally able men, but even in their youth, like Bismarck, ready for any sport and foolhardiness . . . wild fellows, diving off bridges into the Rhine for bets after champagne parties and so on.

Milner himself, though normally cautious and serious where his work was concerned, was to prove not incapable on occasions of impetuous action.

He had early shown liking for the young, and readiness to help them with advice and also in material form. Goschen and Ilbert had broods of small daughters who greatly enjoyed his visits and became his regular correspondents. Ilbert's eldest daughter Lettice, later the wife of H. A. L. Fisher the historian, Fellow of New College and its Warden at the end of Milner's life, was a special favourite. One of her sisters recollected Milner's visits of these years to their Somerset home as follows,

> we little girls adored and revered him, and never felt him to be the kind of grown-up who is best kept in the drawing room. He had a most pleasant voice to which a slight lisp lent an added charm. . . . His tall and handsome presence lent a touch of glory to every entertainment. . . . [Her mother talked to him about everything] and he excelled as a listener.[12]

In the years which concern this chapter he was thanked by a Charterhouse boy for 'the many helps material and spiritual you have freely given me', and he made it possible for another boy, with no claim on him except friendship years before between Milner's and his parents, to go up to Oxford from Harrow. His success at the Treasury meant an assortment of relations and acquaintances, some of them far from deserving, soliciting money or help to get jobs, and it seems that he seldom failed them. Joe Postlethwaite, for example, some connection of Marianne Malcolm's, had a lawsuit which Milner wrote

> entailed on himself financial ruin, and on me the loss of £200 I have lent him. The sum of my losses through friends and relations amounts by this time to something serious.

Postlethwaite, nevertheless, kept sponging on him.

Whatever his social diversions, to be Goschen's right-hand man at the Treasury continued to mean steady grind. When Parliament rose in the summer of '88 Goschen left town, but Milner stayed on with some intervals in the country. Besides visits to the Readys of Hickling ('the nicest part of my holiday, so homey, and air splendid!') and to the Rendels, he spent a week-end with Sir Algernon West 'at his charming little country house near Guildford.' West's taking to Milner was to prove fateful since he was a considerable figure in the English official world. Claiming to be the last man to enter the Civil Service 'without any exam whatever', he had been Gladstone's private secretary in 1868–72 and since then a Commissioner and now Chairman of the Inland Revenue Board. Tall, handsome, a conspicuous figure in West End Clubs and a favourite in society he had earned advancement by 'tact, ability and hard work'.[13]

Pausing at Dover for two very hard days' work on official papers, Milner travelled to Tübingen to accompany his stepmother on a holiday. Since his father's death five years before, he had taken on responsibility for her welfare. They went to Interlaken for a few weeks' diet of variable weather, mild excursions and Kursaal concerts.

Back in England he was working with Goschen at Seacox on speeches for a forthcoming Scottish tour. A speech Goschen was to make at Aberdeen, a Gladstonian stronghold, gave special trouble in preparation. But the tour proved a success for Goschen and the Unionist cause, Milner writing to Mrs. Goschen:

> Everything passed off brilliantly. That product of much labour, the Aberdeen speech, has had a great effect in Scotland. . . . The London papers give you no impression of the effect here.

With the opening of the autumn session his work was what he called 'of the usual diverse and scrambling character' with much attention to Parliament. Balfour's success as Chief Secretary in applying coercion to

Ireland had not eased the Government's path at Westminster or its alliance with the Liberal Unionists. The Special (Parnell) Commission was set up, and Home Rule continued to embitter relations in Society and the clubs. Goschen was much concerned with a strongly-contested Irish Land Purchase Bill, the Ashbourne Act extension, and had to submit to the Tories rejecting the wheel and van ('veal and ham') tax of his Budget. Milner was experiencing difficulty ('owing to the constant change in the orders I have got with respect to it') in getting a Probate Duty Bill into shape. When the session was wound up just before Christmas he noted he had had a rough time.

After a holiday at Eastbourne with Clinton Dawkins and his newly-acquired wife 'Loulie', riding on the Downs, then some days of skating at Hickling, his life in London resumed its accustomed pattern. An awful drive when Goschen arrived for a few days at the Treasury, week-ends at Seacox preparing his speeches, then a new and almost equally troubled session. Ireland, he noted early in 1889, was, as usual, the centre of interest, though he himself was getting bored with the controversy. Goschen was an unbending opponent of Home Rule and had not, it appears, responded much to Milner's argument for a Liberal Unionist policy of conciliation. Milner was helping Balfour to counter the Plan of Campaign by granting temporary exemption from estate duties to the so-called 'test landlords'. And, as his papers reveal, was taking part in Balfour's secret scheme for syndicates of wealthy English and Irish landlords to buy up selected estates.[14]

Jowett, who had never been hopeful about Liberal Unionist policy, had written a year or so earlier from his Balliol vantage point to a friend,

> though the Government can keep in order the Irish, they cannot keep in order the Irish and the English. The question turns upon the growth or change of the Liberal Party in the next year.[15]

The celebrated Pigott confession of forgery exploded public confidence in the Parnell Commission, and began a steady drift of Liberal Unionists back to Gladstone's fold. In conditions of party disarray Milner unburdened himself in a revealing letter to Birchenough.

The Government, he wrote, was in for a big fight over the naval building programme, but it would be a relief to have a fight in which 'every argument [on the Irish Question] is not sickeningly stale.' Adverse election results might make it difficult for them to outlive the session. He hoped that 'our fellows will keep their colours flying and smash, if we must smash, on bold lines and clearly as the Imperial party, the party of strong government, national defence and a forward colonial policy.' By Conservatism or Unionism – he cared not what name was adopted – he meant the sane and manly policy of men like Hartington and Balfour. What he especially feared was the corrupting influence of the pseudo-democrats of the Churchill type, the people who grabbed at immediate popularity by stealing their opponents' clothes. If Unionism would only 'play the long game it must win' . . . the forces opposed to it would fall to pieces from their intrinsic incoherence.

A little earlier the forceful Joseph Chamberlain had figured with Randolph Churchill in Milner's condemnation of what he most disliked in the political game, 'the Radicalism of pure opportunism', which tried to outbid the 'Radicalism of conviction'. In view of his later close association with and admiration for Chamberlain it is interesting that he ceased about this time to include him in these strictures, at least by name. The two Ishmaels were just engaged, in J. L. Garvin's phrase, in 'a flaring quarrel' over John Bright's Birmingham seat. Chamberlain, reinvigorated by a third marriage, was in his own words occupied in 'cautious steering' to maintain the uneasy Conservative-Liberal Unionist alliance.

Goschen's third budget of 1889 again proved a help to the Government. Recalling this and former occasions Milner wrote to him from Egypt a year from this date,

And *how* I should like to know, exactly, *how* many minutes before the delivery of your speech you had finished the preparation of it. I remember some scrambles without a parallel in human history in the past. But then those were the days when you had an unmethodical private secretary.

The *Annual Register* again commended Goschen's speech for lifting his subject out of the dry realm of statistics and investing his figures with living interest. His previous budgets had reversed the historic achievement of Peel and Gladstone by diversifying the tax structure, and had reduced income tax to 6*d.* His main achievement this year was to meet greater defence expenditure without adding much to taxation. But he introduced a new estate duty of 1 per cent on estates above £10,000 which laid the foundation for Harcourt's radical measure of 1894 with which Milner was much concerned.

Milner added a bedroom to his Duke Street rooms and now rented a whole floor in this desirable quarter for £220 a year. Pressure of work this year had heavily reduced his social life. But he had especially pleasant dinners with the ebullient Stead and with Cook of the *Pall Mall Gazette*. He used to repay hospitality by giving occasional dinner parties at one of his clubs. Recently he had given a dinner at the Reform to, among others, G. W. E. Russell, Eyre Crowe of the Foreign Office and Goschen's eldest son George. He and Gell gave a dinner at the New University Club to a number of Liberal Unionists, including the Warden of Merton, Albert Dicey, Haldane, Cecil Spring-Rice and St. Loe Strachey.

Liberal Unionism was in some degree responsible for an event this summer which affected his future personal life. He was best man at the marriage of Philip Gell to Edith Brodrick, sister of St. John Brodrick (heir to Lord Midleton), then Financial Secretary at the War Office and Secretary for War during the Boer War and after. This lady had acted for several years as hostess for her uncle the Warden of Merton, and has described the Liberal Unionist agitation in which Gell took much part in Oxford between the two Home Rule Bills.[16] Another Edith, the sister of James Rendel, had written to Milner when Gell's engagement was announced, 'I know you will take a gloomy view of it.' Now an eligible thirty-five, Milner did not lack women friends and candidates for the position of his partner in life. But seven years earlier he had confided to his diary that celibacy must be 'the first condition' of his future life.

It is less surprising that Milner, who had left Balliol in a cloud of glory twelve years before, was still unmarried than that he was still an apprentice or without any settled career. New College's gift to him of an Oxford home and a small income certainly helped him to bide his time and weigh the offers he received. The flattering view which many people, including Jowett, held of his abilities gave him confidence that opportunities would continue to open before him. What seems to have been the heart of the matter was his ambition, to quote Toynbee's vision of his future, to be 'a statesman, in the middle of things, a leader of men.' Or in his more modest description in a letter to Stead 'a useful politician in the best sense of the word.' But in what practical form was he to pursue this political goal? It was a crucial question he often found it hard to answer, both at this time and later.

He was now, though he never himself used the phrase, pondering over his next move. It must have been in this spirit, reminiscent of his 'wild thoughts of becoming a vagrant and seeing the States and India' after his failure to enter Parliament, that he conducted a correspondence with A. L. Bruce in this summer of 1889 over a plan to visit South Africa.

Alexander Bruce, a Scotsman fifteen years his senior, died too young to figure much in the annals of history. Yet he exerted vigorous, though unobtrusive, influence on British overseas, and especially African, development at this time. In a top position in Younger's brewery in Edinburgh, he had married the explorer Livingstone's daughter and acquired deep interest in Africa. As an ardent convert to Liberal Unionism in 1885 he had induced Goschen to accept nomination for the East Edinburgh seat and become what Elliot calls his 'great standby' in his later successes and defeats. With no personal desire to enter Parliament, he was a man who gave liberally of himself and worked vigorously on his friends in public positions to advance certain causes. Milner, meeting him again in Egypt soon after his own arrival there, called him, to Goschen, 'about the best-informed man living on every phase of British enterprise in Africa.'

Milner was soon to become so closely associated with the British Empire that it is necessary to recall a few facts of imperial progress. The concept of 'Greater Britain' was now in the ascendant. J. A. Hobson in his well-known *Imperialism* chose a date about 1884 for the beginning of a 'vast increase of territory', which in fifteen years added three and three-quarter million square miles to the British Empire; and he took 'the competition of rival Empires', especially Bismarck's Germany, France and Italy, as the main characteristic of the movement.[17] The year 1884 witnessed the formation in Britain of the Imperial Federation League which, though its proposals received only lukewarm support, spread the idea of the essential unity of the Empire. In 1887 the first Colonial Conference seemed to many to mark a new spirit, both in the Mother country's 'deepened sense of the value and claims' of the self-governing colonies and in these colonies' 'wider Imperial patriotism' and recognition of the Mother country's problems.[18]

India, on which Milner had temporarily turned his back, had become the greatest example of British imperial rule as distinct from influence, a huge field for British trade and investment and, as Robinson and Gallagher have shown, 'the grand base of power in the East', with an army employed as an instrument of security over a vast area outside her borders. Africa, to borrow further from these authors, had only lately begun to appear in Victorian eyes as something more than 'a huge, unopened land mass interposed between Britain and the East.' Her chief significance for Europe had until recently been the use of her harbours for strategic and trading purposes; and South African colonies had been the least popular of all her white possessions in the eyes of British officials. In the past few years this indifference had begun quickly to disappear.[19]

In 1882 Britain occupied Egypt, avowedly on a temporary basis, and three years later had failed to extricate Gordon from Khartoum; she then evacuated the Sudan. The next five years, 1885–90, saw the height of the scramble among the European Powers to carve up the continent (on the map). For Britain the issue of actually developing new territories without burdening the taxpayer had been solved by revival of the chartered company method – the Royal Niger Company, the British East Africa Company, and in 1889, the year this narrative has reached, Rhodes's 'Chartered' or British South Africa Company.

In South Africa Britain's hopes of supremacy, for reasons of strategy or imperial sentiment, had for years been meeting the obstacle of Boer nationalist feeling. The Cape was and remained of first-class importance to Britain as a naval base and depot for trade with the East. But self-governing Cape Colony, relatively settled and prosperous, was confronted in the north by the Voortrekker anti-British sentiment of the Transvaal Republic, shared to a large degree by the land-locked Orange Free State and by her own so-called 'Cape Dutch'. Since its triumph in the First Boer War of 1880–1 and its independence under the Pretoria Convention that followed, the Transvaal had become more separatist in outlook. British Governments, determined not to provoke another challenge, had been pursuing supremacy in an indeterminate manner through influence and the agency of their Government at the Cape.

Three years earlier, when British politicians had been immersed in the Home Rule struggle, discovery of gold on the Witwatersrand in the Transvaal had begun dramatically to change the whole balance of South African politics. On a scale much beyond what followed the discovery of Kimberley's diamond fields in the '70s, foreign investors, entrepreneurs and adventurers hurried to this new El Dorado. While Milner was engaged in his grind on Goschen's budgets, the rise in Transvaal Treasury receipts was becoming the most significant single factor for the future of the white settled areas of South Africa.

To speak of any substantial part of this huge area as 'settled' seems a misnomer. It was the fluidity of the South African scene, the large opportunities hardly as yet imagined, the need for development that prompted Milner to consider a visit and apply for expert advice to Alexander Bruce. Cecil Rhodes, whom he appears never to have met at Oxford, had just persuaded the British Government to allow his Company to finance, administer and colonize a huge area to the north of British

Bechuanaland, north and west of the Transvaal and west of Portuguese Mozambique. The Transvaalers, faced with this threat, were counter-trekking and making efforts to create their own eastern outlets to the sea. Germany had lately established a claim on South West Africa. The separate South African white states were also competing among one another for territory and railway and customs concessions.

Milner, though since his undergraduate days a convinced believer in the British Empire, did not hold any 'theory' of Imperialism, unless his strong view that what was now needed was *development* of resources and influence in the territories we already possessed, and not *expansion* into new territories, can be thought of as such. The Empire, he had argued in his major Harrow election speech, was

> so vast and of such great natural expansiveness that our only strength lies in striving for its development rather than its extension.[20]

Bruce sent advice in good measure in letters with itineraries, introductions to politicians, missionaries and business men, even offering help with his expenses. Milner was also corresponding with John Mackenzie, the well-known South African missionary; and must have discussed his project with Albert Grey, his fellow-campaigner against Home Rule in '86 who had just joined the British South African Company's board. Bruce hoped he would meet Paul Kruger, the President of the Transvaal, 'that modern Oliver Cromwell as his friends and admirers call him, who knows English but will not speak it.' Perhaps the most interesting of Bruce's remarks, since they illustrate his view of Milner, concern Cecil Rhodes.

Rhodes, less than a year older than Milner, had fifteen years' achievement in South Africa behind him. He had built up his Kimberley diamond holdings in partnership with Alfred Beit into De Beers Consolidated Mines, acquired stakes in Rand gold mines, served for eight years in the Cape Parliament and just obtained the charter for 'his North'. If Milner did not meet him in Cape Town, Bruce wrote, he would find him in Kimberley walking about 'with slouched hat and hands in his pockets like an overgrown schoolboy.' He added that Milner's meeting him would be

> of immense advantage not only to you in facilitating your enquiries but also to Cecil Rhodes, some of whose views might be modified as you know the European side of African questions, whilst he knows the Colonial and African side. He has an open and expansive mind....[21]

But to use a phrase of which Milner was fond, *dis aliter visum* – Heaven's will was otherwise. His acquaintance with South Africa was to be postponed, and his fate was to take him to the extreme north of the continent. He had heard, probably from Goschen, of a vacancy as Director-General of Accounts in the Egyptian Government. On a holiday in Normandy in September he was studying the French and their economy, working hard to improve what he called his modest command of the language, walking and riding an ancient tricycle. Later he was in Paris with the Dawkinses, trying to find out more about this job and writing to Goschen, who was on holiday in Ireland, about it.

Characteristically, he set out at length the pros and cons of the matter and Goschen, acting as a friend, was not to be rushed into giving advice. Though Sir Evelyn Baring had telegraphed that he would be 'a very good man for it' the job seemed inferior in status and perhaps in interest to posts at home in the Civil Service or elsewhere that he might hope to obtain. Yet he felt that 'it ought with reasonable luck to lead to something better.'

Milner's growing dissatisfaction with party politics in Parliament as obstructing good government, expressed earlier respecting Ireland, had its share in his inclination to accept an offer which gave

as good a chance as I am ever likely to have of getting into the service outside the U.K. where the individual counts for more and the administrator is not so overshadowed and hampered as he is at home by Parliament. [The English Civil Service he regarded, though admitting this was a peculiar view,] as a smaller world than foreign service. . . . [Lastly – and this was perhaps the decisive argument] . . . most men have roots in England . . . but this is not my case, and I shall feel 'at home' wherever I am serving the interests of Great Britain.[22]

Goschen, calling Milner's decision 'a very grave affair', was being pressed by Welby to find him a permanent post in the Civil Service. This would involve consulting W. H. Smith, First Lord of the Treasury, who would have to talk to Lord Salisbury. Milner, as on many other occasions, after fully consulting employers and friends took his own firm decision. Goschen had told him he would like Egypt because he had 'a touch of the adventurous' in his disposition; and once Milner had taken his favourable decision he added,

your heart is with the adventurous appointment and with the independence and individuality of a foreign position.

Was Goschen's 'touch of the adventurous' an understatement? Beneath Milner's dignified appearance and dedication to work lay strong emotions and an element of restlessness. One recalls the Tübingen schoolboy writing of the place as a 'queer little nest' which he saw no prospect of ever being able to leave, his abandoning the Bar and then sitting loose on the *Pall Mall Gazette*. Had he inherited more than appeared on the surface of what his uncle called the wild von Rappard blood? Dawkins, who knew him well, must have been referring to more than his health when, congratulating him on the Egyptian post, he wrote 'some change was absolutely necessary for you.'

Sir Reginald Welby and Sir Algernon West sincerely regretted his leaving the Treasury and a future in the Home Civil Service on personal and public grounds. The former exerted himself to the end to try to keep him, writing,

> if you give up Parliament you should be secured for the Civil Service. You are the kind of man who justifies appointments from the outside. ... I shall miss a friend.

West wrote from Hawarden Castle blaming himself for not having pressed Goschen harder to find him a place on the Board of Inland Revenue, making flattering references to his contribution to the Unionist cause and deeply regretting his going. A Treasury colleague facetiously described him as Roger Wildrake,[23] and credited him with a big share in Goschen's Conversion scheme.

Mrs. Courtenay Ilbert hoped that the pay (which was £1,500 a year) was good, adding 'though you don't care much about that part of the business.' She counted among the advantages of his move that he would be 'getting out of this hideous political strife.' Gell wrote from the Oxford University Press in his exuberant style ('My dear Boy, News indeed!') to give his blessing. The post, he thought, was one from which Milner could be promoted to 'almost anything . . . perhaps to important City positions at home.' Egypt was not, like India or the Colonies, 'an exile' and (optimistically) he must come home on leave at least twice a year. The Oxford Press, he added, was extending its operations in every direction.

Goschen had many years' experience of Egypt, both in his private capacity as a banker and on official missions.[24] This had doubtless contributed to Milner's interest in the country including his idea some years before of writing a book about it. Gladstone's policies over Egypt, culminating in the Gordon tragedy, had aroused his strong repugnance as the height of irresponsibility – an attitude of 'drift' in the face of competition and combination by foreign powers. Egypt, since Britain had chosen to embark on its occupation, appeared to him at this time as a leading case for applying his doctrine of 'concentration', or Britain's standing fast in certain areas. The Salisbury Government had begun by attempting a plan for evacuation, which France and Russia had foiled. Their attitude was still not reassuring.

'Egypt', Milner told Goschen as the date of his leaving approached, 'smiles to me more and more.' His correspondence with him once he had got there was significant in Anglo-Egyptian affairs. Goschen was to continue as Chancellor of the Exchequer until soon after Milner's return to work in London. Since Milner was never again to serve him in an official role it is fitting to add an appraisal of him as man and 'chief' which he sent to Dawkins as soon as he reached Egypt.

Though there were plenty of contenders for the post, he had persuaded Goschen to appoint Dawkins in his place as Principal Private Secretary. Milner wrote confidentially to Dawkins on 1 December that Goschen was 'a very dear creature, considerate, kindly and sensitive . . .' what he needed to make him a complete success was a little more hardness and self-assertion, some of Joe Chamberlain's coarse-grained irrepressible push and importunateness. He was a little too unwilling to push his neighbours off the pavement. His intellectual make-up was a curious mixture of supreme capacity on the critical side and unequal knowledge due to a very defective memory and a certain timidity of judgement in face of new and startling ideas. He had a number of absurd bugbears, like 'Socialism'. His intensely critical faculty made him hard to please; but its worst consequence was to make him 'ignore in practice the great truth that *le mieux est l'ennemi du bien* . . . what might be fairly well done to-day is postponed in order to be perfectly done the next week. But next week brings its own problems' and the matter was apt to be finally 'settled in a great hurry, and then quite badly'.[25] Writing in Shepheard's Hotel, Cairo, Milner ended this description of service under Goschen on the encouraging note: 'as a training, nothing could be better.'

Chapter 5

Egypt

(December 1889 – June 1892)

'Land of Paradox' – Home Leave – Margot Tennant, and
Up the Nile

Two and a half years later Milner unexpectedly left Egypt for a job at
home and at once wrote a book, *England in Egypt*. He described the
country as 'The Land of Paradox', of great antiquity and present chaos,
'altered in so many respects, but unalterably, eternally abnormal'. The
abject poverty of millions existed alongside the great wealth of a few,
and the natives were put in the shade by relatively few turbulent foreigners. East and West 'jostled each other in startling contrast and with
grotesque results', especially in the sphere of government. The Sultan
in Constantinople was the legal sovereign of Egypt's autocratic Khedive,
a member of a dynasty of Albanian descent. Since Napoleon the interest
of Europe's Powers in the country's strategic value and financial possi-
bilities had grown apace, with the interest of Britain and France much
enhanced by the Suez Canal. A modern historian well states that Egypt's
absorption into European rivalries was

> . . . implicit in the aggressive, expanding character of Western
> technology and business. Egypt was in fact a colonial territory
> . . . a poor shadow of a nation in which Westerners could tread
> heavily.[1]

Khedive Ismail's profligacy had reduced the country to bankruptcy
and caused his deposition in favour of his son Tewfik, followed by Arabi's
nationalist revolt and Britain's sole (since France failed to support her)
temporary military occupation in 1882. Already a variety of foreign
agencies had staked a share in governing the country. Ancient Capitula-
tions and Mixed Tribunals exempted foreigners from laws which applied
to the natives. Ismail's entanglements had brought into being the *Caisse
de la Dette Publique*, Commissioners appointed by the chief bondholding
countries, Britain, France, Austria and Italy. A Law of Liquidation
negotiated by Tewfik ordained that about one-half of Egypt's revenue

must be assigned to the *Caisse*, and the rest – under various restrictions – to the Egyptian Government.

Dr. Lutfi-al-Sayyid's *Egypt and Cromer* states with truth that Britain's occupation

> . . . promised to be an unending source of trouble to her on three levels – within the Cabinet, on the international scene, and within Egypt herself.[2]

This trouble was aggravated by the fact that Egypt theoretically ruled the distant Sudan. Seven years after the occupation, when Milner arrived there, Britain's position in the country had, however, been strengthened. She had established the 'Veiled Protectorate', or become the leading foreign influence in Egypt, due to her army and even more to the strength and ability of her Agent and Consul-General, Sir Evelyn Baring (later first Earl of Cromer). Tewfik was a colourless man and felt insecure, so that Baring had become the real ruler, known to most Egyptians as *El Lord* hardly distinguishable from the Deity, and to some of his less admiring British associates as 'Over-Baring'. He took his instructions from the Foreign Office and not the Colonial Office at home, and Lord Salisbury had already acquired much confidence in his judgement.

Milner lived in a furnished flat, less orderly and elegant than Duke Street, with an Arab servant. He told Gell his office consisted of 20 chief subordinates and 200 'indistinguishable quill-drivers', mainly Syrians, Copts and Jews, and did not think his duties as Director-General of Accounts would be very onerous. Over him an Austrian called Blum was Under-Secretary of Finance. One step higher Palmer, (later Sir Elwin) was Financial Adviser, the most important British official in the Egyptian Government's service. The British Advisers were in form similar to Permanent Under-Secretaries of Whitehall Departments, but in practice more influential, since the Khedive and his Turco-Circassian Ministers had become in many respects a façade. The Advisers were usually hand-picked by Baring, of high quality and (including junior officials) much fewer in number than they later became.[3] Milner told Goschen in January that relations between the leading Englishmen there

> . . . were extremely good. They all row in the boat, and are really *a wonderfully strong crew*.

Baring, though he had so far seen little of him, was always extremely friendly.

Baring's speciality, as might be expected, was finance, and after earlier missions to Egypt he had succeeded as Britain's Consul-General since 1883 in bringing the country back to solvency. Service in India on the staff of the Viceroy contributed to his seeing Britain's role as that of trustee, with her first duty the development of Egypt's natural resources and increase of her revenue to reduce taxation of the fellahin and make badly needed reforms. His financial report of early 1890 expressed cautious optimism, but stressed the 'absolute necessity' for British occupation to continue and for Egypt's problems to be treated on their merits without reference to 'unfortunate international rivalries.'[4] Dr. Lutfi's statement just quoted shows that this second condition proved beyond realization. After some years of sharing with Britain dual control of the country, France had begun an 'unrelenting and unreasoning hostility to Britain in Egypt by every method short of war', and maintained this attitude for fifteen years until the Anglo-French Entente of 1904.[5]

These facts were important to Milner not only during his service in the country but for five subsequent years when, in an influential official position in London, he worked hard to further Britain's interests as he saw them in Egypt and the Sudan. His proved aptitude for finance, and the reputation he had now gained at home, gave him confidence to write to Gell that he was in no hurry

. . . to be involved in the general government of Egypt. That will come, I see already, to a dead certainty sooner or later.[6]

Palmer, like many other of the British officials, had served his apprentice-ship in India. Milner summed him up privately as very capable, strong-willed and effective, but narrow and unsympathetic.

Characteristically, Milner began at once to study Egyptian affairs closely and to learn Arabic ('a truly appalling language'). He had arrived at the opening of Egypt's then fashionable winter season. Only five days' journey from London, Cairo was invaded by what he called 'half the civilized world', which meant of course the more notable and prosperous European visitors. This season included the fruitful event of what seems to have been his first meeting with Joseph Chamberlain, who was also engaged in intensive study of the country and who formed a high opinion of him. Garvin maintains that Chamberlain's conversion to the view that Britain must stay in Egypt for a generation completed 'a long process [which] made him whole as an Imperialist.' Back at home on 24 March he made a speech in his Birmingham constituency which marked him out as 'the leader of the new Imperialism'.[7]

Later this season Milner described to Goschen meeting Prince Eddy, the elder son of the Prince of Wales, who had been 'so much run down as next door to an idiot' that he had been agreeably surprised to find him 'just a natural and amiable young man . . . with an inherited grace of manner.' Philip Magnus records that in fact he was causing his parents some anxiety at this time by being dissipated and unstable.[8] He died of pneumonia in 1892, and the place he would have occupied on the throne was filled in the stormy year 1910 by his brother George V.

In spite of his readiness to wait before getting involved in Egypt's higher government, Milner wrote regularly to Goschen to keep him informed and presumably to exert influence on Her Majesty's Government's policies towards Egypt.[9] Goschen, besides his knowledge of finance and of Egypt, was after Salisbury himself better informed on foreign affairs than any other member of the Cabinet; and Baring at least suspected him of being unconvinced that the British occupation should continue. Goschen and the Prime Minister, the latter's daughter writes, had reached 'an easy intimacy [with] a great reciprocal confidence in each other's expert authority.'[10] Europe's scramble for Africa continued, and Milner told Goschen he was 'much more excited over South Africa and the threatened row with Portugal . . . [than over] the most incredibly stale controversy' of Ireland. In fact Salisbury, influenced *inter alia* by Baring's success, had now become convinced (though the fact was not generally known) that continued British occupation of Egypt was essential. He had begun both to replace Constantinople by Cairo as the pivot of his Mediterranean strategy and to aim at keeping other Powers, especially France, away from the Upper Nile. These policies, however, were still in their early stages, and for Salisbury Egypt and the Sudan were only part of a diplomacy embracing the whole African continent. Also, his daughter writes, he 'always preferred a long preparatory interval between conception and action.'

To the end of what was to prove twenty-four years as Britain's Egyptian Agent, Baring adhered to the views that the policy of evacuation was irreconcilable with the policy of reform, and that fiscal and economic reforms had a prior claim over administrative and educational ones. Some historians see the troubles of his era as due to the reinstatement by Europe's Powers after Arabi's revolt of 'pashadom', a despotic, inefficient, corrupt system of rule which maintained an oppressive social order. A Legislative Council and Assembly had been created, but these were advisory and the Assembly met infrequently. After retiring in 1907, Baring wrote in his comprehensive *Modern Egypt* that the main feature of the country's government was that 'legislation has to be conducted by diplomacy.' At the centre in Cairo this meant replacement of the despotism of the Khedive and Ministers by the rule or strong persuasion of Baring and British Advisers.

Milner called the Veiled Protectorate a real masterpiece of political management by Baring. To Gell he wrote,

> ... the essence of the whole situation is a splendid piece of management ... that we should all of us know it and none of us say it, and especially that people at home shouldn't talk about it.[11]

Baring's definition of Egyptian legislation applied equally in the sphere of what he and others called 'internationalism'. Among the international bodies directly concerned with Egypt the *Caisse* was the most important. Milner wrote later that it 'put Egypt into a strait waistcoat of the severest kind.' Under a system of two budgets the Egyptian Government was bound to make good a deficit in the *Caisse*'s budget without the right to share in any surplus. The *Caisse*, on the other hand, while having claims on a Government surplus, could not be asked to help with a Government deficit. The Government was also bound by a legal limit of Expenditure.[12] Baring had just induced the Khedive's Government to take the important step of abolishing (save in exceptional conditions) the Corvée, or heavy burden on the fellahin of forced labour to guard and repair the Nile and the canal banks. If new taxation to pay for this necessary service was to be avoided, France had to agree both to a conversion scheme and to the way in which the money thus saved would be used.

France refused to co-operate. Milner wrote to Goschen in March 1890 that she had 'shown her power in very real manner' and made the Egyptians feel that England was impotent to protect them. He thought the Anglo-Egyptian administrators had shown

> ... a want of strength. ... We do not *resent sufficiently* the wrong they are doing us ... as a natural consequence of our weakness, French pretensions are on the increase.

Goschen wrote that he got on well with Dawkins, though the Treasury was giving him as many worries as ever. At Budget time he had not had 'such a scramble at the last moment' this year, but had missed him very much.

In April conversion negotiations took Palmer to Europe and (Blum, it seems, being away) Milner became Acting Financial Adviser and so

involved in the general government before he had expected. He told
Edith Gell he found this work very interesting since it involved constant
relations with Baring and the Khedive and a seat on the Council of
Ministers. Six weeks or so later his work was again 'an abominable drive',
but should anything happen to Palmer he had now become his inevitable
successor. Baring was splendid, leaving him a free hand but backing him
up fully in a crisis.

This experience at the centre of what he called the 'curious and complicated machine of Egyptian government' had convinced him, he told
Goschen, that Egypt's progress in the foreseeable future had

> . . . one keystone only, the unobtrusive but absolute dictatorship of
> Baring. . . . Despite all his great superficial faults – his brusquerie, his
> conceit, his long-windedness (which you will think is catching) he is
> a statesman of a very big order, a perfectly extraordinary instance of
> the right man in the right place.

He himself had now proved the incapacity of 'even the best of the native
politicians'. Riaz Pasha, the Prime Minister and a Turk, though far the
best, was 'just a petulant child'.[13]

Though France had agreed to conversion, long negotiations followed
on the terms and what was known as 'the application of the economies'.
Goschen agreed with Milner that Palmer was driving too soft a bargain,
and took active steps with Salisbury, as well as using influence with the
bankers at some personal risk, to get more favourable terms. In the
middle of June Milner was telling him:

> . . . with all my pugnacity, I don't want to let fly at the French unless
> they put themselves thoroughly in the wrong, as they will do if they
> make great difficulties over the Corvée.

He added the scheme he would put to the French. If they insisted on
trying to re-establish control, or again raised the evacuation issue, he
would stop the negotiations and *'retire swearing'*. He ended 'it is on you
and Lord Salisbury that we must rely if we are not to be given away
again.'

The French were not treated in this strong fashion by Palmer and
continued obstructing the Corvée plan.[14] Milner became apprehensive
that Salisbury might agree to evacuation discussions, and implored Goschen to prevent him taking any step of this kind without consulting
Baring. He again defined his long-held view of imperialism as the mean

between the two British schools of thought which were either for claiming everything or for sticking to nothing. He considered that

the true Jingo is for limited expansion but unlimited tenacity. Some day perhaps he will be better understood.

By late July Baring and others had left for England on their long summer leave, Palmer and Blum had still not returned and he and Riaz, he wrote, had for a time been 'the government of Egypt'. Riaz was a strong man with 'a profound belief in despotic government', and they got on well personally but never agreed about anything. Milner, though still puzzled about Salisbury's policy, had an inward conviction that Britain was not going to leave the country. If this was so, why didn't Her Majesty's Government give a broad hint to that effect, and so 'quadruple at a stroke the effectiveness of our efforts to establish a rational and civilised system of government?'

Milner then entered a personal crisis when Blum, who had served England loyally, resigned and intrigue began over his successor, Riaz wanting a non-European and the French objecting to an Englishman. On 8 August 1890, after a lapse of over five years, Milner resumed writing his diary and stated,

I am determined not to allow anyone but myself to be put in Blum's place. If this were done, I should resign my present office in 2 or 3 months, but still spend next winter in Egypt, writing a book about the English occupation. . . . At this moment I really don't know which I should prefer, to have the Under-Secretaryship . . . or to have my freedom.[15]

He was, however, offered and accepted Blum's job which he expected to keep him in Egypt for another three years. His diary entry is significant as showing him once again nursing the idea of independence confident, one assumes, that he could maintain himself on his New College income and probably by his pen. It also shows once again his determination to justify Britain's occupation of Egypt to the public at home.

In September he took his first real holiday since his arrival in the form of a trip to the Delta with his friend William Garstin, a British engineer from India engaged under Sir Colin Moncrieff in the crucial task of reorganizing the country's neglected irrigation system. The Public Works Department in which he worked had just completed restoration of the Barrages of the Delta. The river was high, though not yet to the point of danger. Milner enjoyed accompanying Garstin on his landings at some of the more anxious points in his 'long line of fortifications', meeting the mudirs (provincial governors) and sitting up late watching the busy traffic of lighters with their picturesque sails. After only a week Palmer wired that he had been called home suddenly on another conversion scheme, and Milner felt bored by having to cut short his holiday so soon.

He had moved from Cairo to Helwan, a spa in the desert with warm natural springs some 115 feet above the Nile. A nice small house, he wrote to Matheson of New College, was almost unobtainable in Cairo where you could get a 'palace pretty cheap, or a pig-sty very dear.' He loved the desert and found the Helwan air splendid 'and above all the nights most fresh and beautiful.' His promotion had meant an additional £500 p.a. He kept two horses, and looked on daily rides as essential to keeping fit.

Summer was a slack season, but since Blum had been a poor organizer he was again fearfully busy. Riaz invited him for a night to his well-farmed and fertile estate in the Delta. On his native heath he was 'a very great man', and their departure next day from the railway station was like a royal progress. In political matters he remained good-tempered to the end of what Milner called his own 'second interim'. This came in mid-November when Baring, Palmer and 'all our absent notables' returned from Europe, and winter visitors began to pour in.

From visitors and from his large correspondence Milner was well-informed about British politics. He had written earlier this year to Birchenough that he had realized his idea of going

> ... where good work was being done by Englishmen, unhampered by the blighting influence of home politics.

This uncomplimentary comment on home politics did not prevent his feeling intense interest in them. He wrote, for example, in December on the 'breathless interest' of Parnell's recent divorce and the important results it must have on the Irish Question. He was ready to forgive Parnell everything for defying Gladstone and his system of

> ... making use of both God and the Devil ... to lean on the English Puritans with one arm and the Irish lawbreakers with the other.

But he feared that the 'gullible majority of Britons' including Liberals would continue to win by-elections by sticking to the one issue of 'Gladstone, the Great and Good'.

His friend A. L. Bruce wrote from Edinburgh with the encouraging forecast that 'Unionism is undoubtedly growing in Scotland.' The Anglo-German Convention had finally been settled in London with the help of Goschen, who was now Lord Rector of Edinburgh University. In a reference to Goschen's speeches Bruce wrote: 'you are missed, I think, as the literary lapidary.' He added that he was always hearing about Milner, and never anything but what was good. He felt very comfortable about Egypt since he had gone there, knowing that he would gradually imbue others with his high standards and broad Imperial views.[16]

During his second Cairo winter Egypt's finances continued to improve. These were, he wrote home, 'never dull . . . and more than almost anywhere else the very essence of politics. As England is doing some of her best work in the valley of the Nile, I am glad to be of the company.' Goschen was still giving active help over Egypt's financial transactions with Turkey and other Powers. Baring reported early in 1891 another surplus and the certainty, if no substantial change in Egypt's political situation occurred, that more fiscal relief would be possible in the next few years. But since the French had only agreed to using the conversion economies to abolish the Corvée for one year, uncertainty over this matter continued.[17]

Milner had acquired a passion for the desert and tried this winter to combine the fresh air and rides of Helwan with sharing part of a Cairo house with a colleague. This double existence did not answer, partly because, he frankly noted, 'I cannot keep altogether out of the gaieties of Cairo.' His work, first with the Budget and then much concerned with State Lands, was less interesting than in his first year. Deprived of the exercise to which he always attached much importance, and after fifteen months of almost uninterrupted work, he felt stale. He was scathing about 'one of our absurd periodical crises', the resistance of Riaz and others, successfully overcome by Baring, to the appointment of a British Judicial Adviser, Sir John Scott, who became Milner's friend and in time re-created Egypt's whole judicial system.

A letter from Dawkins at the Treasury told him that Sir Algernon West and Welby were as keen as ever to secure him for the Home Civil Service. West was retiring fairly soon from the Chairmanship of the Inland Revenue Board and wanted Milner to become a Commissioner, which might ultimately lead him to the chairmanship. As always when offered a job Milner weighed all the pros and cons in conversation or in writing. He telegraphed refusal, telling Dawkins he would have preferred to talk it over with him and others at home. In a letter he explained that his

. . . chief reluctance would be to leave Egypt before I have had time to make a point of my stay there.

If he left before achieving the ambition of making himself 'an authority on the subject for all the rest of my life, the last arduous year and a half would be more or less wasted.' As later chapters will show he did in fact fulfil this ambition. The position he coveted after two more years or so of Egypt was the Financial Membership of the Viceroy of India's Council, though succession to this would need 'a perfect series of lucky accidents.'[18]

He was due to have three months' leave in early April. He fitted in another week's trip in the Delta with Garstin, exploring drainage operations in a labyrinth of canals, being carried over rivers by native bearers, lunching with Bedouin sheikhs and having endless talks about land. He wrote to Goschen from an inn at Zagazig, a centre of the cotton and grain trades, that though 'the great problem of what we are going to do with Egypt' was still not settled he thought he now knew the whole case thoroughly, and could at least '*pose the question*' with a clearness which he considered largely lacking both in Egypt and at home.

Sailing on 8 April 1891 he reached Athens, the subject of so much reading at Balliol, now seen for the first time. He became lyrical as Athens and Attica surpassed all his hopes. A walk alone up Lycabathis revealed 'the loveliest panorama I have ever seen in my life', and a 26-mile ride on horseback to Marathon called forth historical comment and the sentiment 'it was a great privilege to have lived to stand on that holy ground.' Greece made him feel, as he had felt in Italy years before, that such sights and associations gave him a new intellectual and spiritual vitality.

Crossing to Brindisi and travelling up 'the unlovely side of Italy' he spent some days at Tübingen seeing his stepmother, his young cousin Richard a medical student ('very fine-looking, gentlemanly and intelligent'), his nurse Emma and her daughter Josephine his godchild, now grown up, and other old friends. He found a good deal of support for Bismarck, dismissed by Kaiser Wilhelm II a year before, which he did not share, thinking Bismarck 'so self-willed and egotistical' that total submission to him or dismissal were the Kaiser's only alternatives. Before the end of April he was back in his London rooms at 47 Duke Street.

There followed two months crammed with social engagements, some formal work and – an essential part of his aims – much effort spreading knowledge about England in Egypt. A few days after his arrival a farewell dinner was given, mainly by old Balliol men, to Dawkins, who had just left the Treasury and was bound with Loulie for the local managership of the Peruvian Corporation. He saw them off at Liverpool, calling their leaving 'a great blow, as they were among my dearest friends in England'; South America was, unlike Egypt, a real physical separation. He had sent Goschen an apology for advising Dawkins to take this job, which reveals the similar outlook of the two men. Dawkins, he wrote,

> ... had the spirit which makes men wish to see strange forms of life and work ... he had for years been wanting to go off for any chance ... at the ends of the earth. .... A private secretaryship was of necessity a transitional stage in a man's career.

As with himself, Dawkins's only feeling against the move was 'reluctance to leave your personal service.'[19]

Milner saw an immense number of friends and dined out almost every night. With Gell he attended the Ambarum dinner of dons of both ancient universities at Cambridge, meeting many academic celebrities. He went to Wimbledon to spend a delightful evening with Stead, who talked with his usual brilliance about his hero Cecil Rhodes and hopes of maintaining the political unity of the English race. Small all-male welcoming or farewell dinners of groups of friends at London Clubs were a regular feature of the time; a dinner given in his honour by his friend Bruce at the Reform Club gave him especial pleasure.

Business calls in the City included a formal visit to Rothschilds who were unwilling at that time to take part in converting another Egyptian Loan. He wrote in his diary that he

> ... ought to note, as I believe it is a subject of congratulation, that the Rothschilds, though refusing conversion, were perfectly civil to me.

Later he went to Paris on some business with Alphonse de Rothschild. Though missing de Lesseps, the builder of the Suez Canal, he saw a good deal of Lord Lytton, the Ambassador, and other Englishmen in the city so much linked with Egyptian affairs.

He welcomed news from Egypt of the fall from power of Riaz Pasha, whom he had come to regard as a serious clog on Egypt's progress. His successor as Prime Minister, Mustafa Fahmi, is called by Dr. Lutfi 'a rich, elegant Turk with a weakness for fine shirts which he sent to England to be washed and ironed; but apart from this one eccentricity he never departed from the norm.' Honest and hardworking, he preferred to obey orders rather than give them. His ministry was dubbed the 'ministry of dummies' by the Egyptians, with an exception for Tigrane Pasha, the Foreign Minister and a Christian Armenian who was made of sterner stuff.[20]

Unlike his holidays at home from South Africa in the future, this one was not overshadowed by almost continuous work. Baring spent some months in Britain each year, and Milner was only No. 2 in Egypt's Finance Department, even though that Department was important. He was able to spend carefree June days in Oxford as Jowett's week-end guest, and then see numerous friends and dance till the small hours at Merton Commem. Ball.

A week-end with Jowett at Balliol was almost always shared with eminent guests which on this occasion included the Speaker of the House of Commons and a young favourite of Jowett's, Margot Tennant, the 27-year old daughter of Sir Charles Tennant, a Scottish industrial magnate. Margot was a prominent member of the small company called the 'Souls', witty, eager for knowledge and attention, with a ready tongue, a pronounced ability to shock, and many men friends from Jowett and Gladstone to those nearer her own age such as Balfour. This seems to have been Milner's first meeting with her; he met her again at a later house party and commented that though her conversation was occasionally excellent 'Margot talks too much to be always clever.'

After dinner on the first night at Jowett's he had to rush off to address the Palmerston Club on 'Imperial Questions, especially Egypt', later writing that he thought his audience was interested and that he did some good. A very gay party and capital talk till the small hours of the morning in All Souls' common room followed. He lunched with Willie Goschen, Goschen's younger son, then an undergraduate at New College and later a partner in the family bank, and his parents, and had a long and interesting talk with Goschen. Visits followed to Mrs. Arnold Toynbee, now Treasurer of L.M.H., and the Gells at Headington, as well as a 'water-party' to Godstow, reduced in number by some trouble at Balliol which had caused the College to send down about twenty men.

Milner's love of the Thames was indulged by several days of rowing, south of Oxford, at least one of them in the company of a lady of some mystery called Cecile.[21] He had to refuse an invitation from the Joseph Chamberlains to spend a week-end at their Birmingham home, Highbury. He talked to George Parkin, his Canadian friend, about the policy the Imperial Federationists should adopt, agreeing with him over

. . . the increasing urgency of a definite move forward, as well as the decidedly slow growth of national interest in the question.

One night he thoroughly enjoyed himself at a large dinner given by Asquith at the House of Commons. At about this time and possibly at this dinner Margot Tennant first met Asquith, who had married more than a dozen years before and, besides a promising career at the Bar and as a Liberal M.P., had fathered five children. She wrote much later in her *Autobiography* that she was 'deeply impressed by his conversation . . . [and] made up my mind at once that this was the man who could help me and would understand everything.'[22]

Milner gave an interview on Egypt to the *Pall Mall Gazette*, now edited by E. T. Cook, Stead having left to found his illustrated popular monthly *Review of Reviews*. Milner's object was to give publicity to the 'advantages bestowed on the *people* of Egypt by the English occupation.' In spite of big interest at the time in the sensational Tranby Croft baccarat scandal involving the Prince of Wales, Cook devoted the whole front page to Milner's facts and arguments.[23] On his last night in England Milner dined at the Commons, and sat up until 3 a.m. in Duke Street talking to Gell and writing letters. The next morning he was cordially received by W. H. Smith, First Lord of the Treasury, who was pleased with the progress made in Egypt and to whom, Milner noted, he did not hesitate to express his views

. . . pretty frankly [explaining] why, while interested in Egypt and liking my work there, I did not think that was my ultimate career.

After visits to the India Office and the Treasury on 1 July he went to Dover where he enjoyed rest and sea air for two days. Then, travelling via Paris, Brindisi and a comfortable boat, he reached Alexandria on 9 July.

It still being the long summer lull he was again Acting Financial Adviser. He called on the Khedive, who was very friendly, and had long talks with the new Prime Minister and Tigrane Pasha about relations with the French. He thought the situation greatly improved by the retirement of Riaz and others; but with the very personal system of government characteristic of Egypt he foresaw trouble ahead. With Scott practically Minister of Justice and Kitchener at the Ministry of the Interior, Britain was now for the first time 'really responsible for the whole country.' Yet with the Khedive's personal position now much enhanced, his opposition to British policies could prove awkward. The Prime Minister was terribly weak, Tigrane was openly hostile to British influence, and Milner was nervous about his chief, Palmer, who had excellent qualities but was frightfully precipitate and lacked ability to see things as a whole. But he admonished himself in his diary against

. . . a very natural but no less detestable jealousy [since] absolute loyalty to one another among the English is the secret of success in this country.

Only a few of the senior British officials were in Egypt. Cairo was intensely hot and noisy and mosquitoes interfered with his sleep. He found satisfaction in exerting himself to find a new Cairo house. This took time to furnish, eventually containing 'a huge Arab drawing-room all carpets and embroideries, a study which is violently Chinese', an early Victorian dining-room, an Arab cook and a scullion. He told Fanny, Goschen's young daughter, that he had taken to driving a dog-cart.

Life was not eventful. He found that his new Turkish or Egyptian Finance Minister took little part in the work, but when he did was a good influence. He was himself sitting on two Commissions dealing respectively with cholera and rebuilding the burnt-down Abdin Palace. He went with Garstin on still another trip down the Delta, this time on the Rosetta or western branch of the Nile. He found that his chief interest outside his own work was Kitchener's struggle to get the police in order, on the success of which he suspended judgement. The Ministry of the Interior was called by Cromer in *Modern Egypt* 'the centre of gravity of Egyptian misgovernment.'[24] Responsible for appointing local officials as well as for the police, it was a big fount of patronage and therefore of special interest to Egyptian Ministers. Kitchener, already Adjutant-General of the Egyptian Army, had been created in addition Inspector-General of Police. Though aloof and unpopular with his British brother-officers, he worked prodigiously hard and was successful in cultivating influential friends at home. He had just had a serious difference with the Khedive about relations between the mudirs and the police which Milner had managed to smooth down. Milner called him

. . . certainly ruthless in his treatment of other interests . . . not easy to keep in check. A strong self-willed man, *not absolutely straight*, he might very easily cause great trouble not only with the natives, but among the English themselves.[25]

Kitchener had developed a secretiveness, remarked on by many people, which proved lasting. But without attempting any major reforms he much reduced serious crime, and more than doubled the total number of convictions. His reward was his appointment six months from this date on Baring's recommendation to succeed Sir Francis Grenfell as Sirdar (Commander-in-Chief) of the Egyptian Army; an appointment, his biographer Magnus writes, which the entire Egyptian Army received with surprise and disgust.[26]

In October Baring, Palmer and others returned from Europe. Milner told Baring he thought Egypt's condition wonderfully improved, but he was worried by recent emphatic statements by Gladstone and Morley supporting evacuation. In a long letter to Goschen of 11 October he claimed he was 'not at all a fanatic on the question of the occupation'; but if British troops left it was absolutely essential to maintain the predominance of British influence in the country. His conviction that Baring's measures were of great benefit to Egypt's ordinary *people* was equalled by his conviction that withdrawal of British influence would make the country again a genuine danger to international peace. He could not conceive how the 'peace party' at home failed to understand this. I always say, he continued, that

... if you were to load a Metropolitan Tramcar inside and out, it would amply suffice to carry off all the people who stand between Egypt and another smash and I think you would find that I must be one of the passengers, though perhaps the last to be asked to mount.

He added that, deeply interested as he was in Egypt, he had not lost his keenness about the bigger things at home. A General Election could not be long delayed, with Gladstone's return almost a certainty. In the coming fight he hoped Unionists would not despair of 'sanity and moderation as a policy' and try to outbid the 'Radicalism of conviction by the worse Radicalism of pure opportunism.'[27]

In late November Margot Tennant arrived with her parents in Cairo. For a few days Milner constantly saw them, and his friendship with Margot ripened rapidly. When the Tennants left for a three weeks' tour up the Nile the two kept up a lively correspondence, and Margot's letters, like her talk, were ample, vivid and entertaining. She wished he was with them. Returning to Cairo for Christmas the Tennants spent four more weeks there, when Milner saw much of Margot at parties, sightseeing and sharing with her long walks and rides; 'we saw as much of one another as was humanly possible,' he wrote. Margot danced a *pas seul* at the Barings' Christmas party, and accompanied Milner to the New Year's Eve service at the English church.

Milner jettisoned his earlier declaration of celibacy and proposed to Margot, but was rejected. He was 37, and had lately heard from Sir Algernon West of a possibility that he might be appointed not a Commissioner but to the important post of Chairman of the Inland Revenue Board. Though Margot admired and was fond of him, she had no lack of suitors. In particular, Asquith's wife had died of typhoid a few months before, and he wrote to her in Cairo of his undying love for her. Yet a year from this date West, one of her fervent older admirers, wrote while a guest at her home The Glen, in Perthshire, 'she has no intention of marrying at all at present – which is wise.' In a few years she chose Asquith, and in time as the wife of the Liberal leader and Prime Minister made a large and often tactless contribution to domestic politics.

Milner told Margot he was too lucky in friendship to be lucky in love. She wrote to him on her way to Alexandria that she had never heard anyone spoken of with such 'genuine admiration and warmth', and wrote again with much self-criticism on the boat to Europe.[28] Soon afterwards Milner realized a long-cherished ambition to go up the Nile as far as the Sudan frontier. On the river, catching up with his diary, he wrote that his love for Margot had been

> ... momentous in a unique degree.... Hitherto I have doubted whether I was capable of that single and absorbing love which alone could make marriage desirable in a life so busy and full of interest as mine. Now I know that I am capable of it, but I also know that the only person who has ever inspired me with such a feeling is one whom I shall never marry.

He continued that though perpetual celibacy had become an 'almost certainty', his inner condition of heart and mind had undergone radical change. He felt less restful, with that intellectual and spiritual vitality he had experienced on his recent first visit to Greece. On a high moral note he asked himself whether his life would now become 'more useful, more unselfish and nobler.' Margot's notable lack of reserve soon made his romance a topic in letters arriving from home. To one such he replied he would have married her without hesitation, but unlike her he was 'by nature very reserved about such matters' and would never discuss the affair with any third person.

Shortly before the Tennants left Egypt Khedive Tewfik, still in the prime of life, died of pneumonia. The event, Milner wrote, was a great shock both on personal and political grounds. Though he had felt a real liking for him and believed he sincerely wished to work with the English for Egypt's good, anti-English prejudice was still very strong in the Palace. There was a 'curious irony', he continued, 'about this Egyptian business'. Riaz Pasha's fall and Egypt's decided material progress had made it seem as if the game was really won. But now Morley and Gladstone's folly, persistent French Anglophobia and the Khedive's death combined to suggest 'all is once more in the crucible.'[29]

With Baring's unobtrusive management making its usual contribution Tewfik's son Abbas II was installed in the Abdin Palace with impressive Anglo-Egyptian ceremony. Barely 18 years old, he had spent his formative years in Switzerland and Vienna, where he had a French teacher and had observed the working of Franz Josef's absolute monarchy. He was dignified and good-mannered and made a favourable impression on Milner and Cromer, who reported to Lord Salisbury that his judgement appeared to be sound for so young a man. He was destined, however, to add to the crises which formed so constant a feature of the Veiled Protectorate; and to remain Khedive until Turkey joined Germany in the First World War in October 1914.

In his personal life Milner lost, besides Margot, the appointment of Chairman of the Inland Revenue Board which West had been trying to arrange. Goschen wrote that the Deputy Chairman, who was thought to be retiring, had now changed his mind. His letter, however, was more full of his failure to obtain the Leadership of the House of Commons, after acting for W. H. Smith in the previous session, in competition with Arthur Balfour. His confidence in Milner's judgement and sensitiveness about his own standing in Parliament and with the public are again clear. As a Liberal Unionist he was aware, Milner wrote in reply, that after his success in Ireland the Tory Balfour had 'established himself as a statesman of the first order.' Milner told him that his acceptance of defeat showed 'uncommon fineness of feeling and devotion to the [Unionist] cause.'[30]

Milner was not cast down for long either by his failure to secure the Inland Revenue job, or by what he now saw as his very moderate usefulness when Palmer was in Egypt. He was captivated, as he had been from the start, by 'the wonderful interest of this land of physical and moral miracles', and the reaction which followed the Margot affair was reduced by intense enjoyment of his voyage up the Nile. Leaving Cairo on 19 January by train, he embarked at Asyût on the *Takhta*, a comfortable new steamer lent to him by the Public Works Ministry, with an excellent captain and crew and his own cook. His only fellow travellers were a Major Jackson of the Egyptian Army, and a clerk called Socrates Spiro whose role was to teach him Arabic. He began days of 'sunshine, bracing air, gorgeous sunsets, lovely starlit nights and refreshing sleep.'

For five weeks he combined these luxuries with sightseeing, meeting friends and study of conditions in Upper Egypt. 'As a habitable country', he wrote later, 'Egypt is only one thing – the Nile.' Every square foot of cultivable land had at some time or other been brought down by the river, from April to June a sluggish stream and then for some months 'a sea itself, spreading in a vast lake.' The distance from Cairo to the Sudanese frontier at Wadi Halfa was 800 miles, with frequent high banks, a narrow belt of cultivable soil and beyond this the desert.

In a few days he reached Luxor, where he dined with Edward Tennant, Margot's brother, and other English friends. Besides writing his diary he was filling a notebook with facts and figures.[31] When an American tourist asked him naïvely why England didn't 'internationalize' Egypt he reflected on paper:

> England is between two fires. If she's to be true to the mission of raising the native, she must resist not only France but other foreign attempts at encroachment and make an enemy of everybody.

To 'internationalize', if this meant inviting other Powers to share more fully in Egypt's government, would, it was clear, strengthen the already heavy foreigners' yoke on Egypt.

Aswan he found a grotesque sight with two large Cook's steamers, the bank swarming with tourists beset by donkey boys and a fantastic medley of races. The British officers of the Sudanese Regiment paid their respects to him, he visited the government offices and primary school, and next day walked all over Philae and returned shooting the rapids of the First Cataract which ran between magnificent granite rocks. To proceed further south he had to transfer to a very uncomfortable gunboat which took him through one of the proposed sites of the much-discussed reservoir, which in time became the Aswan Dam. The creation of this, he wrote, was now 'the burning question' of Egypt's irrigation, less for its site than for how the £E2–3 million or more it would cost could be raised.[32] With British capital and engineering this first Aswan Dam was in fact begun six and a half years later.

Milner read a great deal, wrote to Margot and many others at home, was much impressed by the British development of Karosko, saw the temples of Abu Simbel and arrived at the frontier post Wadi Halfa where two Egyptian and two Sudanese battalions were stationed. The Sudanese infantry, he noted, were very expensive since besides wives 'an immense number of other women' moved with them. He was much impressed by the British officers, thinking they compared very favourably with their brothers in arms at home.[33] He got a good view of the Second Cataract, and penetrated some thirty miles south to the extreme limit of Egyptian advance towards a huge area of barbarism. The Mahdi had been succeeded as ruler of the Sudan by the Khalifa in 1885.

Beginning to turn north he rode on a donkey to the celebrated battle-field of Toski where some two years earlier General Grenfell, the Sirdar, had frustrated the Khalifa's big attempt to invade Egypt. At Aswan he rejoined the comfortable *Takhta*. His return to Cairo was much occupied with investigation with British officials into questions of irrigation and land, inspection of public buildings and reception of native deputations. Lighter moments included more meetings with British friends on tour, seeing Karnak by moonlight, riding across country to Abydos and entertaining on his steamer at Tell Amarna the eminent Egyptologist Flinders Petrie and his young assistant Howard Carter. Petrie, who showed him his discoveries, he called 'a remarkable man, as enthusiastic for his speciality as anyone I have ever known'. Howard Carter became Inspector-in-Chief of Monuments in Upper Egypt and with Lord Carnarvon discovered Tutankhamun's tomb in 1922.

It was characteristic of Milner to spend his penultimate day on the Nile working hard to note more facts about irrigation, have an Arabic lesson and reduce his arrears of correspondence.

Though conscious that he had to give 'High Politics the go-by' he was finding his new house a success, bought a magnificent horse and wrote home that Cairo had a lot of lively visitors. His aims were, as ever, to become an authority on Egypt and make the public at home aware of the country's problems. He followed up his *Pall Mall Gazette* interview of the summer with two anonymous articles in *The Scotsman*, republished as a pamphlet.[34] He wrote to Birchenough that, though Britain had much improved her position in Egypt,

. . . the danger at home increases. Unless English public opinion can be radically changed, you will kick the bucket over yet. Egypt must be saved, if she can be saved, in Grub St, not on the banks of the Nile.[35]

The colourful figure Wilfred Scawen Blunt, well known as a poet, traveller, breeder of horses and anti-imperialist, was perhaps the most vocal British critic of our occupation of Egypt. A lively host at his home Crabbet Park in Sussex and married to Byron's granddaughter, he wintered at a house outside Cairo which he called his 'Earthly Paradise', living more or less as an Arab. He had known Milner in his *Pall Mall Gazette* days, saw him quite often in Cairo and liked him. His account of Milner's current activities, though grotesque, contained an element of truth. Milner's appointment in Egypt, he alleged, had been nominally for administrative work,

> . . . but in reality a mission of organizing a Press campaign in London in favour of a continuance of the Egyptian occupation. For this work no man could have been better chosen. . . . No man better than he knew the length of the electoral foot.[36]

So far from any official involvement, Milner took on himself, from political and moral conviction, the publicizing of Britain's work in Egypt. Free from the restraints of his Treasury job, his years as a journalist and links with British politics and the Press made him a self-appointed propagandist for a British imperialist cause. He succeeded, for example, in influencing Baring to write more reports on Egypt's affairs and give these a more popular form. He became friends with Edmund Garrett, now Assistant Editor to Cook on the *Pall Mall Gazette* wintering in Egypt as a sufferer from phthisis, who later as editor of the *Cape Times* gave useful support to his South African work.

This April of 1892 another of Egypt's crises, called 'the firman episode', occurred. A difference on the timing and terms of the Sultan's official consent to the young Khedive's accession seemed, in Western eyes, long-drawn-out and ludicrous. Milner told Gell that every Egyptian from the Khedive downwards 'stands in awe of the Turk'. Baring as usual scored a success, and he himself was delighted that proof had been given of the Turkish danger in Egypt.[37] Kitchener was appointed Sirdar this month and chose as his Director of Military Intelligence Major Reginald Wingate, a very able officer, who was to serve in reconquering the Sudan and, when Kitchener left for the Boer War, to replace him as Sirdar and Governor-General of the conquered province. He had already become one more of Milner's firm friends, and later on one of his best informants on Egyptian affairs.

Milner wrote in April in confidence to Goschen that 'West's little plot' to get him appointed his successor as Chairman of the Inland Revenue

Board was after all bearing fruit. Since his preference was for service abroad he would leave Egypt with divided feelings. But the offer of such a post now, apparently, about to be made was too great a compliment to be set aside, and one he felt it his duty to accept. He also looked forward to being able to paddle his own canoe in a job 'in which self-effacement (though I am good at it) is not the only cardinal virtue.' In a further frank sentence he added,

I don't care to be seen in connection with the work I am doing, but I do like to feel that I influence it.

In sending congratulations Goschen wrote that Salisbury was extremely pleased with Baring, who in June was created Viscount (later Earl of) Cromer. He forecast correctly that the general election would take place in about late June and result in a small Liberal majority. At about the same time Milner left Egypt, ostensibly on leave since his probable succession to West was still secret. He settled almost incognito in the Grand Hotel, Eastbourne, with a secretary and an enormous library, writing *England in Egypt*. On 1 July he told Gell for the first time of the Inland Revenue prospect, saying he aimed to finish his book by the end of August for 'the next publishing season . . . [to be ready] when the Egyptian Question comes bubbling up again next autumn', after the election excitement had subsided.[38] At this date the interval between an author's completing a book and its appearance in the bookshops was still usually short.

In July Gladstone's Liberals and the Irish obtained a majority of only 40 over the Tories and Liberal Unionists. In August Gladstone formed his fourth Cabinet; those members who most concerned Milner were the Chancellor of the Exchequer, Sir William Harcourt, and the Foreign Secretary, his Liberal Imperialist friend Lord Rosebery. Milner was striving to write his book while having to pay visits to Somerset House where, since West's retirement, 'things were getting out of hand.' He told Matheson of New College that his time was much occupied by 'that beastly book', which he felt hampered in writing by his official position which would soon be made public and occupy all his time. He was sending his manuscript in instalments to his publisher, Edward Arnold, and batches of proofs to Gell at the Oxford University Press for correction and expert advice. By early December, however, the book was on sale in the bookshops. With little desire for personal publicity, but much eagerness to inform and influence others, he sent copies to Sir Francis Knollys for the Prince of Wales's perusal, Lord Rosebery, Joseph Chamberlain, Cecil Rhodes and a good many other acquaintances and friends.[39]

Chapter 6

Somerset House
(July 1892 – April 1897)

England in Egypt – 'We are all Socialists now' –
Opportunity Beckons

Though Blunt's account of the origins of Milner's book was wrong, he rightly called it 'an entire success in England'. Early in January the first edition was almost exhausted and further editions soon followed. In some ways it formed a new genre, an account of imperial work in one area brought alive by the writer's own share in the venture and aim to convince without lecturing readers. Arthur Godley, now and for many years Permanent Head of the India Office, told West that it stated the facts and premises while leaving the reader to form his conclusions. Courtenay Ilbert, Milner's friend since Balliol days, told him he had succeeded in 'extracting champagne from blue books and sparkling about finance and public works.' Jowett wrote to Morier, the eminent diplomat, that he thought the book would 'produce a considerable effect on the foreign policy of England.'[1] Reviewers, for example in *The Times*, were generous and often lavish with praise.

Magnus notes the book's contribution in focusing British attention on Khartoum and the Upper Nile valley, writing that it

> ... touched the pride of a great imperial people which had been smarting under a sense of failure and frustration since the disastrous mismanagement of the Nile Expedition [to rescue Gordon] of 1884–5. It declared that Britain's missionary task was as yet only half-done.

He quotes Winston Churchill's praise in *The River War* that Milner had stimulated a wish in Britain to know more about Egypt, and by explaining the difficulties of her position there had enhanced her achievement. The book, Churchill thought,

> ... was more than a book. The words ran like a trumpet-call which rallies the soldiers after the parapets are stormed, and summons them to complete the victory.[2]

State education was barely twenty years old, and one-half of Britain's male voters had only possessed the vote for eight years. 'New Imperialists' had first to aim at increasing support from the influential minority in Parliament, the Press and elsewhere. This would, it was hoped, in time guide and educate the majority which lacked knowledge, experience and usually interest in foreign and imperial matters. A few years later Milner wrote from Africa that 'it is the educated class alone which counts', expressing a distinction, not today much in favour, between educated leaders and the led.

No attempt can be made to summarize the book. Ilbert's description of it as a kind of effervescent blue book is singularly apt. It covered the whole range of Egypt's political system and economy in a clear straightforward style which had a sparkle which Milner (apart from private letters) was apt to reserve for special travel diaries. The feelings he had privately expressed about French behaviour, and about Egyptian personalities, were all but suppressed. He showed more optimism than Cromer did later about the possibility of introducing in the not-too-distant future more education and self-government in the country.[3] He kept the book up to date by periodically adding a final chapter by himself or others until it achieved a 13th edition in 1920.

He told Bertha Synge, his childhood friend, that his new job was of much better status than the one he had left. At Somerset House in the Strand he was working in more architectural grandeur next door to King's College, which must have held many memories for him. While Smirke had added an eastern wing to Chambers's eighteenth-century building for the College, the architect James Pennethorne had added a western wing in the '50s for the Inland Revenue Board. Expressing Victorian ideas of splendour he had adorned its main entrance with statues over seven feet high of a seated Britannia, female figures to represent History and Fame, and the kingdom's six principal cities, perhaps thinking these would endear the operations conducted inside to taxpayers.

Milner was for the first time an established full-time civil servant. But the Board had its own constitutional existence, and enjoyed in the words of a recent Chairman 'a considerable measure of independence.'[4] Though relations with the Treasury were naturally close, its responsibility was to the Chancellor of the Exchequer alone. Milner's salary was £2,000 a year, a good income for a bachelor in the early 1890s. The Inland Revenue was then almost the largest Government Department with a staff of about 5,500, salaries and expenses amounting to over £1½ million and branch offices throughout the United Kingdom. The Excise, the most profitable of its duties, remained its concern until 1909, and stamp duties were still larger, in terms of both work and receipts, than income tax. Sir Algernon West was pleased with the fact that not long before, after a battle royal with the Treasury, he had been the first head of a big Department to introduce what were then called 'women typewriters'.

Sir William Harcourt, Milner's new master, was sixty-five with success, at the Bar, a Law Professorship at Cambridge and office in Gladstone's three previous governments behind him. Built on a generous scale, he was often referred to as 'Jumbo'. Exceptionally able, his quick temper and sharp tongue inspired awe and sometimes fear in his colleagues and officials who served him. A Home Ruler, the most radical of the chief Liberals and popular in the country, he appeared the most likely successor to the octogenarian Prime Minister. He received the devoted help as his private secretary of Lewis ('Loulou'), his thirty-year-old son by his first wife who had died giving birth to him.[5] He had since remarried.

Milner's change of occupation must have had something to do with his resuming a diary, which he kept with only a few interruptions for the rest of his life. This is less revealing than the spasmodic, often introspective, diaries quoted in previous chapters. It was mainly a record of the day's engagements which he normally wrote up each night; highly discreet, it contained little comment and seems to have been intended solely for his own practical use. He noted in January 1893 that Death Duties were very much the first item in his working life. Harcourt had inherited from Goschen 'a miserable mouse of a surplus' and a steady rise of Government expenditure. His plan (much less familiar then than it has since become) was greater dependence on *direct* taxation to increase the contribution of the richer classes. Milner was much engaged in Death Duties talk with Sir William and Loulou in Downing Street, at the former's home Malwood in the New Forest, and with Treasury and other officials.

It was soon apparent, however, that a Death Duties Budget could not be combined this year with the second Home Rule Bill, introduced by Gladstone on 13 February. A humdrum budget did little except raise the current 6*d.* income tax by 1*d.* Gladstone carried his Home Rule Bill's Second Reading by 43 votes on 22 April, and then took personal charge of its exceptionally long further progress. Milner was concerned with the Bill's financial clauses. The Inland Revenue miscalculated Irish excise figures, with results which were temporarily serious and much annoyed Gladstone. But when Milner's Treasury colleagues, Welby and Edward Hamilton, accompanied him to give Gladstone an explanation he was nice to them all and later told Hamilton he was '. . . most favourably impressed by Milner whom he had not seen before.'

West records Gladstone telling him at this date that he had always had the highest admiration for the Inland Revenue Board and regarded it as the ideal of a public department.

Though his Inland Revenue work was exacting Milner gave much time in the following years to Egyptian affairs, in a semi-official capacity and as a freelance. He used to receive a huge Egyptian post, he read the weekly *Egyptian Gazette* and Cromer, Palmer and other Cairo figures and friends kept on coming to London. Lord Rosebery the Foreign Secretary, unlike Harcourt, had known Milner for a long time and was only seven years his senior. In January a fresh crisis had arisen in Cairo and Rosebery summoned Milner to his house in Berkeley Square. Young Khedive Abbas had dismissed his Prime Minister and appointed a successor and other Ministers without consulting Cromer – an act Dr. Lutfi ironically calls 'as good as a coup d'état.' At Cromer's request Rosebery registered British displeasure, and a compromise settlement included the return of Riaz as Prime Minister. The Liberal Cabinet, however, was deeply divided over the evacuation issue with Gladstone, Harcourt and others ready to leave Egypt and draw closer to France, and Rosebery taking the opposite view. Cromer's further request for more British troops caused some Downing Street storms, but was successfully backed up by Rosebery.[6]

The acceptance and secrecy of Cromer's 'management' of the young Khedive, which Milner and others looked upon as essential, almost vanished and were never regained. The veil which masked the unofficial protectorate had worn very thin. Finances under Cromer's direction still improved; but Abbas's action had encouraged some nationalist stirrings. Rosebery asked Milner to get his friend E. T. Cook, now editor of the Liberal *Westminster Gazette* to reply to an interview in his paper with Abbas.[7]

Blunt thought that *England in Egypt*, by its success and its candour, had 'blown the gaff' or exposed the real situation; in the *Nineteenth Century* for April he poured scorn on what Cromer himself had admitted to Milner was 'an artificial system of government.' Garstin, now Under-Secretary for Public Works and as concerned as ever with irrigation, the most popular of England's activities with Egyptians, wrote that anti-English feeling was spreading. Wingate reported a worsened relationship between English and Egyptian officials and French intrigue as active as ever; 'everything', he added, 'is reflected from the head in this country.'[8]

Since returning home Milner had seen much of Parkin who was still in the country lecturing and writing on the Empire. Winston Churchill who heard him as a schoolboy at Harrow records that he had the knack of transmitting his enthusiasm to his audience. When the Imperial Federation League expired Parkin joined a group of young Oxbridge volunteer speakers. Milner made up his mind to arrange a liberal subsidy for his work and approached various friends about this; they included Rosebery, A. L. Bruce, Mrs. Montefiore and his younger wealthy friend Thomas Brassey, later 2nd Earl Brassey and a large benefactor of Balliol and the Bodleian Library. A memorandum recorded agreement to pay Parkin at least £450 p.a. for three years to spend a fair but undefined share of his time in promoting the Imperial Federation idea.[9] It was characteristic of Milner to tell Gell he did not want this plan generally known since he thought this might reduce Parkin's influence.

Milner's New College fellowship was something, he told Matheson, that he 'cared more for than you perhaps know.' He supposed that his new employment would make its retention impossible; but correspondence with Robinson, the Bursar, and legal opinion on the College Ordinances proved that this was not the case. He voluntarily surrendered all emoluments from the College but retained other Fellow's rights – as it turned out to the end of his life.[10] Whenever he could he attended College meetings. In London he kept up, in association with Goschen, his membership of the Council of the University Extension Society and lectured sometimes at Toynbee Hall, the Working Men's College and elsewhere. He added to his clubs and societies by election to Brooks's, the Literary Club and Grillions.

Complaining occasionally of a 'jumpy heart' and 'seediness', his recipe in London for fitness was a morning ride in the Park or the Grosvenor Riding School. His burden of work had not stopped him, once his book was completed, from resuming the social life he relished. A bachelor approaching 40 with a comfortable income, a flat and three clubs in St. James's, the next four or five years were probably the peak of his Society life. If lack of family influence and Balliol had trained him for a life of hard work, a strong strain in his nature craved friendships and social relations. A large correspondence and frequent efforts to help friends in need with money and in other ways were a price he was always prepared to pay.

Clinton Dawkins, who had known him well for ten years, wrote from Peru, with his health mainly in mind,

> . . . don't be rushed . . . by Society, and continue to eschew country Saturdays to Mondays which is about the most tiring thing for a busy man under the modern country house system.[11]

He did not go very far in taking this advice. If not quite accurately to be labelled a 'Soul' he was, as a wit of the time remarked of someone else, a 'parasol'. His week-end hostesses in the country included Mrs. Horner of Mells (called by Beatrice Webb 'High Priestess' of the Souls), Etty Grenfell (later Lady Desborough) whose sons he had taught, and the Cowpers of Panshanger. His hosts included West, now Gladstone's unofficial secretary and so still at the heart of affairs, Lord Rothschild at Tring and Lord Salisbury at Hatfield. He often saw Margot; and on one London Sunday afternoon in June left cards on eighteen ladies. He did not neglect to keep up with many friends like Gell, Rendel, the Glazebrooks and Birchenough of his younger days, his relations and many others lower down on the social ladder. He told Gell in August 1893 he had had

> . . . a wild season . . . *not* crushes (I do draw the line there) but endless dinners.

In a hot summer Gladstone, with inexhaustible energy, kept Parliament sitting to consider the Home Rule Bill, which like its predecessor of '86 virtually ignored Ulster, until late September. This prevented Milner from getting a long holiday, though his job and his habits made his working hours flexible. He spent many August days on the Thames. Sharing a house at Shiplake with his Chelsea boyhood friends the Blunts, he had plenty of his favourite sports of rowing and canoeing and 'water parties.' Reminding one of the Thames of Jerome K. Jerome's *Three Men in a Boat* he told Mrs. H. M. Gaskell, of Kiddington Hall, Oxfordshire,

> . . . there is no mob in these quiet reaches even on Sunday. I have a perfect flotilla at our boathouse . . . and two delicious backwaters quite close, so I moon about endlessly in the afternoons and thoroughly appreciate the rest.

In September he spent three weeks inspecting Inland Revenue offices in the north of England, Scotland and Ireland. On the 1st of this month the Commons passed the Home Rule Bill by 40 votes, but one week later it was killed with a crushing adverse majority in the Lords. The issue lay buried for some eighteen years, when Milner was to play a vigorous part in opposing Asquith's third Home Rule Bill. He now discussed in Belfast and Dublin taxation and excise affairs with collectors and surveyors, and visited warehouses, distilleries and Guinness's Brewery. Back in

London he found plenty to do at Somerset House, and Cromer, Judge Scott and Garstin were eager to talk to him about Egypt.

On 2 October he read of the death in office of Jowett, whose residence in Balliol had lasted since 1836 and his Mastership since 1870. Recent illnesses and his having reached the mid-seventies made the event not unexpected. Milner wrote that his life was 'a pleasant thing to think of', and often referred to him later with gratitude as 'my wise old friend'. He attended his funeral in Balliol Chapel and presumably his burial in the secluded cemetery of St. Sepulchre's off Walton Street, Oxford. Gell was appointed with Abbott and Lewis Campbell (Jowett's official biographers) a literary executor as well as a trustee of his Memorial Fund. To this Milner gave the generous sum (well above the average contribution) of £50.[12]

Milner went to Edinburgh to inspect the Inland Revenue Board office, stay with the Bruces and give an address which, as usual, he had prepared with much care. A week or two later George Parkin wrote to say that Bruce, by no means an old man, had died suddenly of influenza, adding 'you cannot in all your list of friends have had any one more genuine and sincere than he was.' Retiring by nature and wealthy, Bruce had played a significant part in the growth of Unionism in Scotland and in Britain's African ventures. Milner's answer to Parkin is most revealing about his own approach to politics and intentions. Bruce's life, he wrote, had

> ... made a deep impression on me. I feel that a man can do any amount of good public work, and be of the greatest service without joining in the fray – can, in fact, *be of greater service because he keeps himself in the background* [author's italics]. . . . I have an independent position, a great number of influential friends, and, I fancy, that sort of influence myself which disinterestedness always gives.[13]

Though dedicated to Empire and the State he knew that he lacked the art of popular political oratory, and felt repugnance for what he saw as the compromises and manoeuvres of party politics. One recalls the Balliol contemporary writing after his death that as an undergraduate and at Toynbee Society meetings his wide knowledge of domestic and foreign politics gave him great authority but

> he showed no affinity with any British political party . . . had he been returned to Parliament he would have felt unhappy there. He was always impatient of the haphazard character of 'its legislation'.[14]

The cross-benches, it seems, were his place in his twenties and with few interruptions remained so.

He regularly visited Lizzie at 54 Claverton Street, and later arranged that his German god-daughter Josephine Eberle, a Swabian peasant girl, should better herself by working in London as Lizzie's assistant. But this experiment does not seem to have been a success.

His many friends in fairly humble social positions included a girl of some mystery called Cecile living somewhere near Croydon. Milner usually alludes to her in his diary as 'C' and often in these years in England spent single nights with her.[15] On two occasions at least he helped her to hunt for a house in South London, and one August they spent three nights together in Marlow. Milner sometimes made rough notes in his diaries of his gifts and loans (often marked 'irrecoverable') of money to friends and others. 'C' figures often among them, but was this Cecile? He records that on one of his last days in England several years later, before sailing to Africa, she was living in Brixton and he bought her a bicycle; and that he wrote to her from Africa. Later documents show her to have originated from the Channel Islands and to have been an actress.

It can be deduced that, in a discreet and mutually satisfactory manner, Cecile was his mistress. Before he returned from Africa in 1905 she seems to have married and settled in Seattle. But they met again after this in London, and on his death Milner left her an annuity.[16]

He spent the night of 22 December with her and for once spent Christmas in Duke Street, visiting Malcolm and other family graves in Brompton Cemetery on Christmas Day. A New Year week-end with the Goschens made a break before work on the 1894 Budget which, with Home Rule at last out of the way, was to be the new session's main feature.

The Death Duties talks of a year before with the two Harcourts, the Treasury, the Solicitor General, Parliamentary Counsel and Milner's own officials were resumed and continued to be his major concern until the high summer. His continuous interest in Egypt necessitates first a mention of a further crisis there in January 1894 caused by Khedive Abbas making adverse comments on his Egyptian Army to Kitchener its Sirdar, who was not the sort of man to take kindly to such action. Rosebery again sought Milner's opinion, and accounts of the matter from Egypt soon poured into Duke Street. Abbas had to yield and retract his criticism, the

Prime Minister changed again, and much later Cromer called the affair a turning-point with

> . . . the battle for British supremacy virtually fought and won during the eventful period when Lord Rosebery presided at the Foreign Office.[17]

The Liberal Government's progress was not helped by the tension between its three main figures. Edward Hamilton, promoted by Harcourt to second place in the Treasury, was on close terms with them all and also with Milner.[18] Gladstone, much exercised by the rise of the Navy Estimates, harangued his colleagues about this, and rumours of his resignation appeared in the *Pall Mall Gazette* and elsewhere. Hostility between Harcourt and Rosebery was thus sharpened by the issue of the succession.[19] On 3 March the G.O.M. went with his wife to Windsor to tender his resignation, and the Queen at once asked Lord Rosebery to form a government. Harcourt had decided to accept the second place of Leadership of the Commons combined with the Exchequer. But bitterness grew between the two men with long and unhappy results for their Party.

Margot wrote to tell Milner in February that she had made up her mind to marry the rising younger star of the Party, the Home Secretary Herbert Asquith. Too busy with Budget affairs to attend their wedding in May, Milner sent them a present worth £40, and three Prime Ministers signed the register. An official committee was now drafting the Death Duties scheme and finding the task far from easy. Loulou converted his father to a plan for a graduated income surtax, but gave this up when Milner sent him 'an extremely able memo' of objections. The core of the Budget remained a new Estate Duty, which Hamilton called

> . . . a terribly complicated measure . . . so difficult that I doubt if during the last half-century any other man but Harcourt, Mr. G. and Goschen could have tackled it at all.

Harcourt, he added, taunted Milner and himself with undue tenderness towards landlords and millionaires.[20]

Loulou records a long Cabinet meeting of 2 April with Rosebery 'fighting like a demon' against graduation of Death Duties but not being supported.[21] His father made a Budget Speech of nearly three hhurs on the 16th without even sustaining himself with a glass of water. The Estate Duty's principal features were: first a levy on the total wealth of an individual at death without reference to its later distribution; secondly, this wealth was to be taken at capital value; and third, it was to be graduated. It was only expected to yield £1 million in the current year and from £3½–4 million in subsequent years, which contributed to the Budget's initial favourable reception by the House and the Press. The Chancellor also proposed to raise income tax to 8*d.*, add 6*d.* per gallon to the tax on spirits and the same sum on a barrel of beer. Due to agricultural depression the landed classes were given some alleviations.[22]

Milner, in addition to Budget work, was writing an extra final chapter to bring *England in Egypt*, now in its fourth edition up to date, a practice he continued for years. He soon noted 'a very hard day, as indeed all previous days for the last three weeks' and exceptional tiredness. Debate on the Budget Resolutions and the Finance Bill meant his constant evening attendance in the Commons from late April. On 7 May the Second Reading began and Rosebery celebrated his forty-seventh birthday; Milner told a friend that though he did not support his Government he had a very considerable admiration for him. Before long he offered to put Milner's foot 'on the first rung of titular honour' by proposing him for the C.B. Milner spent the Whitsun Recess partly at Henley, then rowed from Reading up to Streatley and went on by train to Oxford to stay with the Gells and dine at Balliol and New College.

He used this visit to consult that remarkable self-made expert on land valuation Walter Gray, Mayor of Oxford. A Lincolnshire stationmaster, Gray had been brought to Keble College as steward when it opened in 1871. Learning that restrictions on the marriage of dons might soon be removed' he began to buy property in North Oxford. Leaving Keble he made a fortune, and became the leader of Conservative City politics. After seeing him Milner returned to London and wrote a long memo for Harcourt on land valuation before going to bed.

Sir Henry Lucy, the contemporary historian of Parliament, writes that the Finance Bill's Second Reading attracted 'all the giants of debate'. The subject was dry, and its intricacies unintelligible to the great majority of M.P.s. But uncertainty about how the details would affect the Government's slender majority maintained excitement.[23] An oversight in the Resolutions caused a fierce row between Harcourt and Balfour, and suspicion that one of Milner's chief officials was helping a Tory M.P. to defeat the Bill. With the Second Reading carried by 14 votes, amendments then threatened to smother the Bill in Committee which lasted for twenty-three nights. The frequent back-room official consultations about these were christened by Loulou 'the Bear-pit', from the number of rows they evoked.[24] Henry Hobhouse proposed an amendment about estates passing between husband and wife which gave those in charge of the Bill a bad scare. 'The Bear-pit' pressed Sir William successfully for one day's relief in each week from what Milner called 'incessant Budgeting' in the Commons. Discussion with Conservative leaders brought compromise on the valuation of agricultural land. But 'the Bear-pit' was still, Milner wrote, 'very busy all day preparing answers to amendments' and usually at the House until midnight.

When the Bill passed the Commons by 20 votes on 17 July, Loulou noted his father 'bubbling over with joy at being "quit" of it and humming to himself at intervals "no more cram".' The Lords could not, of course, alter the Bill. But when 170 Liberal M.P.s gave Harcourt a celebration dinner he made a strong attack on certain peers, especially the Liberal Unionist Dukes of Devonshire and Argyll, for their hostile speeches.[25] He had written to Milner the day after victory thanking him for

> ... the splendid and unwearied aid you have given me in the Budget ... without you the ship could not have floated for a day.[26]

He felt this gratitude years later when Milner's South African policies, though the opposite of his own, came under bitter attack. Edward Hamilton concluded that

> ... without Milner this year at Somerset House I don't know what Harcourt would have done ... I don't believe the Budget would even have been carried.

Harcourt's triumph lay in the fact that the Budget had emerged from Parliament with small alteration. Though Balfour called the Death Duties Act 'financial revolution' it seems that few people then saw it as usch. It had, as a modern successor to Milner at the Inland Revenue Board points out, to contend with the special complexities of the British law of property and trusts. The Unionists mistakenly thought they could easily recast it. During the storm which the 1909 Budget raised, Milner said that the 1894 Act had been 'intended to have the character of finality.' It took time for people to realize that a big direct tax, independent of income tax, had been introduced which was capable of almost indefinite increase by simple turns of the screw.'[27] Harcourt's jest about 'Socialists', made in another connection, was a forecast which only later took on significant meaning. The Budget in time adversely affected both him and Loulou as inheritors of the Nuneham estates.

Milner told Edith Gell that after the Bill passed the Lords it would take some weeks to give the 'new system of plunder' a first shove off. There was fuss and misunderstanding about extra staff at the Inland Revenue Board. He could not begin his holiday until the last day of August, riding westwards on a mare accompanied by a groom. He spent a week with the Ilberts in Surrey and nights with the Tennysons, the Horners of Mells and the Jeunes. With a party he watched cavalry manoeuvres on the Berkshire Ridgeway, then rode past the White Horse and over the downs to Marlborough. Sending his groom with the horses back to London he went on to Minehead for two weeks' stag-hunting, introduced to this sport by a Balliol friend Henry Seymour and much enjoying it. On returning he visited more friends and helped Goschen, at Seacox with his *magnum opus*, the *Life and Times* of his grandfather, the eighteenth-century Leipzig publisher.

His working life became for a time less hectic. Three personal events of this autumn need mention. Asquith had praised Milner highly to Hamilton, regarding (like Dawkins) the Ministry of Finance in India as his true goal. In September, though not hopeful he would accept, he offered him the Permanent Under-Secretaryship at the Home Office, adding,

> . . . there is no man in or out of the Civil Service whose qualifications for the place compare with your own, or whom on every ground I should so delight to see there.

Milner's aim, however, as Asquith suspected, was higher employment in the Empire. After more time at Somerset House he wrote that framing Estimates was 'rather tame compared with empire-making.'

Of greater importance was his delivery late in November, at Toynbee Hall, of a talk on his friend after whom this was named. He consulted Charlotte Toynbee and as usual spent much effort in preparation. He spoke for an hour with a good many old friends in the hall. Both Charlotte and Gertrude, Arnold's sister, were delighted with the talk and urged its publication. This took place in 1895 as *Arnold Toynbee: a reminiscence*, the most personal and perhaps the best of Milner's few books.[28] Toynbee had died twelve years before but Milner said that his thought and aspirations,

> . . . his manner of speech, yea, the very expression of his countenance and the tone of his voice, are so vividly present to me, and seem to me still . . . no less noble and inspiring than they did in the radiant days of youthful idealism, when we first were friends.

The third matter was Milner's success in bringing Dawkins nearer home. When sailing for Peru, Dawkins had extracted from him a willing promise to 'use your eyes for me.' They had kept up a regular correspondence and Dawkins had written 'we are playing the game together' – firm friends with similar views on the Empire and both the wish and the talents to serve it in high positions. He had caught 'African fever' and had written with prescience,

> . . . we have got an Africanus in Brummagen Joe. That fellow will do great service yet to the Empire. He has a capacity of growth.

He hoped Milner would either succeed Cromer, who was offered more than one ambassadorship in these years, or become the Viceroy of India's Financial Minister. Milner tried without success to get Dawkins the City Editorship of *The Times*, and then was probably the main agent in getting him what he most wanted. By early 1895 he was seated in Milner's old chair of Egypt's Under-Secretary of Finance under Palmer in Cairo.

At Seacox again for Christmas Milner, with the help of Teddie Goschen, made his first attempt to ride a bicycle. He was soon talking Budget Estimates again with Harcourt. Loulou describes him as much depressed at the prospects of income tax yield, and shocked at the sum which Lord Spencer, First Lord of the Admiralty, required for the Navy. Different friends, including both Goschen and Gell, wrote to him at Somerset House for advice about their personal tax problems. It was probably compensation to be told by Jumbo in March after some transaction that the Inland Revenue was 'a great horse when called upon with a good jockey up'.[29]

Milner's private activities of the earlier part of 1895 included dining at St. John Brodrick's with Balfour and Alfred Lyttelton to meet Curzon just back from his Afghanistan tour, seeing Oscar Wilde's plays, Sunday walks with his trade union friend Fred Rogers, a visit to Holy Trinity, Pimlico, to see the window he had given in Marianne's memory, nights with Cecile, a New College meeting and a cruise with the Readys on the Broads. Among his usual loans and gifts of money to friends, relations and spongers, Henry Birchenough had a bad business year and was helped with a loan, Joe Postlethwaite and a young Ready cousin were in more trouble and never stopped asking for and receiving what Milner entered as 'irrecoverable' loans.

With no idea that any one of them would ever officially concern him he dined at Brooks's with Albert Grey, Lansdowne, Rhodes and Dr. Jameson. Grey, the reader will recall, had been his Liberal Unionist colleague in '86, and had just succeeded his uncle as 4th Earl. A staunch admirer of Rhodes, he often discussed South African matters with Milner. The Colonial Secretary, Lord Ripon, had just asked the elderly Sir Hercules Robinson (later Lord Rosmead) to return to that country to replace Lord Loch as High Commissioner and Governor of the Cape – to the equal annoyance of the anti-imperialist Harcourt and the new imperialist Chamberlain.[30] Milner said good-bye in April to Edmund Garrett of the *Pall Mall Gazette* going out for health reasons to South Africa to edit the pro-British *Cape Times*.

Harcourt introduced his third Budget on 2 May. It was not a memorable one, though Harcourt and Eddy Hamilton were both appalled at what the latter called huge and increasing expenditure due mainly to the Navy's demands. The yield of the Death Duties was some £14m, almost exactly what had been estimated and winning for Milner a half-crown bet with a colleague. He was busy for many weeks even over a humdrum budget. His Whitsun holiday illustrated a newspaper comment that 'the mania now, especially among ladies, is bicycling'. The safety bicycle and the pneumatic tyre had introduced an exhilarating bisexual sport not yet interfered with by the danger and dust which motor cars created. With five friends, including Etty and Willie Grenfell, and four servants he spent a week cycling from Rouen to nearby places in Normandy and returning by Le Havre and Dieppe. He studied the guide-books, kept the common accounts and wrote up a common journal which he later circulated to the others.[31]

In late June Rosebery's Government, for weeks very shaky, was suddenly defeated. Lord Salisbury formed his third Government; and in the July general election his majority of 152 included 71 Liberal Unionists. Though they retained their separate party machine other Liberal Unionists besides Goschen now joined the Government, and the term 'Unionist' was henceforth used to describe both Government parties; the Unionists' power was to last under Salisbury and then Balfour for over ten years. At Harcourt's request, Rosebery had before resigning written to Milner 'to K.C.B. you'. A spate of congratulations included one from someone at 10 Downing Street who called him at 41 the youngest knight of this Order, and Hamilton wrote that no honour in Rosebery's list was better deserved. Milner told Gell:

I simply love Jumbo and weep to lose him. He is the most unprincipled old politician . . . but a most humourous, kindly fellow in private life. Excessively clever and most grateful.[32]

He wrote in the same vein to Goschen, who, disagreeing with Harcourt's financial ideas especially graduation, now chose not to return to the Exchequer but to go to the Admiralty, where he had been a successful First Lord in the early 1870s. Milner asked him if he thought he himself would get on with Jumbo's 'sour-visaged successor', Sir Michael Hicks Beach. A Tory, Beach had almost as long an experience of office as Goschen, including the Exchequer and the Colonial Secretaryship. Tall and thin with a large black beard, his temper, like Harcourt's, was quickly aroused; but he lacked Harcourt's humour and sociable nature. Someone said he 'thought angrily', and he was widely known as 'Black Michael'.[33] As Milner soon learnt in connection with Egypt, and later with South Africa, he felt much aversion to what he considered any squandering of Treasury funds. Lord Salisbury again combined the Premiership and the Foreign Office, Lord Lansdowne went to the War Office and Chamberlain, who had played a big part in the election, to the surprise of many chose the Colonial Office. Lord Wolseley, with whom Milner was also to be concerned, soon replaced the old Duke of Cambridge as Commander-in-Chief.

Milner spent nights and week-ends after June at Henley, sometimes punting on arriving from London for an hour before dinner. Bicycling in August to stay with the Rendels he had a bad spill approaching Redhill. So a week in Duke Street with his leg in plaster was followed by a month with the Rendels recovering the power to walk. He read a great deal, and Margot wrote that he ought to write more himself since 'you do it *really well*.' He watched a cricket match at Reigate in which both W. G. Grace and Ranjitsinhji played. Rosebery had declared Uganda a British protectorate, and Milner's host Sir Alex Rendel was now appointed the engineer of its railway.

In the autumn Milner saw a good deal of Reginald Wingate in London with Rudolf Slatin, the Austrian who had made a sensational escape from the Sudan after being the Khalifa's prisoner for eleven years. Milner helped with the publication by Arnold of his story *Fire and Sword in the Sudan*, which was a best seller and stirred up British public interest in this area, dormant since the humiliating failure to save Gordon.[34] He found his work up to Christmas very heavy, noting 'I can hardly keep pace with it.' The Death Duties Act proved full of flaws and difficult to apply, and Beach's intentions about it were uncertain. No more able than others to foresee its ultimate impact, he told Dawkins in Cairo it was 'in essentials right.' His strain of radicalism was shown by his adding that he could render no better service

. . . to the revenue or to our own side in politics . . . than prevent the plutocrats [a section of Tories] from using the national uprising against a fussy and destructive Radicalism to further their own selfish ends.

He expected the amendments of detail the Act needed to be his main work for two years.[35]

On 2 January 1896 he heard the sensational news that Jameson and some men of Rhodes's Chartered Company had invaded the Transvaal Republic, and next day that the Boers had beaten them soundly. At dinner at Brooks's a few days later Chamberlain and Selborne were at the next table; there was much talk of possible war with Germany and he noted: 'the situation is serious.' He had no inkling that Jameson's impetuous action, and Rhodes's collapse as a Cape Colony statesman, would one day much concern him. Perspective on Imperialism at this stage can be gained from the comment of Edward Hamilton, a balanced, informed observer, on Chamberlain's first public appearance as Colonial Secretary only two months before. There was always, he wrote to Milner,

something extraordinarily crisp and attractive about his speeches . . . [he had called the colonies] undeveloped estates, and it was very remarkable how 'the Imperial idea' (as it may be called) has caught hold of the imagination of the Englishman at home and overseas. No one wishes to get rid of any of the Colonies now; and no Colony apparently wishes to cut itself aloof from its mother country.[36]

Milner was more concerned with crises in Egypt than with those in South Africa. Dawkins, like Cromer and Milner, saw Egypt's problems as above all fiscal and diplomatic – the relief of a much overtaxed people, and Egypt's position as 'a principal card in a big European diplomatic game.' Two plans on which Cromer's mind was now working raised difficult problems of finance. First, the big project of a dam on the Nile near Aswan to enlarge the whole country's prosperity by irrigation control and make more tax reductions possible. Second, some cautious advance up the Nile to forestall French designs.

A less urgent occupation for Cromer was what Wingate called 'his immortal work', published many years later as *Modern Egypt*.[37] He was sending instalments of this large book to Milner for criticism. Milner told him that it overdid its attack on Gladstone and the French, and that temperate criticism was more effective than violent language. This was not inconsistent with the strong criticism in Milner's *private* letters often quoted above. Throughout Milner's career the distinction between his private and his official letters was of major importance. Milner could express himself easily and was more liable than most persons to blow off steam when writing private letters.

Hicks Beach was described by a Treasury official as, unlike Harcourt, a man of few complimentary words but decisive and prompt in his work. His Budget of 16 April Milner thought a good one; it made no important change in Death Duties but gave further relief to the agricultural interest. Its preparation and the Finance Bill gave him plenty of work, inside and outside Parliament, until mid-July. He was, however, again sitting loose on the job, conscientious, absorbed and yet restless and telling a friend,

> I always hope to get out of my present place – hard, important, boring – some day or other.

A few personal matters in this first half of 1896 influenced his future. Gell had a row with a Delegate of the Oxford University Press which later ended in rupture. E. T. Cook became editor of the Liberal *Daily News* and in time served Milner well, as did Alfred Harmsworth (later Lord Northcliffe) who launched the cheap, popular and imperialist *Daily Mail*; Milner's friend Iwan-Müller was promoted to be a leader-writer on the *Daily Telegraph*. He sought Goschen's help for another journalist friend, Spenser Wilkinson, whom he called 'the gadfly of naval and military officialdom', an expert strategist who became the first Chichele Professor of Military History at Oxford. Milner's younger half-brother, Charles Cromie, died in China. His oldest friend in Shanghai, who had known Milner's mother long before in Chelsea, wrote that Charles shared her exceptional popularity and kind heart.

On 1 March Italy's crushing defeat by the Abyssinians at Adowa spurred Salisbury's Government to authorize Kitchener's advance up the Nile as far as Dongola. Dawkins came home on leave and like Rosebery, Milner and others thought this action premature. Lord Wolseley, who had led the abortive campaign ten years before to save Gordon, appears to have prevailed on the Government in the matter. Dawkins and Milner did not yet see reconquest of the whole Sudan, if this was the ultimate aim, as a practical prospect. A railway of several hundred miles had to be built from Halfa to Dongola; the Khalifa's strength was uncertain, and as usual finance was a difficult problem.

Milner lectured the Clifton schoolboys on Egypt and wrote an anonymous article on the subject in the *Edinburgh Review*, edited by Arthur

Elliot, the biographer of Goschen.[38] The domestic condition of Egypt still imposed on Britain, in his view, 'the inexorable alternative, Retirement or Reform.' He thought the Sudan should *in time* be returned to Egypt since the frontier between the two countries represented division between 'civilization and the most savage barbarism.' He learnt from Dawkins that Cromer had decided to stay on indefinitely in Egypt; and Dawkins had grown more critical of 'El Lord'. He thought he patronized young Abbas too much, paid insufficient attention to Egyptian education, and was growing to believe 'that he is absolutely indispensable here, which he is not now.' Yet Abbas, he later wrote, had 'a fatal attraction' for Turkey, his formal master, and seemed to have made himself generally unpopular in Egypt.[39] Nationalism, expressed in the view that self-government at whatever the cost is preferable to good government by some outside Power, was still, it must be recalled, in an early stage. Dr. Lutfi, who best puts the case against Cromer, shows Abbas as a fickle supporter of nationalist stirrings with 'no real intention of ruling as a constitutional monarch.' What she calls nationalist 'tributaries of thought' under leaders with various aims did not merge into one effective nationalist movement until 1919.[40]

Milner rented Henley Rectory for August, entertaining numerous guests and later commuting to London. He was kept well informed by Wingate, who sought his support, about Kitchener's progress (after various hold-ups) in reaching Dongola on 23 September. The Khedive approved, and no British troops or money had yet been involved; but the *Caisse* began legal action to stop use of Egypt's money for the campaign. If it won would the British Parliament pay? Would a further advance, now finding favour in Egypt, be possible? What also would happen to the cherished aim of an Aswan Dam? In response to appeals from Palmer and Dawkins Milner took pains with a letter to Balfour which eventually bore fruit. For military reasons a pause at Dongola for a year or more was inevitable. Palmer wrote that Egypt's revenue was buoyant and they were rapidly paying off debt. But in December the Mixed Court of Appeal ordered Egypt to pay back the £E½ million spent on the campaign. Egyptian finance, Hamilton noted in the Treasury in London,

> ... bristles so with difficulties and is so tied down by Conventions that only an expert can follow it.[41]

Dawkins came home again, he and Milner saw Lord Salisbury and the Chancellor and got affairs settled. The British Government undertook to repay the £E½ million spent, and promised a loan for an ultimate further advance. This seems the result of Milner's proposal to Balfour and Beach by which Dongola and other Sudan provinces could be temporarily 'loaned' by Egypt to Britain and so produce revenue which would escape the *Caisse*'s control.[42] In February of the New Year Beach announced that Britain intended to advance to Khartoum. By the time Kitchener moved on in the summer to Abu Hamed Milner was fully occupied at the opposite end of the African continent.

Another problem occupied a good deal of his time in these years. On Gladstone's initiative an inquiry into the Financial Relations of Britain and Ireland, especially the equity of Ireland's taxation, was made by a Royal Commission which examined Milner and many others, produced six reports and an agitation lasting some years.[43] In contrast to the views of Irish landlords and nationalists Milner argued in an anonymous article in the *Edinburgh Review* of January 1897 that 'Ireland does very well by the partnership.' He added, however, that as a poor country she deserved 'helpful generosity' with public funds for such projects as Horace Plunkett's agricultural schemes.

Milner spent an autumn week-end with Jumbo at Malwood. He had previously sent him an improved type of Inland Revenue Report evoking Sir William's comment that his 'overweening modesty' and 'failure to puff himself more' caused lack of appreciation of his efforts. One December day he accompanied Goschen and his daughters to Portsmouth to see the new battleship *Prince George*. Soon afterwards his friend Selborne, now Parliamentary Under-Secretary to Chamberlain at the Colonial Office, asked him if he would consider the Permanent Under-Secretaryship there, and Milner wrote in his diary 'I practically answered "No".' Since he hoped for employment abroad it seems strange that he asked Mrs Gell and other friends at this time to help him find a small country house he might buy. After settlement of the Sudanese problem he spent a week of fresh air with the Gells at Salcombe, picnicking on the shore, walking along the cliffs to Bolt Point, reading Mahan and much else. On the day this holiday ended he was told that Chamberlain would like to see him at the Colonial Office.

On 18 January 1897 Chamberlain asked him if he would become Permanent Under-Secretary to the Colonial Office. His staff, he had lately told Salisbury, had gone to pieces; he had also been looking for months for a successor to Lord Rosmead as Governor of Cape Colony and High

Commissioner of South Africa. Milner turned down the first offer; but when Chamberlain then offered him the successorship to Rosmead he replied without hesitation 'I'll do it.' Since the date of Rosmead's retirement was uncertain Chamberlain imposed a pledge of strict secrecy. Salisbury told Chamberlain that the appointment 'would be a success.'[44]

The appointment, Garvin comments, 'defied routine'. There was, however, still relatively little convention about or restriction on the Colonial Secretary's patronage over high Colonial appointments. Recruitment of lower ranks is called by one authority 'ramshackle'; which helps to explain Milner's efforts, soon to be noted, to obtain a friend as Imperial Secretary, his chief future subordinate. Milner, however, with his academic record, his journalism and his service abroad confined to a few years in Egypt, was clearly not a run-of-the-mill High Commissioner and Governor. One Colonial Service friend wrote it was strange to think of him, 'so different from any that I at least have met', in this role.

C. W. De Kiewiet, the noted historian, writes that Milner was to test again 'the rule of South African governorships that no man, however great, had thus far been great enough to cope with its problems.' A quite different authority, Mark Twain, visiting the country soon after the Jameson Raid, decided that 'the South African Question was a very good subject for a fool to let alone.' Milner wrote to his friend Michael Glazebrook

it is an awful job, tho' I never hesitated when asked to undertake it, and without the favour of the High Gods, it cannot be successfully dealt with. Shall I have that?

He was nearly 43, and in an episode of early February defined his personal aims with his habitual frankness. His master Hicks Beach had shown annoyance at Chamberlain's failure to consult him about the appointment and an inclination to refuse his consent. Milner sat late into the night writing at length to him, and to Chamberlain and Balfour. To Hicks Beach he explained in a way he called 'rather stiffly' that he had never wanted a permanent job in the Home Civil Service and never concealed this fact. Though he preferred the job he held to any other in this Service, he had always hoped that success in it would procure him a post in the Foreign, Indian or Colonial Services. He would rather quit the Crown's service altogether than

. . . spend all the best years of my life in a London office. To that prospect I prefer my freedom, and my position, which is one of complete independence, would enable me to resume it at any time . . . I may be wanted [here], but I cannot be kept – for any great length of time.[45]

To Balfour he dramatically wrote: 'I have arrived at a crisis in my life.' But Beach dropped his opposition, and the Queen gave approval. While spending a week-end with Lord Rothschild at Tring, a Press leak about the job gave him a sleepless night. But on Monday, 15 February, his appointment was officially announced, and within a few days he had received 5–6,000 telegrams and letters of congratulation, and almost unanimous Press approval. The opening on 16 February of the postponed 'Committee of No Inquiry' into the Jameson Raid brought fresh public interest in the South African Question.[46]

Why Milner's new post had become, as Welby wrote, '*the* post of difficulty in the Empire' must be briefly discussed. Queen Victoria's Diamond Jubilee that year appears to some modern writers as the peak of the Empire's development, though this view seems a product of hindsight. There is surely much truth in G. M. Young's dictum that what constitutes history 'is not what happened, but what people said (and thought) about it when it was happening'.

For Chamberlain, Milner and other new imperialists, 1897 was not a peak but a foothill – one, as they hoped and saw things, of a series of higher foothills. South Africa, one of the Empire's chief areas of white settlement, presented obvious complications not offered by, for example, Canada or Australia. Larger in size than France and pre-1939 Germany combined, it contained in 1890 less than 600,000 Europeans and some 3–4,000,000 non-whites. Huge space thinly occupied by *white* people was, from the standpoint of Europe's chief Powers, its main feature. Its Europeans had been divided for almost a hundred years between seventeenth-century Dutch settlers (with some French and German additions) and the British. The non-whites were composed of Africans, Coloureds (of mixed race), and Asiatics. With Cape Colony as their base, British Governments had unhappily failed for years to pursue a consistent policy. The Boers who had trekked north had been given independence in the 1850s as the South African Republic and the Orange Free State. The South African Republic had then been annexed in the late 1870s, had rebelled and defeated a British army at Majuba, and been regranted its freedom by Gladstone, subject to restraints in the Pretoria and London Conventions of 1881 and 1884.

The scratch, pastoral, farming of much of the country offered small attraction to new white settlers. But discovery of diamonds near Kimberley and then in 1886 of the goldfields of the Transvaal completely transformed the position and created new, tense conflict between Boer pastoral life and European economic ambitions. Rhodes had made a fortune from diamonds, become Prime Minister of the Cape on good terms with the Dutch, obtained his Charter to develop the north and was striving to realize his vision of a unified British South Africa. Paul Kruger, a man of granite, was prepared to let foreigners work the goldfields – since his people lacked both the capital and the skill to do so – but was determined above all else to maintain his country's independence. Central to this aim, a Transvaal law of 1890 in effect deprived foreigners of the franchise. It extended the residence qualification of the foreigner (Uitlander) – who had to become a Transvaal citizen and reach the age of 40 – as a voter for the First (or main)Volksraad and for the President from 5 to 14 years. It gave Uitlanders with 2 years' residence voting rights on a new Second Volksraad which had very limited powers. Joseph Chamberlain, for eighteen months Britain's Secretary of State for the Colonies, was, with Rhodes and Kruger, the third giant dominating Southern Africa at this stage. As the historians Robinson and Gallagher well put it, he shared Rhodes's belief that the Empire would not grow of itself but had to be 'urgently manufactured'. It was central to Milner's South African career that Salisbury and the Cabinet gave Chamberlain

. . . something like a free hand. Throughout the life of this Ministry indeed, his Conservative colleagues disliked to interfere with him in the colonial field. . . . The respect of Balfour and Selborne for him was personal as well as tactical . . . he was the most powerful Colonial Secretary of the century.[47]

'South Africa' was, of course, a geographical expression, a mosaic of white and black states. The British owned, besides Cape Colony, the 'true-blue' but less rich and populous self-governing colony Natal, and supervised as African protectorates Bechuanaland (now Botswana), Basutoland (Lesotho) and in part Swaziland. Rhodesia sprawled for an undefined distance to the north. The Transvaal had an ally in the more purely Boer and pastoral Orange Free State.

Professor Walker calls South Africa in 1897 'above all a divided land, full of frontiers and all uncharitableness.'[48] The scramble for territory in Africa by Europe's Powers still continued. Besides Britain, Germany was interested in the south, and Portuguese Mozambique with Delagoa Bay harbour had become Kruger's single non-British outlet. The division Walker stresses is best shown in the difficulty the four British and Dutch

M.—E

states found in reaching agreement over customs and railways. A Customs Union had been formed between the Cape (with the British Protectorates) and the Orange Free State, though Natal refused to join until 1898 and the Transvaal showed no interest. Railway construction is described by a good authority as a 'laggard enterprise . . . carried on by the four governments without co-ordination and with conflicting aims.'[49] With the Rand goldfields now their chief market, these states had only been linked by rail in the first five years of the '90s.

Chamberlain had been in office six months when the Jameson Raid foreshadowed disaster, giving Kruger and all he stood for a large bonus. Rhodes resigned from the Cape Premiership, though he eventually managed to save his Charter. Worst of all, the alliance he had formed with the Dutch of Cape Colony, skilfully led by Jan Hofmeyr, was now shattered. South Africa's politics and parties had reached something like dissolution. Kruger distrusted Rhodes more than ever, was convinced that Chamberlain had approved the attempted rape of his country and imported more arms. The new Cape Prime Minister J. G. Sprigg, a Progressive, had no real following and oscillated between the two parties, angling for support from the Dutch Bond, which regarded him as Rhodes's tool.

Rhodes's fall left a vacuum in the struggle for British supremacy which, as Chamberlain and others saw it, only the Imperial Government could fill. 'Influence' by Downing Street had now to proceed to some form of 'intervention'. As Robinson and Gallagher write,

> for six years the empire [in South Africa] had ridden gratefully upon Rhodes's coat-tails. . . . Once the two South African rivals and their systems became irreconcilable, Chamberlain, like Ripon, had little choice but to follow and support Rhodes.[50]

Having failed to lure Kruger to London for discussions Chamberlain and Lord Selborne his Under-Secretary presented the Cabinet on 30 March 1896 with an important memorandum. The Transvaal, they argued, was now 'the key to the future of South Africa, was the richest spot on earth' and would become far more populous. The aim of creating a British South African Federation was gravely threatened by external pressure and internal (i.e. white race) rivalries. If the disaster of the country becoming an independent 'United States of South Africa' was to be averted, firm action to restore British supremacy must be taken.

The British Government was agreed over the aim; the problem was the methods to be used and, above all, their timing. In essence practical methods boiled down to two: to extend Rhodes's policy of encircling Kruger in his 'kraal' by obtaining control of Delagoa Bay, and to increase pressure on him to move towards genuine enfranchisement of his Uit-landers. The fortunes of the Uitlanders, the Trojan horse in the kraal, were crucial. Kruger needed white aliens to finance and work his mines, but through industrial monopolies, taxation and in other ways had made their task very difficult. Though he had recently ameliorated their lot, for example over education, their handicaps and grievances remained strong.

Britain's legal restraint on the Transvaal's independence was limited by the London Convention to her requiring Her Majesty's Govern-ment's consent to the making of foreign treaties. Kruger now made no secret of aiming to get rid of the Convention. Britain's remaining legal ground for intervention over Uitlander conditions was the vague one of maltreatment of British subjects. What other form of pressure was left? Would public opinion in the Cape, or in other states in South Africa, influence Kruger? Would some show of force have any effect?

Milner stayed at the Inland Revenue until late in March. But at the Colonial Office on 9 March he 'found them all in a great fluster over South Africa'. Chamberlain had sent Kruger a stiff despatch on 6 March pro-testing against what he claimed were breaches of the Convention. Kruger formed an alliance with the Orange Free State on 17 March and was still increasing his armaments. Chamberlain considered an ultimatum, but his Cabinet colleagues would not swallow this, though agreeing without much enthusiasm to a naval demonstration and reinforcement of the mere 5–6,000 British troops in South Africa to somewhat over 8,000 in April. Milner noted on 2 April a very serious talk at the Colonial Office, and the decision that he should sail for Cape Town a fortnight earlier than had been planned.

Milner's life in past weeks had been, to use one of his favourite words, a 'scramble'. Besides Inland Revenue work he had talks with Chamberlain and Selborne and with other South African experts including star witnesses at the Raid Inquiry ('a very long one' with Rhodes, the chief star at a dinner party), Lord Loch, a former High Commissioner, his friend Edmund Garrett, and 'South African goldbugs'. The important position of his right-hand man, the Imperial Secretary, hitherto held by Commander Graham Bower, would probably fall vacant after the Inquiry. Philip Gell, now wanting to leave the Oxford University Press, proposed himself for this job; and it seems strange that Milner's loyalty should extend to doing what he could (though in vain) for such an amateur in this sphere. Milner also suggested Garrett for this post, but Chamberlain had for some reason formed a poor opinion of him.

As his Military Secretary Milner chose Major John Hanbury-Williams and as his private secretary Ozzy Walrond, the young son of a friend, who was destined to serve him in South Africa for seven years.[51] Trying out horses outside Somerset House, engaging domestic staff, buying a carriage, plate and furniture, dining and sleeping by royal command at Windsor and visiting the College of Heralds for a grant of arms were other necessities.

Farewell lunches and dinners were a common feature of the time. Milner dashed up to Oxford for a New College farewell dinner which included Balliol friends. A New College don, Prickard, records that pacing in the gardens next morning Milner 'spoke gravely of the risks [to his career and public usefulness] he was facing in going to Africa.'[52] Later, after Chamberlain's public statements had further increased South African tension, Hamilton of the Treasury recorded that on a farewell visit Milner seemed anxious and almost willing to throw up the appointment.

Elected under Rule II to the Athenaeum he dined there with Moberly Bell, manager of *The Times*, Rhodes and Kipling, also newly elected and at 31 far the youngest member. His American friend Harold Frederic, in a party which included Dilke, Augustine Birrell and Frank Harris, and the Inland Revenue staff gave him farewell dinners. Best known of these functions is the dinner at the Café Monico, London, on 27 March, organized by Brodrick, Curzon and Gell, with Asquith presiding and some 140 guests – leading Cabinet Ministers, M.P.s, civil servants and others representing most shades of political opinion. Sixteen of the guests were former Presidents of the Oxford Union, eleven of these from Balliol. The occasion was remarkable for two reasons. First, as evidence of the number of influential people who considered, to quote Harcourt's opinion, that 'things now looked very black' in South Africa. Second, as proof of these people's faith in Milner's ability, and his capacity to deal with a delicate problem on a national non-party basis.

Milner noted that he had a tremendous reception. Asquith in his speech called his new post 'the most arduous and responsible in the administrative service of the country – beset in every direction with embarrassing problems and formidable personalities.' Yet he was sure that Milner with his clear intellect, sympathy and 'power of tenacious and inflexible resolution' would succeed. Chamberlain, Milner later wrote, 'astonished us by a very political and rather bellicose speech' clearly aimed at Pretoria.

Rosebery sent apologies for absence, paying tribute to Milner's 'union of intellect with fascination which makes men mount high.'

Milner had taken great trouble preparing a 15-minute reply which he thought went down fairly well. As usual, he frankly put his cards on the table, admitting he was

> ... cursed with a cross-bench mind. ... My mind is not so constructed that I am capable of understanding the arguments of those who question the desirability or possibility [of imperial unity] ... we should maintain religiously the ties which exist, seize every opportunity of developing new ones, spare no effort to remove misunderstanding and mistrust. ... It is a great privilege, to be allowed [to serve] as a civilian soldier of the Empire.[53]

On 17 April he was off at last – 'a great relief', eluding the Press and joined by his staff and seen off by Gell at Southampton. He was not a good sailor. It was not perhaps a good omen that they sailed in rather rough weather which later got worse.

Part II

OPPORTUNITY

Chapter 7

South Africa – Peace or War?
(April 1897 – October 1899)

Appreciation of the Problem – Decisions and Leave –
Time Runs Out

Gell records a heart-to-heart talk of February in which Milner gave his own explanation of his success. He was not, he said, 'one of the brilliant men' and did not work rapidly, but was industrious, laborious and had gifts of expression. Lacking money and influence his rise, he thought, had been due to tenacious hold on to one idea since youth – the British Empire and Race. He had learnt with difficulty the need for limitation, and was quite indifferent to being out of the swim. He could not account for his undoubted popularity.[1]

In this spirit he was facing the 17 days needed for the run from Southampton to Cape Town, with a stop at Madeira. Besides visiting his horses, taking lessons in Dutch and enjoying varied reading, he worked a good deal and wrote many letters. To Selborne he wrote, for despatch from Madeira, begging him

> . . . to hang on like grim death to the decision to send reinforcements and not let the Government slip out of it on any account. As to the absolute necessity of not playing these high games with no adequate force behind us, I shall never have but one opinion. I desire peace – honestly – and I hope to maintain it.[2]

But they could not answer for the other side. A Boer incursion into Cape Colony, and a rising in support of it, *'might be chanced.'* What ought never to be risked (he correctly deduced) was our being turned out of Natal. Though it might cause some Boer commotion, reinforcement of the existing garrison of under 6,000 troops by 2–3,000 was too small for any British aggressive purpose.[3]

To Parkin in Canada he wrote acknowledging the influence of his ideas upon him, adding 'S.A. is just now the weakest link in the Imperial chain.' He was conscious of his big responsibility in trying to prevent it from snapping. Any elation he might feel at being given so big a job was swallowed up in his 'solemn sense of the great national interests at stake.'

He reached Cape Town on 5 May. Sprigg, the Prime Minister, came on board and drove him to Government House to take the oath, with addresses presented to him *en route* and what he thought a 'magnificent reception'. Sir James Rose-Innes, a leading Cape politician and eventual Chief Justice of the Union, recorded his impression of Milner at the ceremony thus – 'a friendly smile and a pleasant manner, in appearance a scholar rather than a man of action, but with an air of grave assurance which indicated fixity of purpose, a man more apt to give than to take advice. Certainly a Governor of a different type, and in a different class, from either of his predecessors.'[4] His friend Garrett, editor of the *Cape Times* and his constant future supporter, wrote that with his arrival the Imperial Factor (Rhodes's term) was in the saddle.

An important figure in Milner's official life was Conyngham Greene, a regular diplomat of Milner's age and of Irish extraction. His appointment late in 1896 to the key job of British Agent at Pretoria had been a feature of Chamberlain's stiffer policy towards Kruger. Before leaving London Milner had defined with the Colonial Office his relations as High Commissioner with the Agent. Briefly stated, these allowed the Agent to address confidential reports to the Colonial Secretary in London 'under flying seal to the High Commissioner' who could add his own comments. Milner secured power to summon the Agent to confer with him, and to get into direct communication by interview or letter with the President of the Transvaal.[5]

On 15 April Greene had read Chamberlain's March despatches to Kruger and reported him 'greatly excited' over Britain's naval demonstration. Milner wrote to Bertha Synge that on his arrival at Cape Town things looked 'desperately bad . . . we were within an ace of a blow-up.' But though the Boers had not changed in their hearts and 'things all round were in the most rotten condition' there was now a respite.[6] Kruger had sent Chamberlain a conciliatory note. Milner told Lord Grey in June 'things are quieting down. The Boers, as usual, give way a bit when they see we are in grim earnest, and will not defy us.' He told Chamberlain he was quite sure that 'the two measures between them averted war in S. Africa . . . within a fortnight of my arrival the Government of the S.A.R. made a distinct retreat.' He could proceed to a close study of the situation, and the policy agreed with him of patience and an effort to improve relations between Britain and all Afrikanders.[7]

It was South Africa's autumn and Milner lived and worked, with Mrs. Hanbury-Williams as his hostess, in Government House, a long unpretentious mansion in Cape Town built by the Dutch in the seventeenth century for the C.-in-C.'s guests and known to them as the 'House in the Garden' for the lawns, trees and flower-beds surrounding it. The landscape was dominated by the towering precipices of Table Mountain and the Lion. When summer began in October Milner moved to Newlands some six miles away, close to Rhodes's mansion Groote Schuur and the slopes of Table Mountain. He called Newlands in a letter home 'our little country house, inconvenient to get at and *a mere box*, tho' awfully pretty.'

Sir William Harcourt, convinced that due to the Jameson Raid Rhodes had irreparably ruined South Africa, wrote to Milner that in his arduous enterprise he was on the anvil 'under the triple hammer of a self-governing Colony, an ungovernable "chartered" libertine and a sagacious Kruger'.[8] Milner's dual position of High Commissioner, responsible in varying degree for all British South Africa, and Governor of one Colony always aggravated his problems. With the Imperial Government's relations with Kruger improved, his chief preoccupation now lay with Cape Colony, of which more must be said. In an area (with British Bechuanaland) over twice the size of the United Kingdom this had a population at the 1891 census (excluding Bechuanaland and Pondoland) of about 1,500,000, three-quarters of whom were either African or Coloured. Of the white population of some 376,000 about 130,000 were of British origin and 230,000 of Dutch (a term including the small numbers of German and French descent). Cape Town and its suburbs had a population in 1897 of about 90,000.

Milner had told Iwan-Müller before leaving England that his fear was how the Cape people would take his appointment since they had probably never heard of him. Supposedly this was a reference to the British, known later as the 'loyalist', section. What mattered equally at this stage was his ability as Governor to get on good terms with Cape politicians and the Colony's Dutch political organization, the Bond, led by Hofmeyr. Basil Williams, the historian, in his *Rhodes* describes the Cape Parliament as lending itself to tolerance, more like the English House of Commons of the eighteenth than of the late nineteenth century, a small society with high standards of debate. In the years after Milner's arrival, however, the growth of more organized parties led to an increase of Parliamentary intolerance and bitterness.

Besides his despatches (which might or might not be published) Milner wrote to Chamberlain, Selborne and their Colonial Office subordinates frequent, usually long, confidential letters. He wrote Chamberlain such a letter in May commenting on Cape politicians who would soon attend the Queen's Jubilee in London. Sprigg, the caretaker Prime Minister, was 'a good official . . . an honest man, but far from strong'; Sir Henry de Villiers, the Chief Justice, was 'the ablest and most persuasive of the Dutch party' and would assure him that the Dutch in the Colony were thoroughly loyal.[9] He had already made it clear to de Villiers, Jan Hofmeyr and others that 'if they wish to prevent war it is not with Gt. Britain they ought to remonstrate. The centre of disturbance in S. Africa is in the Transvaal.'

The Afrikander Bond, now confined to Cape Colony, played a central part in the story which follows. Its historian calls it 'the only political party for much of its existence' which had begun at Graaff Reinet in 1882. Its aim was frankly nationalist, a South Africa united under the Dutch flag. But this was hampered by the vigorous rivalry, apart from racial feeling, between Boer and British states emphasized earlier in this story. Though the 'Raid' produced new impetus for Afrikander union, 'the Afrikander national movement', T. R. H. Davenport writes, 'failed to get real momentum'; for example, the Bond had still failed by the outbreak of war in 1899 to give unreserved support to Kruger's Transvaal.[10]

Another essential fact is that the Bond was an extra-Parliamentary movement. Hofmeyr now sat in neither the Cape's Legislative Council (23 members) nor its House of Assembly (78 members). Under his strong leadership a Parliamentary caucus supported whichever candidate for the Premiership was ready to comply with the Bond's legislative pro-gramme of the moment. Hofmeyr needed skilled Parliamentarians, of whom W. P. Schreiner, Sprigg's successor as Premier, is the best known example. He also had to appease what Davenport calls 'English Colonial sensitivity to any manifestation of Afrikander nationalism' by making power appear to lie in other hands. Of Sprigg's Ministry of five three were nominal Bondsmen though only one was a Hofmeyr man.

Used to Whitehall, Westminster and St. James's it is not surprising to find Milner calling South Africa to Rendel 'new, huge and very raw'. A Colonial Office expert on South Africa who had been involved, at the Whitehall end, in the Jameson Raid fiasco and was probably thinking especially of Johannesburg called it a country with 'very different moral meridians' to those of Britain. It was unfortunate, though not surpris-ing, that Milner found some of the standards obtaining among the Boers as well as the British much to his distaste. He illustrated this clearly after the War when he told an Afrikander who admired him that the fault among the Boers with which he had come most in contact was

> . . . the tendency not only to overreach in a bargain, but to assume that the man, with whom you are bargaining, is also trying to overreach,

that it is impossible that he should be straightforward . . . and must be trying to 'do you down'.

He went on to admit he was 'a poor diplomatist' and had 'often been baffled and perhaps unduly irritated' by this Dutch characteristic. He also very truly described himself as 'a poor hand at concealing my feelings.'[11]

This moral distaste was combined with what Leo Amery, his friend from the Boer War to the end of his life, called 'a certain background of quiet reserve . . . always something of himself which he kept withdrawn and apart', perhaps due to the circumstances of his boyhood, his need to rely on his own unaided abilities, and his failure to marry.

He made no attempt to conceal in private letters, even that to Parkin before his arrival, that one of the job's disadvantages was that he would be living with 'most uncongenial people'. He told Dawkins in August that 'apart from the work the life here bores me to death. It is 100 thousand times less amusing than Egypt.' To Rendel he even made the statement that he thought it an advantage in his job as a Governor that 'I loathe the place as a man'. It made him fearless of 'coming to grief', and unhampered by personal anxiety in dealings with 'local people and the Colonial Office . . . my only *personal* interest is in my English friends and my only amusement hearing from them'. His private letters were usually fluent and often impetuous, a carefree exercise in 'letting off steam'.

Professor Walker calls him in this period rigid and solitary, with his work hindered by his failure to inspire affection or even understanding in the South African common man. He was often the alert official of his portrait in the Civil Service Club at Cape Town, with close-shut mouth, shrewd eyes looking a little sideways through narrowed lids, weighing up the situation, sizing up his man.[12] It was unfortunate that he failed to establish more friendly relations with leading Cape statesmen. Sir Henry de Villiers, whom Milner admired, was self-contained and austere. But after some attempt he made to influence Kruger had failed, Milner developed a distrust for him which 'prevented him from ever discussing politics alone with his Chief Justice'. Jan Hofmeyr's hostile biographers see Milner as 'a square peg in a round hole' who behaved from the start 'with the spirit of an Eastern autocrat'. Though this picture is overdrawn, Milner, it seems, was assuming too much his High Commission role by failing to consult Hofmeyr more, especially in the critical weeks preceding the Boer War. Also, in declining to take Schreiner, his Prime Minister at the time, to the Bloemfontein Conference with Kruger.

The element of reserve in his nature did not prevent his enjoyment of a stream of visitors to Government House, or the genuine devotion to him of his staff. His diary now included such items as 'heavy business on hand' and 'a great hustle' to get despatches written in time for the weekly mail-boat. He presided over the Cape's Executive Council, had frequent talks with Sprigg and his Ministers, and as High Commissioner many duties and problems outside the Cape. He told a friend that 'the ceremonial part of the business was amusing for about one day, then utterly boring', and Charlotte Toynbee that he was 'fearfully bored by my ceremonial duties, and deeply interested in my real work'. From the start he had been taking Dutch lessons from Adrian Hofmeyr and reading the Dutch press.[13]

It was months before the Colonial Office provided him with an experienced Imperial Secretary; with a rather incompetent Acting Secretary of this kind he relied much on his private secretary Ozzy Walrond who, he found, had lots of ability. Major and Mrs. Hanbury-Williams proved excellent at running the social side of Government House; and his A.D.C.s were agreeable companions in his daily exercise of rides, walks or bicycling in the gardens, and evenings of whist or billiards.

He had made clear to Chamberlain and others that he was going to the job with a perfectly open mind, and characteristically

. . . would not attempt to formulate, still less to express, a definite opinion upon the problem until I have had at least twelve months' experience in S. Africa.

This open mind did not, it need hardly be said, include the general aim of attaining British supremacy which, Müller wrote to him, 'lay outside discussion'. He had no illusion that British federation of what he called South Africa's 'chaos of colonies, protectorates and republics' could be anything but 'a long way off'. It was clear to him from the past two years' events that the situation was inherently one of British–Boer conflict, and that the High Commissioner's post ('the only factor worth mentioning on the Imperial side') had become 'a *fighting post*'. He did not shrink from the fact that the outcome of the long disagreement with the Transvaal might be war, but was sincerely convinced that a reasonable strengthening of the South African garrison would prevent this disaster. His job, as he saw it, was to show all South Africa that 'we mean to be masters and to exclude foreign interference', without taking away the various states' local independence.[14] One may recall that his subject in the Balliol scholarship essay twenty-five years earlier had been 'Are wars more likely to diminish as nations become more civilized?'

On the war against the Khalifa again in progress at the other end of the continent Wingate, Kitchener's Director of Military Intelligence, wrote him vivid accounts. He described the Rodd Mission to Abyssinia ('Prester John') designed to counter French influence on the Upper Nile and Kitchener's capture of Abu Hamed and Berber, 'a nasty position to hold' against dervish forces of unknown strength. Another British pause was then needed. Hicks Beach was now inclined to agree on an advance to Khartoum but stressed Britain's 'costly undertakings' elsewhere overseas.

Details of the complex negotiations which continued with Kruger can be found in the South African J. S. Marais's *Fall of Kruger's Republic*, which gives Kruger much credit for readiness to reform. Marais relies mainly on Chamberlain's papers, Colonial Office records and other British sources. As President Kruger and his colleagues conducted their government so much by word of mouth and also destroyed files during the war, the student (it seems) has few Boer MS. sources to draw on. One can agree with Professor Mansergh that Britain began to adopt 'a posture of menace, deliberately intended to force the pace and the issue', but also with his conclusion that other factors making for war included 'the still insufficiently analysed ambitions of the Boers.'[15]

Although often seen by Chamberlain and others as too much given to pessimism, Milner's nature had its optimistic side. 'If we can pull through next year without disaster,' he told Parkin, 'I believe the situation may be saved.' With the earlier crisis resolved he was fighting on three principal fronts: first the Cape, where he hoped his influence might halt the tide of Afrikander sentiment and cause Ministers to apply pressure on Kruger; secondly Rhodesia, where revision of the Company's charter was his immediate concern. He told Graham of the Colonial Office in September that the success of British policy in South Africa depended 'largely upon getting the development of [Rhodes's] North on to the right lines. The thing is in an awful tangle at present';[16] third Kruger's Transvaal, which he hoped his 'semi-official' pressure (as opposed to Downing Street's heavier touch) might persuade to set itself in order.

For a time this last aim seemed to be succeeding. Kruger lifted his ban on the pro-British Johannesburg *Star*, and gave the city a limited form of municipal government; he also appointed commissions on Constitutional Reform and the Gold Industry, and allowed appeals under the Aliens Expulsion Act, 1896.

Milner had told Grey in June that, though conditions were better, the Transvaal would remain a centre of disturbance. By August he was telling Chamberlain that Kruger's state was 'in a terrible mess, social, political and financial'. W. Leyds, a strongly anti-British active Hollander, had been its roving ambassador in Europe, and tried in vain to secure a loan there. This, Milner thought, made internal reform almost inevitable and he was anxious not to hinder what he saw as a process of disintegration. So he dissuaded Greene (who sent him long and frequent reports) from worrying Kruger over Chamberlain's despatch on the meaning of the London Convention, declined to pursue minor problems and, above all, shelved the major issue of Kruger's Dynamite Monopoly.[17] On the debit side, however, Chamberlain's whitewashing of Rhodes in Parliament after the Raid Inquiry in July had increased Kruger's distrust. Chamberlain had also failed to make progress over Delagoa Bay, or arrange for a South African Immigration Conference.

Milner made a four weeks' tour in September with Pieter Faure, the Secretary for Agriculture of the Eastern Province, his first experience of the country outside the Cape Town area. Crossing the vast dry Karoo ('its air brilliant and most bracing') he turned south to the British strongholds of the eastern ports, visited the famous Lovedale Mission and spent arduous days by spider (a four-wheeled sprung wagon), ox-cart and horseback through mud and drifts to reach the top of the Zwartberg Pass and rejoin the railway. He found his tour 'rather fun on the whole bar the speeches', but returned to an overwhelming mass of correspondence. He moved to Newlands, and went daily by train or rode through Groote Schuur's park into Cape Town.

In October he at last acquired a competent Imperial Secretary, George Fiddes, a Colonial Office official about his own age with knowledge of South African affairs. This enabled him to give more attention to Rhodesia and visit it in a tour of six weeks. Leaving late in October he kept a special notebook intended to supplement the mere outline of his diary, but unfortunately this was not sustained for long.[18] Kimberley, he wrote, was De Beers and 'the De Beers people are violent Rhodesites to a man – not his followers but his servants.' The company was 'magnificently organized . . . a huge and unscrupulous monopoly . . . but giving munificent funds to public purposes', with good native compounds and paying liberal wages. Prospects for profits were good for a long time to come.

After a short stop at Mafeking, where he opened the railway's extension to Bulawayo, he had talks with African chiefs including the celebrated pro-British King Khama at Palapye. He visited the Tati minefield, and entered the British South Africa Company's territory. Talks and functions followed at Bulawayo, 'a city just springing up in the wilderness.' At Victoria in Mashonaland he concluded that 'regular administration' must await large European settlement, of which there was still no sign in these 'vast districts'. Travelling rough he eventually reached the capital Salisbury for talks about the new constitution with Rhodesia's Acting Administrator, Sir William Milton. He then went some 200 miles by mule cart to Umtali for long talks with Rhodes, whose farm at Inyanga lay nearby.

Rhodes had been given a rapturous reception at the Cape on his return from the London Inquiry and had had talks with Milner before going north. He was, Milner wrote to Selborne, 'undaunted and unbroken by former failure, but also untaught by it', and in his much-quoted summing up, 'men are ruled by their foibles, and Rhodes's foible is *size*.' Rhodes was occupied with attempts to acquire the Bechuanaland Protectorate and plans for extension north of the telegraph and railways. Milner, Rhodes's latest biographers write, 'was surprised at Rhodes's readiness to accept a radical revision' of the Company's constitution, and this meeting 'seems to have made a beginning in the removal of grounds for suspicion between them.' It took almost a year for this new constitution, largely Milner's work, to come into force. A Resident Commissioner appointed from home and reporting to the High Commissioner would represent the Crown, and the police would be under Imperial control. New Executive and Legislative Councils would represent the settlers. General administration, however, would still rest with one or more Administrators appointed (with Her Majesty's Government's approval) and paid by the Company. There was added, at Rhodes's insistence, a famous customs clause preventing Rhodesia from putting higher tariffs on British goods than the existing ones at the Cape; and this, Rhodes's biographers write, was 'the almost unconscious starting-point' of Milner's and Chamberlain's own dedication to the idea of an Imperial tariff system.[19]

Taking the train through Mozambique Milner reached Beira ('steamy heat awful') and after a four days' sea-voyage (often 'bilious and miserable') reached Cape Town on 30 November where for a week he was very seedy, 'my stomach being all out of order.' Without changing his view that the Transvaal's internal state was the chief danger to South Africa, he told Chamberlain that improvement in relations with the Republic had been reaffirmed by Kruger's moderate tone in the recent 'suzerainty' debate, and that its internal troubles included growing opposition of sections of Boers to Kruger's autocratic rule.[20] For a time he was more anxious about the Cape. Sprigg's Ministry was losing the Bond's confidence without gaining real support from the mainly British groups. 'Progressive' forces, including Rose-Innes's followers, lacked cohesion. The extreme and new pro-British South African League looked in vain for leadership to Rhodes, who had too much to do in the north, and to Milner, who was not going to be hurried.

On Christmas Day Milner wrote a long letter to Edward Hamilton on the general position, intended for the eye of the Prince of Wales. Next day he climbed with Ozzy to the top of Table Mountain. Before the year was out alarming news arrived of unrest in Basutoland, which remained disturbed for weeks to come.

In January 1898 there were signs that the Boer Republics were considering some amalgamation of their railways, and that Leyds's activities were inclining European governments to greater interest in the Transvaal. Far the worst blow, however, to Milner's faith in improvement of conditions for the British and other foreigners in the Transvaal and the success of the policy of patience was Kruger's election as President for the fourth time, at the age of 72, in February. His majority was a record, double the combined votes of his more liberal rivals Schalk Burger and Vice-President Piet Joubert. With this large vote of confidence, Kruger at once rejected the reforms proposed by his Industrial Commission and dismissed his Chief Justice John Kotze. The Cape Bond by a unanimous vote congratulated him on his re-election.

Marais writes, with some over-dramatization, 'Milner's mood changed now – unalterably – from over-optimism to extreme pessimism. He was willing to wait no longer.'[21] Milner certainly sent Chamberlain on 23 February a despatch and a long private letter in which he thought it a great probability that relations with the Transvaal would now worsen, adding the much-quoted sentence: 'there is no way out of the political troubles of S. Africa except reform in the Transvaal or war.' His despatch listed the many still-unresolved questions in dispute with the South African Republic, and concluded that they seemed to be entering 'a fresh period of strained relations . . . which is evidently fraught with peril.'[22]

Judge Kotze retired to the Cape and Milner (as High Commissioner) felt strongly that his treatment, i.e. the assault on the Transvaal judiciary's independence, concerned not only Transvaal subjects but indirectly all South Africa. Her Majesty's Government at home took a less climacteric view, Chamberlain telegraphing in March that the

. . . principal object in S. Africa at present is peace. Nothing but a most flagrant offence would justify the use of force.

Britain was also, as Milner was inclined to forget, much involved at this time with West Africa, the Sudan and China. Agitation in Kotze's favour, from which he expected too much, failed to produce lasting local interest.

Cape elections for both Houses were due in 1898 and Rhodes, after some persuasion, returned to the Colony in January and threw himself whole-heartedly into the campaign. It has been seen that the Progressives had no leader to compare with Rhodes in force or popularity. The constituency arrangements of the Colony favoured the country districts where Boers predominated as against the towns which were mainly British. Rhodes, like Milner, 'saw a real danger that the Cape Parliament would be captured by pro-Kruger Boer candidates, who would take their orders from Pretoria.'[23]

From some writers one would conclude that South African elections were fought in the friendly, leisurely, spirit of an English village cricket match. The two Cape campaigns, which continued for months, were the most bitter hitherto known, and the effective beginning in the Colony of two organized Parliamentary parties. On 8 March Rhodes finally broke with the Bond by attacking it in an interview. On 3 March Milner made a famous speech at Graaff Reinet, a Dutch farming centre and the scene of the Bond's birth sixteen years before.

On arrival there to open a railway he was unexpectedly given an address from the Bond's local branch. He records a 'tremendous scramble' to prepare his speech in intervals between functions. This lasted for 35 minutes at an official dinner and, he thought, 'passed off successfully.' It was the first deliberately controversial speech he had made since his arrival 10 months earlier in South Africa.

> What reason [he asked in reply to the Bond's loyal address] could there be for disloyalty? . . . Of course you are loyal. It would be monstrous if you were not. [But in differences between Her Majesty's Government and the S.A.R.] a number of people in the Colony . . . without even the semblance of impartiality espouse the side of the Republic.

He denied that Britain had any 'occult design on the independence of the Transvaal.' He criticized the Republic for its unprogressiveness, and failure to see that the danger facing it was not Britain's aim at possession but its own internal state. He urged his hearers to use all their influence to induce Kruger's Government to assimilate 'the temper and spirit of its administration to those of the free communities of South Africa.' For he had constantly uppermost in his mind the contrast between Kruger's discrimination against foreigners and Cape Colony's equal treatment of the Dutch as citizens.

This speech made a big impression in South Africa, and also at home, where the Press in general praised it. The Progressives won control of the Cape Upper House by a small majority in March. What really mattered was to gain decisive control of the Lower House in a campaign which lasted from June to September. Besides Kruger's re-election, disillusionment since his tour there with Rhodesia's material and mineral prospects contributed to Milner's declining faith in the policy of patience. A change for the better in British–Transvaal relations seemed likely to follow the substitution in April of the more pliant Francis Reitz for Leyds as Transvaal State Secretary and the appointment of Jan Smuts, also a lawyer and Cape Colonist by birth, educated at Cambridge and only 28 years old, as its State Attorney. Yet complaint and counter-complaint between Cape Town and Pretoria continued. For a fuller account than can be given here of Uitlander grievances and Kruger's limited efforts to meet them the reader should consult in addition to Marais's pro-Kruger version, Basil Worsfold's *Lord Milner's Work in S. Africa, 1897–1902*, and E. T. Cook's *The Rights and Wrongs of the Transvaal War*.[24] The latter contains many references to despatches and blue books, and Cook, Milner's friend since Oxford and their work on the *Pall Mall Gazette*, was regarded by people of many opinions as in the top class of contemporary journalists. For two years or so he had edited the liberal *Daily News*.

The Basutoland crisis died down due to the skill of its Resident Commissioner, Godfrey Lagden, whom Milner later made his Commissioner for Native Affairs in the Republics after the War. In April Milner spent four weeks touring this isolated 'Switzerland of S. Africa', with its bracing air and absence of Europeans, railways and roads. He told Mrs. Horner in England: 'we scramble over grassy downs and up steep rocky mountain-sides on rough but very good-tempered and sure-footed ponies.' He once camped at almost 9,000 feet; and besides conducting much business found his tour 'a tremendous joke and a first-rate holiday.'[25]

Back in Cape Town his days were still rigorous, and he wrote asking Chamberlain for autumn leave at home. Holding a levée and ceremonies to mark the Queen's Birthday, arranging with Sprigg for a tribute to Gladstone, giving a small dance at Government House ('the cotillion, rather experimental, was not a success, but otherwise people seemed to enjoy themselves') and occasional hunting of jackals were breaks in a life filled with interviews, despatches and letters. Once Basutoland had calmed down, a serious situation arose in northern Swaziland. A Convention of 1894 had given Kruger the right of administering this small African country, though the majority of its resident whites were

British subjects. Its problems provided one more continuous bone of contention.

Milner had been engaged since his arrival in much correspondence with Greene about Kruger's treatment of 'Cape Boys' (i.e. coloured persons) whom he chose to treat as Africans or Bantu. Cape Colony contained some 250,000 of them, in general more educated than the Africans and granted the vote. Those working in the Transvaal were thus British subjects, though the London Convention was ambiguous about their precise legal status there. By pegging away at the subject Milner, Greene and his substitutes in Pretoria obtained from Kruger improvement in his treatment of these 'Boys'. Though it must be said that their disabilities, and also those of Britain's Indian subjects in the Transvaal, remained substantial by British standards up to the outbreak of war.

It is important to notice Milner's general views on the Native Question, (now known as the Colour problem), which in South Africa was a complex multicolour problem. The most-quoted of his statements on the question is his letter to Asquith of 18 November 1897. He affirmed that it 'horribly complicated' the cardinal Dutch–English problem. In general, he said with some foresight,

. . . you have this singular situation that you might indeed unite Dutch and English by protecting the black man, but you would unite them against your policy of protection. There is the whole *crux* of the S. African position.

In the Colony he could only use personal influence, doing all he could 'to encourage the minority, which is for fair treatment of the Natives. . . . By far the worst [in this matter] is the Transvaal. Here the black has no rights whatever . . . [and is treated with] neither kindliness nor wisdom.'[26]

The question was still, to use Walker's apt phrase, 'below the surface' of the Anglo-Dutch conflict. To quote British politicians at opposite ends of the British political stage, Balfour, not an unqualified admirer of Milner, decried all forms of racial arrogance and agreed with Asquith that 'the great blot and stain on the Boer Government . . . was its treatment of the native races'; yet he denied absolutely that the black and white races could be brought soon to equality – 'men are not born equal. They cannot be made equal by education extending over generation after generation within the ordinary historical limit.'[27] The historian Bernard Porter in *Critics of Empire: British Radical Attitudes to Colonialism in Africa, 1895–1914* shows that Liberals and Radicals felt small concern for

South African 'natives' before or during the Boer War. What they were most concerned to do was to attack Imperialism as a state of mind. The post-war Chinese Labour controversy was almost the first issue which added to the Anglo-Dutch conflict awareness and sympathy in Britain for the non-white peoples.

It is well known that Milner bitterly regretted, too late, neglect of the chance in the Vereeniging Peace of combining with the promise to the Boers of eventual self-government some guarantee of the franchise to Africans. In his 'Watch Tower Speech' at Johannesburg of May 1903 he publicly expounded his views. The rule of the white man could only be justified on 'the ground of superior civilization.' His example and educational efforts were the only means of 'raising the black man . . . up to a much higher level than that which he at present occupies.' He wrote in the next year: 'for the civilized native, *a coloured man*, . . . all colour disabilities, political or other, should be cancelled. Property and a high education test would be essential conditions.'

In June the vital Cape Assembly elections began to hot up. On the 6th Milner thought the political situation still very uncertain and on the 14th noted 'a good rough and tumble debate' in the House when Schreiner moved a vote of no confidence. Soon afterwards Sprigg's Government was defeated; *Ons Land*, the chief Bond paper, had a flaming article attacking him and 'all sorts of wild rumours were flying about'. Milner got more disquieting news about Swaziland, and an important telegram from Chamberlain about Delagoa Bay.

Early in July Rhodes had long talks with Milner about the still unsettled boundary between Rhodesia and the Bechuanaland Protectorate. His diary on 1 August noted Bismarck's death and on 2 September Kitchener's victory at Omdurman. Wingate had sent him full news of the Nile campaign, reinforced since early this year by British troops and since August by Winston Churchill, both officer of the 21st Lancers and *Morning Post* correspondent.[28] Khartoum was occupied. Hicks Beach had agreed with Salisbury that if the war ended there he would find the money for the Aswan Dam; so work on this, using British capital and skill, soon began.

Milner, however, was more concerned with Cape Colony elections. Rhodes had been very active, spending lavishly and speaking often on a programme of anti-Krugerism, redistribution of seats to help the towns, and federation. Schreiner, not a Bond member but the chief Parliamentary representative of its aims, named his following 'the South African Party', fought back ferociously and also spent freely. Contemporaries agreed that the bitterness between the white races was unexampled.

The result was very close. Schreiner's Party won a narrow majority of seats, while the Progressives won a majority of electoral votes. This gave further support to the recurring Progressive demand for electoral re-distribution. Their leaders, now including Dr. Jameson, tried hard to persuade Milner to let Sprigg retain office and defer the opening of Parliament in the hope that they would win more Progressive seats on a scrutiny. Milner would not countenance this, had lively interviews with Rhodes and Sprigg and had to postpone going on leave. His constitutional correctness prevailed. Parliament was opened on 10 October and Sprigg resigned; Schreiner took his place and remained Prime Minister until the Boer War had lasted nine months. Milner tried to educate Rhodes in the role of Parliamentary Opposition leader, but the Colossus left for Kimberley and then for England to further his railway and telegraph plans. Garrett was one of the successful Progressives and proved a persuasive speaker in the Assembly.

Schreiner was the son of a German missionary, a lawyer like so many South African politicians, and brother of Olive, whose *Story of an African Farm* had been a big success in Britain fifteen years before. His biographer calls him shy, and his South African Party Government precarious. Though dependent on Bond organization its six members contained only two Bondsmen though two others, J. X. Merriman and J. W. Sauer, were strong Colonialists and active opponents of the Imperialist Milner and his views. Schreiner was greatly opposed, Milner found, to his forthcoming leave and, with the suspicious Merriman, was 'wondering where precisely the urgency lay.' Both men well knew the defects of Kruger's regime, but asked, 'hadn't the Johannesburgers patience?'[29]

Milner only knew the date of his leaving on 1 November when a telegram came from London decisively calling him home. His main object, of course, was to get Her Majesty's Government to listen to him as 'the man on the spot' and to convince it that his diagnosis was sound. He sailed two days later, and as usual on voyages he got through much reading, learnt that France was climbing down over Fashoda, and thought Chamberlain's report of his conference with Colonial Premiers the year before 'decidedly interesting and important.' The Commander-in-Chief of South Africa's garrison had died in October and Milner wrote on board ship to his successor, General Sir William Butler, who was unknown to him and would in his absence be Acting High Commissioner; the two men passed one another at sea. By 18 November Milner was back in the familiar Duke Street he had left 19 months before.

His leave in England was to last $2\frac{1}{2}$ months and consist of a full social life and plenty of work, between which it is often hard to distinguish.

He was commanded to dine and sleep at Windsor, spent week-ends at Sandringham, Hatfield, Highbury, Seacox and other country houses and attended or gave endless lunches and dinner parties. These included the brilliant function of a farewell dinner at the Hotel Cecil to George Curzon, appointed at the early age of 39 Viceroy of India. Dawkins was in England, having now left Egypt on promotion to the job of Financial Member of the Viceroy of India's Council. He discussed with Milner future editions of *England in Egypt*, and the offer made to him by J. P. Morgan, the foremost American banker, of the much better paid job of partner to look after his English business. Milner discussed with several people the future editorship of the Johannesburg *Star*. Once he had to have 'a huge bella-donna plaster on my chest to keep my heart quiet', and another anxiety was some defect which developed in his eyesight, involving a minor operation. By late January he wrote 'the pace was getting tremendous towards the end.'

In his first talks with Chamberlain Milner left him in no doubt about his preference for 'an active and resolute policy even at the risk of its leading to war.' But Chamberlain wished to do nothing to precipitate further crisis; his answer was: 'our policy is not to *bring* things to a crisis. Let them *come* to a crisis. The Boers must put themselves in the wrong.'[30]

The British public, Milner wrote in December to Schreiner, were not in the least interested in anything South African. Then, as so often, fate intervened with a minor event. On Christmas Eve Milner read 'a very ugly telegram about a row in Johannesburg, the death of an Englishman at the hands of the police, followed by a Uitlander demonstration and much local feeling.' This event became notorious as the Edgar Case.

General Sir William Butler was an Irishman of 61 whose memories went back to the Great Famine of the '40s and who had known much varied military service. His wife was a noted Victorian painter of military subjects. It is now more to the point that the General held strong liberal political views. In Egypt in 1882 he had praised Blunt's *Secret History* and helped to save the rebel Arabi from execution. He had been appointed to Cape Town without any consultation with Chamberlain, probably by Lord Wolseley alone. Like that of many soldiers before and since, his view of the War Office was a low one. He claimed he had been sent to what he called 'the central stormspot of the world . . . without storm-chart, or direction of any kind . . . I went out blindfold [but] the bandages soon fell off.'[31]

What he saw differed radically from Milner's picture of South Africa and her needs and what followed was a passage almost of farce. He found

Rhodes and his followers, Edmund Garrett and others of Milner's associates and the Johannesburg so-called 'magnates' the arch-villains of the scene. He agreed with a Cape politician who called Johannesburg 'Monte Carlo superimposed upon Sodom and Gomorrah', and made up his mind that Kruger's Transvaal was being shabbily treated. Marais calls him 'a High Commissioner after the Schreiner Ministry's heart.' Butler's biographer, in a useful and more objective study, calls his appointment 'one of those ironies of history which must wake the laughter of the gods.'[32]

The Edgar Case was a Johannesburg brawl between a Uitlander of this name, who seems to have been drunk, and a Boer policeman (*Zarp*) who shot him dead, was then charged with murder but finally acquitted. Greene was on leave, so that the Acting British Agent was the less experienced Edmund Fraser; and Smuts was the Transvaal State Attorney. What mattered most was the agitation backed by the Transvaal South African League which at once arose among the Uitlander rank and file, who produced a strongly-worded petition to the Queen. Butler censured Fraser and refused to accept the petition which, according to Headlam, 'by its existence had opened a new era in the history of S. Africa.' Chamberlain's first reaction was that the affair 'may be very important', giving Her Majesty's Government 'the right of remonstrance and action.' Butler cabled a number of times to London, and the case continued to cause trouble long after Milner's return from leave.[33]

The Anglo-German convention of August 1898 had freed Britain from possible German interference in Mozambique and the South African Republic; and the Fashoda crisis was a thing of the past. But the British Cabinet was deeply divided over Chamberlain's South African policies, Balfour and Hicks Beach disapproving with Salisbury, though often doubtful, sometimes supporting Milner's general distrust of the Boer proposals. A modern historian has revised Garvin's picture and decided that Chamberlain was

. . . vacillating, at times even weak . . . with a fatal gap between his vision and his practical statesmanship . . . [but] Milner was made of sterner stuff. It was Milner's, not Chamberlain's policy, which prevailed and it was Milner who dominated their fateful partnership.[34]

Milner, at least, was convinced that as 'man on the spot' he knew the South African situation better than Downing Street, and persuaded Chamberlain that Kruger must be directly challenged on some broad policy ground. In December the Transvaal Raad proposed an extension of the Dynamite Monopoly, perhaps the mineowners' main grievance and Kruger's favourite concession. Chamberlain sent Kruger a despatch protesting that this violated the Convention, and this opened the way to a more challenging British policy. Alarmed over this and the Uitlanders' Petition, Pretoria tried to make terms with the 'magnates', and to discuss a 5-year foreigners' franchise scheme.

Milner sailed again on 29 January, accompanied by Greene and young Lord Belgrave ('Bendor'), George Wyndham's stepson, as a new A.D.C. who before long succeeded his grandfather as 2nd Duke of Westminster. He wrote to Gell from the ship that he had had to use his leave to 'convey in person' his impressions of *all* the South African problems he could foresee, and was fully satisfied with it 'except as a holiday'. This recalls Churchill's writing to his mother at about this time, 'this is a pushing age, and we must push with the best'. He met on board a Mrs. Chapin, an American whose husband had South African mining interests, a woman of much intelligence who became still another of his permanent friends.[35]

He now had little hope that, as he had written to Selborne before his leave, 'two wholly antagonistic systems – a mediaeval race oligarchy and a modern industrial state, recognizing no difference of status between various white races' – could live permanently side by side. Pretoria's attempts to make terms with the magnates and discuss a five-year franchise are seen by Marais as the start of close contact between Chamberlain and the magnates, and a revival by Milner and Greene of 'the reform movement of pre-Raid days.'[36] Garvin and others see them as a clever 'double move' by Kruger's Government – to square the capitalists by a direct deal, and divide the Uitlanders by a mere 'distant prospect of a very limited franchise extension.'

The 'capitalist negotiations', as the first moves became called, began in February and collapsed four weeks later in a flood of mutual recrimination. Percy Fitzpatrick of the Wernher-Beit firm, the son of an Irish immigrant and judge, and Milner's main go-between with the magnates, had been the main negotiator on their side and had small belief in the frankness of the Boer offers. It was then the turn of the Uitlander rank and file to try to improve their conditions by a Second Petition to the Queen, again sponsored by the South Africa League, signed by some 22,000 British subjects on the Rand and sent on by Milner to Chamberlain on 28 March. This called their state 'well-nigh intolerable,' with complete absence of political rights, over-taxation, no real local government, and other grievances. Kruger countered with his own petition which he claimed was signed by 23,000 Uitlanders, and Milner sent Fiddes to Johannesburg to investigate the position.[37] The Uitlander petition, which did not reach Chamberlain till mid-April, is described by Garvin as presenting him with 'a crux', since its acceptance would raise the spectre of war and its rejection disintegrate Transvaal British loyalty. Though the Uitlanders, British and otherwise, it must not be forgotten, were not unanimous in supporting drastic action.

Since his Graaff Reinet speech Milner had in some measure publicly identified himself with a political cause. The dualism of his two roles sometimes resulted in his regarding his High Commissionership as approximating to leadership of the whole 'country'. He well knew that any unification of the country would take time, but the vision of an ultimate, coherent, British South Africa always dominated his thoughts. As he put it in 1904, his work was always to help towards the creation of

> . . . a great and civilised and progressive community, one from Cape Town to the Zambesi – independent in the management of its own affairs, but still remaining, from its own firm desire, a member of the great community of free nations gathered together under the British flag.[38]

Chamberlain's despatch of 10 May embodied Her Majesty's Government's decision to accept the Second Petition. Though such action involved a risk of war, it did not bar more conciliatory attempts to achieve a genuine settlement. On 4 May Milner sent Chamberlain his famous telegram known as his 'helot despatch'.[39] Garvin calls this 'a daring and impassioned burst of outspokenness' in which Milner's claim that 'the case for intervention is overwhelming' was the salient phrase. When the cable was later published much was made of Milner's statement of the bad effect on Britain's reputation of the sight of 'thousands of British subjects kept permanently in the position of helots'. As Professor Walker has remarked, Milner's gift of expressing himself included a command of pungent phrases that sometimes stuck and recoiled strongly upon him. The word 'helots' had in fact been used in a similar context a few years before in the Transvaal by Charles Leonard, a leader of British agitation, and on the eve of the Jameson Raid in a leading article in the London *Times*.

In April influential Cape politicians made stronger efforts to make Kruger adopt more reforms, and to ward off a possible war. De Villiers, for example, went to Pretoria, and Schreiner had many talks with Milner. Chamberlain, in his (still unpublished) despatch of 10 May, proposed a conference between Milner and Kruger to which Milner agreed, but which he would have preferred to occur after publication of a Blue Book on the

Transvaal's discriminations. This time-table was upset by Jan Hofmeyr. At dinner with Milner on 9 May, broaching the scheme of his meeting Kruger at Bloemfontein, the moderate President Steyn of the Orange Free State offered to act as their host. Milner told Selborne he was 'not hopeful of the result of the conference', though he would do his 'very utmost to get *any* settlement, which has the possibility of improvement in it.' The Orange Free State and Cape Afrikanders were, he thought, 'thoroughly frightened' and ready to put heavy pressure on Kruger to give way, but he added 'it is more than doubtful whether he will.'[40]

Milner was almost certainly mistaken in declining to accept Schreiner's offer to go with him, and was attended only by Fiddes, Ozzy and Belgrave. Bloemfontein, the setting, was described by Amery later as little more than a large village,

> It was mainly a vast oblong market square, filled at busy times with great ox-drawn farm wagons, a primitive hotel or two, a few stores and a handful of pleasant bungalows. A fairly imposing Gothic mansion to house the President, and a few other Government buildings. . . . An outer fringe of 'indescribably sordid hutches' housing Kaffir labourers.

Milner met Kruger for the first time at Steyn's house on 31 May and, as Merriman said, 'two more opposite men could scarcely be brought together.' Frank Harris, unreliable as a man but an able writer, had met both men at some time and describes them unflatteringly. Milner he calls 'tall, thin, with shaven, stony face, calm direct regard and immaculate attire, the type of clean, intelligent efficiency' contrasting with Oom Paul's appearance of 'a sick gorilla, with a heavy animal face and small hot eyes glinting out under bushy brows.'[41]

On the Boer side prospects of settlement had not been improved by the Raad's recent cancellation of some selective franchises, the invention of a transparently bogus conspiracy at Johannesburg, and the substitution for Leyds's diplomatic finesse of the pliable, less experienced State Secretary Reitz. Milner fastened firmly at the outset on the franchise, demanding for the Uitlanders a 5-year full retrospective franchise. Though in law an internal Transvaal matter, the Uitlander franchise was the heart of what Chamberlain and Milner saw as South Africa's problem – the denial of white racial equality and the fight for political supremacy, i.e. voting power, in white South Africa as a whole. He was fighting, Milner had said and written countless times, for the Transvaal British to be given the political rights which the Dutch majority had always enjoyed at the Cape. He repeated again that his aim was not conquest but the aim of all liberal-minded Englishmen of the political right of the vote for white peoples.

The story of the conference, a real confrontation, is well known. Milner stuck to the franchise question and refused to be drawn by Kruger into genuine discussion of the numerous other unresolved contentious issues. Some historians see his behaviour as a prime example of his tendency 'to see a complex situation entirely in black and white'. To many contemporary British observers, Kruger's aim seemed to be to rush Her Majesty's Government into a franchise scheme which would look liberal without effecting essential change, and perhaps accomplish his prime aim of inducing her to abandon her suzerainty claim. Hofmeyr's biographers blame Milner for failing to recognize that Kruger was 'a slow-thinking seventeenth-century Puritan farmer'. It would certainly be hard to imagine two men of exceptional power who were so different.

Milner was not ready to accept Kruger's offer of a 6-year franchise hedged round with numerous restrictions, without giving this more detailed study. With a Sunday intervening, the conference broke up on 5 June on the day Chamberlain telegraphed (too late) 'I hope you will not break off hastily'. Milner told Mrs. Chapin, 'I am fearfully tired, and disappointed, but not *beaten*'. To Chamberlain he wrote a long report on 14 June frankly admitting that he might have been wrong in breaking off the conference 'quite as quickly as I did. Perhaps extreme fatigue had something to do with it.' It seems futile to speculate on how a different result might have been reached or whether either or both men wanted agreement. The franchise and other issues had been argued *ad nauseam* in despatches, and by the British Agent in Pretoria with small positive results. Milner and Kruger were both implacable men, each filled with distrust of the other. The reader will recall Milner's special dislike, quoted earlier, of the Boer's assumption that anyone with whom he was bargaining was 'trying to over-reach him'.[42]

Shortly before the Conference Milner's relations with Chamberlain for the first time became strained. Professor J. Grenville quotes the latter's minute, which his Colonial Office officials approved, that 'if Milner is to keep in close sympathy with Her Majesty's Government I think he requires to be restrained rather than to be encouraged at this moment.'[43] Garvin notes Joe's 'disapproving astonishment' at the quick end of the Conference, and his minute 'this is a serious matter. It seems clear to me that Sir A.M. has been overworked. Hence some natural depression.' He notes that Chamberlain's private letter of 7 July, though giving Milner staunch personal support, contained an injunction of restraint which could hardly have pleased Milner.[44]

The publication in London on 14 June of a South African Blue Book (Cd. 9345) which included the Uitlanders' Petition, Milner's 'helot' telegram and Chamberlain's 10 May despatch made the possibility of a war for the first time clearly visible to the British public.

Gell told Milner there had been criticism of him at home for breaking off at Bloemfontein too abruptly, but that publication of this Blue Book marked the height so far reached of his public reputation. Previously limited to politicians, officialdom and the Press, this had now reached the man in the street with the Bloemfontein Conference as big news, 'everyone interested in your despatch . . . your name on all the posters.' Since Milner's departure Gell had worked hard to champion his policies, keep him informed about British opinion and proffer advice. On the last day of May, backed by Lord Grey, he had secured a seat on the board in London of Rhodes's Chartered Company. From this date his letters to Milner included much about the Company's plans, personalities and affairs in Rhodesia.[45]

Gell's influence may well have played a significant part in Milner's failure to realize what was obvious to Chamberlain: the effort required to bring the British public to support a war over issues which were far from simple and which few people outside a small circle clearly understood. Neither 'goldbugs' with foreign names and Park Lane mansions, nor the distant rank-and-file Uitlanders, nor even the spectacular Rhodes and his sometimes barely reputable hangers-on made obvious appeal to the average Briton's common-sense view that some moral, intelligible, cause alone justifies the sacrifices of war. Most of all, and of crucial importance to Milner's whole outlook, was the conclusion Professor Max Beloff, the modern historian, reached that

> . . . the British were not an imperially minded people; they lacked both a theory of empire and the will to engender and implement one.[46]

Chamberlain, Garvin writes, well knew that British public opinion in 1899 required a masterly handling and that the conflict between his 'sinewy gradualness and Milner's ardent chafing would have to continue for some time'. Selborne wrote to Milner on 25 June that 'the idea of war with the South African Republic is very distasteful to most people.' But Chamberlain's speech to his Birmingham Unionists on the following day had a strong effect on M.P.s and did much to convince ordinary people that a war might have to be faced. Frequent Cabinet meetings concerned with South Africa now began.

For details of further complex negotiations with the Transvaal on the franchise the reader must consult the histories referred to. The Transvaal Raad introduced a Franchise Bill on 13 July, but for reasons of prestige refused Britain's request for the opportunity to verify the reality of its concessions. Chamberlain then proffered the olive branch (as De Villiers called it) of a Joint Inquiry into the franchise law, to be followed by further talks between Milner and Kruger. The South African Republic was advised by Leyds from Europe to play for time – the Johannesburgers' nerve might give, or the British Liberals still checkmate Chamberlain's pugnacity. Kruger then injected into the argument an arbitration proposal aimed at excluding all future British interference. In mid-August Smuts and Greene engaged in Pretoria in new informal franchise talks, with Chamberlain asking Milner to be conciliatory and telling Salisbury he was 'unnecessarily suspicious and pedantic in his adherence to form.' State Secretary Reitz then told Greene that any new franchise concessions were expressly conditional on three guarantees, which (as he knew) the British would be unable to accept. Chamberlain, trying again in a Birmingham speech on 26 August to use threats unrelated to force, made the famous criticism 'Mr. Kruger procrastinates in his replies. He dribbles out reforms like water from a squeezed sponge.' The Transvaal then reverted to its previous seven years' franchise offer.

By early September Lord Salisbury had concluded that war was probable, and the Cabinet became mainly concerned with the practical military problem. The Prime Minister and his colleagues, it has been seen, had left Chamberlain much freedom over colonial affairs. Salisbury, in his 70th year, was acutely aware of the European inconvenience of a war in South Africa; he disliked both financiers and jingoes, and did not want to be rushed into a war for their sakes. On 31 August he sent Lansdowne his well-known comment on Milner:

> His view is too heated, if you consider the intrinsic significance and importance of the things which are in controversy . . . but what he has done cannot be effaced. We have to act upon a moral field prepared for us by him and his jingo supporters.[47]

On 4 September Smuts told his Government that 'humanly speaking war between the Republics and England is certain' and, Sir Keith Hancock records, set his fertile mind 'furiously at work upon grand strategy . . . which was his true bent.' He produced plans of political warfare, economic mobilization and military operations. The mills of God, represented in this context by the Cabinet, the Commander-in-Chief and War Office in London and General Butler in Cape Town, ground more slowly, and with considerable mutual friction.

The British garrison of regular troops in South Africa in 1898 was some 8–9,000.[48] The War Office paid little attention to its Intelligence Department's estimate that the total Boer force in the field might reach some 48,000, though at the end of the year it had asked General Butler to report his defence plans. Butler's subsequent actions again bear a strong touch of farce. Determined above all to avoid provoking the Boers, he made a plan which was essentially defensive but refused to report this to the War Office (which he thought his most formidable foe) until finally forced to do so in June 1899. He refused to support Milner's view that troops should be stationed on the vulnerable Natal and Cape frontiers; and Milner told him 'it can never be said that *you* precipitated a conflict with the Dutch.' Milner wrote to Chamberlain that the General was

. . . unfortunately quite out of sympathy with my policy. No doubt he is making all strictly military preparations, but cordial co-operation between us is impossible. This is a great source of weakness.

On 21 June Butler sent Lansdowne at the War Office a long despatch which was mainly a rehash of his personal views on the political impasse. Milner then noted: 'things have become very critical now. Butler or I will have to go.' Butler finally went home at the end of August and was replaced as the C.-in-C. by General Sir Frederick Forestier-Walker.

McCourt charitably comments that Butler's resignation had 'an element of grandeur' in its throwing away of the coveted chance to head an independent command in the field. Julian Symons, admitting that Butler was mistaken in vital matters, thinks he may have been right in considering war was not inevitable and that an agreement, temporary like all agreements, could still have been reached.[49]

Milner, of course, was now quite convinced in the opposite sense, though since his arrival he had believed that an early and adequate show of force might have prevented a war, at least for a time. After the failure at Bloemfontein the British Cabinet had rejected Lord Wolseley's proposals for mobilization of Britain's one Army Corps on Salisbury Plain, and accumulation of supplies and transport in Natal, but had authorized Lansdowne to appoint General Redvers Buller Commander-in-Chief of a possible Expeditionary Force. Lansdowne ordered the small South African garrison to be put into a state of efficiency as regards equipment, transport and stores; and in August the Cabinet decided to send out an additional 2,000 men to a garrison still under 10,000. In July a few Special Service officers including Lord Edward Cecil, the Prime Minister's fourth son and a regular soldier, were sent secretly to South Africa to help Baden-Powell form a corps of irregulars to garrison Mafeking. It says much of the situation prevailing at home that Lady Edward Cecil (aged 27) and her husband, though seeing the Prime Minister daily, left England 'unaware of the urgency of the Cape situation.'[50] After arriving in Cape Town Lady Edward wrote often to Balfour, her husband's cousin, supporting Milner's opinions and actions.

Violet Markham had arrived slightly earlier in Cape Town to convalesce, met Milner and became his admirer and practical helper. She found him 'a reserved austere personality on whom the burden of great events rested heavily' with a mind 'narrowed down to one issue – the upholding of British rights in S. Africa.' Though a Liberal with strong social sympathies she thought Butler's view of the Boers (widely shared among Liberals at home and in Europe) as 'a little pastoral people very badly treated by a great imperial power' essentially shallow.[51]

Milner had to wrestle about military preparations almost as much with Schreiner, his Prime Minister, as with Butler. What he most dreaded, as it proved rightly, were serious reverses in a war's opening stages, particularly the Boers' over-running Natal and invasion of north-east Cape Colony. Debates in the Cape Parliament after August took on new ferocity, and relations between the Governor and his Ministers became strained. Schreiner and his colleagues, however, thought Kruger's Government were playing their cards very badly. The main argument between Schreiner and Milner was over Kimberley's defence. Agreement was soon reached that the role of Cape Colony's own troops should be confined to defence of their own soil, and the Government was ready to provide police and volunteers under Colonial Officers but not the additional irregulars Milner wanted. Schreiner fought hard, believing that if he resigned an increasing number of Cape Dutch would side with the Transvaal. He was in a very difficult position; Mrs. Chapin, though an admirer of Milner, was not alone in seeing Schreiner as a 'very big man, misunderstood.'

Leo Amery of Balliol, All Souls and *The Times* reached Cape Town on 11 September, having left England two weeks before to write up, as he thought, the peaceful settlement. He was under 26 and this, so far as the writer knows, was his first meeting with Milner, whose life-long friend and intellectual partner he became. He found the situation greatly changed for the worse since he had left England, and Milner harbouring no illusions about the danger which the Boers' numbers and military skill presented.[52]

On 8 September the Salisbury Cabinet agreed both to a despatch of Chamberlain's offering the Transvaal one more chance, and to the sending of 10,000 troops, mainly from India, to Natal. The correspondence between the two governments was now only a method of gaining time for war preparations. On the 22nd the British Cabinet sanctioned a grant of £860,000 for supplies and transport, and purchase of these began. English public opinion was on the whole backing the Government, with an anti-war 'demo' in Trafalgar Square on the 24th proving a total fiasco. On the 26th Milner wired to London that the Orange Free State and the South African Republic were likely to take the initiative. The next day Transvaal's burghers were called out and the Orange Free State Raad resolved to stand by its ally, though Schreiner continued to beg President Steyn not to invade Cape Colony.

Refugees from the Transvaal, British and sympathizers with Britain, were arriving in large numbers in Cape Town and Durban. On 31 August Milner had reported to Chamberlain that Johannesburg was already suffering severely, especially from the loss of labour to the mines. A few days later Greene reported to Milner that panic, even in Pretoria, was 'something terrible'. A Johannesburg Relief Committee was set up to organize wholesale evacuation and by September nearly all the Uitlanders other than the riffraff had left.[53]

Curzon's promptness and Boer delay due to Orange Free State hesitation over mobilization allowed the first reinforcements from India to reach Durban on 3 October. On 7 October mobilization in Britain of the one Army Corps of some 47,000 men was ordered, though its first troops would not sail until the 20th. On 9 October Milner received a report from Greene in Pretoria that the Transvaal had got in first with its intentionally unacceptable ultimatum – a point, of course, to Britain's political advantage.

The rains had come, so that grass was now growing again on the veld; and the main force of Boer commandos under Commandant-General Joubert invaded Natal on 13 October. Few people, either British or Boer, had any notion how much more grass was to grow, be consumed, wither and grow again before an end would be brought to the fighting.

Chapter 8

The Second Boer War

(October 1899 – May 1902)

Cape Town via Ladysmith to Pretoria – 'Flight in Full
Courage' and Move to Johannesburg – Home Leave and Peace

On 13 October the Boers' main force of 24,000 burghers invaded Natal,
to be faced by 16,000 British professional troops. Leo Amery had been for
days at the centre of events in the Orange Free State and the Transvaal,
interviewing Fischer, Kruger and Reitz and then trying in vain to get
Joubert to allow him to accompany the invading force. Two comments
of his deserve notice. First, the optimism he found among Boers that
Majuba was going to be repeated and the war finished in a matter of weeks;
it never entered their heads that the British soldier could seriously compete with the 'well-armed, straight-shooting, mobile burgher.' Second,
his assessment of the invaders led by Vice-President Joubert as 'a very
formidable force'.[1]

The British at home were equally confident that the war would be short
though, of course, with a different ending. General Buller, the Commander-in-Chief, when saying good-bye to the Queen at Balmoral, is said
to have told her that the war was not likely to be a long business or
include much hard fighting. George Wyndham, Milner's friend and now
Under-Secretary for War, kept writing for weeks to his parents and
brother, a professional soldier on the staff in Natal, in the strain: 'we
don't know Buller's plans. But he seems serene and his troops are in
good form.'[2] Buller sailed for South Africa on 11 October; and, Symons
writes, it was 'almost a point of honour with him not to talk to newspaper
men.' He made no exception for his fellow-traveller Winston Churchill,
who had left the Army and was going out as chief war correspondent of
the *Morning Post*.

By the time Buller reached Cape Town on 31 October a good deal
unfavourable to the British cause had taken place. It is not, of course,
possible to record here in detail complex military operations which
finally lasted not far short of three years. What must be uppermost are the
work and anxieties of Milner. Britain's last war against white people had
been in the Crimea in the '50s, in alliance with a larger French army. One

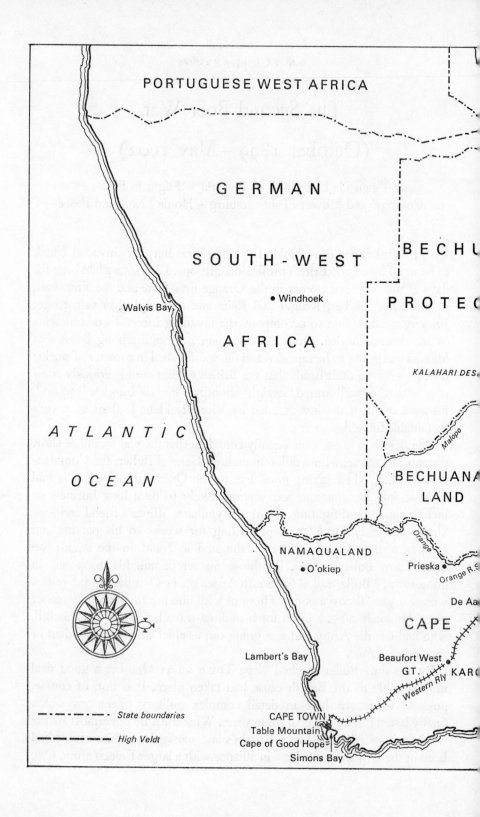

PORTUGUESE WEST AFRICA

GERMAN

SOUTH-WEST

AFRICA

• Windhoek

Walvis Bay

BECHU

PROTEC

KALAHARI DES.

ATLANTIC

OCEAN

Malopo

BECHUANA
LAND

Orange

NAMAQUALAND

• O'okiep

Prieska

Orange R.S.

De Aa

CAPE

Lambert's Bay

Beaufort West

GT.   KARO

Western Rly

CAPE TOWN
Table Mountain
Cape of Good Hope
Simons Bay

·—·—·—·—·—· State boundaries

━━━━━━━━ High Veldt

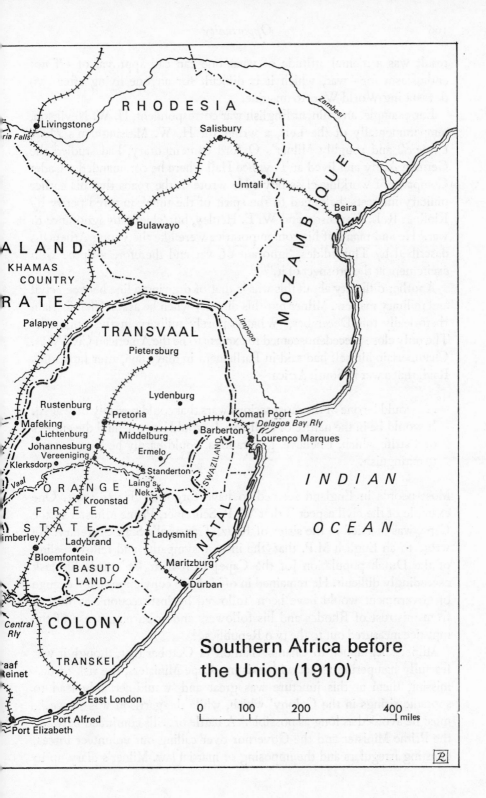

Southern Africa before
the Union (1910)

0   100   200   400
                    miles

result was a mental attitude of what one can call approval of – if not enthusiasm for – war, which it is difficult for anyone living after two devastating World Wars to imagine.

For example, an eminent English war correspondent, H. W. Nevinson, temperamentally of the Left, a writer for H. W. Massingham's *Daily Chronicle* and roughly Milner's Oxford contemporary, had studied the German Army and lived at Toynbee Hall where he commanded a Cadet Company of working-class boys. He wrote in the 1920s that his earlier military interests 'belonged to the spirit of the time', inspired partly by Kipling, R. L. Stevenson and W. E. Henley, but 'chiefly by ignorance of war.' He and many of his contemporaries were like the young Athenians described by Thucydides, 'ignorant of war and therefore a-tiptoe with excitement at the prospect of it.'[3]

Another difficulty about this war is that of drawing a line between civil and military matters. Milner put this directly when he asked Chamberlain rhetorically this December, 'What is purely military in this country?' The only close precedent seemed to experts to be the American Civil War. Chamberlain himself had said in Parliament in May 1896, after Jameson's Raid, that a war in South Africa

> ... would be one of the most serious wars that could possibly be waged. It would be in the nature of civil war. It would leave behind the embers of a strife which, I believe, generations would hardly be long enough to extinguish.

Most people in England seemed to have forgotten this forecast. One example of the civil aspect is that W. P. Schreiner, Prime Minister of the Cape, was married to the sister of Reitz, Transvaal's State Secretary. He wrote to an English M.P. that 'the intense sympathy and fellow-feeling of the Dutch population [of the Cape] with their kin' made his task exceedingly difficult. He remained in office from conviction that a change of government would have been 'followed by insurrection', as well as from mistrust of Rhodes and his followers and 'a burning sense of the injustice measured out to the two Republics.'[4]

Milner telegraphed to Chamberlain on 11 October that, though it was fearfully hampering to act with existing Cape Ministers, the risk of dismissing them at this juncture was great and 'would certainly lead to sporadic risings in the Colony' which, while the garrison was so weak, must be avoided as long as possible.[5] A battle of wills continued between the Prime Minister and the Governor over calling out volunteer forces, enlisting irregulars and the imposing of martial law. Milner's diary up to

Christmas is peppered with entries like 'intolerably long conversation with Schreiner' and 'got complete control of the Colonial Armoury out of Schreiner'. Like nearly everyone else Schreiner expected the war to be short; his policy of preserving Cape neutrality, called 'quieting', was all of a piece and inevitable from his point of view.

In the first week of war the Boers, in addition to invading Natal, laid siege to Mafeking and Kimberley (with Rhodes in it) and occupied Cape Colony's long extension north of the Orange River. In Natal Joubert's burghers advanced to defeat Sir George White, with British losses of 1,200 men, on 30 October at the battle of Ladysmith, the war's first large-scale engagement. Buller, just arriving at Cape Town, made the first of his many mistakes by approving White's decision to shut up his army in Ladysmith.

Lady Edward Cecil, it has been noticed, had arrived in South Africa with her husband in July. With Lady Charles Bentinck, whose husband like Lord Edward was shut up in Mafeking, she lived at Rhodes's invitation at Groote Schuur, entertaining his friends, working for hospitals and the thousands of refugees from the north. Her one book, *My Picture Gallery, 1886–1901*, gives a good account of Cape Town life in the first months of the war. Milner and his staff, she records, were 'stretched to the full' though assisted by voluntary helpers; and the Government House ballroom was used as an office. Many people in Cape Town society

> . . . meant to be on the winning side whichever this was, and were clinging round the knees of the Governor and swearing fealty.[6]

She writes that General Buller was 'always good company'. He agreed to Milner's proposal that the Colony's Volunteer force should be strengthened and put under his own immediate command. More important, he took, in the words of a modern historian, 'a desperate decision, threw the War Office's plan to the winds for the moment and split the Army Corps [which had not yet arrived] into three unequal parts.' One part would relieve Ladysmith, another relieve Kimberley and the rest march to contain the invasion of Cape Colony by the Orange Free State which, in spite of Schreiner's efforts, began on 1 November, becoming known as the 'First Cape Rebellion'.[7]

It is difficult, at this distance of time, not to look upon General Buller's subsequent actions as comedy, in the sense of a light or amusing performance which, unlike tragedy, eventually has a happy ending. The happy ending, however, was a long time in coming and a long way from

Cape Town: in 1902 at Vereeniging on the faraway Transvaal border.

Milner made ample comment on Buller's actions and strategy. He strongly but in vain opposed his withdrawal of garrisons in north-east Cape Colony, the area of the Orange River boundary with the Free State. He was taken aback to learn that Buller, without letting him know, left Cape Town on 22 November to take personal command in Natal. He had previously tried to dissuade him from such action and told Chamberlain,

> It was a great mistake Buller going to Natal. I always thought so. The military situation there is no doubt difficult, and bad. But it is comparatively simple. Here it is intensely complicated. He cannot judge the position here from Natal.

Among other things Buller's action left Milner, already busy enough over Colonial Office correspondence, censorship, arranging use of railway and shipping resources and other civil matters, carrying an undue share of the military burden. Boer invasion of the Colony was beginning to make headway, and rebellion in some form over much of its area was becoming a serious threat. The G.O.C. of the Garrison, General Forestier-Walker, Lady Edward Cecil called 'a charming man, desiring, above all things, a quiet life.' Milner heard on 9 November that the first transport of the Army Corps (which was expected to win the war quickly) had arrived. The Corps's 47,000 men continued arriving and being deployed until December.

In the gathering gloom of the war it is refreshing to note Winston Churchill, after talking to Milner (on an introduction from Chamberlain), introducing some realism by telling his mother as he went to the front in Natal,

> ... we have greatly underestimated the military strength and spirit of the Boers ... a fierce and bloody struggle is before us.

Also that the Boers were very confident of victory.[8]

It is a big understatement to add that in England in late 1899 there was no clarion call to arms, such as Churchill was to make in May 1940. The trouble was not that which afflicted Ben Battle who – as the consequence of a cannon ball – laid down his arms. It was rather that senior officers (up to Buller at the top of the local tree) and many of Britain's civil leaders forgot that the Boers had any cannon balls, and felt confident that their own arms would prove adequate. There were many reasons for this, including the misfortune that many British senior officers (from Lord Wolseley, the Commander-in-Chief, downwards) were misled by South African or other African experience against only native forces. Another was the rivalry existing at this time between the British Army command in London and the command of the British and Indian armies at Calcutta.

Buller reached Maritzburg, the capital of Natal, on 25 November and spent a week organizing transport for the operation of relieving Ladysmith. The over-cautious Joubert became ill and returned to Pretoria, leaving the younger and abler Louis Botha to command the Boer forces facing Buller on the Tugela River. Buller had a *penchant* for changing his plans, and decided on 12 December to make a frontal attack on Botha's position at Colenso. Two days before General Gatacre, though showing much energy and courage, had been defeated at Stormberg, in the sensitive north-eastern Cape Colony. On 11 December Lord Methuen, trying to relieve Kimberley, was defeated by General Piet Cronje at Magersfontein, suffering big casualties especially among the gallant Highland Brigade. As news of these defeats reached England there was still confidence, including that of the well-informed like George Wyndham, that Buller would put matters right.

'Sir Reverse', as many of his officers now called Buller, did not deserve this confidence. On 15 December he was beaten at the battle of Colenso and almost incredibly heliographed to General White in Ladysmith suggesting that he should surrender. Botha telegraphed to the Volksraad 'the God of our fathers has given us a great victory.' These three successive disasters in three vital areas produced what became known in Britain as 'Black Week', and some sardonic laughs among Britain's enemies in Europe. Was this the future Kipling forecast when he wrote at the Diamond Jubilee two years before in *Recessional*:

> Lo, all our pomp of yesterday
> Is one with Nineveh and Tyre!
> Judge of the Nations, spare us yet,
> Lest we forget – lest we forget!

Was God quite so enamoured of the Boers as Botha assumed? Kruger certainly thought so and telegraphed his commanders to look up the Psalms which read 'be of good courage, little band of god-fearing ones', and 'the Lord would arise and scatter His enemies.' Jan Smuts, who was to play a significant soldier's part in this war and on the British side in 1916–18, expressed in the 1930s a different view. Discussing the problem of Hitler he wrote with the advantage of hindsight, 'I keep believing in God, but I don't forget that He favoured the English rather than the Boers, although then we thought He would stand by our righteous cause.'[9]

The news from the fighting areas took time to reach Milner in Cape Town. On 16 December he recorded 'a week of disaster . . . Buller severely defeated yesterday in attempting to force passage of the Tugela'; and next day 'complete upset of all plans consequent upon Buller's disaster.' A few days later he received an immense mail from home, commenting when this left that the war was looking more hopeful in England. 'What a change since then.'

It is useful to bear in mind that the theatre of war was a huge one, local military censorship strict, Cape Town 6,000 miles from London and the electric cable not then very efficient. Gell wrote to Milner almost weekly from London with views, *inter alia*, on British public opinion. On 9 November he wrote that 'public feeling was much more resolute and less complicated than that of the politicians.' On 2 December he said that St. John Brodrick, his brother-in-law and now Under-Secretary for Foreign Affairs, had bet him a case of champagne that 'serious fighting (defined as an engagement or siege in which 3,000 men were employed on either side) *will be over by Xmas Day*!!!!' He added that Brodrick was 'in the closest touch with the War Office and the Cabinet.' On 15 December he was reporting on 'this depressing week' (Black Week) and a feeling in England bordering on panic. No one thought, he contended, that Lord Lansdowne was strong enough to 'hammer the professionalism of the War Office.' He thought that 'a grimmer and harder man than Brodrick was needed to knock those frock-coated [War Office] officials into shape'; though Brodrick did in fact replace Lansdowne as Secretary for War about a year later.[10]

Queen Victoria, Lady Longford has told us, had from the outbreak of war brought austerity into her household, kept a stiff upper lip and suppressed her own feelings. Later in the war she visited Ireland for the first time for thirty-nine years and created a new regiment of Irish Guards with the motto of the Order of St. Patrick, *Quis Separabit*. She had told Balfour,

> Please understand that there is no one depressed in *this* house; we are not interested in the possibilities of defeat; they do not exist.

Shortly before Christmas the Government acted decisively in the spirit of this sentiment. They took steps to speed up reinforcements to South

Africa, to enrol volunteers at home and in the Colonies, and above all appointed Lord Roberts to replace Buller as C.-in-C. in South Africa with Lord Kitchener (still in Egypt) as his Chief of Staff.

Lord Roberts of Kandahar reached Cape Town with Kitchener on 10 January 1900. Aged almost 70, he belonged to an Anglo-Irish family long settled in the south. He had served almost his whole career in India and was 'Bobs' of Kipling's poem –

a little red-faced man [who] rides the tallest 'orse 'e can . . . what he does not know o' war . . . you can arst the shop next door.

Lord Kitchener was a very different man. Aged 49, born in southern Ireland of English parents, he was tall, slim and of striking appearance. He had done most of his service in the Levant especially Egypt, and some notice has earlier been taken of his relations with Milner. His exploit of conquering the Khalifa's dervishes at Omdurman, his diplomacy at Fashoda and Governorship of the Sudan had raised him to the height of popularity in Britain. Roberts was married, had only one son, who had just been killed in a gallant action at Colenso and awarded the V.C., and two daughters. Kitchener was unmarried, though he skilfully cultivated both sexes in high British Society.

The two officers got busy in Cape Town remodelling the Army for what was almost a new war. The new strategy Roberts was evolving needed much reorganization of transport and supplies. Milner remarked in private, 'I feel now that at least we shan't be shot sitting.' To Chamberlain he wrote on 17 January,

Things are rather on the mend in this Colony and unless we have some hideous disaster in Natal, I look forward to a turn in the tide shortly. We are all very anxious about this relief of Ladysmith. . . . There is for the first time since trouble began a vigorous control of matters military. . . . I am relieved of the futile and perhaps dangerous effort to do other people's work. . . . And so my mind is turning once more to my own proper business.[11]

On 6 February Roberts and Kitchener left secretly in a brougham from Milner's door for 'the front', which at this stage meant the neighbourhood of the Orange River Station where the British Army was concentrating. It is necessary to describe South Africa's railway system since this played a vital part for the British in early 1900 and throughout the war. The country's large area was served by four lengthy trunk lines: first, the *Western* which linked Cape Town (via De Aar and the Orange River Station) with the Cape Colony towns of Kimberley and Mafeking and then ran on to Rhodesia; second, the *Central* (and most important) which starting from Cape Town ran up to De Aar and merged with three lines from the other important Cape Colony ports in what must be called this Colony's 'North-East': this merger was completed in the Orange Free State just across the Orange River, whence the line ran due north to Bloemfontein, Johannesburg and Pretoria; third, the *Pretoria-Delagoa Bay* line, Kruger's independent outlet to the non-British world; fourth, the *Durban–Johannesburg* line, shorter and less important in the war than the other three. It was important that the whole country was badly supplied with links between these trunk routes, so that carts of some sort, usually drawn by oxen, were indispensable forms of travel.

Roberts's strategy was to concentrate his army on the stretch of the Western Railway south of Kimberley, march east across the veld a hundred miles or so to take Bloemfontein in the flank and regain the Central Railway, with Pretoria as his ultimate objective. With the capital of the Orange Free State in his hands he assumed (like many people) that the battle for Pretoria would be the culminating one. His flank march to Bloemfontein began on 11 February under blazing sun, with inadequate water supplies and against stiff Boer opposition. Five days later Milner noted a 'very memorable day. First sign of a turn in the tide . . . French reached Kimberley last night.' There was wild rejoicing in Cape Town, and a large crowd outside Government House insisted on his showing himself. General French had got out of Ladysmith just before its investment, and now commanded the Cavalry Division sent by Roberts to relieve the Diamond City.

The main army, continuing to advance, fought a long battle (with Kitchener in command due to Roberts's illness) at Paardeberg which culminated in the surrender of the Boer General Piet Cronje and some 4,000 burghers on 27 February (Majuba Day). 'The English,' cried Paul Kruger, 'have taken our Majuba Day away from us.'[12] Kruger happened to be visiting this area at the time; and on the day (7 March) when Roberts resumed his march he and the leading Free Stater Christiaan De Wet were almost captured. Had they been so, the future course of the war could not have failed to be very different. On the day after Cronje's surrender Buller's aim of relieving Ladysmith in Natal was at last successful. The news of Lord Dundonald's entry into the town caused, Milner noted, 'the wildest excitement and delight.' In London there was corresponding rejoicing. A few days later Bobs reached Bloemfontein, and soon optimistically told Milner that the whole of the Orange Free State to the south of the capital was 'gradually settling down.'[13]

He happened to write this, with other optimistic forecasts, on St. Patrick's Day. Roberts's optimism, it is necessary to stress, survived until his departure from South Africa at the end of this year 1900, and the consequences of this were important. His reassurance about the southerly Orange Free State soon proved to be mistaken. On 19 March Milner made a two weeks' trip to north-east Cape Colony and on to Bloemfontein. Hearing news of a British defeat in a minor engagement at Brandfort, near the capital, he wrote, with some prescience,

> . . . another bad day. The Boers are certainly dying hard, if they are not coming to life again.

By 6 April he was writing that Boer commandos seemed to be 'running all over the south of the Orange Free State.'

On 4 April Winston Churchill had achieved his famous escape from the Boers. After some weeks in Natal he arrived in Cape Town to try to wear down the objections of Roberts and Kitchener to his being attached to their army. His account of a talk with Milner introduces two themes which must occupy attention later in this story. He got into bad odour in England and Natal by a despatch he had cabled from Ladysmith urging generous treatment towards Natal rebels. He wrote later,

> Sir Alfred Milner was far more understanding, and spoke to me with kindness and comprehension. [He said] 'I thought they would be upset, especially in Natal, by your message when I saw it . . . now passions are running too high' . . . I was impressed by hearing these calm, detached, broad-minded opinions from the lips of one so widely portrayed as the embodiment of rigid uncompromising subjugation.[14]

The first of the themes is the rebels, British subjects from Cape Colony and Natal who fought at some stage on the Boer side. The second is the related one of potential rebellion in Cape Colony. Milner from the outset of war was anxious about this threat and earned a good deal of reproach from officials at home for making it a King Charles's head. Among modern historians Professor A. P. Thornton may have had this fear partly in mind when he wrote that Milner 'saw emergency everywhere, and was ever inclined to lose his head while all about him were keeping theirs'.[15] It seems more true to say that Milner was inclined to foresee troubles which did in fact occur.

Before Roberts's flank march began General French and his cavalry had contained the Boer forces and by 'an almost unbroken series of small successes' checked invasion of the Colony which had an important effect on morale. The advance towards Bloemfontein had then caused withdrawal of Boers from Cape Colony. But on 8 April Roberts, revising his view, told Milner he was 'much concerned' over the rapid and sudden return of the Boers to the Orange River. He had ordered Kitchener to stamp out incipient rebellion in the west of the Colony round Prieska, and then to move east into the Orange Free State near Bethulie. But he declined to grant Milner's two wishes for first, mobile columns to be permanently stationed in the Colony to guard against further rebellion, and secondly, complete pacification of the southern Free State before his further advance to the north. Bobs was set on advancing as soon as possible, with the Central Railway as his axis, on a front extending from Kimberley to Ladysmith, into the Transvaal.[16]

Various reasons, especially enteric among his troops and the slow arrival of much-needed remounts, caused his pause in the Orange Free State capital to last for seven weeks. This, of course, gave valuable breathing-space to the Boers. As mixed military–civil government began to function in parts of the Free State Roberts consulted Milner freely. He felt a respect and liking for him, which was reciprocated. Milner sometimes, however, gave private expression to impatience. His main interest, of course, was in the renewal of full civil government as early as possible. On 6 May he wrote 'Roberts is getting on at last.' The northward advance had been resumed on 1 May, at least one month later than expected. Roberts's army consisted of about 170,000 men against a Boer army of about 30,000.[17]

As Roberts marched northwards President Steyn and the Orange Free State Government retreated but kept in existence. This advance in the centre was publicly overshadowed on 19 May by the relief at Mafeking of Colonel Baden-Powell and those in his charge. This event, not of much strategic importance, became a sort of symbol in Britain of light at the end of a long tunnel. The maffickings and rejoicings that took place in London and throughout England have been described many times. The slow speed at which South African news was travelling is illustrated by the fact that Milner in Cape Town heard of Mafeking's relief from London on 19 May but it was not until 21 May that he got confirmation of it from Mafeking itself or from Kimberley.

Roberts advanced with his main force through Kroonstad, which was on the railway and was the second town of the Free State, proclaimed this country – retitled Orange River Colony – annexed to the British Crown and crossed the Vaal River. Botha had replaced Joubert, who died in March, as Commandant-General of the Transvaal, one cause of the infusion of more vigorous blood into Boer leadership. He first made and then abandoned an effort to defend Johannesburg, which was surrendered unconditionally by its mayor to Lord Roberts on 30 June. Winston Churchill, who had been riding on a flank with General Ian Hamilton's mounted infantry division, describes his journey on a bicycle through the nearly deserted Gold City, still containing some Boers, to inform Lord Roberts of Hamilton's arrival at nearby Florida and also telegraph to his newspaper in London.[18]

On 2 June Milner commented on the innumerable uncertainties of the situation, and that news from the north got through slowly and in fragments. Roberts entered Pretoria (evacuated by Kruger and his government) ceremonially on 5 June, and ordered the hoisting of a Union Jack worked by Lady Roberts. Winston Churchill was met by his aunt who wrote that he had contrived in a short time 'to acquire influence and authority . . . he was most amusing, and a general favourite.'[19]

Milner wrote a year later in a memo to the Cabinet that 'at every stage of the war it was always expected that it would only last a few months longer.'[20] This described most British opinion from Lord Roberts downwards. After the capture of Pretoria he expected a quick finish to the war by forcing submission of Botha's army on the 250-mile stretch of railway from Pretoria to the Portuguese frontier. Lady Edward Cecil, no mean judge of events, wrote from Cape Town to Balfour, 'now at last we are beginning to see the end.'

Some backward look must be made at Milner's preoccupations before and after Roberts reached Cape Town in the previous January and he told Chamberlain that his mind was 'turning once more to my own proper business.'[21] This was in essence making plans for the situation which would follow peace. Implementation of these depended on how soon the war could be brought to an end, and the support which the Chamberlain–Milner policies would receive at home. The appointment of Roberts and Kitchener had much encouraged Britain's well-known capacity to rally after defeat. Volunteers, British and Colonial, had flocked to join up. Dawkins wisely wrote to Milner on 15 February from Calcutta that though he hoped this was 'the darkest hour' in South Africa, there might be still a darker one to come. The satisfactory feature so far, he wrote, was that

... in spite of all the military incompetences and muddling, [there is] the temper of the nation, and the courage of our men . . . the nation is determined to fight out the controversy on the true issues whatever may be the sacrifices demanded. . . . You say that your personal feelings, interests, and reflections, have faded to nothing, so thoroughly are you absorbed in the great question. That is a right feeling. . . . If the question at stake had not been made clear and brought home to the nation now, the fate of S. Africa would inevitably have been decided against us.[22]

The Colonial Office had been discussing post-war settlement of the Boer Republics with Milner since November 1899. His own chief concern at that time was 'the much graver question of the Cape.'

What [he continued] is to be done about the constitution of the Cape Colony when the war is over? . . . What the Bond is must now be evident to the crassest. In all the revolted districts leading Bondsmen, including in many cases (not in all) the local members, have been foremost in rebellion. Throughout the country the vast majority of the Dutch population . . . have given the enemy the strongest, most unfaltering, moral support. . . . I am appalled to find how widely the influence of a Bond Ministry . . . has sapped the loyalty of the Civil Service. . . . If, when our troops have withdrawn, the Government remains in the old hands, the Colony will be part of the British Empire only in name.[23]

Milner's anxieties about the loyalty of *the* Colony, Britain's base, continued to be a major element of his planning. Besides Schreiner's guidance regarding rebellion, fomenting this in the Colony had been a major item from the outset of Smuts's grand strategy of the war. Milner wrote to Chamberlain at the end of January 1900:

The critical time is still before us, and a pinch of sorts is bound to come, however the war goes. . . . If the enemy begin to lose (it being assumed that the scale will only turn against them very slowly) then will be the time for their sympathisers in the Colony to come to their aid. The *modus operandi* will be a loud and general outcry for peace – peace at this stage necessarily meaning a compromise very unfavourable to Great Britain.[24]

This was exactly what happened once Roberts's flank march had begun and achieved some success. In early March the two Boer Presidents made overtures for peace, and Salisbury gave them a curt reception. Her Majesty's Government, he cabled, was not prepared to assent to the independence either of the South African Republic or the Orange Free State. He observed that the two Republics 'claimed to treat the inhabitants of extensive portions of Her Majesty's dominions as if those dominions had been annexed to one or other of them.' About this time, the Bond's historian writes, the word 'conciliation' began to gain practical importance. With an Englishman, Ernest Hargrove, as the moving spirit Conciliation Committees were formed in the Cape to preserve the Republics from annexation and secure peace on this condition.[25] Hargrove was small fry, but in England there were bigger fish who supported a Boer Conciliation Movement. G. B. Pyrah, an authority on the attitudes to the war of the Opposition in Britain, records that the Liberal Party was split into three broad, though somewhat fluid, divisions: first, the Radicals, numerically the weakest but including Harcourt, Morley, 'the independent and eccentric Courtney' and two younger men, Lloyd George and Sir Robert Reid (later Lord Loreburn); secondly, the small but powerful group of 'Lib. Imps', and third, Campbell-Bannerman who led the largest group of Liberal moderates, backed by 'a mass of weighty opinion outside the Party' and whose chief advisers were Ripon and Bryce.[26]

C.-B.'s dislike of Chamberlain's 'new diplomacy', and his refusal to regard the war as inevitable or support any transfer of blame from the Government to the soldiers have been seen. But the bulk of the Liberals shared with Unionists a policy of maintaining and strengthening the Empire. Where they parted from them, once war had begun, was in the *methods* by which the war was being fought and the war's ultimate aims. At the end of November 1899 C.-B. had written to Bryce about Chamberlain, adding 'behind him stands Milner, and it is doubt of Milner that is the unpardonable sin.' His official biographer writes,

. . . he attributed a large part of his difficulties with his colleagues and especially those of them who were Balliol men to what he characteristically called the *religio Milneriana* . . . this blind belief in a Balliol hero he regarded as a psychological infirmity of the Oxford mind.[27]

C.-B. had been at Trinity, Cambridge, and was some eighteen years older than Milner. His College, in spite of its size, could not match Balliol men's remarkable success in attaining influential positions.

Cronje's surrender at Paardeberg had produced the first substantial haul of Boer prisoners, and invasion of the Cape had now netted a number of rebels. Milner had pressed on Chamberlain his need for a legal adviser to deal with constitutional problems. So Harry Wilson, another Cambridge man and a Colonial Office Legal Assistant, came to Cape Town in March 1900 to fill this role. He wrote home that Milner looked 'rather worn and aged, and no wonder, but they say he's borne the strain remarkably well, especially since Roberts and Kitchener arrived.' Milner seldom left the grounds of Government House except for a short ride or drive and often worked in his room into the small hours. He gave Wilson the job of identifying, and organizing the trial of, the 3,000 or so Cape rebels already in British hands.

Milner's continuing as Governor after the war and his views about Reconstruction had also been discussed by him informally with the Colonial Office since November. It was obvious even then that a phase of military government would have to follow annexation of the Republics. By the time Roberts moved forward from Bloemfontein in May military government of the southern Orange River Colony had begun to be hampered by the first of De Wet's many brilliant successes as a guerrilla leader. Milner told Chamberlain: 'with few exceptions, wherever soldiers are now doing civilian work, things are going badly', including muddles over Martial Law in the Cape.[28] To Roberts he wrote less strongly with the advice he had asked for on military civil affairs. The C.-in-C. said his own thoughts were 'much occupied' over making a proper start in the Transvaal when we reached it; there would be 'an immense mess' to clear up, and he had always maintained that the war would last until August. Milner offered to lend Fiddes, his Imperial Secretary and principal helper, to him as his 'all round civilian adviser', and this offer was gratefully accepted.

Milner told Chamberlain they were 'working away steadily in whatever time is left to us from the urgent preoccupations of every day "getting up" the several questions which will confront us on the threshold as soon as the Boer power is absolutely broken.' At the end of May he wrote to him privately agreeing to go to the Transvaal as its Governor

> ... taking my High Commissionership with me ... I should not care to stay in South Africa on any other condition ... I am, as I think you know, not desirous of remaining very long in the Public Service, and am not a candidate for any other post ... if we make the Transvaal what it ought to be, the Colony will matter less, and in the long run with the heart sound the whole body will be saved ... I should like my appointment to the Transvaal not to be for any definite period.

In view of the heavy expenses of moving his furniture, horses, etc. and the high cost of living in the Transvaal he asked that his salary as High Commissioner should continue to be £4,000 p.a. and that as Governor of the Transvaal should be £7,000 (the salary, incidentally, paid to Kruger). The total of £11,000 would, he thought, free him from anxiety and loss. To all these conditions Chamberlain readily agreed.[29]

Meanwhile Lord Roberts in Pretoria was anticipating an early end to the war. The unforeseen battle of Diamond Hill, east of Pretoria, on 11 June hardly seemed vital since Botha's force (far smaller than his own) was the only large Transvaal force still in existence. But though he pushed back the Boers he failed to beat them. Sir Ian Hamilton called the battle 'the true turning point of the campaign', and the historian Rayne Kruger points out it was one of the last major pitched actions of the war. Hancock records that by June the experienced Smuts thought that 'his people' (the rank and file burghers) were on the brink of physical and moral collapse and suffering 'a terrible process of disillusionment.' What then happened to make Diamond Hill far from a Boer collapse? Roberts's delay of a week or more at Pretoria had given the Boers time to rally and Botha was showing undoubted powers of leadership. Most important of all, it seems, were the moral effects of De Wet's introduction in the Free State of the tactics of employing small mobile groups to attack British forces (the *rooineks*, or *khakis*) with rapidity and then withdraw with equal speed. This became known as 'Flight in Full Courage'.

Its significance seems not to have been realized by Roberts and most British commanders for some months to come. It was aggression ideally suited to Boer skills, and which meant that to retire was to be alive to fight again another day. A friend of Milner's had written to him from the field six months before, with prescience, that the striking feature of the Boers as soldiers was their combination of courage and judgement in seizing the moment for retreat; but he showed up British military limitations by adding 'this comes, no doubt, from their having no professional pride.'

Botha and his fellow Transvaal leaders decided to make De Wet's brilliant improvisations a calculated plan of warfare. After Diamond Hill they scattered and rebuilt commandos by bringing back burghers who had taken a neutrality oath, or simply gone back to their farms. Farm-burning in the Free State had been started by Roberts as a defensive tactic some months before. But his proclamations about this of August and September (whatever their justification) stiffened burgher resistance and helped Botha and De La Rey's work of recruitment.

Military operations developed in many areas which it is misleading to call 'fronts'. The British, from beginning to end, were largely tied by their numbers and by logistics to the four trunk railways. The two Boer commands became more or less independent, with Botha, De La Rey and Smuts the leading figures on the Transvaal side, and De Wet (and later J. B. M. Hertzog) their counterparts in the Orange Free State army. Roberts chased Botha's army and Kruger east along the Delagoa Bay railway with Buller lumbering up from Natal to give him some help. On 11 September Oom Paul left his country, officially on six months' leave but in fact destined never to see it again. A burgher described him not long before as 'seated at a table in a railway station with a large Bible open before him – a lonely, tired, man.' The Lord had not, so far at any rate, delivered his people from Pharoah.[30] He sailed in a Dutch warship from Mozambique to Marseilles, had triumphal receptions in Paris and Cologne, but was snubbed by the German Emperor and settled in Holland.

A successful battle at Bergendal (sometimes called Dalmanutha) on the railway on 26 August seemed to Roberts more or less to end the war, and on 1 September he proclaimed the Transvaal annexed. His army reached Komati Poort, the Mozambique frontier, on 24 September. In mid-October he told General Neville Lyttelton he was soon going home and that Kitchener would succeed him until 'about Xmas, when the war would be over' and that he, Lyttelton, would then succeed Kitchener as Commander-in-Chief.[31] *The Times History* concluded later that though the Boers had suffered in many ways the British had hardly made any impression on 'the really strenuous members of Botha's commandos.'

One must turn again to Milner's activities since June.[32] The chief one, perhaps, was continuous argument with Schreiner and Bond sympathizers in Parliament about the treatment of rebels. On the 11th he considered that the affairs of the Cape Ministry were 'in a most awful mess' with the Cabinet split on this question. Two days later Schreiner resigned, to be succeeded by the elderly Sprigg as Prime Minister for the fourth time. Milner wrote to Fiddes in Pretoria of Schreiner that

. . . at the last moment [he] could not rise at a fence. Het ook a very courageous, very conscientious, and very correct line. But he was too divided in his own mind . . . I think on the whole, he is not sorry to be out of it. But I am sorry to lose him.[33]

Sprigg formed a Progressive Ministry; but most of his followers distrusted him as concerned above all else with clinging to office. Rhodes, the natural Progressive leader, had turned again after Kimberley to 'his north', with no wish to re-enter Cape politics and strong feelings against an autumn election.

Of Rhodes at this date it is necessary to add a serio-comic train of events. Princess Radziwill, a lady aged 41 of Russian–Polish extraction, separated from her husband and interested in money, official secrets and journalism, had travelled to Cape Town with Rhodes in July 1899. She presented herself to Milner with a letter of introduction from Lord Salisbury, ignoring etiquette by remaining seated at their interview. Her later behaviour might be dismissed as comic had she not aimed at creating distrust between Milner and Rhodes. Through her skill at intrigue she might have succeeded. Though she failed to do this she remained a nuisance to Rhodes until his death. She reappeared in Cape Town in August 1900, but the effects of her intrigues were the opposite of what she intended. The relevant letters can be found in Cecil Headlam's second volume and Brian Roberts's *Cecil Rhodes and the Princess*.[34]

Milner's private June letters included another general survey to Eddy Hamilton at the Treasury intended for the eyes of the Prince of Wales. 'Even now', he wrote, 'the war is, in my opinion, not over', and continued,

> we can make South Africa British now if we set the right way to work about it, and there is not sentimental folly at home. There are two quite separate problems, though they must be dealt with together as part of a whole.

The first was a phase, once the Republics were conquered, of 'paternal despotism' to allow them to settle down, and the British to return and to immigrate. The second was the clouded future of Cape Colony. Its rebels he now estimated as at least 10,000. Substantial Dutch farmers, mainly loyal and sick of the war, lacked the courage to resist the Bond's 'tide of racial and religious prejudice'. The Dutch Press, and Ministers of the Dutch Reformed Church, exercised a pernicious influence on the bulk of the people, who did not even understand English. Through Sir Francis Knollys the Prince sent Milner thanks and good wishes.[35]

Four separate Commissions came out from home to assist preparations for peace. Sir David Barbour came to look into financial prospects in what were now called the 'new colonies'. A Hospital Commission came to report on military hospitals, the poor conditions of which had created a rumpus in England. Hugh Arnold-Forster, a Unionist M.P., came to examine future Land Settlement. Alfred Lyttelton, Milner's friend and a barrister, came with his wife Edith to report on the important pre-war Transvaal Concessions. Edith Lyttelton described Government House in Cape Town as

. . . thronged with people all day long [and noted] the adoration of everyone about Milner is very remarkable . . . his quick sympathy often makes people think he's weak in personal matters [but it's really] one of the sources of his great strength, for he is quite capable of overriding his leanings when necessary, and on the other hand his sympathy often helps him to find a way out.[36]

Alfred wrote home that Milner was generous about his English opponents such as Bryce, and thought their views on South Africa natural for those who knew 90 per cent of the case but, through being in Britain, did not know the last 10 per cent. His official report contained ample proof of the corruption and inefficiency of Kruger's Concessions system.[37]

Believing the war to be virtually over Salisbury announced dissolution of the Imperial Parliament and a general ('Khaki') election was held in October. This was bitterly fought, with Chamberlain making full use of pro-Boer Englishmen's letters found at Bloemfontein and Pretoria. The *Annual Register* stated that the settlement of South Africa when the war ended 'still held the public mind', and that many voters doubted whether a Liberal Government would maintain Britain's annexation of the ex-Republics with vigour. The Unionists, in any case, secured a comfortable majority. Salisbury resigned the Foreign Office in favour of Lansdowne, who was replaced as War Secretary by St. John Brodrick. Goschen retired from the Cabinet, was made a Viscount and was succeeded at the Admiralty by Selborne. Hicks Beach and Chamberlain stayed at their posts. Selborne wrote to Milner that the election was 'the ratification by the nation to the hilt' of his and the Colonial Office's policy.[38]

Many soldiers and others were returning home. Buller – to Milner's relief, since he distrusted his politics – was 'kicked upstairs' to the Aldershot Command. Lady Edward Cecil sailed away in October after a farewell party in Government House, and in the following year had a second child, Helen. Lord Roberts, detained in Pretoria by the illness of one of his daughters, handed over command to Lord Kitchener on 19 November, and left Cape Town on 10 December after some days there of public rejoicing.

Fiddes had written to Milner from Pretoria calling conditions there chaotic and adding 'for heaven's sake get rid of military government as soon as possible.' Milner was, however, still 'Administrator' of the two ex-republics, only able to initiate civil government in the degree which Kitchener and the state of the war would allow. But he paid the ex-capital and Johannesburg a visit in the autumn before Roberts's departure, taking Lionel Curtis, just back in South Africa, as a temporary private secretary.[39] Pretoria he described in a letter to Lady Edward Cecil as

. . . a lovely little spot of water, trees and gardens, ruined by . . . German architecture of the Bismarckian era at its worst . . . [as regards civil business] *chaos* is a mild term for the state of things here.

In the Cape, Sprigg passed an Indemnity and Special Tribunals Act in much the same form as the Act which Schreiner had planned. Milner wrote in September, 'I have been frightfully overworked now for months.' Rose-Innes, as Attorney-General and in official contact with him for the first time, was 'astounded by his capacity for work', with his ante-room never empty and the calls on his time far 'greater than those of an ordinary Governor under ordinary circumstances.'[40] There is small doubt that overwork and fatigue sometimes distorted his judgement. His diary entries express natural impatience over 'the interminableness of the war', and the fact that 'the state of the Colony is extraordinarily bad.'

For months he had been corresponding with Chamberlain and others about his successor as Governor of Cape Colony when he went north. He wanted 'a strong man . . . a striking appointment' to console the Cape for the loss of its former 'premier position'. Many eminent men were approached, but in vain. So eventually Hely-Hutchinson, not regarded as an outstanding Governor, was asked to move from Natal, when the time became ripe, to take the office.[41]

Milner's comment about Cape Colony's state was soon to be visibly justified. He had told Lord Roberts that the Dutch had been 'excited to fever pitch' by De Wet's guerrilla successes. A 'People's Congress' at Worcester (near Cape Town) on 6 December 1900 was attended by numerous Bondsmen including 12 M.P.s, and censured Milner and demanded his recall. He received a deputation from it on 11 December and, in his words, gave this 'rather a rough time of it'.[42] Five days later Boer forces under Hertzog and Kritzinger crossed the Orange River into the Colony, and the 'Second Cape Rebellion' was in full swing. General Sir H. Settle reported to Kitchener that pronounced disaffection prevailed in the Colony, and soon many more districts were placed under Martial Law. In late January De Wet himself made a second raid on the Colony, but turned back to the Free State. Later in 1901 Smuts realized his long-cherished aim of invading the Colony with considerable success, penetrating close to Cape Town and then advancing to the mining area of Namaqualand in the far west before he was called away to the Peace Negotiations in April 1902.

Milner's departure to reside in the Transvaal had again to be postponed.

At the end of 1900 he said good-bye to his Military Secretary, Hanbury-Williams ('we both felt parting a good deal'), chosen by Brodrick as his private secretary at the War Office.

On New Year's Day 1901 he noted the year had begun with a clouded political outlook. Attacks on him in Westminster and Fleet Street included the description of him in one paper as 'the German Satrap', inaccurately claiming that his father had been a Professor and so automatically a German citizen. These prompted Chamberlain to include him in the New Year's Honours List and Milner chose to be raised to the rank of G.C.B. He had written to a friend:

> I *did not want* to be made a peer. . . . My feeling is that for a man not rich, or well connected, and by nature a Bohemian, a title would be an encumbrance . . . I don't aspire to anything except to bring this job to a clear finish. . . .

He also declined Chamberlain's offer of immediate leave, told him he had decided to move to the Transvaal on the last day of February, and sent him a despatch of prodigious length on the general situation.[43]

In January he was visited by Emily Hobhouse, a cousin of his Balliol friend Henry Hobhouse, a spinster of forty, who had courage, determination and advanced liberal views. She approached him, she wrote, in a state of 'torture of mind'. He asked her to lunch, talked to her for an hour and readily gave her (subject to Kitchener's approval) permission to visit the Refugee or, as they were sometimes called, 'Concentration' Camps. She wrote that Milner's 'singular charm and sympathetic manner [are] so calculated to put one at ease.'[44]

Kitchener's summer campaign had begun in December but a sketch of it must be left until later. What faced him is described at length in *The Times History of the War*.[45] It is enough to say that the war was now more than ever 'a War Against Space', that it became henceforward more ruthless and that Kitchener did not really regain the initiative until April. Queen Victoria died at Osborne on 22 January, and is said to have asked Princess Beatrice on the previous day, 'What news is there from Lord Kitchener? What has been happening in South Africa these last days?'

Milner at long last went north in a 'yeomanry special' on 28 February. He was met at Bloemfontein by Kitchener on 2 March for long discussion of the Middelburg Peace talks he had been holding with Botha but had so far told Milner little about. No attempt can be made to summarize the proposals. Kitchener in general favoured these talks, while Milner thought them premature. On 16 March, Botha, without offering any explanation, broke them off.[46]

Milner moved on the previous day to a house called Sunnyside in Park Town, Johannesburg, found for him by Lionel Curtis. A guard of honour of the Rand Rifles lined the streets. Since he was to live there until he left South Africa it is worth quoting his description of it to Mrs. Montefiore as

> . . . a villa, which might be the residence of a prosperous tradesman at Hendon or Chislehurst. It is on the outskirts of Johannesburg, on the top of a hill to the north of the town, well away from mines and places of business, and looking over a magnificent rolling country north towards Pretoria. The climate is splendid, and we are nearly 6,000 feet above the sea.

He was due to go on leave in six weeks, and his views on the Reconstruction problem had ripened in his mind. In April he noted that Johannesburg was still strongly guarded as there were a few fighting Boers hanging about on all sides. He paid special attention to the South African Constabulary, formed in October under Baden-Powell as a police force for the new colonies. He appointed the main heads of the Transvaal civil departments – Sir Richard Solomon from the Cape as his Legal Adviser, Fiddes reinstated as Imperial Secretary, Patrick Duncan from England as Transvaal Colonial Treasurer and others. He began work on the problem of municipal government for Johannesburg and the Rand, and particularly on efforts to get the gold-mines restarted. The Orange River Colony under Major Hamilton Goold-Adams and with Harry Wilson from the Cape as Colonial Secretary was – so far as guerrilla warfare allowed – making progress.

Kitchener was to take over his work as High Commissioner. Milner's train journey to Cape Town was, as often before, interrupted by Boers making raids on the line. On 8 May he went on board the *R.M.S. Saxon*, feeling 'mentally quite torpid'.

On reaching Madeira he found a telegram from Chamberlain about the offer of a peerage and a big reception awaiting him, which he mistakenly took to be a hoax. Docking at Southampton on 24 May (Empire Day) he found numerous friends to greet him. At Waterloo Station Lord Salisbury and most of the Cabinet, Lord Roberts and others did him the same honour. He was then driven with the Prime Minister and Chamberlain in an open landau to Marlborough House where King Edward conferred a Barony upon him. The next day Chamberlain presided over a big lunch of welcome at Claridge's, and he answered his toast to his health. He was then commanded to spend two days at Windsor Castle.

This welcome had its political as well as personal aspect. The *Annual Register* notes 'a curiously obstinate tendency' at this time in some quarters to interpret Milner's leave as his recall. The war's renewal after Pretoria's capture and Kruger's exile had proved a bitter disappointment to the British public. In spite of success in the Khaki election Salisbury's Government had failed to become popular. 'Saki' wrote an amusing parody of Lewis Carroll, illustrated by the brilliant drawings of the cartoonist F. C. Gould. Balfour is shown as the 'Ineptitude', with the view that 'you mustn't interfere with the inevitable. Slide and let slide, you know.' Lansdowne (the White Knight) went to war 'but not under modern conditions.' Alice sings Kipling's 'Recessional' as the 'Intercessional':

> Voice of the People, lately polled,
> Awed by our broad-cast battle scheme,
> By virtue of whose vote we hold
> Our licence still to doze and dream,
> Still, falt'ring Voice, complaisant shout,
> Lest we go out, lest we go out.[47]

Milner's leave in England was again a rich mixture of work and social engagements. In June he attended a big parade in Hyde Park when the King presented medals to 3,000 South African troops, and he received one himself after Lord Roberts. Later, after another long audience with the King, he took his seat in the House of Lords with Lords Manners and Revelstoke as his supporters. In July he received the Freedom of the City at Guildhall in the presence of a large gathering. He was examined by his English doctor, Philip Gell's brother Henry, whose report was satisfactory.

After about 2½ months in Britain (the double voyage took more than another month) he wrote to Dawkins that he had no 'holiday'. Some days' work with Chamberlain at Highbury was followed by more audiences with the King, attendances at the Cabinet and Defence Committee and many visits to the Colonial, Foreign and War Offices. While continuously busy, as he wrote to Kitchener, 'sucking in opinion' he was characteristically active trying to influence his friends in influential positions. The three chief 'Lib. Imps', Grey, Asquith and Haldane, were still objects of his special attention.

King Edward, an historian has remarked, again made London a genuine capital; and week-ends out of town in what proved a hot summer were as popular with the ruling classes as ever. In spite of the war's depressing continuance and its cost, the British continued to be 'prone to easy distraction.' Milner enjoyed again week-ends at country houses like Hatfield, Walmer Castle, Taplow Court and Mells; as well as the humbler establishment of his cousins at Yarmouth and the sanatorium in which his friend Edmund Garrett was now confined. At the big houses he often combined pleasure with business – it was still what Kenneth Rose has aptly called 'the age of gun-room diplomacy.'[48]

He had a good deal of correspondence with Kitchener, telling him in June that British opinion was '*as sound as a bell*. The pro-Boer ravings produce astonishingly little effect . . . on the other hand there is a very natural impatience . . . at the want of clearly visible progress.' Kitchener replied in July:

> We are pegging away as hard as we can, but the Boers will not stand at all. . . . After the recent decision to carry on the war, I do not expect there will be any serious peace again before September . . . [and he ended] I am not too enamoured of the army after 6 years' continual war, and would give a good deal to sink into oblivion and peace. . . .[49]

This last sentiment one might think a curious one to be uttered by a Commander-in-Chief. But the letter, like many of Milner's quoted in this story, was, one must remember, *private and confidential*. This war, unlike the Sudan campaign, had not yet been successful. Kitchener, with some 240,000 men against the Boers' 13,000 or so in the field, can be called a sledgehammer cracking a nut. He had adopted two principal tactics: first, so-called 'drives' of large well-equipped columns over great areas of both ex-Republics and the Cape, and secondly, building small forts called blockhouses on the railways, and after July in the area Pretoria–Johannesburg and the Western Transvaal. This amounted to construction of a massive, complex military machine, not unlike the huge American build-up against North Vietnamese forces in the 1960s and '70s.

One part of this machine, the Refugee or 'Concentration' Camps, stemmed partly from the tactic of farm-burning begun on a small scale about April 1900. In a huge country of isolated farms it was easy for Boers – who might or might not have surrendered – to use these as strongpoints. Lionel Curtis, young and idealistic, had been indignant about this tactic and quotes serving officers sharing his views. Milner defended it when treachery had been proved, but disapproved strongly of indiscriminate destruction of houses and crops as barbarous, ineffectual and likely to produce (as it certainly did) lasting bitterness.[50] Late in 1900 Kitchener had tried the propaganda experiment of a 'Burgher Peace Committee' offering lenient treatment to Boers who surrendered. This had failed, and he issued a proclamation creating the Refugee Camps for Boers and their often destitute families on the railways, which provided besides greater safety easy access to food and other essential supplies. Unhappily they were often badly sited, still more badly administered and overcrowded and insanitary.

His biographer, Magnus, writes that once the Middelburg negotiations broke down in mid-March 1901 Kitchener 'at once started to recommend the employment of draconian methods'. The large-scale 'drives' just mentioned caused great devastation and became a permanent feature of his strategy; as the countryside became less habitable the importance of the Refugee Camps naturally grew. Botha and other Boer leaders expressed gratitude for relief of anxiety over their families.

Mention has been made of the visit of Emily Hobhouse to Milner in January this year. This intrepid lady was allowed by Kitchener to visit a proportion of Orange River Colony Camps which she did the hard way, in an army truck. She often wrote home and happened to sail home on the same ship as Milner in May. Her young cousin Stephen, the eldest son of Henry Hobhouse and a Balliol undergraduate at this date, forecast correctly that of all existing Hobhouses she was 'most assured of a niche in the temple of history.'[51] He had, incidentally, joined the recently formed Cyclist Corps which paraded in the Broad under the command of the Professor of Logic. Emily got quickly to work at home, interviewed Brodrick, published a very adverse report on the Camps (price 1d.) which she circulated to Peers and M.P.s and, most important of all, had a long interview with Campbell-Bannerman who gave her his rapt attention.

This resulted in C.-B.'s famous speech of 14 June condemning 'methods of barbarism', a phrase he repeated in Parliament which had big repercussions. The Liberal Party became even more split; Lloyd George bitterly attacked Milner, which incensed the 'Lib. Imps', and Labouchere called him a 'wretched penny-a-liner'. In July the Government decided that a Committee of Ladies under the chairmanship of Mrs. Millicent Fawcett, widow of the Cambridge economist, should go to South Africa to report on the Camps; but they would not include Emily Hobhouse in it.

One must add Botha's famous remark, some eight years later, that 'three words made peace and Union in South Africa, "methods of barbarism" '; C.-B.'s courage in using them had touched the Boers' hearts.[52]

One must balance against C.-B.'s phrase some defiant answers to pro-Boer factions Milner made at the welcome luncheon to him on 25 May. He castigated the 'Utopian dogmatizing' which proposed various means of conciliation, adding 'to conciliate what? – panoplied hatred, insensate ambitions, invincible ignorance.'

In what Hancock calls 'a near-desperate military situation' Botha called a conference to draft armistice proposals. But a Boer Council of War at Waterval in the Transvaal in June decided against any talks with the British which did not guarantee independence. Steyn, De Wet and other Free Staters proved the most intransigent on this issue until the day peace was signed. On 7 August Kitchener issued a Proclamation demanding unconditional surrender by 15 September under pain of perpetual banishment of Boer leaders, and a tax on burghers to help maintain their families in the Camps. He was ready, Magnus writes. 'to make a clean sweep of the Boer population of South Africa [and thought it] a mistake to regard the Boer as a civilised race.'[53] Rayne Kruger and others suggest that Kitchener's Proclamation was ineffectual; much later Milner thought it had greatly increased the number of rank and file who surrendered.

Milner's many talks with the Government at home achieved results which must be listed: first, he urged a policy of 'protected areas', which will be further explained; secondly, he secured Chamberlain's full agreement to his future railway schemes and to grants-in-aid for administration, restocking the railways and Land Purchase; third, he got consent for tax revision to include 10 per cent on the gold mines' profits and for a Transvaal War Contribution of £50m.

He sailed back to Cape Town on 10 August, doing much work on the ship with Ozzy and others, and Sandow's then-popular physical exercises. He wrote to Dawkins that he thought his visit had been a political success, and to Parkin that 'the heart of the nation is sound.'

Arriving at Cape Town on 27 August he drove through cheering crowds to the mayor's reception. After hard work and interviews he went north to Bloemfontein and reached Johannesburg again on 10 September. He wrote to Mrs. Montefiore that he had had an adventurous journey, continuing:

The state of the country is horrible, death and devastation everywhere, as the continuance of this wretched and senseless guerrilla warfare has forced the military to sweep the country from end to end. The Orange

River Colony is virtually a desert, almost the whole population living in refugee camps along the railway line.[54]

Judged by his correspondence with Milner, Kitchener, especially in contrast with Roberts, was querulous and hard to work with. Milner did not lack tact or due awareness of his temporarily subordinate position. But *he* not Kitchener was the man who was going to have to rebuild the country out of the ruins the war was creating. Kitchener was impatient to get away from Africa for his desired goal in India, as well as now quite ruthless towards the 'uncivilized' Boers. Milner kept on pleading with him without much success for his own solution of 'protected areas', fair-sized districts surrounding places like Bloemfontein, guarded by troops or the South Africa Constabulary, which could be made exempt from the process of sweeping people and all stock indiscriminately into Refugee Camps.

He had returned to find a serious row going on between Kitchener and Sprigg's Government over the former's wish to extend martial law to the Cape Colony ports. He personally detested martial law 'not because it is a severe law, but because it is no law at all', arbitrary and indefinite. After much argument a compromise was reached early in October.

The new campaigning season had begun with the spring rains of September. Kitchener's large-scale drives went on, the blockhouse system began to attain its final widespread nature, and futile De Wet hunts had almost ceased to be a joke. Smuts led his 'Trek of the Two Hundred' brilliantly to the far west of the Cape and in February assumed the self-appointed office of Commander-in-Chief, Cape Colony. From the standpoint of Britain's many infantry columns the war is immortalized in Kipling's

> Boots-boots-boots-boots movin' up an' down again!
> There's no discharge in the war!

From another standpoint the war appeared in retrospect to Josiah Wedgwood, a young member of the porcelain family, and later a prominent English M.P., as 'a nightmare of animals', ox-teams and wagons crawling at 2 m.p.h., a chaos of drifts and the shooting of his own horses; he also found it full of 'prehistoric Army starch'.[55]

The second anniversary of the outbreak of war had come and gone and it still required much self-control by Milner to exercise patience. His statement in a speech that 'in a formal sense the war might never be over' brought denunciation of him by Rosebery, in his famous Chesterfield speech of December, for hunting the Boers to extermination. The allegation might have been more justly directed at Kitchener. The railways were working better, some central districts were pacified, and the theatre of war seemed to be contracting. But Kitchener intended to introduce in January 1902 what was known as 'the new model drive'. Milner wrote that despite many difficulties and discouragements 'the machinery of the Government is getting rapidly into working order'. There were, however, two fair-sized flies in this pot of ointment: he had been pressing Roberts and Kitchener for months to allow the return of sufficient British refugees to Johannesburg to restart the mines, but the process proved slow. Of the Rand's total capacity of some 6,000 stamps only 450 had so far been started; and the numbers in the 34 Concentration Camps in three colonies had grown to a peak in October of 161,000. Much maladministration of these had undoubtedly occurred; the total deaths, the Boers claimed, were about 26,000 (with a high proportion of children) and the mortality rate reached its peak of 244 per thousand in October 1901.[56]

Nearly all the Camps (i.e. those in the ex-Republics) had only been transferred from military to civil control in March, and the few in Natal transferred in November. Improvements then began. Mrs. Fawcett's committee arrived about August, inspected all the Camps except one and reported in early December. It found that the high death-rate was due to three groups of causes: first, the insanitary condition of the country produced by war; secondly, causes within the inmates' control, e.g. the Boer women's 'horror of ventilation' and addiction to primitive medicines; third, causes within the administrators' control. The Committee paid a tribute to Milner as 'not a partisan . . . but a statesman desirous to hear the truth, whether pleasant or unpleasant.'

Milner's remark quoted above that the civil government machine was 'getting rapidly into working order' calls for a little explanation. He continued to live at Johannesburg since the final choice of the Transvaal capital would be left until self-government was granted. He resisted in December His Majesty's Government's proposal that Letters Patent creating him Governor and C.-in-C. of the two colonies should be published, since he thought this would give the civil arm the semblance of power without its substance.

The civil government machine included the well-known Milner Kindergarten, the dozen or so young men whom, he later told Warden Spooner, 'the scoffers here call the *crèche*.'[57] Lionel Curtis, in some ways its most prominent member, says the word (in its German form) was a taunt originating with an English barrister in Johannesburg who 'couldn't resist the temptation to make trouble for Milner.' His early arrival on Milner's staff, preceded only by 'Peter' Perry, had been noticed. Milner made special efforts in 1900 to obtain Patrick Duncan, his former private secretary at the Inland Revenue and still about 30. for the key post of Transvaal Colonial Treasurer. On his recent leave in England he had enlisted the help of Geoffrey Robinson of the Colonial Office in proposing other suitable young men; better known under the name of Dawson – by which he will be called henceforward in this book – Robinson joined Milner later in Africa, and became his lifelong helper and admirer. Amery recruited John Buchan, and when he returned to Africa to report the Peace Negotiations, stayed on for a bit and informally became, as he puts it, 'an extra member of the Kindergarten'. Basil Williams, the historian and biographer of Milner in the *Dictionary of National Biography*, joined after war service this autumn.

A few others of the group joined after the war. Apart from securing Duncan and consulting Dawson, Milner made no deliberate effort to recruit for this group, though Curtis certainly did so. Of the round dozen usually regarded as composing it about 9 were, like Curtis, from New College, Oxford. Amery and Duncan were from Balliol, Dawson and Perry from Magdalen and (like Amery) All Souls; Buchan was from Brasenose.

Allusion to Oxford affords opportunity to refer again briefly to Rhodes, who was from Oriel, and the Princess Radziwill nuisance. He had resisted her effort to sow distrust between Milner and himself; and to re-enter Cape politics. Gell told Milner that eighteen months earlier Rhodes had said to him, 'I can trust Milner, and am quite ready to go as far as he does'. Stead had since visited Gell, who found he had 'passed under the sway' of the intriguing Princess. Though still an imperialist and admirer of Rhodes, the erratic Stead was strongly opposed to the Boer War, and meeting Rhodes in London about the same time said: 'it was Rhodes who championed Milner'.[58] In December Milner heard from Lord Grey that at Rhodes's request he was writing to invite him to become a Trustee of his will. Milner was glad to accept, but added that while he remained South Africa's High Commissioner he would be unable to take any active part as a Trustee.

Rhodes did not return to South Africa until the beginning of 1902, according to Headlam to 'face the music' in the form of giving evidence at the trial of Princess Radziwill for the forgery of documents related to his business affairs. He died soon afterwards in March, at the age of only 48, in his small cottage by the sea at Muizenberg south of Cape Town. Sarah Gertrude Millin writes that 'his body passed along the path of his spirit' to a cave in the rocks of the Matoppo Hills where he had wished to be buried. The hill was swarming with Matabele warriors 'who gave him, alone of white men before or since, the royal salute of *Bayete*'.[59]

His death was a serious setback to more harmonious British–Dutch relations in the future; and more immediately to a scheme cherished by Milner since late in 1899 – what he called to Chamberlain 'some temporary suspension of the Cape Constitution.' By mid-1901 Milner considered that the constitution had suspended itself, in view of the number of Cape M.P.s who were rebels and the fact that the date for a new register had expired. The Parliament had not met for eighteen months, and the Cape was *de facto* a Crown Colony with the Prime Minister Sprigg responsible to no one. However, the logic of this did not appeal to either Chamberlain or Selborne, both of whom thought suspension much too drastic a step. Rhodes, on returning in January, had talked most of the Progressive M.P.s into signing a petition for temporary suspension. But his death again left his party with no effective alternative leader. Milner called the issue the only important one regarding South Africa over which he and Chamberlain were at cross purposes.

The next stage of this story merges with the Peace Negotiations. At the end of April Milner was staying with the architect Herbert Baker at Muizenberg. Under pressure he met the Committee of Progressive M.P.s preparing the Suspension Petition. Unfortunately he then allowed a private letter of 19 May to Hely-Hutchinson supporting the Petition to be published in the local Press.

The war continued in a desultory fashion, with the British at home as well as in Africa sustaining deep shock at De La Rey's capture of Lord Methuen and 600 troops at Tweebosch in the western Transvaal on 7 March. On 9 April the Peace Negotiations began in a drama of five acts spread over almost 2 months. A meeting of the Boer Governments on this date revealed what Hancock calls a 'deep cleavage of emotion and thought between them.' The leaders then met Kitchener, who agreed to a conference being held of 60 fighting burghers, while he still carried on the war with ruthless energy. The burghers met at Vereeniging on the Transvaal–Orange River Colony border on 15 May, with the Free Staters still insisting on independence being preserved, while both Botha and most other Transvaalers took a more realistic line. The much-respected General De La Rey, for instance, acknowledged that 'the bitter end has come.' A commission of five of the leaders then negotiated with Kitchener and Milner. After hard bargaining this body reported back to the burghers and two more agonizing days of debate at Vereeniging followed. All but 6 of the 60 burghers agreed to the terms, and the Treaty was signed at Pretoria just after 11 p.m. on 31 May 1902.

There is no need to record once again the story of Kitchener and Milner's disagreements, and the many discussions with London. The two men's roles, *The Times History* writes, were curiously reversed, with Kitchener, who had shown such military ruthlessness, now the 'dove' and Milner, often critical of his methods, the 'hawk'. It is unnecessary to attempt a full summary of the terms, on the finality of which Milner insisted. It must suffice to say they included Britain's promises that

> . . . as soon as circumstances permit, Representative Institutions, leading up to self-government, will be introduced [there will be no] decision about granting the Natives the franchise until after self-government; help [will be given] to the Boers in restoring and equipping their homes.

There would also be various kinds of financial assistance. At the Paris Peace Conference in 1919 Botha told Milner it was 'a generous peace'.[60]

The *Annual Register* wrote that in London on 1 June 'the blessed news of peace in South Africa' was received with 'intense and universal relief'. Hardly a British family had not been in some manner involved or free from anxiety. The generous British temper, however, desired 'the cultivation as quickly as possible of the most friendly relations with the Boers.'

Victory had required from first to last about 450,000 British troops. Fewer than 8,000 had been killed or died of wounds, though a further 14,000 had died of disease. As almost every male Boer was potentially a full or part-time soldier, British estimates of Boer strength varied widely. Milner put the total at 70,000 excluding British rebels. But the official history gives their strength in the field at any one time as never more than 48–50,000 and often much fewer. Some 4–5,000 of these had been killed, and by the Peace 25,000 taken prisoner. The war cost the British taxpayer £200 million. Whether or not the increased bitterness of Anglo-Boer relations would be repaired by a generous peace, the promise of eventual self-government and efficient wholesale reconstruction lay with the future.

Chapter 9

South Africa – Reconstruction
(June 1902 – April 1905)

Repatriation, and Chamberlain's visit – Progress,
Leave and an Offer Refused – Success and Failure

'The surrender, brilliantly organized by Kitchener, the sort of thing of which he is a master, has gone marvellously', Milner wrote. With their leaders' encouragement and in an atmosphere of goodwill the 21,000 or so burghers still in the field handed in their arms. Within three weeks Kitchener left for home, his sights set on India and his baggage containing life-size statues of Kruger and other Boers taken from public squares. On 21 June civil government began with Milner swearing the oath as Transvaal's Governor, and his Executive and Legislative Councils holding formal meetings. Two days later he performed the same duty at Bloemfontein where he found a much more enthusiastic crowd and installed Major Goold-Adams as his Lieutenant-Governor.

Milner, Keith Hancock truly states, 'held in his hand the entire power for which Kruger and Rhodes had contended; yet not quite so firmly as he would have wished.'[1] Nearly all South Africa was now under the British flag and, Judge Rose-Innes told him, he enjoyed to a unique degree the confidence of 'the vast majority of the King's loyal subjects'. But the weakness of his position, as he well knew, was greater than Hancock's qualification suggests. In Cape Colony the effective power remained with the Bond. It was only a matter of time before demands by the two ex-Republics for fulfilment of the Peace Treaty's promise of the grant of 'representative institutions leading up to self-government' would have to be met. The Johannesburgers' political aims and degree of attachment to Downing Street, as when Kruger had ruled, were always uncertain. Milner regarded as inevitable the hostility towards him of the Dutch leaders, and of large sections of Radical and Liberal opinion at home.

While 'roaring confusion and scurry' prevailed in Pretoria, he accepted the defeat of his plan for temporary suspension of the Cape constitution. Chamberlain had only just learnt of the publication of his private letter of 19 May supporting the Loyalists' petition, and sent him what Julian

Amery calls 'a stinging rebuke'.[2] Selborne wrote that he should not have published the letter and that, for the first time since Milner had been in South Africa, he differed from him.[3] After Sprigg's opposition to the plan was strongly supported by the Premiers at the Colonial Conference in London, the British Cabinet rejected the Cape Progressives' petition on 1 July. The Cape Parliament met again on 20 August, with Sprigg's Government existing on Bond sufferance.

Milner was torn between sincere loyalty to Chamberlain his chief and his own strong convictions. In a frank private letter to Jim Rendel he confessed that this unfortunate letter of 19 May

> . . . was not an "indiscretion" . . . it was a *very deliberate*, desperate, perhaps questionable, attempt to prevent a tremendous blunder. I hardly hoped to succeed, but I am glad I tried.

To Chamberlain he wrote impetuously on 27 June proposing to resign on grounds of health at the earliest convenient time. Chamberlain sent a friendly reply saying he hoped he might ignore this proposal, and warmly defended him in Parliament. But on 6 September Milner told him he had not altered his mind. He felt

> out of touch with the predominant sentiment of my countrymen, the trend of opinion which ultimately determines policy, on the South African question. . . . I am anxious to quit the field, while I can do so in peace, without discredit, and with a really good pretext.

The past three years had told on him physically. He thought, optimistically, they would be out of 'the present jungle' in six months' time when a new High Commissioner would have 'immense advantages . . . if he does not trust the Boers (which I pray he may not do), he will be better able to pretend to trust them than I am.' He would besides have 'that robust faith in self-governing institutions' which in his own case had been 'unfortunately dissipated' by his experience of their practical exercise in South Africa.[4]

Many friends wrote to congratulate him on the Peace, and he was advanced in the peerage to Viscount. His views on his future did not prevent his absorption in work which, he noted, was 'getting more overwhelming than ever.' Lionel Curtis, who had worked close to him for over a year, explains this (not unusual) state of affairs as due to the fact that

. . . he lets people bring all sorts of trifling matters to him, with the result that 'his strength is so taxed that the bigger ones sometimes get shoved into the background'. The incentive to consult him was his 'trick' of putting you so much in possession of your wits that you can convey to him in 10 minutes what would take 30 minutes for you to express to other people.[5]

Perhaps this explains his success, amounting to genius, in administration. John Buchan calls him 'the most selfless man I have ever known.' He often worked with him when he was desperately tired but never recalls an impatient or querulous word. He was a stern judge of himself, but lenient to other people.[6]

On the Rand, which was the key to Milner's whole reconstruction plan, the white population was nearing its pre-war figure and the mines were starting to recover. Almost everywhere else the two colonies, as he later described them, 'were a total wreck, with half their population in exile, and no administrative machinery whatever.' Whatever view one may take of Kitchener's tactics they had left much of the country, especially these new colonies, a wilderness stripped bare, intersected by lines of block-houses and barbed wire, with the livestock driven away, the veld un-tilled, railways torn up and townships and houses destroyed. Repatriation and resettlement on their farms of 200,000 Boer burghers and their families – over half of them in concentration camps and 24,000 overseas as prison-ers of war – was the civil Government's most pressing problem.

Big official Repatriation Departments were formed while the permanent machinery of Resident Magistrates and South African Constabulary was starting to function. July being winter, forage as well as vast quantities of food and equipment had to be imported. The damaged railways were carrying, as well as this essential northbound traffic, most of the British army of 200,000 going south to the ports. Milner and his subordinates had to haggle with the Army for the purchase of equipment, horses and oxen, many of which were in poor condition. Josiah Wedgwood records his appointment after war service by Milner as R.M. of Ermelo, the principal town of the eastern Transvaal high veld, a country as large as Wales. There were hardly any whites yet in the area, and Ermelo was 'a city of the dead' which he and his staff began to rebuild with their own hands.[7]

The thirty-odd concentration camps proved valuable in this process of large-scale repatriation. They served as natural centres for the reunion of families and the concentration of animals and stores which preceded the burghers' trek by ox-cart for often long distances to their farms.

In September Sir Arthur Lawley, chosen by Milner as the Lieutenant-

Governor of the Transvaal, arrived in Pretoria. A former private secretary to the first Duke of Westminster, Administrator of Matabeleland and Governor of Western Australia, he proved a most competent deputy until the end of Milner's South African career.[8] His arrival freed Milner from much detailed work and allowed him to make treks of some 2,000 miles during the next three months to see for himself the progress of repatriation.

Delighting in spells of freedom from his office Milner travelled mainly on horseback, with servants, wagons and Cape carts in attendance, and usually slept in a tent on the veld. His special journal contains frequent references to 'melancholy spectacles' of devastation, ruined farms, absence of stock and areas 'fearfully harried'. In October the Government assisted the burghers in reviving their farms by the provision all over the colonies of its own ploughing teams; Milner noted the difficulty of 'getting enough oxen to plough sufficient land to keep people alive.' His own treks were intended to show the Boer farmers that the Government was not indifferent or aloof. Besides meetings with repatriation officials, Resident Magistrates and police Milner received many burgher deputations and talked to individual Boers in what he called 'broken Dutch'.

From one of these treks he wrote to Lawley in Pretoria that, keen as he was to make the use of the English language universal,

> I want also to use Dutch where it is clearly a great convenience to people, and in purely agricultural districts there are still many who can read nothing else.[9]

In talk with a British friend he again distinguished between the town-Boers, lawyers and politicians whom in general he distrusted, and the farmers whom he called

> ... the landed aristocracy, and gentlemen in the best sense; dignified, courteous and hospitable, and amazingly self-controlled. They 'think behind their eyes', and give nothing away.

But he also felt that

> ... deep down there is a stratum which one cannot penetrate, beneath which are sealed convictions ... [including] their amazing oneness as a race to which all others are alien.

John Buchan, a countryman from the Border, working enthusiastically over large areas on repatriation and seeing much of the farmers, reached similar conclusions. In a book on his experiences he called the Boer the representative on a grand scale of 'the ordinary backward countryman' with the countryman's faults of 'doing lip-service to principles he does not understand', suspicion, meagre imagination and 'incurable mendacity'. He also, however, had the countryman's virtues of few needs, adaptability, dignity and hospitality. He thought the Boer naturally law-abiding and 'the easiest creature in the world to govern.' The war had broken his former arrogance, and 'he now waits to make up his mind on the new regime.' Buchan optimistically concluded that 'once won to our side he'll make a great colonising force.'[10]

Soon after the transfer to civil government Buchan had written home that he was preparing to put on 'kilt and lace and siccan vanities' for a great Pretoria levee when news arrived of King Edward's illness. Postponement of the Coronation would cause great disappointment in Johannesburg which had been 'saving up for months for a really big show.' Lord Salisbury resigned the premiership in July and was succeeded by his nephew Arthur Balfour. Chamberlain, the one British statesman who had 'gained greatly and lost nothing by the war',[11] suffered a bad cab accident in Whitehall, but reappeared in the Commons at the end of July to explain the plans for South Africa's reconstruction.

The three chief Boer Generals, Botha, De La Rey and De Wet, arrived in Britain on the day of the Naval Review which followed the postponed Coronation, and were received by the public with a warmth which surprised them. Prompted by Kruger and his so-called Hague Delegation, they made demands to Chamberlain for what amounted to a new Peace Treaty but got nowhere: a demonstration of Milner's foresight in insisting on finality at the Vereeniging negotiations. Chamberlain's invitation to the first two (Milner would not contemplate De Wet) to join the Transvaal Legislative Council were met with refusal. From The Hague the Boers then issued an 'Appeal to the Civilized World' for funds; this failed in its purpose, alienated British opinion and earned them a rebuke from Chamberlain. Botha, at least, learnt that Europe could not be counted on to give their cause concrete support. The sum they raised was £105,000, much of which had been subscribed before their tour.

Soon after peace Milner told Chamberlain he wished he would visit South Africa (which no Colonial Secretary had ever done while in office) to see things for himself. By September Chamberlain sought his views on his intention to take 'the new step of a rather sensational kind' of visiting all the self-governing colonies beginning with South Africa. Milner replied,

It would be the best thing that could happen for all of us, and I earnestly urge you to carry out your plan.

Chamberlain's announcement of this was greeted with much approval in Parliament, and by the pro-Boer as well as the Unionist Press.

Everybody in South Africa was wanting something done at once and screaming like mad if it wasn't, Milner wrote to Lady Edward Cecil. Besides dealing with many day-to-day issues he was writing long despatches on major matters requiring decision by His Majesty's Government. In early September, for example, he worked before breakfast and just managed to catch the mail-train with a long despatch on finance which was to him at this stage the crucial question. With Duncan and W. J. Wybergh, his Acting Commissioner of Mines, he had been unravelling Kruger's complex official finances. Soon after peace was declared he had obtained Chamberlain's approval for an immediate 10 per cent tax on the profits of the mining industry. But all parties at Westminster were demanding a large contribution from the defeated colonies to the war's costs; and neither the amount of this nor the way to finance reconstruction had yet been determined. With the Transvaal's industrial growth in his view the main hope for the future, Milner argued for expenditure to develop the sources of revenue, and revenue to be drawn from an increase of what was taxed rather than from high taxation rates. He proposed a Consolidated Transvaal Loan of £30 million to provide for the first of these, and thought that the Transvaal should be able to assist substantially in extinction of the War Debt. The Orange River Colony would only require a loan of £8 million, but would be unable to contribute to the War Debt.[12]

Railways and Customs rates have been shown as continuous causes of pre-war conflict between South Africa's white states, British and Dutch. The plan for a Central South African Railway would clearly give opportunity for some mutual arrangement for pooling railway receipts. Much rivalry over this matter had, however, still to be overcome. Natal, for example, still feared that the Transvaal's development of the Delagoa Bay line and port would threaten her plans to enlarge Durban, about a hundred miles further from the Rand market. Kruger had made preferential agreements with the Delagoa Bay line, and Milner believed that its terminus 'is, and always must be, the natural first port of the Transvaal', and was depending on Mozambique for revival of its supply of native labour for the mines. He tried to convince Natal that South Africa's total trade would before long be taxing the capacity of the whole country's four major ports. While he sent home proposals for new railway construction, he was only beginning late in 1902 to sound Natal and the Cape about a joint Customs Conference.[13]

Two more imperial matters need mention. Notice has been taken of Milner's plan that South Africa's permanent garrison should in future take the form of another 'Aldershot', or training camp, of at least 30,000 troops, preferably in the northern Cape, who would be learning 'the system of tactics which English armies are most likely to require in the future.' General Sir Neville Lyttelton, elder brother of Alfred and Milner's choice for the job, had succeeded Kitchener as Commander-in-Chief and supported this plan, as did Chamberlain at home. Unfortunately it was a scheme on which both the Cabinet and the War Office were much divided. Milner continued to fight for it though commenting, it proved correctly, 'it will not be done. Habit and *vis inertiae* are too strong for new departures of this kind.'

The other imperial matter was the future of Rhodesia without Rhodes. Gell continued to send Milner copious news of the British South Africa Company's affairs, stressing its bad relations with Chamberlain and the Colonial Office. Some Rhodesian settlers began a movement for abrogation of the Company's Charter and union with the Transvaal. Lord Grey arrived on a visit to South Africa, saw much of Milner and later sent him a glowing account of Rhodesia's improved 'moral atmosphere', agricultural resources and prospects. Though Milner did not rule out future union, he was too busy with more pressing questions to give much thought to Rhodesia or to help, as he put it, 'to untie some of those needless knots into which the Colonial Office had got the thing.'[14]

Lady Sarah Wilson visiting Cape Town, which she knew well, in August found it much altered by the war. The British Government's refusal to suspend the Constitution had not extinguished much Loyalist support for this step, so she found that 'political feeling was running very high; it almost stopped social intercourse; it divided families.'[15] Rhodes's absence from the Cape Parliament was acutely felt. Sprigg was allowed by the Bond, in effect his masters, to pass Indemnity Acts but did little else. Milner saw these events as endorsing his views on suspension, though he told Basil Worsfold, editor of the Johannesburg *Star*, that he was not in favour of renewing the agitation. 'The Cape,' he said, 'will always remain the Achilles heel of the British possessions in South Africa.'

A steady flow of official guests and personal friends visited Sunnyside. The Governor-General of Mozambique paid a state visit. Milner was host to members of all the local Colonial Governments, to Lord Alverstone's Martial Law Commission from home, to Bendor (the young Duke of Westminster) and his wife and to the teams of South Africa's cricket match with Australia. Games of bridge with his guests were usually the prelude to more work until a late hour. Riding and an occasional race meeting were his chief recreations. Though he wrote in November that the 'strain of ceaseless work was beginning to tell a bit' his doctor gave a favourable report. He was either more strong-willed or more fortunate than some of his staff. Lionel Curtis had been invalided home for months earlier in the year. Ozzy Walrond, his faithful secretary, was in hospital before Christmas with some sort of breakdown and Milner felt very anxious about him. Now E. B. Sargant, his gifted Director of Education, was similarly afflicted, quarrelling with his subordinates, overworked and sent home on long leave.[16]

Chamberlain had told Milner that his South African tour was intended for 'business not show.' He hoped to limit the number of his speeches and get some recreation. He arrived at Durban on Boxing Day, 1902, with Mrs. Chamberlain and his staff, to find that his presence aroused an unexpected amount of interest. On reaching Maritzburg, the Natal capital, he also found a 20-page memorandum from Milner describing the political situation and listing seven matters on which the Imperial Government's decisions were urgently needed. In spite of much achieved in six months in the ex-Republics, Milner had to report 'an appreciable increase of bad feeling' against Crown Colony Government. He attributed this to the return of 'the more undesirable section of the Boer population', including the most truculent of the prisoners of war and 'political agitators, notably parsons of the Dutch Reformed Church' who had been deported. The only remedy he could see for the unpopularity of British rule was the development at the highest possible speed, by efficient administration, of the two colonies' resources.[17]

After spending the morning of 3 January 1903 riding up Majuba Hill with a Boer guide who had taken part in storming it in 1881, Milner and Lawley met the Chamberlains in their train. For three weeks in Pretoria and Johannesburg Chamberlain spoke at official banquets, attended garden parties, received deputations, negotiated with mining magnates and had long talks with Milner. His engagements and speeches were incessant. But he proved, Milner wrote, 'a wonderfully vital sexagenarian' and Mary Chamberlain was 'adored by everybody.'

Chamberlain called himself 'a missionary of Empire', and the main themes of his speeches were the reconciliation of British and Dutch in the common Empire citizenship, and the privileges and duties this entailed.[18] A Pretoria banquet, though marred by two tactless Uitlander speakers, was significant for the presence of the three leading Boer generals; Chamberlain's speech was called by John Buchan, writing home, 'very good – the old professional among amateurs.' Chamberlain later received a deputation of a hundred leading Transvaal Boers whose address, drafted by Smuts, contained grievances and demands many of which amounted to revision of the Treaty. He replied that the Treaty as it stood was for the time being the Boer nation's 'charter', speaking in a fashion Milner applauded, 'inflexible and yet very courteous in manner.' Worsfold maintains that he left the hall with Milner and Lawley to the sound of Boer cheers. Smuts, on the other hand, wrote to L. T. Hobhouse, for publication in English papers, that his speech

could not but be considered insulting and was so considered by everybody present.[19]

The Boer address showed that financial arrangements, real or imagined, bulked large among their complaints. The £3 million free grant of Clause 10 of the Treaty was being used by Milner as immediate aid for repatriation combined with compensation, a fact not generally understood. The Army proved slow in meeting the many Boer claims against them, so Chamberlain cabled for the transfer by the War Office of another £3 million to the civil administration to handle these claims. He then spent a fortnight as Milner's guest in Johannesburg negotiating with the mining companies, the outcome of which he announced at a banquet on 17 January. After placing of the Guaranteed Loan of £35 million a second loan of £30 million would be issued, secured on the Transvaal's assets and treated as her contribution to the War Debt. The much poorer Orange River Colony would not be asked to contribute to this debt.

The Chamberlains had a magnificent send-off from Johannesburg for a trek west to Mafeking and Kimberley, where Mrs. Chamberlain was presented with a silver casket of diamonds. Chamberlain was much struck by the widespread devastation and destruction, exceeding everything which he and the English in general had imagined. They trekked back to Bloemfontein where Milner rejoined them for more ceremonies and talks. When Hertzog presented a petition to Chamberlain on behalf of De Wet's section of 'wild' (or extreme) nationalist Boers he 'fairly demolished him.' At a banquet on February 7 Milner announced two major decisions. The railways of the two colonies were to be amalgamated into a 'Central South African Railway' system. And a new body, the Inter-Colonial Council, was to administer this joint railway system, the South African Constabulary, and the service of the Development Loan.

Among the many decisions reached between Chamberlain and Milner two others need mention. The introduction of non-official members into

the Legislative Councils proposed by Milner in July was agreed, and
fresh invitations sent to Botha, De La Rey and Smuts. Declining to serve,
the Generals publicly stated that the good work of reconciliation so far
achieved would

> . . . almost certainly be jeopardized by this [Transvaal] Legislative
> Council, which would throw almost every apple of discord in the arena.

This was chiefly disappointing as regards De La Rey, who was thought to
have given an affirmative answer to Chamberlain and was the only one of
the three for whom Milner felt real esteem.[20]

The other decision, which Chamberlain's later biographer calls 'the
most enduring single result of his whole tour',[21] was that Milner should
stay on the job. He did so, however, on condition that he should take
leave that year and return for what (public grounds permitting) was to
be *one* final year. Chamberlain agreed to his continuing to live in Johannesburg since Lawley now resided in Pretoria. He paid many tributes to
Milner in his speeches, denying in particular the image of him as a hard
man inclined to arbitrary methods. More significant, perhaps, was his
testimony in letters to King Edward to Milner's unique combination of
authority, knowledge and drive, and 'the unlimited confidence' he inspired.

After saying good-bye to the Chamberlains at Bloemfontein, Milner
wrote to a Progressive M.P. at the Cape that their visit had so far been
'an unmitigated success', though he was anxious about its last (Cape
Town) phase. To Lady Edward Cecil he showed his reasons in more
vigorous language,

> You can imagine my feelings, if Joe does forgive and bless the Bond
> before he leaves S. Africa. You may be kindly to the Dutch, even the
> rebels, if you will. . . . But it is a blunder *even to receive* a Bond depu-
> tation. As many Dutchmen as you please, but *not as Bondsmen*.[22]

Travelling by train Chamberlain had enthusiastic welcomes at Grahamstown, Port Elizabeth and even at Graaff Reinet where he transgressed
Milner's maxim by receiving a Bond deputation. After stops at Middelburg
and Paarl he reached Newlands to stay with the Governor. In a final busy
February week he obtained Sprigg's promises that no attempt to re-
enfranchise rebels would yet be made, and that as soon as the new register
was ready an election would take place and a new Parliament called. He
had several meetings with Hofmeyr in an effort to heal what Hofmeyr's

biographers call 'the plague-spot in the situation – the almost frantic distrust of two sections of the population of each other.'[23] At a Bond deputation Hofmeyr promised to issue a circular to the Dutch urging them to stop insulting and boycotting loyalists. Chamberlain and the Governor, for their part, undertook to release more prisoners still held on political grounds.

Milner, confined to his room for a week with congestion of the bowels and in Buchan's opinion 'much overworked', was displeased with Chamberlain for carrying reconciliation to these lengths. Kipling, on his usual winter visit to the Cape, wrote that Chamberlain had been 'spoofed. The Bond are almost stupefied with their good luck.' Milner's friend Iwan-Müller later sent him an account of an hour's interview with Chamberlain in London. His 'whitewashing of the Bond', he had said, had been a question of tactics. He had 'genuine affection, admiration and gratitude' towards him, but significantly added 'Milner is a very great man but he has his limitations. He does not suffer fools gladly and unreason makes him angry, while it only amuses me.'[24]

With basic issues settled and Chamberlain leaving much to his discretion, Milner felt able to increase his speed. He was normally called at 6.30 and aimed to achieve six hours at his desk before lunch, refusing to be interrupted except by most important visitors. Though the bulk of his work was administration Leo Amery called it 'fantastically untrue' to label him a bureaucrat, writing 'the whole essence of his mind was not bureaucratic but political' and Reconstruction was never an end but only a means.[25] Milner restated the end to Spenser Wilkinson:

> ... it is no longer war with bullets, but it is war. Still ... we now hold the winning cards, but it is not true that we have won the game, and we cannot afford to lose a single trick. We are fighting for something immensely big.

If they could only develop a spirit of wider British patriotism South Africa could become 'by far the most valuable of all the distant portions of the Empire.'[26] He was suffering one of his periodic phases of doubt of Parliament at home ever understanding South Africa's problems.

Two factors, at least the first of which could not have been foreseen, now threatened the economic progress on which all his plans were based.

The rains normally due in South Africa's spring months of September to November had in the previous year not come until mid-December. This had seriously hindered the Government's ploughing programme to provide the food for 1903, and brought more disease to livestock already in poor condition. It was followed in early 1903 by further drought which, continuing through the year and into 1904, proved the worst for about 40 years. Much of the Repatriation Department's work had to be done again, and the cost of Government help and complaints of the farmers both increased.

A special repatriation problem arose with *bywoners* (squatters), the numerous poor, white and black, who were landless and lacked special skills. Their plight had been aggravated by the war, and the hostility of the 'bitter-end' burghers towards the 'hands-uppers' (early surrenderers) and those who had fought for the British. The political Dutch Reformed Church, for example, at two post-war synods virtually excommunicated the National Scouts.[27] In the autumn the Government had created, mainly in the Transvaal, 'Burgher Land Settlements' to help National Scouts run by syndicates on lines like the French *métayage*. These, proving successful, were opened to all white *bywoners* and, Milner noted in January, were 'assuming very large proportions.' In the Orange River Colony the *bywoners* were usually engaged in irrigation and public works and lived in Relief Camps.

By March 1903 repatriation to their homes of the 200,000 men, women and children was completed, and almost all of the overseas prisoners had been brought back. The Refugee Camps had fulfilled their last function and been closed and dismantled. Milner could now hope to get on with his plans to obtain 5–10,000 British settlers on the land, and improve the low state of agricultural knowledge and practice in the colonies. He had decided to give first preference for any Government land available after peace to disbanded soldiers, especially Australians and New Zealanders who were more likely to cope quickly with South Africa's special conditions than settlers from Britain.[28] Boards in each colony were acquiring land, and Agricultural Departments, unknown before the war, were offering technical help. Young Bendor was privately financing the settlement of Cheshire yeomen on a large estate he had acquired near Ladybrand, one of the best areas for cereal-growing, in eastern Orange River Colony.

The second, and at least as important, factor threatening Milner's plans was a shortage of labour for the gold mines. This problem, like the *bywoner* problem, was not new,[29] but the size of it after nearly three years of war was only now becoming apparent. The labour force of the Rand on the outbreak of war had been 119,000, of which some 12,000 were white and 107,000 African, three-quarters of whom had been recruited in Mozambique. Milner's negotiation of the *modus vivendi* with Mozambique in December 1901 has been noticed, and he went to Lourenço Marques in August 1902 in part to try to improve the recruitment of labour. By March 1903, however, less than half the pre-war figure, or only some 50,000 Africans, were at work in the mines. The unsettlement of the war, the work available to Africans repairing railways and on other reconstruction tasks and the wages policy of the companies all contributed to this serious shortage.

The core of Milner's reconstruction policy was thus put at risk. A prosperous Transvaal must, he was convinced, be the basis of South Africa's federation, and a prosperous Transvaal could only mean a steadily rising output of gold. In a speech of early 1904 he replied to the 'wiseacres overseas' who said that the pace at which gold was produced didn't matter:

> It does matter enormously at what pace we get it out . . . the faster we get it the greater is the over-spill, if I may use that word, over what is necessary to remunerate the capital invested, and which benefits the local community and fills the coffers of the State, and can be used for the general advantage of the country.[30]

He considered that this *'over-spill'*, or surplus, was the one means of ensuring the development of the country's otherwise limited resources and creating new industries.

He had inclined with some others towards an experiment in importing Chinese to relieve labour shortage in Rhodesia; but had found Chamberlain during his visit against this on the ground that it would be most unpopular in Britain and all over South Africa. In 1903 the Rand Companies began to favour importing such labour as a *temporary* means of overcoming the shortage, but this at once aroused strong opposition. The issue was bitterly fought in South Africa for over nine months, and at home for much longer, relentlessly pursuing Milner long after he had ceased to be responsible for the country. In April 1903 he told a friend he had almost concluded that African sources would be unable to supply the mines' needs and that

> we must have some Asiatics – not necessarily Chinese – here for our industrial development. I am dead against the Asiatic settler and trader, but I do not believe the indentured Asiatic labourer would prove uncontrollable.

Without this help he could not see how they could get 'that great influx of British population – for skilled work, trades, professions, and agriculture – which is the ultimate salvation'. He wrote in the same vein to Chamberlain stressing that, besides the mines, agriculture and other industry would soon be short of labour. In the spirit of his aim that the Transvaal, though temporarily a Crown Colony, should be treated 'wherever possible as if it were self-governing' the Transvaal Government would adopt 'an attitude of neutrality' and take no action until 'the trend of public opinion was quite unmistakable.'[31]

Milner worked hard to improve the administrative structure and create what one historian calls 'an inchoate federation' of the two northern colonies. In March he presided over a two weeks' Conference at Bloemfontein of these colonies together with the Cape and Natal (represented by their Prime Ministers), Rhodesia and Mozambique. Though debates were sometimes stormy and the conference was sometimes on the verge of a breakdown substantial gains were made. Internal tariff barriers were abolished, and a new common tariff gave Britain an imperial preference. A Native Affairs Commission was created to form the first joint South African survey of this vital problem.[32] Approval was given to importation under certain circumstances of indentured Asiatic labour. Milner's friend Henry Birchenough, in South Africa to report on trade prospects, wrote that he had heard on all sides how much these results owed to Milner's personality and prestige. Milner told Hely-Hutchinson he was 'satisfied without being enthusiastic'. In particular he had *no illusions* that a federation of South Africa, British or otherwise, was anything but remote, though the conference ended up with 'a gushing resolution' to discuss federation further. The meeting had made him feel more than ever 'how great are the obstacles to any real Union. Not only the character, but the material interests of the several Colonies are so widely divergent.' In general discussion they were all Federalists, 'but no sooner did any definite proposal crop up than Particularism was rampant'.[33]

Milner's correspondence with friends in England and elsewhere gave him continuous pleasure; but inevitably this burden was increased by constant requests for jobs for the writers or their relatives and friends. These were seldom the settlers on the land he so much wanted. His staff, Kindergarten or not, engaged in responsible administrative work could only be small. Ozzy Walrond, his private secretary since April 1897, broke down again this April, was sent on six months' leave and replaced by Geoffrey Dawson of the Colonial Office referred to above. Sargant, his able Director of Education, wrote from England that he had recovered and wanted to return, which Milner arranged to his advantage.

Perry, the first of the Kindergarten to join him, now left him to become chairman of the Rand Native Labour Association. John Buchan had left earlier on completing his agreed term, and Milner took pains to help him to get what he then wanted, a job in Egypt. Fauconnier, the chef whom Milner had brought out from England six years before and whose wife had been his housekeeper, left with a tip of £200.

On 14 May a cold morning suggested the beginning of winter, and next day snow fell on Johannesburg. A little later Milner opened a Municipal Congress which might today be called a 'teach-in'. This approved much preparatory work done by Johannesburg's town council, inspired by Lionel Curtis, to introduce elected councils in Johannesburg and throughout the Transvaal.[34] Curtis was promoted to Assistant Colonial Secretary for Urban Affairs and three of his Kindergarten friends worked with him. Richard Feetham, a lawyer, replaced him as Johannesburg's Town Clerk, Lionel Hichens continued as Town Treasurer and John Dove came out from England to be Feetham's deputy.

A few days later the enlarged Transvaal Legislative Council met in Pretoria. Called by Chamberlain in the House of Commons 'semi-representative', this comprised 14 representatives of various classes and interests and 16 official members. It met in public and became very active. The important Inter-Colonial Council of the two colonies met at Johannesburg under Milner's chairmanship in July and drew up its first budget. Chamberlain's approval of this body has been noticed. Leo Amery called it one of Milner's 'most original and fruitful conceptions', a major instrument for his goal of creating 'a South African habit of mind.' Robert Brand (later a successful banker and Lord Brand), of New College and All Souls and a close friend of Perry, had come out from home to be secretary to this body, and continued to be so until the eve of South Africa's Union.

Dawkins, who saw and heard much as J. P. Morgan's London representative, wrote that Chamberlain had returned home to find 'a very demoralized and hesitating Government', though his South African mission had been 'generally applauded in all quarters.' To Chamberlain's and Milner's disgust the Cabinet in the former's absence had agreed to repeal the small wartime corn-tax. In a speech of 15 May 1903 to his Birmingham constituents Chamberlain launched his historic campaign for Tariff Reform and Imperial Preference. It seems he had disclosed his intention to do this to Milner and Fitzpatrick in Johannesburg, when Milner gave him 'intense concentrated attention' and thought that public opinion in England was still insufficiently prepared for such action.[35]

Johannesburg had a very mixed population and it seems, from an entry in Milner's diary, that this included enough old Etonians for a Fourth of June dinner. The Vice-Chancellor of Cambridge wrote offering Milner an Honorary Doctorate which, being in Africa, he had to refuse. His friend Parkin, in Africa organizing the scholarship scheme for the Rhodes Trust, and his wife were his guests. In July he took a few days off for a trek in the fertile eastern area of Orange River Colony getting cordial receptions from the burghers, having much talk about Land Settlement and making speeches he described as composed of 'gubernatorial platitudes.'

In April he sent the Colonial Office reports of a Johannesburg meeting organized by the 'White League' (the small minority of skilled white workers employed in the mines) which defeated the Asiatic Labour proposal by 5,000 votes to 2. This issue was now 'hotly debated and of burning public interest.'[36] Fears as far away as Cape Colony of creating still another colour problem were widespread. That intrepid radical campaigner Emily Hobhouse returned to the country in May, stayed with Olive Schreiner and De Wet and formed a lasting friendship with Smuts. In such circles she naturally found little satisfaction with the Government, and visiting Morley after returning home she 'dwelt very specially [and partially] upon the unbending Boer opposition to Chinese Labour.'[37]

The Transvaal Government appointed a strong Labour Commission to examine this matter and Milner, preparing to go on leave, told Chamberlain that the issue was his one great anxiety. He claimed nevertheless that among thinking men, including the Boers, a big swing of opinion had taken place. He much hoped that

... the Chinese – since they are now our only hope – may come, and come quickly. The Mines have exhausted their efforts, by higher wages, better recruiting and *much better arrangements in every respect* – food, clothing, sanitation, etc. – to get natives, but though they have got *some thousands more* these are not nearly enough.[38]

His own lack of bias and considerable share in persuading the mineowners to make these improvements has been recognized by the historian Walker, who writes:

he took the Mines in hand. He was no man's tool, but a driving force ... with little tenderness for business men and less than none for mining magnates as such.

Besides doubling Kruger's profits tax he had improved the Gold Laws and the laws against sales of illicit liquor, compelled the companies to pay rates to the Johannesburg Town Council and spoke of larger State royalties for future mineral discoveries. From his time dates 'the development of the mines as a model great industry.'[39]

On 7 August he left for four months' leave, sailing in an Austrian steamer up the east coast. His reading included Holland Rose, Anatole France, Haldane and De Wet's recent *Three Years War* which he noted 'seems genuine but so badly written as not to be interesting.' He made a trip into the interior of Uganda and was met at Port Said by his former Egyptian servant. On reaching Trieste he had V.I.P. treatment, stayed at the Hotel Sacher in Vienna, was looked after by the Ambassador and talked with the Minister of Finance. He proceeded to Carlsbad, having noted while still on the ship some threat of a return of '. . . my old intestinal trouble, which now might be very awkward.' Carlsbad, like Marienbad, was at this date popular with the English. It was not long before his routine of drinking the waters, mud baths and concerts was enlivened by an English acquaintance introducing him to Elinor Glyn. This lady was 38 (eleven years younger than Milner), attractive, red-haired, separated from her husband, and a successful author of romantic novels then considered *risqué*. The previous year she had bought a tiger skin with the profits from one of her novels, and wrote later that 'a merciless fate' had decreed her name being coupled for ever with a woman lying on one.[40] She liked 'real English gentlemen of the old school' especially if they were classical scholars, and was a friend of Sir Francis and Lady Jeune, F. H. Bradley the eminent Oxford philosopher and (later) Lord Curzon.

As Milner and Mrs. Glyn walked in the pinewoods their common love of Greek ideas and philosophy helped to make them close friends; he used to read Plato to her in the evenings, especially *Phaedo*, 'the final pages of which never failed to move him to tears'.[41] Milner's company, she wrote, inspired her to write a 'little volume of biting but subtle satire' called *The Damsel and the Sage* published later this year. She kept a diary and some years later, after a London meeting, recorded:

. . . he loved me and loves me still. His stern face grew soft when his eyes rested upon me . . . and at last was full of wistful pain. . . . At last he went away. . . . I cannot love him – I love only one.

There is little evidence that Milner, having loved and lost Margot Tennant twelve years before, was really again in love. We have only Elinor's word for it, and she was nothing if not a romantic. Milner was, however, much attracted to her and she became one more of his permanent friends. Helen, the daughter of Lady Edward Cecil, writes that she 'got into terrible trouble' when her mother found her reading Elinor Glyn's works.[42]

On 18 September Milner noted 'an exciting stir everywhere owing to rumours of Chamberlain's retirement', and telegrams from London confirmed that he had indeed left the Cabinet to be free to campaign for Tariff Reform. Milner had been warned to expect Balfour to offer him Chamberlain's vacant chair, so was not taken by surprise when a King's Messenger arrived in Carlsbad for this purpose. He had not, however, expected the Messenger to convey the King's personal hopes, expressed through Balfour who was at Balmoral, that he would accept. He sat up late writing a refusal to Balfour, and wrote an answer to the King's personal message next morning. This was by no means, however, the end of the matter. A wire from Balfour asked him to reconsider his decision, and 'very much upset by this' he offered to travel to London to see him. He was accompanied to Nuremberg by Elinor Glyn, who later recalled their 'joyous day' there, and to London by Geoffrey Dawson who was staying at Marienbad.

Milner has been seen on a number of occasions taking much time consulting friends and conscientiously weighing pros against cons when offered promotion, and this occasion was no exception. Those who wrote urging him to accept included Chamberlain himself, whom he had called in his letter to Balfour 'the greatest Colonial Secretary our country has ever had'; but a roughly equal number of letters urged him to refuse. He consulted Dawkins and Iwan-Müller and on 29 September ('a most agitating and eventful day') had two long sessions with the Prime Minister. Sleeping on the matter, he wrote to him on the 30th his final refusal, and left that evening for Dover and the Continent. J. S. Sandars, Balfour's confidential Secretary, called it a 'poignant situation.'[43]

The Government was of course shaky, and a Cabinet job was likely to be a fairly short-term affair; it was also most likely that a Liberal Government would replace Milner in Africa by somebody else. Gell had urged his acceptance as 'the best thing for the Empire . . . and a happy way of leaving South Africa.' There is, however, no reason to doubt Milner's sincerity when he wrote in his last letter to Balfour that 'the one great reason' for his refusal was:

I do not think I ought to abandon the work, to which I have devoted so many years, at its present necessarily very incomplete state.[44]

He felt morally committed to finishing the job so far as he could, to those who were helping him to do so and to the British loyalists in South Africa.

He went for a fortnight to Tübingen to arrange a new monument for his parents' grave and the acquisition of permanent rights in this. He could not foresee that thirty-five years later Hitler's Nazi régime would obliterate this grave. After visiting friends in the town he went to nearby Heckingden to see 'old Emma' and her family. He visited his stepmother Elise whom he found 'terribly aged and broken' in a mental home near Stuttgart, and stayed with his cousin Richard in Bonn, walking one day to the top of the Drachenfels.

Back in England for six weeks he stayed with Clinton and Loulie Dawkins in Queen Anne's Gate and in Kent. He worked at the Colonial Office and elsewhere and enjoyed many social engagements. He was once again commanded to dine and sleep at Windsor, playing bridge with the King. He stayed with the Goschens at Seacox and the Chamberlains at Highbury, saw many friends and, helped by the prosperous Dawkinses' 'motor-brougham', squeezed in a visit to 54 Claverton Street. He saw a good deal of Lady Edward Cecil, something of Elinor Glyn and gave a dinner with Dawkins to a dozen civil servants and journalists.

Balfour had appointed as Colonial Secretary Alfred Lyttelton, Milner's friend and three years his junior, who had not hitherto held political office. Milner's chief work in these weeks, in his own opinion, was convincing the Cabinet, to which he was summoned on 16 November, of South Africa's shortage of native labour for the mines and other essential needs. He attended the Defence Committee to discuss South Africa's garrison, had talks with Rothschild and Friedrich Eckstein and attended a B.S.A. Company board meeting. On 27 November the familiar entry 'tremendously busy' appears in his diary.

The next day he was outward bound for Cape Town on the *Dunnottar Castle* with Dawson, Walrond and other friends. Walrond had become engaged to a South African girl and was due before long to leave Milner's service. A storm flattened Milner out in his cabin, made everyone miserable and lasted for days. When the ship was steady enough for him to take pen in hand he began strenuous letter-writing and conferences with his staff, recording:

. . . every moment of the day [was] occupied, as I don't believe in idling on board ship especially in hot weather. But there was no prodigious result.

They docked on 15 December at Cape Town, where in spite of poor weather a large crowd in the streets gave him a good reception. After many interviews he travelled non-stop to Johannesburg.

Milner's 'one final year' on the job after leave which he had agreed on with Chamberlain was going to prove nearly sixteen months. Professor Walker describes his career in South Africa after the war as

. . . always a race against time, while his prestige could still sway volatile Johannesburg; but the work went on, hopefully throughout 1902 and 1903, then with a sense of urgency and even of desperation in 1904.[45]

The drought noticed earlier as persisting was one cause of continuing economic recession; and settling British immigrants on the land proved a slow process. There were signs of impatience by some of the British in the Transvaal with Crown Colony Government, as well as of Boer political revival. Both Milner's health and his popularity were wasting assets. 'Pace', he wrote to a South African friend, 'is everything.'

One of his first acts on reaching Johannesburg was to examine fully the two colonies' financial situation with Lawley and Patrick Duncan. He telegraphed to Lyttelton on 27 December,

. . . the immediate prospects are very bad. There is complete stagnation owing to the labour difficulty.

Faced with deficits in both the Transvaal and Inter-Colonial Council budgets he urged some deferment of the War Contribution, to which His Majesty's Government agreed, and further reduced the size of the South African Constabulary.[46]

He had written to Gell from the ship that though great difficulties were involved over Asiatic Labour he would leave nothing in his power undone to obtain it; 'the hard school of life' had hammered him into 'one of the most *dogged* of beasts of burden.' After two days' debate and long speeches the Transvaal Legislative Council carried by 22 votes to 4 on 30 December 1903 the motion of Sir George Farrar, a mining magnate, favouring importation of 'indentured unskilled coloured labourers'.[47] Milner told Lyttelton the vote faithfully reflected local public opinion and the Executive Council unanimously favoured going ahead in the matter.

After His Majesty's Government had proposed some amendments and given its sanction the Labour Ordinance was passed on 10 February 1904. There were, however, two fences still to be crossed. The first and chief one was to procure the Chinese to whom, as everyone knew, the formula just quoted referred. This meant diplomatic negotiations in London, and some difficult work over recruitment in China by 'Peter' Perry and others. The second and, at this stage, smaller fence was winning support for the measure in Parliament and by British public opinion.

This study has only been able to pay small attention to current views on South Africa of British parties and public opinion. In the standard book on this topic G. B. Pyrah has shown that the Liberals approved of the principles and 'statement of aims' of the Vereeniging Treaty. Their criticism during and just after the war had been confined to the Government's methods, and now to the manner and timing of granting self-government to the two ex-Republics.[48] By Liberals is meant here, of course, Campbell-Bannerman and the bulk of the party. Though Rosebery and the other 'Lib. Imps' formed a powerful group, C.-B. had strengthened his position and moved in a Gladstonian direction. His and his followers' faith from afar in the Boers was, as the reader is now well aware, precisely what Milner lacked.

Milner's attitude when offering Chamberlain his resignation in the summer of 1902 was expressed in a letter to Rendel,

> I am, and always have been, rowing against the stream. The tendency of public opinion and feeling in England is to go wrong about South Africa. It needed an ultimatum to *wake them up*, and they will go to sleep again on the first opportunity.

Lyttelton as Colonial Secretary was not in the same class as Chamberlain, and it is clear that he saw himself more as Milner's disciple than his master. Milner's correspondents from early 1904 were forecasting early dissolution followed by a Liberal Government; Chamberlain's Tariff Reform campaign was splitting the Unionists and beginning to consolidate their opponents.

Selborne proved a good prophet when he wrote to Milner on 14 March that the Government were doing all they could to help him over Chinese Labour, but the consequences 'will be disastrous to ourselves.' The Government was bound to be beaten (in the election), but he was anxious over the Radicals' probable 'very big majority . . . and the cry (now become "Chinese Slavery") was the most criminal and remunerative electorally he had known.' There were anxious times ahead at home and abroad. But he wanted especially to assure him that 'your friends are sticking to you.'[49]

Lyttelton, as the result of this issue, took some severe blows on the chin in the Commons. Goschen wrote that the Lords 'have had a time over the Chinese Labour question. Such rows, and such battles over your body! All your critics became frantic.' When the Bishop of Hereford made a violent attack he had taken the opportunity of 'giving him such a dressing as I expect no Bishop has had for years in the House of Lords.'

In February the scene had been brightened for Milner by the victory in the Cape elections of Jameson, now leader of the Progressives, over the Bond by 50 votes to 45. Sprigg, now 74 years of age, was eliminated for the time being. Kipling, from his usual resort near Cape Town, wrote to Milner that 'things are going not so badly here.' The Progressives were really being led by Dr. Jameson. But 'to think that after such a war we should be rejoicing here to have defeated "constitutionally" the declared aims of declared rebels!' In a reference to an outbreak of bubonic plague at Johannesburg he ended 'I congratulate you on the plague. Otherwise you might not have been certain that the last straw had been laid on your burden.' Milner, it must be added, would not accept that Jameson's victory had shown that his fight for suspension of the Cape's constitution was mistaken. To Dawkins he wrote that British supremacy at the Cape had only been maintained by stirring up 'all the old racial animosities.' Now two fairly evenly matched parties were 'fighting for power on *the racial issues alone*', and the racial feud must soon spread to the new colonies.[50]

The last twelve months of Milner's career in South Africa, from April 1904 to April 1905, may be used to attempt some balance of his successes and failures. Throughout its three years his work of Reconstruction was a race against time. As the result of the war he had to contend with what Basil Williams has called 'a sort of instinctive distrust between himself and the Boers he was called on to govern'; and also with much indifference and misunderstanding at home.

He clearly perceived that, given the nature of the country, material restoration was the first essential object. The gold mines alone could produce the wealth upon which other industries, education and all social progress could be built. The first 1,000 indentured Chinese, on a 3-year contract, did not reach the mines until June 1904. A year later they numbered 40,000 and eventually 50,000. The available new African labour continued throughout 1904 to be small (a bare 8,000 or so) and only began to pick up in mid-1905. Gold output, however, doubled in four years from the Peace. The Chinese workers, as Milner had hoped, created openings for skilled white and later unskilled African labour, gave confidence to shareholders and increased the flow of immigrants. Professor Walker concludes that before the last of the Chinese left the country in 1910 they had given the Transvaal the surplus which 'helped it to dominate the National Convention [of 1909–10] that made the Union'.

Milner saw the first and most important use of any 'overspill' the gold mines might produce as being to 'fill up some of the most flagrant gaps in the [inadequate] railway map of South Africa'. He was still engaged in early 1904 in fighting a 'preposterous' War Office claim for £1½ million of capital spent on the lines during the war, which he eventually managed to settle for £½ m. In June he succeeded after much effort in persuading the Treasury at home to permit the issue of the last £5 million of the Guaranteed Loan. He had given close attention since the war ended to railway extension schemes, but Sir Percy Girouard, director of Railways throughout the war and then Commissioner of the new Central South African Railway, did not succeed in the latter capacity, was publicly attacked and evoked from Milner the comment 'the whole thing is horribly disagreeable'. He retired, and his work was entrusted to a Railway Committee of the Inter-Colonial Council guided by its capable secretary Robert Brand.

Milner held discussions in June with the Governors and Railway Ministers of the Cape and Natal to discuss the vexed question of Delagoa Bay traffic and other matters of common interest. These led to a Railway Amalgamation Conference in February 1905 which reached some agreement over Delagoa Bay, and passed a resolution favouring pooling of receipts. Milner's programme called for doubling the Transvaal and Orange River Colony mileage by construction of more than 1,000 additional miles. His achievement in creating the Central South Africa Railways is called, in *The Times History of the War*, 'one of the most enduring instruments of his constructive policy'.

Others claim that in the three post-war years a complete agricultural revolution was inaugurated. More impressive is the fact that Milner's extensive aid to agriculture was, according to Botha's biographer, the one subject about which the general, a farmer and not one of Milner's admirers, praised him.[51] This aid included Agricultural Departments in both colonies, grants, importation from England of experts for work on experimental farms and the study of irrigation and afforestation, introduction of new varieties of cattle, sheep and cereals and intelligence about locusts.

Even his harshest critics will concede Milner's success in introducing, for the first time, competent administration and orderly reform of the law in both ex-Republics. Kruger's oligarchy had, partly through his own nature and long career, been notably deficient and corrupt in all that concerned the machinery of his state. Then his defeat had been followed by inexperienced British military government. There is no doubt that Milner, as one historian writes,

> . . . gave the North, for the first time, clean, efficient and boundlessly energetic administration which proved of great value to the future Union.

This structure placed finances on a sound footing; and the organization in a democratic manner of the municipalities and local government in general. The native population was organized under competent district commissioners, as a real part of the community.

Much credit for all this is due to the Kindergarten, though the Boers' slowness, Biblical respect for age and (as one of them wrote) 'disbelief in the hasty, impetuous ways of youth' inclined to make their employment another cause for blaming Milner. These dozen or so young Oxford men have tended to elbow out of the history books others of Milner's young and not-so-young British helpers from the early war days onwards. Goold-Adams, for example, a regular soldier, Henry Wilson, a rather older classical scholar from Cambridge, and young Lord Basil Blackwood of Balliol, not usually mentioned in Kindergarten lists, all played a major part in the reconstruction of the Orange River Colony.

Some Kindergarten lists justly include the architect Sir (as he became) Herbert Baker. In South Africa as a young man he was befriended by Rhodes and rebuilt Groote Schuur in 1896 after its fire. Milner asked him to help in the Transvaal's reconstruction, and his notable buildings included a new Government House at Pretoria as well as the Union Buildings and part of the Anglican Cathedral. After work in New Delhi and in London he built Rhodes House in Oxford in the South African Dutch style.[52]

Any outline of Milner's successes must include education, which, since its beginning by Sargant in 1901 in the Concentration Camps, has been given too small attention in this story. When peace was signed some 42,000 children in the new colonies were receiving education, about double the number receiving it when they were independent Republics. Development was then faster, with teachers imported from England and elsewhere. In 1903 a policy was promulgated in which primary education was free though not compulsory, religious teaching was undenominational and, to quote from a later despatch of Milner's,

While the Dutch language is to be thoroughly well taught, the medium of instruction is, as a general rule, to be English.

Education merges with the important (perhaps decisive) topic of the Dutch cultural–political revival. The Dutch Reformed Churches were decidedly hostile to Milner's educational plans, and set up in both colonies what they called 'Christian National Schools' which gave primacy to the Dutch language, but were not on the whole a success. Milner's offer in 1904 to create local boards with a majority of elected members, if half of the cost of the schools was raised locally, was rejected by the Transvaal *predikants*, but had more success in the Orange River Colony. Advances in secondary and higher education included two 'Normal Colleges' to train teachers, the foundation, on land given by Alfred Beit, of a Johannesburg Technical Institute and expansion of the Grey College at Bloemfontein.

Little need be said about Rhodesia and Swaziland which, especially the former, were on the periphery of Milner's labours. With Rhodes dead and the war over, Beit and Jameson visiting Rhodesia found its colonizers bitter, with trade languishing and many grievances in the air. An Order-in-Council of 1903 gave equal representation on its Legislative Council to official and unofficial members. Milner had recently called Swaziland to Chamberlain a country of 'pacific chaos' with a 'hopeless tangle' of concessions. After much correspondence between him and the Colonial Office His Majesty's Government decided in 1903–4 to continue Swaziland's close connection with the Transvaal, establish civil government there and appoint a Concessions Commission.

Among Milner's partial or total failures, one can be quickly disposed of. As he had expected, he failed in his plan to make South Africa a large-scale training camp for Imperial Troops. Amery wrote articles in *The Times* and others at home did their best to foster this scheme. But Chamberlain wrote in July 1903 that the most he could get from a Cabinet Committee was approval for a garrison of 25,000. A further reduction early in 1904 caused Milner successfully to enlist the help of Lord Roberts, the Commander-in-Chief, in resisting still more reductions.[53] But Whitehall's economic objections eventually triumphed.

The question of the status of British Indians had occupied Milner's attention before the end of the war. The matter was complicated in the Transvaal by past British protests to Kruger over discriminatory laws, and the need to take account of colonial sentiment. Milner felt unable to prejudice a future Transvaal government by allowing new Indian immigration, so that little was done.

A far more important problem, since it lay, with restoration of the mines, at the core of Milner's general plan, was that of Land Settlement by the British in the two colonies. This proved, for a number of reasons, one of his principal and lasting disappointments. A good deal of land which the Government inherited at the peace was unsuitable. Then land which it sought to buy in the open market proved expensive, and competent staff in this sphere was hard to come by. Milner told Bendor early in 1904 that his settlement in the eastern Orange River Colony was 'the only important assistance we have had from private sources', and they had now got some 5–600 British citizens on the land in this colony sponsored by the Government. In the Transvaal the difficulties were greater. When Milner departed in April 1905 there were only some 700 male settlers, the survivors of a considerably larger number, in each colony.

In April 1904 Lyttelton told Milner that Balfour considered 'a dissolution is to be expected next spring, when almost inevitably we shall be beaten'. He was convinced that the Liberals would 'extricate themselves from a painful dilemma (Chinese Labour) by granting self-government to the new Colonies *sans phrase*'. Did he think that 'in our remaining year, [we] should make a cautious move in that direction?' This letter crossed an important despatch from Milner of 2 May putting forward the same idea. He defended the policy of deferring responsible government, but now underlined

... the extreme undesirability of deferring it for too long, especially in the case of the Transvaal.

One reason for this view (often overlooked) was that returns were becoming available of the first scientific census ever held in the Transvaal or Orange River Colony.[54] In the Transvaal the whites numbered 290,000 (90,000 of these adult males); the Rand accounted for some 117,000 of this total, and Johannesburg alone for 84,000. Some estimates showed that potential voters amounted to 58,000 British and 34,000 Boers. In electoral terms this meant, from Milner's endless psephological calculations, a small Boer majority in the Transvaal, and a larger one in the Orange River Colony. Immigration might in a few years, he told Lyttelton, 'turn the balance [in the Transvaal] in favour of the British'; but the rate of the influx had 'greatly decreased and is still decreasing'.

The two men began work on a scheme of representative government designed to last only two or three years, known to history as the Lyttelton Constitution. It occupied Milner, including despatches of 5 and 24

December, for the rest of his time in South Africa, and the relevant Orders in Council were only published on 31 March 1905. Since the Constitution never came into force no details need be given about it.

Among reasons for their work on the Lyttelton Constitution were the Boers' cultural and political revival, and political agitation by some of the more volatile and unco-operative British Transvaalers. The Bond's historian writes that in 1902–3 the Boers were preoccupied with their post-war problems and 'riven with discord among themselves'. Then in Cape Colony Jan Hofmeyr, still the outstanding leader there of his people, retaliated for Milner's making English the official language in the north by helping to revive the *Taalbond* and then to achieve with others the remarkable feat of mixing the Taal and High Dutch to create a new language, *Afrikaans*. The Bond by a new constitution was married to the (Parliamentary) South African Party. In the Transvaal a meeting of Boers under Botha at Heidelberg in July 1903 to discuss grievances, led to the foundation in January 1905 of a party political organization *Het Volk* (the People). Meetings in the Orange River Colony under Hertzog brought the creation, soon after, of its counterpart *Orangie Unie*.

Paul Kruger, Milner's greatest Afrikander opponent, may be said to have shared by his death in this revival. Expiring in Switzerland aged 78 in July 1904, his body was brought to Cape Town where it lay in state, and was buried with ceremony on 16 December (Dingaan's day) in Pretoria, with Milner represented by his Military Secretary. The next day Botha, De La Rey, Smuts and other Boer leaders, inflexible as ever, reaffirmed to Milner their opposition to temporary representative government. Though not demanding change in a hurry, they would accept nothing less than full responsible government.

Milner overestimated the patience, always an uncertain factor, of his countrymen in the Transvaal; and also the prospects for British immigration and land settlement. He seems not to have foreseen the degree in which the strain of war and the bitterness of defeat would exacerbate Boer nationalist feeling. The reader can find the case for 'the failure of Milnerism' up to 1907 presented in full in G. H. Le May's *British Supremacy in South Africa*.[55]

In the aim of uniting the country under the flag of Great Britain alone it is true to say Milner failed. But, as Smuts was soon to remind him, time brings reconciliations as well as revenge. He had laid strong foundations for Union, and the Kindergarten he had trained continued his work for Dutch masters. He left South Africa, Professor Walker (himself a South African) writes,

... knowing that much of his work was endangered, but confident that something of it would stand .... He had even builded for Union better than he knew. In a very real sense the greatest of the High Commissioners can claim to be one of the Fathers (or was it the stepfathers?) of the Union of South Africa.

His basic conviction that the unity of the country could best be achieved by freedom and security within a united British Empire was an ideal translated into action by Botha and Smuts within four years.

On 17 November Campbell-Bannerman in England had pledged to grant 'a full and honest measure of self-government' to the ex-Republics. Stimulated by this and by news of Milner's constitution-making, two Transvaal British bodies, the Progressive and the Responsible Government Associations, were formed and began agitations. The former included some mining magnates and was content with Milner's gradual proposals, while the latter had stronger aims similar to those of the Boers. The Orders in Council for the Lyttelton–Milner scheme were published on the last day of March, two days before Milner's final departure. Campbell-Bannerman's Liberal Government replaced Balfour's Unionists on 5 December; and two months later decided to ignore the Lyttelton Constitution.

Since returning from leave in England in December 1903 Milner had not left Johannesburg except for two short treks and working visits to Bloemfontein and Cape Town. A few personal events of his last sixteen months must be mentioned. Getting wind of his approaching retirement, Macmillan's solicited a book on his South African experience, and Moberly Bell of *The Times* asked him to write the official life of Disraeli. He refused both offers, telling Bell that if he ever took up his pen for another book it would be to try to

... draw some profit for others from my own experiences, sufficiently peculiar and unpleasant as they have been ... Dizzy was a vastly more interesting personality than Gladstone.

Goschen, Chancellor of Oxford since 1903, had written that when Milner was next in England it would give him much pleasure to bestow Oxford's D.C.L. upon him. Tom Brassey wrote to ask for a contribution to his Balliol Endowment Fund. His guests at Sunnyside included Lord Roberts with his wife and daughters, and Princess Christian. He attended the inaugural meeting of the South African Association for the Advancement of Science. And he gave a ball for about 1,000 people in Johannesburg.

It had not proved easy to find a successor to Milner, who had been in correspondence about this for over a year.[56] As late as February 1905 Balfour was pressing him to 'do a Cromer', that is, to stay in office for an indefinite period. He firmly resisted any such idea, in part because 'reasons of health are decisive'. Late in February Balfour wrote again to say that he had netted Milner's first choice for the job, Lord Selborne, who 'goes reluctantly, and out of a sense of public duty'. Milner noted that the Press contained the 'glorious announcement' of this.

Shortly before leaving, his doctor's report that his heart was rather 'worried' gave him some cause for anxiety. While official addresses and letters poured in he celebrated his 51st birthday. He made three important farewell speeches at Germiston, Pretoria and (most important as a summary of his Imperialist views) the leading city of the country, Johannesburg.[57]

When he left on 2 April 1905, a Sunday, with a heavy rainstorm in progress, Johannesburg station was crowded and hundreds of people insisted on shaking his hand. He sailed, as on his last leave, from Delagoa Bay, taking the east coast route to Europe. He was not to see South Africa again until almost twenty years later, in the last winter of his life.

Viscount Milner, after being gazetted a peer. Portrait by Hugh de T. Glazebrook

Milner's Kindergarten

Part III

OPPOSITION

The City and Political Bouts

(May 1905 – August 1914)

South African Backlash – Constitutional Crises – Fighting Home Rule Again

Milner steamed north with Dawson, whom he had helped to obtain the editorship hitherto held by Basil Worsfold of Johannesburg's *Star* and who was going on leave. As usual, lack of exercise made him feel 'seedy', so with Dawson he took to dumb-bells and skipping on the captain's deck. A sea-voyage was always a time for reading old issues of *The Times* and the literature he enjoyed. This did not prevent him briefing Selborne, 'in sweltering heat on a rolling ship' in the Red Sea, on South Africa's state in a memo of thirty-five pages, with a P.S. of sixteen pages added later at Venice.[1] A Dutch fellow passenger had earlier given him what he found 'rather an odd letter' from Smuts. His arch-enemy among the Boer leaders wrote: 'I am afraid you have not liked us.' But he hoped time would bring them both to appreciate better

> ... the contribution of each to the formation of a happier S. Africa.... History writes the word 'Reconciliation' over all her quarrels. . . .[2]

A stop at Mombasa made possible a brief visit to 'the little town' of Nairobi. Then landing at Suez en route for Cairo he found intense interest in watching 'the old familiar life' of rural Egypt. As the guest for a week of the Cromers he was received by the Khedive, called on Ministers and saw former colleagues.[3] He travelled de luxe to inspect the great Aswan Dam formally opened only six months before. Returning to Alexandria en route to Venice he found Walrond there suffering from a stroke and took trouble to see he was cared for.

His great aim was a long rest, and he envisaged a leisurely trip through the Balkans to Constantinople. But fate intervened in the form of a message that Dawkins had had a bad heart attack and was ordered abroad. He gave up his travelling plans and joined Dawkins, Loulie and their daughter on Lake Como for over five weeks. His days were passed reading to his bedridden friend, answering heavy budgets of letters and walking. In May he told Lyttelton that the chances were good for Dawkins to resume his usual life. He himself, though unwilling, might have to revisit Carlsbad 'for the intestinal trouble which has worried me for several years.' Through his New College friend Matheson he declined Oxford's offer to confer on him an honorary D.C.L. in June. Besides needing a long rest he knew he couldn't come home for one purpose without 'becoming involved in all kinds of things.'[4]

Though no longer a public official, his burden of correspondence with friends, obligations incurred and duties to one cause or another kept mounting. This fact and some illness made him spend a week in June under a false name at the Lord Warden Hotel, Dover. He sent his servant, Axten, to London to collect an immense mass of correspondence from Brooks's, ate his meals in a private room, read much Shakespeare and took solitary walks. He went to Paris, again used a false name and visited Walrond, still ill and for some reason at Aix-la-Chapelle. A week alone at Reading, seeking a country house in the area, followed. On 19 July he joyfully noted that his bachelor quarters at 47 Duke Street, St. James's, could house him again. Next day his return to England appeared in the Press.

As the first of three leading 'Prancing Proconsuls' to come home his views were much sought. A 'longish interview' with the King and a command from the Queen, talks with Balfour, the Chamberlains and Margot were items in scores of engagements. His lean face proved the truth of Garrett's judgement that eight years of South Africa had 'strained his physical constitution, notoriously unequal to the will that drove it', almost to breaking-point.[5] He wrote to Violet Markham and others that he was 'far from rested' and intended to continue his holiday abroad. It was ironical that this state of mind and body caused his refusal in August of the Empire's most glittering prize. The resignation this summer of Lord Curzon brought strong pressure from Brodrick, on the Government's behalf, that he should succeed him as Viceroy of India.

He had 'no political interest worth mentioning', he had written from Africa to the Imperial Federalist Association, 'except the maintenance of the Imperial connection.' He intended in time to get enough work in the City to give him substantial independence. It was the vision agreed years before with Dawkins of gaining enough wealth to work outside party politics for Imperial union. He now made Dawkins's fine Regency Villa, Polesden Lacey near Dorking, his base for a wide search for a small country house ('a home of sorts'), to establish roots in England.

Accepting an offer from Lionel Curtis and six other New College Kindergarten men for his portrait to be painted by another New College man, Maxwell Balfour, and hung in the College hall, he called his interest in South Africa 'inextinguishable'. In the months to come he sat to Balfour and the portrait reached its appointed place where it hangs today. His Imperial interest impelled him to start work at once as a Rhodes Trustee. Though Rosebery was the Senior Trustee, Milner's financial skill and constant attendance made him in practice more active; this and the chairmanship of Toynbee Hall Council were the only offices outside politics he retained when he joined the War Cabinet in 1916. He replied to the toast of Rhodes at the annual Scholars' dinner at Oxford and helped to elect the first Beit Professor of Colonial History, Hugh Egerton, at the university.[6]

His one other working entanglement at this stage was Lord Roberts's National Service (or conscription) campaign, which he saw as a non-party aspect of Empire defence. This occupied a good share of his time in the years preceding the War and beyond. He was introduced once more (as a Viscount) to the House of Lords with Goschen a supporter, and with no intention of hurrying to impress that assembly.

Unknown to him his apprenticeship there was going to prove far from pleasant. Balfour's Government had been cliff-hanging for months; and some Radicals had revived in stronger form the agitation against Chinese labour on the Rand, now made sensational by the crimes and homosexuality of some Chinese, and the flogging of some found guilty. Lyttelton at the Colonial Office was astonished to learn that Milner appeared to have sanctioned flogging without previous recourse to the law. Balfour, rightly apprehensive over Chinese labour as a Liberal electoral asset, was furious about what he called to Selborne 'Milner's amazing blunder'.

For Milner a personal matter bulked larger at this moment than politics. Dawkins had fallen ill some weeks before while in Paris with Loulie and himself, but seemed to have recovered on returning to England. He had a relapse and died, aged 46, on 2 December. Milner's note in his diary was 'one of the worst days of my life.' Dawkins and Gell were his most intimate long-standing friends; and Dawkins appears as the man with the larger experience, greater wisdom and moderation in counsel.

On 4 December Balfour resigned and next day Campbell-Bannerman led the country. Milner's three 'Lib. Imp.' friends held the key places of Chancellor of the Exchequer, Foreign Secretary and Secretary for War. More important to Imperial matters were C.-B.'s almost Gladstonian views, the choice of the elderly Lord Elgin as Colonial Secretary and of the brash Winston Churchill, aged 31 and a recent convert to the Liberals, as his Under-Secretary in the Commons. The importance the Liberals attached to South Africa was made clear by C.-B. in an Albert Hall speech of the 21st which included a promise to stop the importation of more Chinese labourers forthwith. Milner spent Christmas at Seacox where Lady Edward was one of the guests. On 8 January 1906 the King dissolved Parliament, and in a few days election fever began.

Though free trade was the principal issue, what was inflated into 'Chinese Slavery' played a big part. Lord Samuel claims credit for his share as a young Liberal in using this question as a symbol of the war and the Rand 'money-grubbers' so successfully that 'the country caught fire'.[7] Leo Amery, far better informed on the topic, saw the agitation as emotional and ill-informed, ignoring indentured labour elsewhere in the Empire and little related to the real issues disturbing South Africa. It was an unedifying aspect of an election which in essence was a recoil from years of Conservative rule. Lyttelton was stoned, spat upon and abused; hoardings showed chained Chinamen being flogged and maltreated.

In mid-January Milner went to Hyères in southern France for three weeks. His solitude, letter-writing and climbing did not exclude close attention to the Unionist débâcle. The Liberals won 377 seats, an overall majority of 84; Unionists saved only 157, of which 109 were Chamberlain-ites or Tariff Reformers. On 5 February Milner was back in London talking with Balfour on the Unionist Party crisis. Neither man, nor anyone else, could foresee that the Liberals would stay in power, though with decreasing public support, for almost ten years. Nor did Milner and Balfour know that three days later C.-B. would gain Cabinet consent for the grant of self-government to the defeated Boer colonies at the earliest date. This policy was included in the King's speech on 19 February.

A week later Milner made his maiden speech in the Lords, called by the *Annual Register* 'impressive and pessimistic'. As he had so often said, he believed in self-government for the Boer colonies at no distant date but only when preceded by a vital half-way stage. He repeated that 'a prosperous and loyal Transvaal is the key of the whole South African situation' and the right policy 'a cautious line in constitutional development, and full steam ahead in material recuperation.' He did not wish 'to seem to make a party attack.'[8] The Government sent the Ridgeway Committee to South Africa to report on the future franchise and constitution. The Lyttelton Constitution had been killed not only by the Liberals, but by what Selborne called the 'fissiparousness' of the British Transvaal parties. Even Botha's *Het Volk* was not anxious for immediate responsibility. It considered as fair the arrangements made in London by the end of the year for a nominated Upper House and a franchise expected to produce a small British majority.

In the meantime Lord Portsmouth, an Under-Secretary, had asked Milner in the Lords on the day after his speech if he had (as a Blue Book stated) given oral sanction through the Superintendent of Chinese Labour, one Evans, experienced and sympathetic to the Chinese, for 'slight corporal punishment' for some offences. Milner did not hesitate to take full responsibility and so by implication admit the charge; the event occurred on the eve of his leaving Africa and he told his friends he had no recollection of the matter. His reply, of course, delivered him into his enemies' hands. Some Liberal papers made scathing attacks, and Churchill accused him in the Commons of 'grave dereliction of public duty'. On 21 March Byles, a Radical M.P., made his well-known motion of personal censure which was amended by Churchill in somewhat insulting language on behalf of the Government. Led by Chamberlain the Unionists gave Milner ardent defence.

The affair was by no means over. For both parties Milner had become an Imperialist symbol. In the Lords Viscount Halifax moved a resolution approving his South African rule which evoked much support and was carried without a division. On Empire Day, 24 May, a big banquet was held in his honour, when Chamberlain called him one of the Empire's great assets. A Public Address was arranged which was signed, by its presentation in August, by over 370,000 persons; and another Address came from 25,000 citizens of Cape Colony. Duncan, among the most shrewd of Milner's Johannesburg officials, wrote that the censure motion had made people there angrier than anything in his previous experience.

Some historians see this affair as the first round in the conflict which was soon to make the relations between the Houses of Parliament so bitter. To many contemporaries it seemed more an assertion of Imperialist faith against 'Little England'. Milner himself, well inured both to blame and to praise, was most moved by the prospect of early self-government which he regarded with undue pessimism as destruction of all his South African work. The Government found it impossible to stop importation of Chinese for whom licences had been issued. Churchill's scheme for their repatriation failed, and he found, as Milner had done, that no adequate alternative sources of labour existed. A solution was left to the future Responsible Government.[9]

Milner's social–political engagements included evenings with the 'Coefficients', a dining club for informal discussion of serious topics, where H. G. Wells found him 'bold-thinking but hampered by political reservations.' More important and united in aim were the 'Compatriots', a ginger group of Imperialists active until 1914. He attended the Pilgrims' welcoming dinner to Curzon, with whom later his political fortunes became closely involved. Erskine Childers, the Irish Republican leader of later years, discussed with him a volume of *The Times's* Boer War history of which he was editor. In May he started his first City job with the London Joint Stock Bank, later amalgamated with the Midland Bank. Though his number of directorships grew this was his chief one until 1916.

In spite of much search he had not yet found a country house to his taste. So he rented for the summer Norman Hall, Sutton Courtenay, which he described as despite its name 'a tiny house in a beautiful back-water of the Thames.' Days of work in London were relieved by his passion for exercise on the river. In June Oxford gave him his honorary D.C.L. together with Aberdeen, Haldane and Plunkett and he noted that he 'certainly had the best reception.' His close touch with Oxford had been revived by his Rhodes Trust activities.

Among his guests Beatrice Webb, an acquaintance rather than friend and not always a reliable critic, came to lunch and found him in sombre mood: 'stern, rigid and brooding . . . he would not be comforted' and insisted that 'my house of cards is tumbling down', self-government in South Africa would dismantle his work. She conceded his public spirit and uprightness, but concluded that in spite of great virtues without a God or a wife he fell short of greatness.[10] He spoke in the Lords to urge the Government to act to protect British land settlers in South Africa, and on 10 July backed a motion by Lord Roberts on National Service. The next day Joseph Chamberlain, just 70, had a stroke and never again entered the Commons. By pretending his illness was gout his family managed to hide the true facts for some time; his brain remained clear, and the Tariff Reform movement kept up strongly.

In late summer Milner heard of 'a little tumbledown manor-house', Sturry Court, a few miles from Canterbury. On the site of a much older building, this sixteenth-century mansion had declined into a small farm-house. Milner bought it cheap with its estate of some 200 acres on the banks of the Stour, its magnificent barn, two mills and various fields and buildings. In November he moved there, with Lady Edward's help with decoration and picking up antique furniture. He employed a leading architect, Reginald Blomfield, for restorations over some years. Although 52 and with plenty of work in London, he devoted any time he could spare to planning its gardens and renovating its buildings. It was a home he much cherished till his death there nineteen years later.

Though indebted to A. M. Gollin's *Proconsul in Politics*, the writer cannot share without qualification his theme of 'a man with a problem' growing more and more bitter in these nine pre-war years. His problem, of course, was how to reconcile strengthening the Empire with his lack of the personal gifts needed to lead a political party. Quite early in life Milner realized this lack and decided to work indirectly through influence – persuasion of leaders, encouragement of the able young, full use of the Press and the grind of much writing of letters and briefs. He had proved that apart from this serious limitation he had high intellectual ability and traits which commanded much respect and affection.

An essay written after his death by 'Ned' Grigg, at this date a young man on the fringe of his inner circle, supports this analysis. He understood much better, Grigg wrote, 'what it was desirable to do than how, in a democracy, to get it done.' Influence of the type he exerted was losing ground in these turbulent years (as they turned out to be) of British party politics. In a mood of pessimism in 1908 he told Gell that, though public affairs took up much of his time, he had grown 'half-hearted about them.' He doubted whether either of them could do much good in their lifetime in Imperial politics. Though the next generation might make something of them, 'men of our time are useless for this job.'

Grigg added that beneath his external calm and readiness to hear other points of view burned intense convictions and a decisive spirit. He hated incompetence. His temper was not easily kindled, and against real challenge to his faith 'his resolution froze rather than flared.'[11] He made, however, as will be seen, occasional outbursts in public. For the most part his letters show him soldiering on, with optimism in the long-term future and bitterness limited to the Liberal Government's lukewarm Imperial views. Amery got him to speak in December on the Empire to Unionist audiences at Manchester and Wolverhampton when he said:

I neither occupy nor aspire to a place among party leaders . . . I am a free lance, a sort of political Ishmaelite.

Early in 1907 he joined the boards of the Bank of Egypt and an insurance company and, rather reluctantly, became Warden of the Anglo-Colonial Masonic Lodge. Lord Goschen, whom he called 'my political godfather, always a most affectionate loyal friend', died aged 75. He spent months settling Dawkins's estate, which was strangely awry, on Loulie's behalf, including disposal of Polesden Lacey. He joined his rich friend Tom Brassey in launching a scheme for an Oxford University Endowment Fund. The Grocers' Company made him an honorary freeman.

In the Transvaal election of February, to the general surprise, *Het Volk* won a comfortable overall majority. Selborne offered the premiership to Botha at once, and Smuts exclaimed: 'we are in for ever.' Through his

Rhodes Trust work and visits and letters from friends, Milner was well informed on South Africa's progress. Dawson in Johannesburg looked in vain for any record of his sanction of Chinese flogging and concluded that Evans, under mine-owners' pressure, had covered himself by telling Lawley that Milner had given his approval.[12] Botha made a good impression at the Colonial Conference in London in April. He obtained a Government guarantee for a loan which meant independence from the immediate prosperity of the mines; and agreed not to import more Chinese in return for the system remaining in force for another three years. On wider issues the Conference achieved little beyond agreement to meet every four years with the title 'Imperial' and to style the self-governing colonies 'Dominions'. For Milner and other Imperialists the Government's aversion to more formal Imperial ties or tampering with free trade was no surprise.

This autumn the Boers also gained an easy victory under Fischer in the Orange River Colony and a few months later Jameson fell from power at the Cape. Selborne was no more regarded as a reactionary than Milner had been by those British who served him. For some time he had approved of the Kindergarten planning to revive the vision of Rhodes and Milner of a unified (though now Boer-controlled) country. Since the Kindergarten met at Feetham's Johannesburg house called' The Moot' they chose this name for their discussions. Lionel Curtis ('the Prophet') supplied the main driving force. Financed in part by the Rhodes Trust he left the High Commissioner's staff, toured the four colonies and drafted a memo (called the 'Egg') for his colleagues' discussion. They knew that their plan must appear a response to South African demand, and persuaded Jameson, still Prime Minister at the Cape, to ask Selborne officially to prepare it. Hence its publication, after scrutiny by the Colonies, in July 1907 in South Africa as the 'Selborne Memorandum'.[13]

The achievement owed much indirectly to Milner's inspiration and, though he lacked Selborne's faith in the plan, to his advice in response to Kindergarten requests. Amery visited South Africa late in 1907 and concluded that Botha and Smuts, though scrapping some good things, were too busy and wise to tear Milner's system up root and branch; the War and Reconstruction had laid the indispensable foundations of Union.

Some events at home in 1907 and later need mention. In June, Cambridge gave Milner an honorary degree together with Elgin, Haldane and Curzon. J. A. Spender writes in his life of C.-B. that the company in the Senate House 'made it abundantly clear that Lord Milner rather than the Radical P.M. was the hero of this hour'.[14] Lady Edward had declined to make her home in Egypt so that her marriage had now virtually broken up. With her husband's financial help she bought a house called Great Wigsell, dilapidated like Sturry but more imposing, on the Kent–Sussex border close to Bateman's, the Kiplings' home. Only forty miles from Sturry, Milner in future saw more of her than of any other lady friend. He employed Arthur Steel-Maitland, who had had a distinguished Oxford career, as a 'sort of political private secretary'. On visits to Oxford he and Loulie Dawkins persuaded Strachan-Davidson, Master of Balliol, to erect a bronze plaque to Clinton's memory in the College ante-chapel; and he opened a 'Sweated Industries' exhibition. His week-end visits to country houses, though much reduced, embraced Hatfield and Taplow Court. He took voice-production lessons, and made Liberal Unionist speeches at Edinburgh and Rugby. Though he henceforth made many speeches their manner was not usually up to their matter. His voice, it was said, lacked resonance, and he sometimes got mixed up with large sheaves of notes. But he was capable of inspiring large crowds through his clarity and sincerity.

In the New Year his regular medical check-up was favourable; and he turned down an offer from A. F. Walter to join *The Times* board. Soon after he went on bank business to Egypt, staying in Cairo with Gorst, Cromer's successor, and travelling south to Khartoum where the Governor-General and Sirdar, his old friend Wingate, and Slatin showed him Gordon's College, Omdurman and the Mahdi's tomb. Somewhat later he began a long business association with Sir Ernest Cassel, the financier, in some Egyptian project.

C.-B. resigned from office in April, to live only two weeks longer, and Asquith replaced him. Milner had seen little of Asquith in recent years, though he called on Margot quite often and lunched with her at 10 Downing Street in June. He wrote to Asquith to congratulate him 'as an old friend' on attaining the highest office and to recommend another friend, Spenser Wilkinson, a non-party man with 'quite exceptional' knowledge of defence affairs, as a useful adviser. His judgement was soon confirmed by Wilkinson's appointment as the first Chichele Professor of Military History at Oxford. Milner wrote to Lord Roberts, for whom he worked hard in the background, that he had 'too many irons in the fire' and must soon go abroad for rest from perpetual business, private and public. Haldane's Army Reform scheme was on paper complete; Milner advised giving help to his organization but campaigning that it was inadequate.[15] What he and those who thought like him meant by National Service can be summed up as: first, compulsory training in the new Territorial Army for 4–6 months of one year for youths of 18–21, with less training for a further 3 years; and secondly, these men to be liable for

Home Service only till they were thirty. A visit to Windsor Castle for
Ascot and brief visits to Sturry gave him rest. On Whit Monday he
canoed up the Stour against a strong current to the centre of Canterbury
in nearly three hours. His plans for restoring Sturry's buildings, plan-
tations and so on would, due to their cost, take some years. But he
arranged his bulky South African papers in the 'oast' and allowed historians to use them.

Lord Blake has said in his life of Law that the fact that even left-wing
Tories saw wholesale exercise of the Lords' veto as a quite legitimate
tactic was 'a remarkable feature of the political climate and intense
partisanship of the time.' One reason was the extent, now hard to imagine,
to which 'Socialism' was thought of as revolution. In amending or rejecting the Commons' Bills many Peers thought it their constitutional duty
to check the tendency of the Lower House to rush through half thought-
out measures, especially those which they thought required an appeal to the
people. Conscious that the composition of their House needed reform
and active over schemes for this, they nevertheless clung tenaciously to
their powers. Asquith's Government, of course, took an opposite view.
The most hard-hitting Tories, the Tariff Reformers, saw Imperialism (embracing foreign affairs and defence) as in conflict with lukewarm Liberal
interest in these matters; and also as a way of financing social reform.
Liberal defeats in the 1908 by-elections seemed to promise an early return
to office, one Tory writing that 'the atmosphere radiates optimism.'

Milner attended the Lords fairly often but spoke mainly on his causes of
South African land settlement, the Empire, Tariff Reform and Defence.
He served on the Port of London Committee and supported Old Age
Pensions. He was preparing to pay a first visit in September to Canada, upon which, more than any other Dominion, Imperial integration depended.
With Steel-Maitland he travelled all the way to the Pacific with short stops
for sightseeing, visits to further Ready cousins and Canadian friends. He
made his first speech at Vancouver, followed on his return by others at
Winnipeg, Toronto (his most elaborate) and Montreal. He stayed with
his friend since the '80s Lord Grey, a popular Governor-General and
shrewd in his judgements of Canadian opinion. By chance he met a
fellow-Imperialist Lord Northcliffe, who wrote that except for Milner
Canada had hardly seen an English public man of position. His speeches
and informal talks needed tact, since Laurier's Liberal Government was
in power and Canadians resented both anything looking like stronger
rule from Britain and suggestions by some English papers that they lacked
Imperial feeling. He emphasized the aims of equality of the Empire's self-
governing states, and co-operation on practical problems before the

creation of more formal ties. Lord Grey wrote of his tour as 'a great success' which had sown Imperial seeds in every city he visited, and informed Canadians about Britain's true contribution to South Africa.[16]

By mid-November he was back in England talking of Canada to Chamberlain at Highbury. He found him 'physically very broken, but mentally all right and still keen.' With staunch help from his wife and Austen he still exerted much influence from his sick room on the Tariff Reformers. Milner joined a fourth City board; opposed as a tactical error the Lords' rejection of a Licensing Bill, and began with others the detailed preparation of a Tariff.

His South African letters showed his Kindergarten's leading part in the difficult work of steering the four States into union. Curtis as chief propagandist travelled widely, founding 'Closer Union Societies', and established, with funds from Abe Bailey and Philip Kerr as its editor, a monthly journal, *The State*, to promote the same object. At a national Convention which began this October Brand and Duncan, as Smuts fully acknowledged, did conspicuous work for the Transvaal delegation. By May a draft Constitution, owing much to the Selborne Memorandum, but aiming at union not federation, had been signed. Brand, Dawson and others wrote to Milner with optimistic hopes of a future South Africa, part British and part Dutch, realizing the great material benefit in belonging to the Empire. Milner's distrust of the Boers had not altered, though he conceded that 'the [Union] Constitution isn't so bad.' Any aim of extending the African or Coloured franchise had, needless to say, been dismissed by the Convention. When the South Africa Bill passed the Commons in August 1909, Asquith called the problem of adapting free institutions in a white–black society 'a modern one which remains unsolved.'[17]

Early this year Milner went again to Egypt on business, with a week's holiday on his return in Perugia with Mrs. Gaskell. Home in April he was dining alone on the 29th at Brooks's when members came in full of Lloyd George's long Budget speech with its startling proposals. This complex measure aimed both to furnish the means for social reform despite big naval demands, and to force on the issue of Lords' obstruction. Both Churchill and Lloyd George, the former's son writes, 'positively relished the prospect of a fight'; though neither expected the resistance which they met. Among many items the innovation of Super-Tax and Land Value duties caused most excitement. Some saw the Socialist threat coming true; the Tariff Reformers saw removal of the revenue motive from their plan and Northcliffe brought his powerful hostile influence into play. In a few days Milner attacked from a platform at Bristol, alleging as an expert that the Budget would 'eat up capital' well beyond the limit of profit to the Revenue. An uncompromising stand by Unionists in the Commons prolonged the debate till November, and allowed Lloyd George to make nation-wide speeches with the wealth of the dukes, including Milner's friend Bendor, among his main targets.

In May Milner began work, due to last four years, on the London University Commission. At a working week-end with Lord Roberts at Ascot he met General Henry Wilson, Commandant of the Staff College, with whom later he had much to do. He sometimes attended large parties with a strong political flavour at Curzon's country home, Hackwood, and at Taplow Court. He was now writing of feeling 'very hard driven' and doubting his ability to keep up the pace. One wonders again at the will-power which drove him to undertake so many duties and so many engagements. Moral fervour, the importance attached to his advice by so many people, and his sociable inclinations all played their part. His inveterate habit of over-taxing himself sometimes led to failures of judgement.

With Dawson, who had come from South Africa, and Amery, he did what he could, by a speech, attending receptions and private meetings, to influence the Empire Press Conference held in June. When in Canada, as earlier in Africa, he was shocked at the inadequacy of the news imported from home. A year earlier Northcliffe had become Chief Proprietor of *The Times* and suggested to Amery that he might succeed Buckle as editor. Since he wanted to enter politics Amery turned down the offer, but he obtained Northcliffe's further interest in promoting Milner's ideas.

Of greater significance was the return from South Africa, suitably begun by Curtis in July, of Selborne and most of the Kindergarten. Of the best-known members only Duncan and Feetham, both lawyers and the former ultimately to become Governor-General, had decided to stay in the country. Discussions began with Milner over 'Curtis's scheme', which led to a full-scale conference in September at Lord Anglesey's home Plas Newydd. Though Milner continued for a time to use the term Kindergarten, the word 'brotherhood' perhaps better describes the group, now larger and based on London. Those who joined without having previously served under Milner included F. S. Oliver, the apostle of federalism, Lord Lovat, with special interest in overseas settlement, and later Waldorf Astor. What Curtis proposed was to use the methods that had proved so successful in Africa, to form in every Dominion groups like their own of men dedicated to unifying the Empire.

Milner was looked on by the group as their master. He presided regularly at their Moots, and did more than anyone else to procure and supervise their funds. But as Kerr wrote to Curtis, who had gone to Canada, it was harder in London than in Johannesburg to get members to do 'regular mooting work'. Brand, for example, was perpetually busy as a City banker and Oliver as director of the drapers Debenham and Freebody; and

> ... of course Lord Milner is far worse than anybody else. You generally have to wait a week to get even an hour's appointment with him.

For this reason and because of his own special gifts Curtis soon again became a main force. Philip Kerr, the first editor of their quarterly *The Round Table* which appeared in 1910, in part financed by the Rhodes Trust, was again his chief colleague.

Curtis's methods and views began, however, to take on some differences from Milner's approach. The former were a complex, long-term mixture of selecting sympathizers and study. By travel he, Kerr and others formed groups in each Dominion of small numbers of people of local influence who favoured the Empire's 'organic union'; the equality of status of these with the London-based group, and the confidential nature of their studies, were stressed. The fruits of these studies would be collated by Curtis in another 'Egg'. He would then send this to all groups for comment and redraft the replies into what he called 'omelettes', or a set of agreed conclusions which would one day be published and could, in his words, '. . . be used by those that adopt them as a guide in practical political affairs'. This scheme was almost a global tutorial system for a small number of hand-picked, enlightened students linked together by correspondence. It is not surprising that in many Dominion centres, for example Toronto, most members were academics; and that before long Curtis himself was Beit Lecturer in Colonial History at Oxford.

In the years before 1914 no version of Curtis's 'Egg' got accepted, though his efforts achieved much effective Empire propaganda. *The Round Table*, to which Dominion groups contributed regularly, was undoubtedly a success and still survives. The Kindergarten members were now often called 'Round Tablers' and were active in recruiting younger members. But Milner, Selborne and others of the older members were less optimistic than Curtis over early achievement of any formal Imperial Union.

Some, notably Amery, were more concerned with Tariff Reform and others began to lose interest, while Curtis began to emphasize more the Dominions' ignorance of foreign affairs and lack of participation in naval defence. A special restraining force on him, according to a later editor of *The Round Table*, was exerted by Bob Brand, 'perhaps the best brain in the group'.

In September Milner was again at Highbury talking politics with Joseph and Austen Chamberlain and especially the tactics the Lords should adopt when the People's Budget reached them. The Bill was still in course of its passage (which took over 70 Parliamentary days) through the Commons, with Churchill conspicuous in attacking the peers. The Unionists were divided over whether the Lords should take the strong step of rejecting the Bill, and Balfour also went to consult the Highbury sage. Lansdowne's biographer claims that by early October both leaders were convinced that compromise was impossible; but Sir Almeric Fitzroy records finding Lansdowne much later full of 'grave misgivings' over a policy of rejection forced on him by the Tariff Reformers and the Unionist Press. The fighting policy was an exercise of effective leadership by the elder Chamberlain, convinced that his party should force an election which would end in victory for Imperialism.

Milner agreed and prepared for the first of his three main bouts of political campaigning in these years. In each case the issue seemed to him and others a constitutional one, on a plane on which national interests transcended the 'game' of party politics. This Finance Bill, as he saw it, was intended by the Radicals to reduce the authority of the Lords over all legislation without any consultation with the people. Though disliking the whole party system, he had, somewhat ironically, to use the Liberal Unionist machine. In October he spoke on Tariff Reform to Liberal Unionist meetings at Ealing, Bradford and Chesterfield. By November 9 the Bill had passed the Commons and he attended a party meeting at Lansdowne House to discuss future action.

The great debate in the Lords on Lansdowne's motion for rejection began on the 22nd and lasted six nights. Speaking two days later Milner called the 1894 Death Duty Budget 'a trivial affair' compared with this one. He claimed that the House had 'expressly reserved the right' to reject a Finance Bill which seemed to him and others less about finance than the groundwork for a social revolution. Dashing up to Glasgow on the 26th, he worked hard on the journey on the speech which contained the most-quoted sentence of his career,

If we believe a thing to be bad, and if we have a right to prevent it, it is our duty to try to prevent it and to damn the consequences. All we claim to do is to refer the question to the nation.

A week-end at Steel-Maitland's home near Stirling was followed by another speech to a big audience there and a return on the 30th to London. Hastening to the Lords he found it 'full to bursting – a wonderful sight' and could not get a seat. Just before midnight Lansdowne's motion was carried by 350 votes to 75. In less than two days Asquith carried a resolution in the Commons to the effect that this action was a breach of the Constitution, and a January general election was inevitable.[18]

This was the first such election in which peers could campaign, and party officials visited Duke Street to arrange with him for a speaking tour. In mid-December he spent two nights at Eaton Hall with Bendor, which included playing bridge with King Edward and Mrs. Keppel. He made speeches at Huddersfield, Stockport and before Christmas to a rowdy audience at Cardiff. When visiting a church near Cardiff he hurt his foot. Returning to Sturry with a swollen knee, his doctor put his leg in splints which he had to endure for a month.

In the New Year he hired a car to make a short speaking tour in the Midlands. He contrived to keep up with his City and other affairs, including long talks in his rooms and at the Rhodes Trust with a Kindergarten committee. When polling began and lasted two weeks he closely analysed the results. As January ended these showed the optimism of the Tariff Reformers much misplaced. Instead of the majority of 100 some had predicted a year earlier, the Unionist party was now in a minority of 124. Their total of 273 almost equalled the number of Liberals, so the Government now depended on the votes of some 82 Irish Nationalists and 40 Labour. Among Milner's friends Amery suffered defeat. Milner spent a week-end with Lady Edward at Great Wigsell and a few nights at Sturry. Back in London he had talks with Lansdowne, Austen Chamberlain and others before travelling to Cairo on business.

The years which followed were years of much confusion in politics, as well as industrial unrest and suffragette troubles. Two constitutional issues, the Lords' veto and Irish Home Rule, were intertwined and surpassed all others. Milner got back to London on 1 April; before the end of the month the Budget had passed the Commons with the help of the Irish and was let through the Lords without a division. Asquith had also introduced the Parliament Bill, which made no attempt to reform the Lords but abolished its veto of a Bill which had passed through the Commons in three consecutive sessions in a minimum period of two years. The sudden death of King Edward on May 6 then suspended party strife.

Milner came up from Sturry to attend the Privy Council proclaiming King George V; later he marched with the Lords to the lying-in-State and motored to Windsor for the 'splendid ceremony' of King Edward's funeral.

The differences dividing the parties were so deep that, on the initiative of the new King, a Constitutional Conference of four leaders of each major party began private sittings in June which lasted to early November. On 31 May the Union of South Africa came into being, with Lord Gladstone (the former Prime Minister's youngest son) as its first Governor-General. Milner's fight with Lord Lovat and others to help British settlers had only succeeded in placing them for 5 years under a Government Land Board which lacked power to add to their number. So in June he attended a dinner to mark the demise of the Imperial South African Association, proposing the health of Bendor, the largest private investor in British land settlement. Another South African matter which continued to occupy his time was his effort to help many British, who had served him or were strangers, 'retrenched' by the Dutch and thus looking for jobs. Many letters to him support the contention of a Cape politician that responsible government had removed all sense of security from these British officials. In private he was bitter over Dutch 'unmitigated radicalism and jobbery'.[19]

Before the election Milner, as ever pursuing his special causes, wrote to Lord Roberts that national defence was 'more important than any of the things we're fighting about', and Liberal neglect of the question was his main reason for wanting them out. A supporter over this, Lord Newton, wrote that 'excellent speeches by Curzon and Milner' and the voting result in the Lords caused much interest and showed that compulsory training was not just a crank's dream.[20] Milner was less sanguine since most politicians and senior soldiers disliked the idea; but helped by Amery and General Wilson he worked hard to give Roberts advice and ammunition for speeches and pamphlets. An uphill battle was not made easier by divisions, this year and later, in the National Service League which he was often called upon to resolve.

This summer and autumn, more withdrawn from politics, he spent much time at Sturry where his architect Blomfield was still busy and was given more advice by Dunstan, the head of Wye College. His help to friends in trouble included looking for work for Walrond and trying to set right the business troubles of Robert L. Chapin, the husband of his American admirer Adèle. He gave Curzon, an active Chancellor of Oxford, advice on University reform and joined his committee arranging Balliol portraits of Asquith and Lord Loreburn. The Rhodes Trust involved him in much correspondence with absent Trustees. George Parkin had remained 'Organizing Secretary' of the Scholars and had been joined later, when the first Scholars got there, by Francis Wylie as the first resident 'Oxford Secretary'. Rhodes had left discretion to his Trustees over spending the residue of his estate after his duty-free gift to Oriel, provision for Scholarships and some smaller matters. This balance proved smaller than expected, and was mainly invested in De Beers which had been declining in value. With some difficulties over reinvestment the Trustees could only offer small sums to a portion of what Milner called to Feetham 'competing claims which are numerous and strong.'[21]

Not surprisingly Milner suffered in September from writer's cramp. He took 'the nearest approach to a holiday I have had this year' of three weeks divided between Pau with Loulie Dawkins and her sister, Paris, and gardening at Sturry. Back at work he was much engaged visiting branches of his Joint Stock Bank scattered over the whole London area. His social life embraced Wingate and Garstin from Egypt, Canadian friends, a large Moot at Selborne's country house, the annual dinner of Rhodes Scholars at Oxford and Leo Amery's wedding. A more unusual event was his meeting Cecile, discussed earlier in this story, now married and living in Seattle. He took her to tea, had a good talk and was to see her again.[22] On 10 November he was dining with Amery and others when the failure of the Constitutional Conference was announced. All the talk was at once of another election, and Crewe told the Lords that dissolution was fixed for the 28th. By 1 December another election was in progress.

It became known that during the Conference Lloyd George had negotiated for a Coalition which (as a minor item) would inaugurate compulsory military training of the type urged by Roberts and Milner. More important was the failure to reach any compromise over the Lords' veto on Home Rule. The election, Lord Newton writes, gave 'no clear indication that the average voter was much interested in the fight between Lords and Commons.' Disunion was marked in the Unionist ranks; many chose to emphasize opposition to Home Rule, while strong Tariff Reformers like the Chamberlains and Milner were aghast at Balfour's tactic of pledging a referendum before introducing Protection. Milner spoke for Amery at his 'bear-garden', Bow and Bromley (which he lost to George Lansbury) and also at Wilton, Bodmin and Newport Pagnell. The results were remarkably like those of January with Liberals and Unionists each winning 272 votes, the Irish 84 and Labour 42. Asquith announced in the campaign that once the Lords question had been settled he would introduce a Home Rule Bill.

Staying with Roberts at Ascot in January 1911, Milner described a discussion with Amery, the foremost of those who urged him to take a more forward political role. He gave reasons why

> I feel less inclined than ever to take a leading part in the game of party politics and why I think the present an opportune moment to commence a gradual but definitive withdrawal from that arena.

One reason was bad health, and another that he was soon to leave for a stay of six weeks in Cairo on business. In his absence Asquith again introduced the Parliament Bill, in the form described earlier in the Commons. Coming home in mid-March Milner concentrated on his business and personal interests, adding a directorship of the Rio Tinto Company to the former. Cecile reappeared and they met several times before he saw her off to her home in Seattle. He attended the Lords to speak in support of a motion by Roberts on the Army, and then to support Kitchener's introduction there as a Viscount. He called Lansdowne's introducing a Bill to change the Lords' character, as a counter to Asquith's Bill in the Commons, 'a chilly proceeding'. Being host at a dinner at Brooks's to twelve Moot members, and a guest at a large Astor party, were more warming. Late in May he dined with Asquith to meet the delegates to the Imperial Conference. His chances to mix with the delegates were small, since in a few days he was operated on for long-standing nose and throat trouble. He then went abroad to convalesce until early July.

Hiring a 'courier-valet' he went to Bad Ems, Goschen's favourite resort, where he took the cure and was host to his cousin Richard Milner. Going south he had a day full of memories at Tübingen with a visit to his parents' grave, a climb to the Castle with its splendid view of the Swabian Alps and his usual visit to Heckingen to see Emma. At his destination in Switzerland near St. Gallen he found heaps of letters awaiting him. His main occupations were 'highland walks', sometimes up to the snow line, and reading. He noted 22 June as Coronation Day in London.

Back at Sturry in mid-July he found intense heat and drought and 'political excitement at its height'. The Lords' amendments to the Parliament Bill were rejected by Asquith with notice to Balfour that, if necessary, he could count on the King's use of his prerogative for large-scale creation of peers. The two Tory leaders showed indecision in the face of Die-Hard revolts in both Houses, but eventually asked the Peers to vote for the Bill or abstain. Milner noted:

> Once more and most reluctantly, I have been dragged back for the moment into politics.

He spoke shortly at the Die-Hards' Halsbury banquet,

> . . . a remarkable gathering . . . to incite as many as possible of the peers to vote against a surrender . . . [though by 1 August] it seems doubtful whether the Die-hard movement will not be a fizzle.

On the famous last night's debate on 10 August the heat was such that Midleton saw the usually immaculate collar of Curzon, who had changed from a 'Ditcher' to a 'Hedger', dissolve in a shapeless mass. Uncertainty of the outcome made excitement intense. About midnight the Bill was carried by 131 to 114. Largely due to Curzon's efforts 30 Unionist lay Peers supported the Government, while Lansdowne and the majority abstained. The ill-feeling which followed, Newton writes, 'gravely impaired the solidity and morale of the party.'

Milner spent most of the rest of August at Sturry. Husbandry, week-end guests, visits to Lady Edward and friends within range filled his days. Amery had now succeeded through Chamberlain's influence in entering Parliament as Liberal Unionist for South Birmingham, a seat he held for the next thirty four years. This removed him still further from the Moot's somewhat academic inner circle; he had taken active part in forming the Empire Parliamentary Association and in fighting the Parliament Bill in the Commons. This September, with one or two others, he got Milner's views on a half sheet of paper of what Die-Hard policies should now be. This, slightly condensed, read as follows:

> (1) Tariff Reform, (2) Imperial Unity, (3) Defence (if possible National Service), (4) Social Uplifting (especially Agricultural Improvement). Milner saw these four as Imperial issues and matters of principle. Two topics of 'machinery' followed – (5) A Sound Constitution with a fully elective Upper House which might eliminate 'ordinary party motives', (6) an ultimate Federal United Kingdom.[23]

A small 'Halsbury Club' was formed in October, not hostile to the Party leaders or organization but aiming to take 'a more vigorous fighting line'. Milner, apart from this club, stayed largely outside political matters. Austen Chamberlain, also a member, wrote to his father ('the only man who has any real influence with Milner') regretting the leaders had not consulted Milner more, but admitting he held 'ostentatiously aloof' and due to his many engagements was 'a very difficult man to get hold of'. In most Unionist circles criticism of Balfour's leadership had been growing, though the Halsbury Club denied that to oust him was one of their aims.

Milner was surprised to learn of his resignation on 8 November. The two obvious successors, Austen Chamberlain and Walter Long, both withdrew in the interests of party unity, and Bonar Law was elected. Like the elder Chamberlain he was a middle-class business man who by vigour in Parliament had made his way to the top in a still largely aristocratic political world. Milner wrote of him as a hard-headed man who would make a good leader. Most important for the years just ahead was that his Scotch-Ulster origins made him feel, in Lord Blake's words, 'more strongly about the Ulster Question than anything else in politics at this time.'[24] In April 1912 Asquith introduced the Third Home Rule Bill.

Some two months before, Milner paid his first visit to the Rio Tinto copper mines in a large valley south of Seville.[25] As usual on his business travels he got V.I.P. treatment. Moving south, he stayed with the Governor of Gibraltar and then sailed to Cairo. Kitchener, now Agent-General, offered him rooms at the Agency but he favoured a suite at the Semiramis Hotel. He combined business, political talk, a close eye on *The Times*, walks and a large correspondence. Back in England in April, his life resumed its usual pattern though with less attendance at the Lords. He renewed an interest of young days by agreeing to be chairman of Toynbee Hall Council which he remained for the rest of his life. To Curzon's annoyance he declined the same office on the Finance Committee of the Oxford University Endowment Fund. Before May was out he wrote 'the London rush is beginning to tell on me' and his throat doctor advised more treatment at Ems. Going there for two weeks, he was visited by another cousin, Karl Milner, a lawyer at Coblenz, and looked up relations at Bonn.

In mid-summer he was much engaged with the Kindergarten, now often called (as well as its meetings) the Moot; he was not much concerned with *The Round Table* apart from presiding over its Finance Committee. With Lionel Curtis much in evidence, he met Borden, now Canadian Prime Minister, and other Canadian Ministers in London. Two further examples of his preference for exercising influence in the wings deserve mention. He employed Charles Boyd, once a secretary to Rhodes and more recently on the Rhodes Trust staff, in what proved the long task of selecting and editing his speeches since the famous farewell London banquet of 1897 for publication. And after talking to Lansdowne he undertook to compile a detailed report on Unionist Land Policy. His interest in Land Policy owed something to his affection for Sturry and all the advice he had sought in developing his own estate. And his formal links with the Party had been strengthened by the recent appointment of his friend Steel-Maitland, aged about 35, as its Chairman. On the different level of his need for the company of friends he offered his young married cousin Oliver Ready, on leave from his job in the Chinese Customs, a house on his estate at low rent as a permanent home, and Oliver fell in with the plan.

A poor August, with rain ruining the cut corn, was part holiday and part work. He toured bank branches all over Yorkshire for a plan of amalgamation his London bank was proposing. For years a keen amateur student at Kew, he slept there and spent a whole day in the Gardens before working next day at Duke Street and returning to Sturry. At the end of the month his installation as Master of the Anglo-Colonial Masonic Lodge involved a long ceremony, a still longer dinner and innumerable speeches. He had little rest until he sailed on September 13 for a second, shorter, visit to Canada, where Borden's success now made the prospect of Empire integration more promising.

Landing in New Brunswick, he had no time to visit Prince Edward Island, where his grandfather had been Governor. Met by old friends, he visited Halifax, St. John, Fredericton and elsewhere, being shown the sights and speaking to Canadian Clubs and students. In a week at Montreal he had many talks, forecast 'a mischievous party fight' on the Navy Question but made no speech. Ten days at Toronto were even more crowded, meeting old friends and Toronto magnates and going to parties. His only speech appears to have been a private one to 70 Round Table young men at the University. He sat on the right of the Governor-General, the Duke of Connaught, at a huge assembly of the Canadian Club. Then, his guest at Ottawa for two nights, he met many Ministers of both parties. He left to pay his first – to prove his only – visit to the United States.

His hosts for a week-end were the Chapins, in the country not far from Albany, New York State. Chapin's business projects, mentioned before, still miscarried and were connected, at least in part, with Rhodes Trust investments.[26] As so often Milner, spared neither effort nor time to help friends in trouble. After one night in New York he sailed home, knowing no one on board, reading much on the Land Question and arriving at Plymouth on 4 November.

In his absence the great ceremony had occurred of the signing at Belfast, under Carson and Lord Londonderry, of the Ulster Covenant. Months before, plans for forming an Ulster Provisional Government if a Home Rule Bill was passed had begun, and a Volunteer Force had been created. In July, Bonar Law made his famous 'Blenheim Pledge' to support

Ulster's resistance wherever it led him. Milner did not yet believe that the Union was in serious danger, though he felt indignant with Asquith for clinging to office with Nationalist votes. Already many Unionists had come to criticize Asquith and some to denigrate him as 'Squiff'. Amery called him:

> . . . temperamentally reluctant to face unpleasant decisions, and inclined to postpone if he could not finally evade them.[27]

Morley, Asquith's colleague, confirmed to Sir Almeric Fitzroy all he had heard of Asquith's shirking a difficulty in the confidence that he could find some solution if a situation got out of hand.

If the Liberals had lost strength as 1913 began, the Unionists had become one party in form (since the Liberal Unionists had wound up their organization), but not in much else. Tariff Reformers in the Party faced Free Traders, with a mass of unsettled opinion between them. A party meeting in January confirmed the Free Fooders' position, a surrender Austen Chamberlain called the 'greatest disappointment' of his public life which proved a severe set-back to Imperial Preference. There were now many, inside and outside the Party, who regarded rejection of the 1909 Budget as a major tactical error and cause of the Party's decline.

Milner wrote in a blank page of his diary a sentence he had found in *The Times* about a Canadian, presumably because he knew it mirrored himself:

> . . . he has perhaps the cross-bench mind, which finds servitude in allegiance to party and satisfaction in devotion to definite objects.

His influence with *The Times* had been strengthened by Northcliffe's appointment of Geoffrey Dawson as editor. He completed his Land Report and sailed in January for another month in Cairo. During intervals he worked hard there on the introduction to the collection he and Boyd had made of his speeches, published later this year as *The Nation and the Empire*. One friend whom he always saw in Cairo was Lord Edward Cecil, sometimes visited by his wife. He had until lately, besides a failed marriage, had unhappy years under Eldon Gorst as Under-Secretary of Finance. But Kitchener, Gorst's successor, had promoted him to Milner's former and influential job of Financial Adviser.

At home again, Milner told Bertha Synge that politics were 'more hopeless than ever', though in spite of economic depression his business interests were in good order. Moot occasions continued to be frequent;

and he spoke at Oxford to a new Raleigh Club, formed for non-party discussion by dons and undergraduates of Imperial questions, sitting next to Vincent Massey, a Canadian of Balliol who later married George Parkin's daughter and rose to be Governor-General of Canada.

He attended with relief the last meeting of the London University Commission. At Sturry on a Saturday just after his 59th birthday he called this 'for once a pleasant and easy day'. A visit to the Readys at Yarmouth preceded days in Dublin with his old friend Sir Horace Plunkett to discuss not Home Rule but the agricultural co-operation Plunkett had done so much to promote. Milner's own Land proposals, emphasizing increase in the number of occupying owners, led to months of Party discussion.[28]

He was inducted as Senior Grand Warden at the Masons' Grand Lodge, and dined with his friend Claude Montefiore, the President, at the Anglo-Jewish Society. Raising money for various causes bulked large in his correspondence, and he owned that writing to raise £2,000 for Toynbee Hall was an 'awful grind'. In June he visited Düsseldorf, presumably for its links with his forbears, then went south to visit his stepmother in her lunatic asylum near Stuttgart and on to old Emma. Back at home he attended a ball to which the Portlands asked 'all the world and his wife' to meet George V and his Queen. On holiday in August at Sturry, mixed with working visits to London, heart trouble caused his comment,

I don't know if it is worse than it has been scores of times, at intervals, during my life for the last 30 years.

He took more of a holiday by hiring a car for a fortnight and visiting an assortment of friends in East Anglia and the Midlands, which included the Gells at Hopton Hall. Philip Gell was still a director of the British South Africa Company but through illness, absence from London or some other reason his meetings and correspondence with Milner had recently much declined.

By September the Home Rule Bill had twice passed the Commons and twice been rejected by the Lords so that, under the Parliament Act, it was bound to be carried in 1914. At the opening of the year Carson moved a resolution in the Commons to exclude Ulster which of course was anathema to John Redmond's Nationalists. Milner's friends, notably Oliver, had been offering varied solutions to Ireland's problems in public. The English parties began efforts at compromise including a famous *Times* letter of 11 September by Loreburn, the former Lord Chancellor, urging special treatment for Ulster. The Unionist leaders and some of the country's

eminent lawyers went so far as to propose that the King should dismiss
Asquith and force an appeal to the people. Asquith and Law negotiated
privately with no fruitful result; and in Dublin the Irish Volunteers were
formed. The officers of the Army, from Lord Roberts downward, were
overwhelmingly Unionist in sympathy and often Irish in origin.

As the crisis grew worse this autumn Milner was too occupied with
other matters, especially the threat of a serious strike at Rio Tinto and
disputes in National Service League councils, to pay great attention to
Ireland. Yet for him and a large number of Unionists, to a degree now
perhaps hard to imagine, Home Rule meant Ireland's eventual separation
and a fatal stab at the heart of an Empire still developing common
interests and aims. In letters to Scott Oliver, Milner stated his general
agreement with Oliver's remedy of 'Home Rule All Round'; but he
insisted that the Government, not the Unionists, had the duty to find a
solution. For himself, he was loath to contribute to a controversy to
which he was sure he 'could not help adding bitterness'.[29]

Before long, in common with many who really knew Ulster's strength,
and with pressure from Lord Roberts combined with deep distrust of
Asquith, the whole situation seemed to him to be one leading straight to
civil war. It was, he decided, essential that action in Britain to help Ulster
should be 'thought out beforehand'. He wrote confidentially to Carson on
9 December 1913,

> ... for all ordinary purposes I have done with politics. But the business
> we have been brought face to face with goes far deeper than ordinary
> party struggles. *I am completely in accord with you about Ulster.* ...

and wanted to know any way in which he could help.

He had entered the ring for his third and severest bout of these years.
After long talks with Carson and Law he ended the year in the gloomy
belief that the Government was playing with negotiations to save time,
and had 'got over their fright'. At the beginning of 1914 he was thinking
out plans and associating with the Union Defence League, a body formed
six years before by Walter Long, a former Chief Secretary for Ireland, to
sustain opposition to Home Rule. His thoughts were then diverted by
more troubles at Rio Tinto which compelled him to go again to Spain.
Reaching Madrid in deep snow he had negotiations with the Prime
Minister, whom he suspected of double-dealing, and an audience with
the King. After reaching the mines he was glad to find much good feeling
in response to some settlement, and once again in Madrid had a fairly
satisfactory visit from the Prime Minister.

Back in London talking to Unionist leaders his idea of action on Ulster's behalf crystallized into a 'United Kingdom pledge', to which Roberts among others was 'most sympathetic'. His object, modelled on his share years before in defeating Gladstone's First Home Rule Bill, was to mobilize sufficient domestic support to force Asquith to hold a General Election. He obtained the U.D.L.'s full backing and began to raise funds and get signatures for a public announcement. At one lunch, for example, he got the consent of Lords Lovat, Balfour of Burleigh, and Desborough and of Walter Long to sign a pledge. In a letter to Selborne he wrote that the pledge's whole object was to reveal those ('the stalwarts') who would do something now. Influential public support was the essential preliminary to obtaining the signature of

> . . . thousands of sober citizens resisting an Act of Parliament through belief it had no moral sanction . . . the crisis was different in kind from other political controversies.[30]

By late February he was writing,

> . . . this Ulster Defence Movement takes up the whole of my time and I had none to spare to begin with.

On 3 March the pledge, now called a 'Declaration', appeared in the Press signed by twenty well-known persons. A preamble forecast 'civil turmoil without parallel in living memory' if the Government passed Home Rule without consulting the people. The Declaration, its name changed again to 'Covenant', invited all citizens to attest that such action would violate the Constitution, and that if it was taken they would hold themselves justified in

> . . . taking or supporting any action that may be effective to prevent it being put into operation, and more particularly to prevent the armed forces of the Crown being used to deprive the people of Ulster of their rights as citizens of the United Kingdom.

Six days later Asquith, moving the Bill's second reading, stated the limit of the Government's concessions; briefly put, any Ulster county might exclude itself from the Dublin Parliament for six years by majority vote. Carson dismissed with contempt this time-limit idea, and the plan weakened Redmond's position. For a year or two past certain Die-Hards, with Lord Willoughby de Broke the foremost, had considered the reckless procedure of the Lords' amending or rejecting the Army Annual Bill due to pass by 30 April. Amendment would deprive the Government of use of the Army in Ulster until after a general election; rejection would suspend all military discipline. The grip which the Ulster issue exerted and the loss for a time of the leading Unionists' balance is shown by Law's conviction in January, which he got Lansdowne, Curzon and Balfour to share, that amending this Act was the only real weapon left to the Party. A few days after Asquith's proposal Churchill, First Lord of the Admiralty, by making a bellicose speech at Bradford and beginning the transfer of warships to the west coast of Scotland, strengthened the view that military coercion of Ulster was imminent.

There is plenty of evidence that, whatever the politicians might do in Parliament, senior officers both in Ireland and Aldershot were very anxious. On 19 March King George stressed to Asquith the awful predicament in which the Crown would be placed by civil war. On the next day Milner described Roberts as 'in greatest distress at the menace of an approaching collision with Ulster.' That evening he was dining at a party when Law was handed a telegram reporting that General Hubert Gough and all officers of the Cavalry Brigade at the Curragh had resigned rather than be sent against Ulster. What is known to history as the 'Curragh Incident' had occurred. The next day, a Saturday, much excitement prevailed, though few people in London knew any details. Unionist leaders, however, had in General Sir Henry Wilson, who was Anglo-Irish and Director of Military Operations at the War Office, a soldier whose loyalties in his view lay with them. Sir Charles Hunter, a former General and now a Unionist M.P., called as his envoy to report to Milner that the War Office was 'in revolt' and backing the Curragh objectors. Milner rushed to see Garvin in Hampstead to ensure that *The Observer* had the story the next day; Dawson came to assure him that *The Times* would take a strong line.

The Incident, which lasted for ten days, is so often described that no summary is necessary here.[31] It ended with General Gough, a Southern Irishman by adoption, obtaining from the C.I.G.S., Sir John French, effectual endorsement of his own and his officers' views (with their resignations withdrawn), and Seely's replacement at the War Office by Asquith himself. Historians, like contemporaries, still differ about whether the Government's intention was only, as it claimed, to send troops to Ulster to guard depots. It could not in any case be concealed that, as F. S. L. Lyons writes, Asquith 'had very nearly had a mutiny on his hands' and could no longer count on the loyalty of the Army if he moved to coerce Ulster.[32]

If Asquith's official biographer could call General Wilson 'a restless and fiery spirit', Milner, when roused by an issue which appeared to him in large degree moral, was hardly less so. With the Home Rule Bill in the Commons and no solution in sight he held a meeting of the British Covenant's General Council in April with Long, Roberts and Carson to get this organization started. A few days later he and Balfour spoke in Hyde Park to very large crowds in the first of a series of protest meetings. The Unionists in the Commons kept up bitter attacks on the Government; and, as in the '80s, social intercourse between Liberals and Unionists became very strained. On the night of 24 April successful gun-running at Larne and elsewhere made the Ulster Volunteers into an armed force, though inevitably swelling recruitment to the Irish (or Nationalist) Volunteers; it also led Asquith to try to wring larger concessions from Redmond. Milner addressed another big meeting with Balfour, this time in Coventry, finding the audience quiet and attentive. Amery, giving fully of his energies and advice, rushed over to Ulster to get fresh news from Captain James Craig, Carson's lieutenant.

Reducing his work in the City and elsewhere, Milner gave much time to the Covenant organization, the appointment of county agents, and writing and speaking to urge National Service supporters and others to sign the pledge. More secret talks between Asquith, Law and Carson proved unfruitful, with Law describing his party as 'growing averse to any kind of settlement'. A separate Amending Bill, aimed to give six Ulster counties temporary exclusion and receive Royal Assent on the same day as the main Bill, failed to satisfy Carson. Amery quickly drafted a detailed plan for Ulster to set up a skeleton Provisional Government; Milner sent this to Carson for his views.[33] On 22 May, after dining with Anson the Warden of All Souls, he and J. A. R. Marriott, the historian, spoke at Oxford Town Hall. His keynote was that Unionists 'must not leave the firm ground of principle'; it was high time the Government stopped 'Parliamentary manoeuvring' and sought the people's opinion on the whole issue. His experience had convinced him this was adverse, a contrast to the view of another Oxford supporter, the constitutional lawyer A. V. Dicey, expressed in *The Times* ten days earlier, that Englishmen were 'wearied out with the subject of Home Rule.'[34]

Was this another lost cause which Milner, with the fervour with which the Imperial cause gripped him, had espoused? With the hindsight of Britain's creation of an Ulster Government six years later one could give a negative answer. Ulster's tragic condition over sixty years later makes one more doubtful. He spent Whit Sunday at Hatfield, where the King discussed the crisis with him at length. Early in June he and Selborne addressed a big protest meeting at Hull and then a larger one, with five platforms, at Leeds. Among many efforts, unofficial and otherwise, to find a solution F. S. Oliver had been tireless in publicly advocating his federal plan; and four other Moot members, Brand, Grigg, Curtis and Hichens also produced a well-thought-out scheme of 'Home Rule All Round'. Churchill invited Curtis to join him on the Admiralty yacht *Enchantress* to discuss this; and Law, Carson and Austen Chamberlain were impressed by it. But Asquith, it seems, swayed by Redmond's losing support in Ireland, was unable to decide on its merits.[35]

Milner was invited by Lansdowne to join a small group of leaders, called the Shadow Cabinet, to discuss urgently the kind of Amending Bill the Party could accept. When Lord Crewe introduced the Government's version on 23 June this proved to be almost identical with the restricted exclusion proposals of March. The Lords then amended this to exclude all Ulster; and Morley confided to Fitzroy that the King's chief anxiety had always been Asquith's 'reluctance to grasp the nettle.' He had put off negotiations on the limits and timing of Ulster's exclusion, which were now, from the Government's standpoint, an urgent necessity. He began these with intermediaries in what Roy Jenkins calls 'an almost over-complicated net.'[36] By mid-July he thought he had made enough progress to secure the King's approval for a conference of eight party leaders, including Redmond, Carson and their chief lieutenants, to be held at Buckingham Palace on the 21st.

Milner was no solitary alarmist in looking on Home Rule as equivalent to secession, and telling the Constitutional Club that the Government's failure to concede more to Ulster could end by

. . . destroying any chance of averting bloodshed and a collision between the forces of the Crown and the people of Ulster which the Empire would never get over.

He continued, in a phrase which proved prophetic, that civil war in twentieth-century Ireland would be 'abominable and unprecedented.'[37]

Earlier this month Joseph Chamberlain died in his 78th year. Milner called him to his wife 'an incomparable chief' and paid a short tribute to him in the Lords.

After three days the Buckingham Palace Conference had failed, since agreement about Ulster's two southern counties with their Catholic majorities proved impossible. Asquith at once sent General C. N. Macready to Belfast; no troops were to move, but the Government would decide on their action if and when a Provisional Ulster Government was formed.[38] Two days later the Irish Volunteers conducted a gun-running at Howth outside Dublin, when the killing and wounding of civilians by soldiers caused deep indignation. Next day, 27 July, Milner first noted the Austria–Serbia conflict which he saw threatened general war in Europe. J. A. Spender, a well-informed observer, says the British mind had been so absorbed by domestic affairs, especially Ireland, that for two years foreign affairs had received less attention than at any time since 1906; and the prospect of war with Germany, 'always before us' up to 1911, had latterly seemed to recede.[39] On the 28th Law and Carson suggested to Asquith that the Lords' Second Reading of the Amending Bill should be postponed. The Government decided to enact the Home Rule Bill as it stood, but to suspend its operation until a new Amending Bill could be passed.

Milner experienced black days in the City, and rapidly moving events in Europe caused divisions in the Cabinet. Belgium's refusal on 3 August to allow passage to Germany's armies brought Law's pledge in the Commons of Unionist support if the British Government entered the war. Unexpectedly and bravely Redmond followed his lead. Though the fact was unknown to the public, the Army Council decided to send four infantry divisions of the six available and their one cavalry division to France. In the evening of next day, the 4th, Milner with Wingate and Lovat, urged Kitchener to see Asquith in the hope that he would be offered and accept the Secretaryship of War. Before midnight Britain had entered the conflict.

Chapter 11

War Service

(August 1914 – December 1916)

Business Partly as Usual – Coalition, Food Production,
Conscription – Attack on Squiff's Government, Imperial
Meetings, Coal Supplies

> For all we have and are,
> For all our children's fate,
> Stand up and take the war.
> The Hun is at the gate!

Kipling's challenge, though appearing in the Press on 2 September, struck hardly a chord in Britain. All would be over, the average citizen thought, in a few months and he would be little affected. The view, with which Kipling continued, that 'our world has passed away' struck him, if he noticed it, as moonshine.

Milner and his friends, having given the reluctant Kitchener a push towards office, gave another one to ensure the immediate despatch overseas of the Expeditionary Force. A few days later Sturry was requisitioned by the West Kent Yeomanry. Milner, with officers in his house and horses in his barns, told Bertha Synge that beyond being in London and looking after his usual interests and his dependants he didn't foresee or desire 'any special part in this job', though he would be ready to look after 'anything which may seem to be being neglected.' Years later Lady Milner described him at this time as immensely depressed. Compared with German energy and preparation, the English, he said, 'had left everything to chance and we shall suffer fearfully.'

The slogan, attributed to Churchill, of 'Business as Usual' for those not in uniform or in Whitehall was bound to grow less attractive to Milner. For a time his business in the City, the Rhodes Trust, Moot meetings, Toynbee Hall and his other attachments were sufficient. But his impulse for action when he thought this essential, and for substituting order for chaos, inevitably grew as the gap between war needs and official neglect became wider. For example, when Parliament reassembled late in August he asked in the Lords about wheat supplies in view of a world shortage expected in 1915, and was given a reassuring response.

Sturry Court, near Canterbury

Lady Edward Cecil, and her two children, Helen and George

For him conscription (still called National Service in Britain) was the principal military need. With war, the National Service League quickly dropped propaganda and devoted itself to help with recruiting and the provision of field-glasses and saddles, supplying interpreters and answering inquiries. 'Bobs', its President, wrote to Milner that although 82 he would, if requested, take command of Home Forces to repel the invasion which he always thought likely.[1] A month later he was visiting 'his' Indian troops in France, caught pneumonia and died at St. Omer. His campaign of the previous ten years was soon to appear well directed. But he never offered self-justification or extended reproach to the scoffers.

Kitchener, though he forecast a long war and the probable need of three million men, enjoyed to what now seems excess the confidence of the public. Opposed to conscription and ignoring Haldane's Territorial Organization he set about raising 'new armies'. With most of his General Staff sent to France he was smothered in War Office detail. His secretiveness, remarked on for years by Milner and others, proved a serious drawback. The Cabinet was unable to get clear-cut military views; and Milner complained that his statements in the Lords gave no information. As Churchill had cause to remember, he disliked the Press, whose correspondents were banned from France till 1915. The strict censorship which prevailed strained morale, and caused rumours to flourish.[2]

It was only on 18 August that the B.E.F.'s safe arrival in France was announced. Keenly interested in its movements, Milner had already one valuable private informant. Henry Wilson, in the new post of sub-C.G.S. in France, asked his wife to show Milner and some others his letters. These disclosed big German advances and by early September 'alarming news' of casualties, poor equipment and poor reinforcement. The disquiet caused to Milner had a personal as well as a patriotic basis. On 12 August Lady Edward had seen off her son George Cecil, just commissioned in the Grenadier Guards at the age of 18, from Victoria Station. A young brother officer wrote: 'the secrecy of our movements is extraordinary.' It later became known that George's battalion reached Mons, came under fire on the 23rd and joined the general retreat. On 8 September Lady Edward received a telegram that he was 'wounded and missing'.

Spending a week-end at Wigsell Milner wrote: 'the uncertainty about George hangs like a pall over everything here.' Lady Edward's distress, did they know it, was due to be shared for over four years in thousands of homes. Milner went to great lengths on his own, and employing others, talking to the wounded, visiting enemy prisoners and chasing a story that George was in hospital at Aachen. It was not till November that Lady Edward's hope was abandoned, with the identification of his body in a grave near Villers Cotterets not far from Soissons. He'd been shot in the head on 2 September in a long, almost sleepless, march to the rear when his whole battalion was wiped out.[3]

In spite of what he had told Bertha Synge, Milner was soon saying he was busy with '100 things, mostly not my job at all. We shall straighten out presently.' The truth is he both thrived on work, and was much sought after, especially as a chairman. The Red Cross, the Officers' Families Fund and Belgian Relief drew him into their councils. One major burden now off his back needs mention as a link with the past and the future. No agreement had been reached at the outbreak of war over Ulster's exclusion. After agreeing to Unionist demands that this should be added to the Home Rule Bill, Asquith gave way to Nationalist objections and the Bill was passed without any addition, though suspended in operation. Carson was active in mobilization and Kitchener soon agreed to the formation of an Ulster Division. But Kitchener's delay in agreeing to an Irish Brigade for the South gave offence.[4]

Leo Amery, never far from the centre of matters, described himself as 'a sort of extra secretary and assistant to General Rawlinson, Director of Recruiting at the War Office' (which was 'chaos'). Milner wrote to an overseas friend that people at home were

... tumbling over one another to join the Army, but the W.O. doesn't know what to do with them. What irony!

The early volunteers' spirit and what followed are ably expressed in *Disenchantment* by C. E. Montague, at Balliol not much later than Milner and a chief leader-writer of the *Manchester Guardian* when he joined up in 1914. While regular soldiers and weapons for training were lacking, Henry Wilson kept on writing for the 6th division to be sent out to France, and a 7th and 8th as quickly as these could be formed. The Germans, he added, were 'proving superb fighters' and had very good war organization. Ex-President Theodore Roosevelt added force to the pre-war National Service campaign by asserting in a letter from New York to Kipling that if Britain had possessed an effective army in proportion to her size 'Germany would not have entered upon the war.'[5]

Another useful informant of Milner's, William Lambton, his Military Secretary in South Africa and now serving the C.-in-C. Sir John French in this post, wrote that, finding the Germans had entrenched themselves in strong force, they had done so themselves. The Marne battle proved the last engagement on pre-war lines. Men in trenches with machine guns, the artillery barrage, gaining yards of ground at high cost, gas attack and the primitive tank were the shape of the future battles in France. Faith persisted in the pressure on Germany of Russia's huge hordes; Churchill tried in vain to rouse Belgian resistance by an expedition to Antwerp. The first battle of Ypres, during 10 October to 11 November, A. J. P. Taylor concludes,

> . . . marked the end of the old British army. The B.E.F. fought the Germans to a standstill, and itself out of existence.[6]

With deadlock apparently reached, Milner's attitude expressed to a friend is of interest. He was labelled by some a pessimist, though perhaps a truer description would be often a pessimist in the short term and an optimist in the long one, or, as Geoffrey Faber concluded, both realist and idealist. His feelings, he wrote, were those he had had in the South African War. In the worst days no one had been less downhearted than he. But he

> always refused to permit or encourage optimistic illusions . . . people's practice of shutting their eyes to unpleasant facts and exaggerating agreeable ones . . . is the only thing by which I am really frightened . . . it would now need great care and effort to prevent things altering for the worse.

He added that he did not say these things in public, but only when his words might have weight and to people whose judgement most counted.

In November Sturry was restored to him with its house in good order but its paddock a quagmire. Another of his South African staff, Fabian Ware, obtained, with his help, an important position with the Red Cross in France, and later directed the Imperial War Graves Commission. A link with a more remote past, his boyhood in London, was broken when Lizzie, the servant of Marianne Malcolm, supported by him as a landlady for years at Claverton Street and then his pensioner, died aged 96. A further break with the past was his leaving 47 Duke Street – the source of one half of his title. For six months he had been renovating 'at considerable expense' 17 Great College Street, an area then as now of politicians and lawyers a few minutes' walk from the Houses of Parliament. To Bertha Synge, to whom he always wrote frankly, he called this

> about as big as a bandbox and rather in the same style . . . an eminently suitable place for an old gentleman, who was born a century and a half too late, to end his days in.[7]

Next door to Alfred Lyttelton's widow's home the house, tall and narrow, had an air of austerity and economy like that of Sturry Court, and perhaps of Milner himself. Though his work in the City brought him what then was considered a good income, his tastes excluded both opulence and ostentation. What he sought was enough space for work and for entertainment on a limited scale. He lived in this house till he firmly put office behind him and married six years later. Within its four walls streams of callers appeared, informal meetings were frequent and issues of high politics were argued at length. His influence was still potent.

Spending Christmas there Milner summarized the year in some gloom. There was something like stalemate, he wrote, in the East and the West. The year, he decided, had been disastrous and the outlook was 'very uncertain'.

At the opening of 1915 he went up to Oxford to attend a New College meeting, heard Kitchener give another uninformative statement in the Lords, attended a meeting of American journalists with Harry Brittain, the founder of the Empire Press Union, and had ceaseless talks with friends, associates in one of his causes and Unionist leaders. One can hazard the statement that through personal (including military and Press) contacts he was one of the best informed men on a wide range of topics in London. He now employed a secretary, Miss Smith, who remained with him till his death; and usually dictated to her before and after a long midday spell in the City. After various evening engagements he had the habit of sitting up until 2 a.m. to prepare a speech, draft a memorandum or deal with more correspondence.

Milner presided regularly over the Moot; these dozen or so well-informed people were concentrating on the present not the future, at the moment the recruiting campaign. The response of the Empire to arms had been swift. But in Britain the view still prevailed that fighting was a professional business; one historian calls it 'not a nation at war, but a nation supporting and encouraging part of itself at war'.[8] Kitchener's 'first 100,000' was already a statistical dodo; and the statement just quoted refers to much besides the men volunteering to risk death in France.

Milner found the Rhodes Trust, which he said he was 'left to run almost alone', occupying some time. Both Curtis and Wylie at Oxford were acting as godfathers to Scholars who had taken commissions and so lost their scholarships and met with financial trouble. Milner wrote to J. A. R. Marriott that the Trustees had no power to exclude German scholarships, which had for a time 'suspended themselves'. Were it not for the decrease of Scholars the Trust's income for this purpose would be quite insufficient. De Beers shares had much declined, and were 'still our principal income'.[9] Uncertainty in the political sphere was the theme of a letter to him from Duncan, most judicious of his numerous South African correspondents. It was doubtful, he thought, whether Botha would renew his majority,

> You can't argue from any ordinary principles of reason about what the Boer will do'. Hertzog and the rebel section might win the inevitable election, and South Africa is 'on the razor's edge'.

In the autumn the Committee of Imperial Defence had been rechristened the War Council, a body with none of the powers of decision of the later War Cabinet. A conflict of opinion prevailed in the Government over plans for knocking out Austria and Turkey and provisioning Russia from the south. An effort to reach Constantinople by sea having foundered, a British and 'Anzac' force under Ian Hamilton landed at Gallipoli late in April. By this date a succession of terrible casualty lists and a criminal shortage of shells had become for the public at home the main features of the campaign in France. Northcliffe's emphasis in the *Daily Mail* on the shells scandal showed the power now exerted by the Press. Though hard to credit, the House of Commons had not yet once discussed the war; and the strict War Office censorship proved counterproductive. Strong Press power was a factor which favoured Milner, and Lloyd George had close contacts with more radical editors and proprietors. By contrast Asquith, according to Spender, could never be got to realize this factor or to meet or make public reply to Press critics.

Discontent of M.P.s over shells, and of Admiral John Fisher over the Dardanelles venture, played their part in the successful effort of Law and Lloyd George at the end of May 1915 to force a Coalition on Asquith. The new Cabinet was composed of 12 Liberals, 8 Unionists and one Labour Minister; Law accepted what for the Unionist leader was the minor office of Secretary for the Colonies. He nursed admiration for Asquith's capacities; this fact influenced events in 1916, though Lord Blake writes that he viewed Asquith's policies through most of this year with 'increasing alarm'. The Cabinet lacked, like its forerunner, what for Milner and those who thought like him the conduct of war needed most, strong co-ordinated direction. General scepticism over the change received an illustration from the success of F. S. Oliver's long polemic, *Ordeal by*

Battle, only published in June. Attacking the P.M.'s capacity and reshuffle, it had a big sale and required a new edition in July. The Coalition's major success, Lloyd George, now Minister of Munitions, like his colleagues ran his own 'show' and provided at speed the weapons the armies most needed.

Lord Esher, an experienced acquaintance of Milner's, wrote regretting that

'Milner's services should be lost to the State [and that] his gifts of character were obscured by clouds of factious and unfair criticism.' In the Boer War he had shown the qualities of 'moral courage and tenacity' now again so much needed.[10]

This opinion was shared by many, inside and outside the Unionist party, who cannot be classed among Milner's close friends or disciples. Less welcome was the revival by the *Daily News*, the *Nation* and by some private correspondents of attacks on him as the son of a German. He told one of the latter that his father and he himself had always been treated in Germany (and taxed) as foreigners. He was never conscripted, and the allegations being made were 'too silly to be noticed'.

Earlier in this year Zeppelin raids had been made on East Anglia and on 31 May the first real attack of this kind was directed at London, causing four deaths. At a later attack, interrupted in his work after midnight, Milner went into the street where the crowds 'showed no fear and seemed to regard it as entertainment.' He went up to Oxford to speak to some 100 American Rhodes Scholars, and called on Warren and the Master of Balliol. He wrote to *The Times* on the subject, again much in his mind, of National Service, and in June the Moot had two discussions on how to proceed in this matter now a new Government had been formed.

One of his best friends in the Government, Lord Selborne, now President of the Board of Agriculture, asked him to preside over a Food Production Committee. In a reference to South Africa as well as his pre-war work for the Unionists he wrote that Milner had done more than most people in 'mugging up' the subject for 15 years and had formed 'some very strong opinions.' He found that his civil servants, as well as the public, lacked all sense of urgency in the matter. So

... the driving power will have to come from you ... and we must inspan our whole reserves of capacity [among experts].

Milner accepted, recruited the foremost authorities in the country (for example R. E. Prothero and Christopher Turnor), and wrote that they must evolve some scheme of guarantee to farmers who proved claims to have increased the food supply and paid decent wages,

> . . . a big Socialistic experiment, of course, but we are neither opposed to *reasonable* Socialism.

From mid-June until late July this committee, somehow added to his other duties, sat almost daily ('a most fearful rush and grind'), and visited leading Unionists to secure their agreement. They presented an Interim Report to the Government as a challenge to introduce the guarantee scheme. But the Government would not do so, and he wrote he was 'very disgusted', especially with the Unionists' failure to back them. 'All life' then left the committee, though they sat to produce a Final Report in October. One result was enrolment at the end of the year of women to undertake agricultural work, though it was not until 1916 that women entered almost every branch of national activity including the Army. The Government appointed its first Food Controller, Lord Devonport, a year from this autumn, though with no system of control as his weapon.[11]

Agricultural needs soon came into conflict with the Army's devouring requirements for men. Milner's prime aim for Britain at war – National Service – was part of the wider problem of manpower to which no one had paid much attention. So coal-miners, farm workers and other skilled men who had volunteered early and gone abroad were increasingly needed at home. Public feeling was by now much frustrated by the unfairness and lack of direction of the voluntary system; Northcliffe had long made National Service one of his causes and Press controversy on the issue became even more violent. In the Cabinet, Curzon, Churchill and Lloyd George pushed hard for the change though with little support. On 20 August the Press published a manifesto by Milner announcing, as its chairman, that the National Service League was compelled by the seriousness of events to resume propaganda; it would advocate compulsory service overseas as well as at home though 'for the duration' only. He contributed a long article to the *Empire Review* for September stating:

> 'Conscription' is not primarily a measure of compulsion . . . abroad it is thought of as a privilege and honour . . . its essence is good order and equality of sacrifice.[12]

At the end of the month he was commanded to a week-end at Windsor.

King George, with whom his relations had always been cordial, respected both Asquith and Kitchener and expressed at some length his own opposition to National Service. A day or two later Milner called on Kitchener, with whom he remained on good terms, but failed to shake his belief in the voluntary system. Men of influence who backed him outside the Cabinet included St. Loe Strachey, editor of the *Spectator*, and Sir Arthur Lee (later Lord Lee of Fareham) who reported from France that every soldier favoured National Service. Leo Amery, his tireless helper not least with his pen, spent some months for the War Office in the Balkans and came home convinced that the Dardanelles effort could only succeed as part of a major operation embracing all Balkan countries. He was then used by General Callwell, Henry Wilson's friend and now D.M.I., to write memoranda on conscription for the Cabinet. When Parliament met in September the Commons debated this issue for three days. Asquith evaded the problem by passing a mere Registration Bill and then asking Lord Derby to set up a voluntary scheme of 'attestation' of all men, unmarried and married, of military age. This proved a failure.

A deal between Kitchener and Joffre, of which the Cabinet was not told, caused the disastrous battle of Loos in October with 50,000 British casualties. Kipling's only son John, in the Irish Guards, was reported missing and then killed. Since Milner was on close terms with Kipling a study of what a discerning critic calls his 'final, most difficult, least understood period' deserves mention.[13] He wrote with a savagery against suffering and death which was new; but he never glorified war for its own sake. His 'authoritarianism' was expressed in the principle of 'give the job to the man who can do it without inexpert interference.'

Milner's views on conducting a war for which Britain was so ill-prepared owed much to this outlook. A foretaste of the future occurred when he met Lloyd George privately for the first time as the battle of Loos was beginning. Lloyd George had made a big contribution at the Ministry of Munitions, introducing regulation both of management and labour and providing the first real example of dealing with the manpower problem. Milner's letters and diaries became filled for two months with disgust at the Government's failure to fulfil Sir Edward Grey's recent promise in the Commons 'to give to our friends in the Balkans all the support in our power.' Bulgaria joined the enemy, and with Greece staying neutral the situation he wrote was 'now very bad'. The Cabinet was divided over whether to send reinforcements to Gallipoli or to the small Anglo-French force just landed at Salonika. It did neither, outraging both Carson, the Attorney General, and Milner.

Milner's patience gave way to what has been called earlier a political bout – blunt public speaking as a substitute for private persuasion. On 14 October after hearing Crewe speak for the Government in the Lords on the Balkans he asked fiercely whether evacuation of the Dardanelles should not be considered, and attacked the failure of Balkan policy. The Press gave prominence to the speech, and Milner received many congratulations from friends, including Steel-Maitland, now Bonar Law's Under-Secretary. Asquith counter-attacked by accusing Milner of having endangered security. Carson's resignation then dealt the P.M. a serious blow by providing hostile Tories with a powerful leader. Unrepentant, Milner went with Lady Edward to speak at Canterbury 'expressing myself very plainly over the muddle of the Government.'[14]

In early November he recorded London as 'full of rumours over a Cabinet crisis . . . we are approaching a general smash, internal and external.' General Ian Hamilton had been replaced; and Kitchener, whose stock in high circles had fallen low, was sent to the Dardanelles to report on evacuation. On his return he found that French had been replaced as C.-in-C. in France by Douglas Haig, and Sir William Robertson ('Wully') installed on his own terms as C.I.G.S. Milner repeated his attack in the Lords in an effort, which failed, to force Bonar Law's resignation (which Law had already offered to Asquith but had withdrawn). Somewhat later he tried with no better success to persuade Austen Chamberlain to resign. He pressed Lansdowne, who was naturally cautious, for news on the Balkans but the Cabinet was still split on the Dardanelles issue and two weeks elapsed before evacuation began.

The Tory St. Aldwyn and Liberal peers such as Cromer and Morley, Milner noticed, felt 'very strongly about the mismanagement of the war.' In December a number of these, including the former Liberal Lord Chancellor Loreburn, formed a bi-partisan group of anti-Government peers and chose Milner as their leader. Soon afterwards Milner's periodical use of rash phrases brought him fresh trouble. His reference in the Lords to rumours 'of some occult German influence' at the centre of government caused a stinging rebuke from Lord Crewe and unpleasant attacks in the Radical Press, which his friends took more seriously than he did, on his own alleged 'German origin'.[15]

At the opening of 1916 Milner once more complained he had 'more work of all sorts than I'm able to get through'. His chief innovation was Monday night dinners – fully treated by Gollin as 'the Monday Night Cabal' of some half-dozen friends convinced that a government led by

'Squiff' and Law was incapable of winning the war.[16] Both Milner and Carson had many admirers in politics but, as Amery puts it, Milner's

> . . . devastating sincerity, dislike of publicity and incapacity to drama-
> tize himself . . . prevented him becoming a popular figure.[17]

He contributed to the group's prime objectives by speeches from time to time in the Lords; but still more by the respect which his personal qualities and intellect earned him from many (taking Curzon as a sample at random) outside his close circle. Persuasion, both personal and in print, was his primary weapon. Carson, by contrast, stood out clearly in the public arena. It is claimed by Amery that outside the Cabinet he was 'the only strong personality in the Commons and the only arresting figure in the public eye.'

The Monday Night Club (as the writer prefers to call it) lasted through-out 1916 and beyond. In view of later events its contribution, except in one major matter, is often exaggerated. Lloyd George, for example, had little to do with it and Beaverbrook nothing. The exception is its powerful links with the Press. Since Amery was in Salonika much of this year, Geoffrey Dawson, as Editor of *The Times*, became its third most active member: Oliver was an able publicist, Waldorf Astor the proprietor of *The Observer* which was forcefully edited by Garvin. Philip Kerr, Henry Wilson and Jameson sometimes joined them. Though they all looked on Milner as leader, Carson led a strong dissident Unionist Committee and some like-minded Liberals in the Commons.

This January the Cabinet gave way at last and by a Military Service Act imposed compulsory service on unmarried men aged 18–41. One result was to extend Lloyd George's initiative and add an exemption for coal-miners and other skilled workers needed at home. Kitchener, compulsion's arch opponent, was back at the War Office but Newton, who had represented this Office in Parliament in his absence, wrote that (due to his failings) it was 'generally believed he'd be employed in some other capacity.' Even Kitchener, at a dinner, now praised Australians for adopting compulsory military training seven years previously. This Act, however, failed to furnish the men needed, and the Cabinet was again deeply split. Asquith offered the Commons one more compromise measure in its first secret session on 26 April. External troubles then made him withdraw this and carry universal compulsion, irrespective of marriage, to the 41 age limit. Taylor's statement that this was the Lower House's only direct intervention in the war sheds light on the role of free-lances like Milner.

One external trouble was the Easter Rising in Ireland, which opened the long and successful career of Sinn Fein; though Milner had little to do with the problem, which further discredited Asquith and exhibited Lloyd George's skill. He made one of his visits to Oxford, dining in Balliol on the day A. L. Smith was elected its Master and sharing next day in long talks there with W.E.A. leaders on industrial problems. On the war situation in France he gained much first-hand news from the visits on leave of his friends. Henry Wilson, now commanding the 4th Army Corps, Hanbury-Williams, since the opening of war the head of the British Military Mission with Russian H.Q., and Ned Grigg in the Grenadier Guards, who helped to teach Churchill trench warfare, were included in these.

On 6 June he wrote that the news of Kitchener's death while sailing to Russia 'spread like wildfire and caused an immense sensation.' For the public, unaware that for months he had been a mere figurehead, the event was a tragedy. A number of people saw Milner, with his knowledge of the Army's 'top brass', as his appropriate successor. But the prize went to Lloyd George, who took office at the start of the bloody and long-drawn-out trial on the Somme of Kitchener's volunteer armies. Now that military compulsion had at last been achieved, the future of the National Service League, which had 50 branches and contained much variety of patriotic opinion, had to be settled. Milner was among those who favoured what he called its 'decent interment' by its amalgamation with the Royal Colonial Institute. But many members, in particular Curzon, strongly favoured its continued independent existence. As chairman of its council, Milner attended many meetings for the rest of this year. These ended with the collapse of the Royal Colonial Institute scheme and the League's closing down until further notice.[18]

Sturry, where he sometimes took week-ends of rest, would, he wrote, be delightful were it not for the 'constant obsession of tragic and anxious thoughts over the war'. This July it brought him, as he gardened and walked, the sound of the firing on the Somme. For the whole of this month delegates of the Empire Parliamentary Association visited Britain, and besides informal meetings Milner addressed them at length, initiating discussion, on 28 July. The war, he argued, had strengthened the need for some new and more formal system than the quadrennial Conferences. He favoured an Imperial Council, indirectly elected by Britain and all the Dominions and not representing existing parties, with power to make or unmake the present Imperial Government; though he realized that for many his action might be too extreme. Failing this, a Convention should meet to thrash out the problem of an Imperial Parliament; or possibly two Parliaments making some division between Imperial (including India and the Dependencies) and local (England and Dominion) affairs.[19]

Lionel Curtis's long-hatching 'Egg' was privately circulated this year, but again failed to obtain universal acceptance. The Canadians, for example, thought his scheme controversial and premature. Milner was critical of the details of his plan for an Imperial Parliament. In a private much-quoted letter to Curtis he wrote that their politics were much less government by the people than by caucuses and machines. Democracy

> ... happens to be the inevitable form for my country and the Empire. Therefore I accept it, without enthusiasm, but with absolute loyalty... and I am quite prepared to make the best of it.

Curtis published as a personal effort *The Problem of the Commonwealth*, an historical survey in depth of experiments in union up to America's War of Independence.

The Round Table, Moots in London and the groups in Dominions kept the effort towards Imperial Unity alive on a propaganda level. The contribution of Dominion troops to the fighting in France and Gallipoli gave, of course, a feeling of Empire solidarity to far larger numbers. Milner accepted the chairmanship of the British Agricultural Section of the British Empire Producers' Association inaugurated this year.

About the same time he agreed with his friend Robert Cecil, Under-Secretary at the Foreign Office, to become 'Supervisor' of the three Coal Committees concerned with different aspects of the industry and reporting to different Ministers. He at once got into touch with the representatives of owners and miners; he and Smillie, the President of the Miners' Federation and once very bitter over Chinese Labour, formed a mutual attraction. Milner wrote later he regretted that earlier in the war the Government had not taken over all the coal output at fixed pit-head prices, and restricted distributors' charges. He now tried unsuccessfully to establish fixed wage rates for the war, which would have saved much later trouble. By December he had persuaded the House to appoint a Commission of three to take over all the mines.[20] In the earliest phase of this work Bonar Law wrote to Milner on Asquith's behalf pressing him to be chairman of the Dardanelles Committee of Inquiry; he declined, though not until after more pressure from Law and Austen. The curious timing gives support to Gollin's suggestion that this was a Government effort to damp down 'their severest critic'. The Monday Night Club, especially Dawson, and Unionists outside it were working for a Government of much smaller size in which Lloyd George, supported by Carson and Milner, would galvanize the war effort.

Among Milner's wide range of private interests he probably counted the Rhodes Trust as the foremost. Insufficient has been said of the doubts which he felt, shared by Parkin and Wylie, about advising Americans to take up their scholarships in abnormal wartime Oxford. They decided to do so; but Wylie wrote later that Scholars had 'a restless and unsatisfying time', apart from the rule (not always observed) that holding a scholarship barred marriage.[21] Much time was spent in 1916 by the Trustees regarding suppression, which would need Parliamentary action, of the German Scholarships. Michell, Rhodes's biographer, was often in Cape Town, very sensitive about being consulted and called by Rosebery 'that queer character'. Milner needed again all his resources of patience and tact. In the end the codicil granting these scholarships was revoked by Parliament.[22]

Milner's visitors, hosts or guests not connected with business this autumn included Bob Brand, now Deputy Chairman of the British Mission in Washington, Fred Perry doing similar work in Canada, Hanbury-Williams from Russia, the Northcliffes, Dunstan of Wye College to advise him on Sturry. He found time for journalism, usually anonymous, and for the more solid reviews; and at this date the preface to a series of *Times* articles on 'Reconstruction'. He was mainly responsible for passage through the Lords of a Municipal Savings Bank Bill.

In mid-November, when the Somme battle had ended with great loss of life and no strategical gain, he made a strenuous tour of ten days covering miles of the French front. He visited Advanced G.H.Q., all the Army H.Q.s, a large section of the front which embraced Delville Wood, the main aerodrome, the South African Brigade and the base camp at Étaples. He returned home convinced, according to Wilson, that we could not beat the Boche on this front, and 'thoroughly depressed and depressing.' A Monday Club dinner which Wilson attended on the 27th urged Carson to persuade Lloyd George to resign taking Bonar Law with him and so smash the Government. Three days later Arthur Lee gave him lunch to meet Lloyd George and Carson.

It happened that while Milner was touring the front Lloyd George was attending a conference on Allied strategy in Paris. This convinced him that the war in the West was a waste of men and equipment and that helping Russia was the strategy to adopt; but Joffre and the generals won the conference over to the opposite view, arousing his great indignation. He agreed with Maurice Hankey that a small War Council, with himself as its chairman, should conduct the military strategy. These decisions were soon to affect Milner's future.

At the end of November Asquith offered Milner the Food Controllership, sending Runciman to press him. When he wrote declining, the Prime Minister countered with a request to him to become Coal Controller. By this time the internal political crisis had become very acute. Of the Milnerites Carson was most closely involved, and on Asquith's side Bonar Law, now facing a split in his party but strongly advised by Sir Max Aitken (later Lord Beaverbrook) against resignation, was the key figure.[23]

Asquith first agreed that Lloyd George should head a War Council, changed his mind, resigned in an effort to rout his opponents and by 6 December had lost the game to the Welshman. The crisis deserves Milner's description of an 'awful rumpus'. He had got the leader and the small executive War Council he wanted. But he was disappointed, he told Lady Edward, that

> . . . the *unexpected firmness* of Bonar Law has resulted in the return of the old Unionist tail . . . so the new Government is really old Unionist hordes, L.G. and *some* new men.

He had no idea whether Lloyd George would include him, and was strongly against this unless he was one of the 'supreme direction'. On 8 December Lloyd George wrote fulfilling this wish. The Admiralty was given to Carson; Milner was offered and accepted at once the post of Minister without Portfolio in a five-man War Cabinet. Besides the Prime Minister his colleagues were Law (as Chancellor of the Exchequer), Curzon and Arthur Henderson representing Labour. Due to hustle he appeared, Sir Almeric Fitzroy records, at the Palace for delivery of his seals from the King unsummoned, an event unknown since the death of Queen Anne.[24]

Part IV
OFFICE

War Cabinet

(December 1916 – April 1918)

Synoptic Member, and Russian Mission – Imperial Counsel,
Shipping, Food – Military Strategy – Supreme War
Council – The German Offensive, and Doullens

Milner entered his first Ministerial office in Britain. It is not hard to see
why Lloyd George chose him, apart from his personal influence and links
with the Press. Milner's gifts, he well knew, were exactly the opposite of
his own – the gifts on the highest political stage of a chief of staff not a
commander. He was also aware that loyalty was a cardinal virtue for
Milner. While he made the final decisions, the special preoccupations of
Law as Leader of the Commons and of Henderson with Labour left
Curzon and Milner to oversee a huge range of work. Where domestic
affairs were concerned they occupied jointly a position similar to that
conferred by Churchill in World War II on his 'willing horse', Sir John
Anderson, though with one vital difference. In 1914–18 the home front
was far less prepared for war and less penetrated by the State. So the peacetime Departments remained, while new ones – concerned for example
with shipping and food – were created on what was intended to be a
temporary basis. Fluctuation in the duties and leadership of these caused
formidable problems of co-ordination.

A War Cabinet could not under these conditions have functioned
without an efficient secretariat to serve it. Colonel Maurice Hankey,
former Secretary of the Committee of Imperial Defence, was appointed
as first Secretary to the Cabinet. He did not know Milner and was one of
many, as he records, to experience surprise when he met him. Instead of
a rash, impetuous 'damn the consequences' person he found one rather
slow to make up his mind but 'very sure'. He soon thought him 'very
attractive and possessed of personality and we got on like a house on fire.'[1]
Hankey was joined by some of his staff but a larger body, to serve the
Prime Minister as a personal staff (the 'Garden Suburb') as well as the
Cabinet as a whole, was quickly needed. Lloyd George turned to Milner
for help in this matter which he knew he was well qualified to supply. It is
not surprising that the talents of Amery, Kerr, Curtis, and others associated
at some stage with Milner, were employed in these groups.

The War Cabinet first met two or three times daily, and then on an average at least once a day for five days a week throughout its career. Milner lost little time in persuading Lloyd George to invite the Dominions and India to some share in its counsels. The precedent of the Committee of Imperial Defence discussing all matters in secret was preferred to that of the hitherto publicized but reticent Imperial Conferences. A beginning in this sphere could not be made until March 1917. From that date a three-fold and flexible superstructure evolved: first, the War Cabinet 'proper' for discussion of purely British business, secondly, intermittent Imperial War Cabinets to include Dominion Prime Ministers or their substitutes, third, larger Imperial War Conferences. Milner wrote that 'avalanches of letters' arrived congratulating him on his appointment. He gave up all his City directorships and functions with unofficial bodies except the Rhodes Trust and Toynbee Hall. He was given an office at 2 Whitehall Gardens and chose as his chief private secretary Major Hugh Thornton, who stayed with him until 1920.

Britain's military strategy and foreign relations, inextricably linked, were continuously under War Cabinet scrutiny. Lloyd George, with all his superlative gifts, had only limited knowledge of either, so depended a good deal on Milner's advice on both topics and Curzon's advice on the second. His experience of the recent summer campaign in the West had caused him to favour some new effort to undermine Germany's strength from the East. So within a few days he asked Milner to lead the British delegation of an Allied Mission to Russia. Before Christmas the War Cabinet paid much attention to Balkan affairs, and to answering a Peace Note, prompted by Germany, from President Wilson which, Milner wrote, 'rather upset us all.' Snatching two nights at Sturry he resolved to grow more foodstuffs there, and commented 'so ends the stormy year 1916.'

He was taken by Lloyd George on 1 January to a full-scale Allied Conference in Rome, at which Lloyd George hoped to persuade the Italians to support the plan of a combined offensive on their front. Failing to do this, Lloyd George had to accept the plan of another Western offensive, and went so far as to make Haig in large degree subordinate to Nivelle, Joffre's successor as the French C.-in-C. Milner, after much preparation which included a talk with the King, left Oban with the French and Italian Missions on 20 January. His high-powered staff included Henry Wilson, whose French counterpart was the impressive General Noël de Castelnau. Landing at Port Romanov near Murmansk, the one entrance in the winter for foreign supplies, they found chaos. The very slow train which took three days to reach Petrograd further depressed them.

The Mission had the two objects of co-ordinating the coming summer's offensives and reaching agreement on supplies of munitions to Russia. From the Ambassador, Sir George Buchanan, Samuel Hoare, engaged in intelligence work, Sir Alfred Knox the military attaché, Hanbury-Williams and others, Milner learnt of the tense political situation existing. The Tsar, who now held supreme command of the Army, was alienated from the members of his Government with 'literally no one except his wife with whom he could freely discuss the political situation . . . and no clearly defined idea' except his duty to maintain autocracy. Liberal Russians brought pressure to bear on the Allied leaders 'and in particular on Lord Milner, to intercede with the Emperor in favour of constitutional reform'.[2] On 31 January the Mission formally visited the Tsar at Tsarskoe Selo when Milner delivered two letters to him from King George; two days later he had a private audience and lunched with the Tsar and Tsarina who made it quite clear they would tolerate no discussion of internal politics. After another two days the whole Mission returned to the palace for a State dinner when Milner had merely a kind word from the Tsar who didn't linger to talk to anyone else.

The plenary meetings of the Conference consisted of 40 or more people, a feature Milner especially disliked. At the first one he remarked to one of the French mission: 'We are wasting time.' Talks with a single Russian Minister or in small groups were thwarted by a series of long formal lunches, receptions and dinners. By 5 February he wrote he was 'feeling the effects of hard work, close air, endless long functions and constant interruptions to business.' The Russians held out no hope of launching a big offensive until months had elapsed. It was evident that their High Command was badly organized, their armament quite inadequate and their transport very defective.

Robert Bruce Lockhart, a live wire who at 29 was Britain's Consul-General in Moscow, turned up to plan Milner's visit to that city. He records that he:

fell at once before Milner's charm, and found him extraordinarily well informed about facts and figures, which he seemed to carry in his head without effort.

Accompanying him south as his guide and interpreter he continued,

to the end of his life Lord Milner never forgot those 3 days in Moscow. They were the last nail in the coffin of his discomfort . . . he was chained to his duty from early morning till late at night.[3]

A huge 'rout' at the Town Duma and a five-hour Anglo-Russian luncheon with interminable speeches were part of this duty. Far more to Milner's taste was a two-hour talk about Russia's internal state with Prince Lvov, a leading liberal statesman, joined by Moscow's mayor.

Milner returned to Petrograd for ten more days of Conference meetings, interviews and receptions. He found that two colleagues had finished their report on Munitions, to which he attached more importance than to any other of the Petrograd proceedings. Wilson returned from a tour of the northern front, judging the situation there better than he had expected. On the 18th Milner went with the two other leaders to say good-bye to the Tsar with whom he had twenty minutes' private talk. He ventured to refer to internal unrest, but told Wilson he had not achieved much. Before leaving he wrote a highly confidential letter to the Tsar.[4] Concerned mainly with supplies, this included what, Katkov writes, would appear to the Tsar 'the humiliating demand' that Allied technicians should accompany supplies to the front to ensure they were properly delivered and used. Milner also made cautious hints about reforms which, in the tense atmosphere prevailing, could be read as lack of Allied confidence in the Government's efficiency.

The Tsar left for G.H.Q. in the field and the Allied Mission left for home on the 22nd. Hanbury-Williams, whom the Tsar trusted and who obtained the approval of Alekseev, the Chief of Staff, wrote an appeal to the Tsar to furnish himself with the 'outlet' of advice from the Duma.[5] The Mission trundled north for three days, found Port Romanov even more congested, and sailed in great cold and some danger. Milner had long talks on the voyage with Wilson who proved over-sanguine about Russia's military prospects and wrote in his diary,

> Milner considers the defeat of the Boches in the field as impossible, and therefore he is prepared to consider terms of peace, which I think quite impossible.

He also had 'a sort of vague hope' that with the help of the Dominions 'we might be able to keep out of European complications.'[6] Landing at Scapa Flow they reached London in the afternoon of 3 March, to be met by Lady Edward, Amery and Thornton. It was a Saturday and he went to Buckingham Palace to deliver a letter from the Tsar to the King; on Monday he returned there for a long talk with the King and Stamfordham about the Mission. In a long Cabinet on that day the Mission was the leading business.

In his report Milner supported the policy of sacrificing some strength in the West to supply Russia's urgent needs. He also expressed the view, shared by most of the British delegates, that talk about revolution in Russia while the war lasted was exaggerated, though the situation might degenerate into chaos. Lloyd George was pleased with his main conclusion, seeing him, though on good terms with the Army's 'top brass', as an ally in his fight which he knew would grow worse with Robertson, Haig and the 'western' generals. The Cabinet was much occupied with discussions with visiting French Ministers and with Nivelle and Haig over plans for the forthcoming Spring offensive. In addition, Dominion Prime Ministers were arriving, and programmes were being drawn up for the first of the Imperial War Cabinets.

On 15 March there was news of disturbance in Petrograd and the papers next day were full of the subject. Late in February (by Russian calendar which was 13 days behind England's) strikes and street demonstrations took place in the capital and the Government collapsed. On 2 March the Tsar, inflexible to the end, abdicated in his train at Pskov and Prince Lvov formed a Provisional Government. Much has been made of the fact that Lloyd George, in his *War Memoirs* published in the '30s, made sarcastic attacks on Milner and Wilson for failure to foresee the event.[7] Though in Petrograd talk of revolution had been constant, few leading Russians believed this would happen until after the war. The Official Court Chronicler, the resident Germans, other interested foreigners, revolutionaries on the spot and Lenin in Zürich were all taken completely by surprise. The position on the front appeared stable, and no major disturbances outside the capital were reported. To Gell, Milner wrote that Lvov was the best of the Liberals, though he doubted whether his Government could last long. The Tsar could have saved it all by appointing less reactionary Ministers himself.

Lloyd George faced new emergencies daily with amazing resilience of mind and spirit. Unlike Milner or Law he loved riding the storm in Cabinet or in Parliament, and in talks with advisers often found a solution by some flash of intuition. Milner, by contrast, could do little good in a stormy Cabinet meeting. Cool and quiet in council, his strength lay in hours of patient work on a brief, first-rate logical judgement, and the power over colleagues these capacities gave him. Though the optimism once felt by British leaders had vanished, it was fortunate none could foresee that the year 1917 was to bring greater trials and distress, in sea and land warfare and on the home front, than the year which had passed.

Dr. Christopher Addison, Lloyd George's chief supporter among Liberal M.P.s, a Free Trader and Home Ruler, had been scornful in 1916 at the suggestion that if Lloyd George supplanted Asquith he should take Milner into his Cabinet. Now Minister of Reconstruction, and later the first Minister of Health, he revised his opinion and after the war summarized Milner's value,

> ... though Milner never came into the limelight ... all through 1917 he did heroic work. The best feature of the War Cabinet system was that it enabled men like him to be set apart to thrash things out with the Ministers concerned and to make adjustments in numberless matters that could not possibly be argued out in Cabinet ... I was privileged to know the real Milner.[8]

Leo Amery, who now held the rank of Colonel, was both an Assistant Secretary to Hankey and a political secretary to the Cabinet. This meant close association with Milner whom years later he testified he had always considered 'my leader, as well as my best friend.' He was given by Hankey the congenial task of making arrangements and planning the agenda for an early meeting of the Imperial War Cabinet. The night before news was received of the Petrograd revolution Milner gave a dinner at Brooks's to Smuts, just arrived from South Africa to deputize for Botha. Smuts's 'odd letter' to him of years earlier about History providing 'the reconciliation of quarrels' proved true.[9] The two men now shared the same view of relations within the Empire and the place of the Empire in the world. They also shared a sense of realities, the power to get quickly to the heart of a matter, and a grasp of how military strategy was related to policy. On 20 March the Imperial War Cabinet held its first session.

For six weeks a flexible three-tiered structure was kept in being. With the 'ordinary' Cabinet still meeting almost daily, the Imperial one met normally three times a week. The difficulty of limiting this body in size was solved by creating two sub-committees under Milner and Curzon dealing mainly with peace-terms. With British experts attending, the problems of manpower, the size of Dominion contingents, war material of all kinds and shipping were discussed with these sub-committees' reports. In a public speech the Canadian prime minister Borden stated,

> ... each nation has its voice upon questions of common concern and highest importance as deliberations proceed; each preserves unimpaired

its perfect autonomy, its self-government, and the responsibility of its own Ministers to their own electorate.

The Imperial Cabinet made history in reaching agreement, made public by Lloyd George at the Guildhall late in April, on the thorny question of Imperial Preference. Each part of the Empire undertook to give specially favourable treatment to the produce and manufacture of all other parts, subject only to Britain retaining her freedom on the question of taxation of food and to showing regard for the interests of Allies.

The Imperial War Conference of Dominion Ministers of lesser rank met several times weekly under Walter Long, the Secretary for the Colonies, and was much concerned with constitutional questions. It resolved that in future the Dominions and India should participate fully in foreign relations, and that better arrangements should be made for Imperial consultation. But the question of closer formal ties, it decided, must await full discussion until after the war.

When these meetings ended in May, Hankey states, there existed 'a strong and unanimous view that the experiment had been a great success.' Much private discussion took place about ways of continuing closer Empire relations. The idea of enthusiasts such as Amery, that Ministers of all the Dominions might be permanently stationed in London, was unrealistic and failed to find favour with Borden and Smuts, though his firm understanding with Botha allowed Smuts to do this and to render great service in Britain. Walter Long's allegation that Milner tried to 'stampede the Premiers into Federation' fails to carry conviction for two reasons. As a colleague, Long was jealous, and even vindictive. All the evidence shows that Milner, whatever he argued in private, was fully aware of the practical difficulties in his way and content to make haste slowly towards some kind of formal Imperial Council. He looked on these six weeks of meetings and the general agreement to repeat them in 1918 as real progress.

Both before and during these meetings Milner had much besides Imperial matters to contend with. Lloyd George had created a Department of National Service under Neville Chamberlain which signally failed to ease the growing difficulties of manpower and recruiting. Violet Markham, the Deputy Director of its Women's Section, told Milner she had spent 'an odious six months'. Milner, who advised Chamberlain to resign, had to reorganize the Department.[10] Lord Derby had replaced Lloyd George as War Secretary and become a strong ally of Robertson, the C.I.G.S., who disliked the War Cabinet and backed up Haig's strategy to the hilt. All these three men had been alienated by Lloyd George's gift to

Nivelle of virtually supreme command over British armies in France. The British won the battle of Arras in April, and Imperial unity was fostered by the heroism of the Canadians in capturing Vimy Ridge. But Nivelle's offensive petered out disastrously in a month, making no strategical gain and leaving the French armies incapable of further offensives in 1917. Soon after the Dominion ministers left Britain he was dismissed and replaced by Pétain. Haig and Robertson, thus vindicated, continued their plans for a summer offensive.

Two other problems made much claim on Milner's energies in the month before the third battle of Ypres. On 1 February the Germans enlarged their prime weapon of submarine warfare against all merchant ships bound for British ports, which became a major concern of the Cabinet. Milner had hardly got back from Russia before he was asked to inquire into the manpower needs of the shipbuilding industry and competing claims of the Army, official bodies and industry for manpower and tonnage. Of the various interdepartmental conflicts that followed, that between the shipyards and the Army was especially hard to resolve. In April some 650,000 tons of British shipping were sunk or, if foreign ships are included, one out of four ships which left British ports. America's entry into the war in this month gave a general boost to Allied morale and did something to relieve this particular danger. But it also drove the Germans to do all in their power to cause Britain's collapse in the months which were bound to elapse before American action, especially on land, could produce much effect. Milner wrote to his American friend Adèle Chapin:

> Just a line to congratulate you on the States' coming in at last! Nothing will ever make me admire Wilson, but one has to be just even to one's antipathies, and I am bound to admit that he did finally leap off the fence in fine style. His speech was an impressive one, and also very politic, for of course he has left no loyal German-American any excuse for not 'playing the game' . . . neither the German Government nor the people are conquered yet. Very far from it.

Shipping losses at the rate now occurring meant some system of imposing import controls, which provided an additional task for Milner. As losses continued he was called on to allocate the imports of this year and (allowing for much smaller tonnage) those for 1918. Gollin rightly describes him as becoming the arbiter of the final solution, of what was unquestionably the war's central issue – how much Freedom must be sacrificed to Control.[11]

'The priorities he now established', this historian states, '. . . decided in good part which industries would continue to function in the country; they decided the volume of food that was imported; and the amounts of military stores available for the armed forces.' His system and the Allied Maritime Transport Council now formed a general staff in this sphere. And Lloyd George was highly pleased with the service Milner had rendered.

The decision to introduce convoys, which in time proved the best way of countering the submarine menace, was taken this April with political consequences in which Milner figured. Carson both lacked real faith in Lloyd George and had strong support among Unionists upon whom the Coalition depended. The Easter Rebellion in Ireland of the previous year was met with repression which caused the rise of Sinn Fein as an underground movement and of De Valera as the nationalist leader. The entry of America into the war had encouraged those Irish who sought independence, while Ulster's Unionists were as hostile as ever to any form of Home Rule. This March, Lloyd George began planning an Irish Convention to include North and South; but Carson advised against this.

The Admiralty, Carson's Department, had been suffering what he called 'a calculated and concerted attack' from the public and Press for its reluctance to introduce anti-submarine convoys. On the last day of April Lloyd George took the unusual course of going to the Admiralty and, in the presence of Jellicoe, the First Sea Lord, but not Carson, commanding this step to be taken.[12] Carson was not the man to take kindly to the criticism his Department and especially Jellicoe had received; when Lloyd George brought up Ireland in public he counter-attacked with the submarine issue and warned him he was ready to fight. Though Carson persuaded the Ulster-men to attend the Convention he kept up his threat to the Prime Minister's authority.

While a close friend of Carson, and sharing his views about Ireland, Milner had definite reservations about his fitness to administer the Admiralty. What decided his action, however, was his view that Lloyd George was the one man in sight who was capable of ensuring the Empire's survival. Haig, who called Milner 'the strongest member of the War Cabinet as well as the best informed', gets support for his view from this crisis. While his War Cabinet colleagues kept silent, Milner let Lloyd George know he would back him, then evolved the idea of promoting Carson to the War Cabinet with the duty of helping Law lead the Commons. When in early July Lloyd George proposed this to Carson, Milner wrote to Carson as a friend in support of the plan. Carson stalled, Lloyd George then back-pedalled, and told him he could stay at the Admiralty if he wished, and for ten days did nothing. It was Milner who acted again by writing to Lloyd George on 16 July,

I am very anxious about the Admiralty . . . cannot the Carson–Geddes business be settled right away ? It is very urgent.

In a short time Carson accepted the War Cabinet post in conjunction with the oversight of war propaganda. Sir Eric Geddes, one of many business men brought into the Government, took charge at the Admiralty. Churchill, shabbily treated by Lloyd George hitherto, replaced Addison as Minister of Munitions.[13] In the meanwhile the first convoys of merchant ships reached British ports without loss.

Milner's second large contribution in domestic matters this year, on a plane with his work over shipping and imports, was to take drastic measures to improve Britain's supplies. When the War Cabinet came into being the country contained grain sufficient for no more than fourteen weeks; by April 1917 wheat was said to have fallen to nine weeks' supply. A Ministry of Food was set up under Lord Devonport, a grocer, who worked out a rationing scheme. In February Arthur Lee, a personal friend of both Lloyd George and Milner and an agricultural expert, was made Director-General of Food Production. Previous chapters have shown that Milner had for years studied agricultural problems, and that in 1915 his plans for increasing grain production had been turned down as too drastic. While Imperial meetings were still taking place the War Cabinet had the first of many discussions of a new Corn Production Bill.

Milner's hardest task was ensuring that the agricultural labour supply was no longer eroded by the constant recruiting demands of the Army. Characteristically he went straight to the man at the top, in this case the somewhat flabby Lord Derby. The problem, his papers show, was by no means resolved by one visit; and he wrote of the effort demanded by 'the eternal manpower question.' The Army Council complained to the Cabinet that in competition for men they were now far too low in the list, and Milner sat up late writing one more memorandum for his colleagues. He refused to accept fewer men than he thought were essential. The C.I.G.S., who on Kitchener's death had wanted Milner to be his successor, was doubtless now glad that the choice of Lord Derby had given him someone he could handle more easily. He complained in his memoirs that 'Milner was all for men for agriculture' and had forced the War Office into 'giving him' too many men.

Milner's Corn Production Bill struck many M.P.s and others as a highly radical measure: first, it suggested minimum prices for wheat and oats in the whole country: when average market prices fell below these the farmers would be compensated by the State – a form of protection which outraged the still numerous British free-traders; secondly, it set up an Agricultural Wages Board to establish nation-wide minimum wages; third, landowners' rights to raise rents were curtailed; and fourth, the Board of Agriculture would be able to authorize landlords to remove inefficient tenant farmers, or, failing their action, to do so themselves. Here was a Milner in no doubt that the plight of the country justified rigorous State action. Lloyd George recalled that when the War Cabinet discussed these proposals Balfour, who as Foreign Secretary was often present, gaped with astonishment.

In July Milner set up a committee on Agricultural Labour in the Lords, but expressed to Selborne and Prothero, now President of the Board of Agriculture, his fears about the shaky Parliamentary prospects of his Bill. The Cabinet decided to pass the Bill before the adjournment, though Milner wrote to a colleague, 'will we stick to it?' A fortnight after the opening of the fourth year of war in August Milner spent much time spread over a week attending discussions, sometimes heated, within and between the Lords and Commons on his Bill. Though he called this 'a great worry' since it upset all his other work he succeeded in carrying it through; and Amery states that he 'always regarded the Act as one of his greatest contributions to national regeneration.' A later historian makes the same point by calling it one of the measures which

seemed to have brought on at a bound social and ameliorative action by the State which in peacetime made way so slowly and against such deadweight of mistrust and vested interests.[14]

The proof of the pudding was Arthur Lee's writing to Milner in March 1918 that winter wheat showed far the greatest increase ever recorded. In May he sent more results, 'as you have helped so much to bring them about', adding doubts whether progress at this rate would continue due to

old forces of obstruction and pessimism . . . now that you have left the Cabinet we have no ally with any stomach for a fight.[15]

Arthur Lee is best known as the Lord Lee of Fareham who gave Chequers to the nation for the use of its Prime Ministers. His offer had been accepted by Lloyd George this August, and Lee sent Milner the draft Chequers Trust deed for his criticism. He stressed that he wanted to offer Prime Ministers

a typically rural life . . . antiquity and calm and the high and pure Chiltern air in a house with 1,500 acres of land 38 miles from Hyde Park Corner. For years his chief outdoor interest had been trying to perfect and make fully productive his various farms. His gift would include the paintings and interior furnishings of the house and an endowment of £100,000.[16]

Milner still managed occasionally to escape for one or two nights to Sturry and sometimes to Wigsell. He had made a small house in his grounds formerly occupied by Oliver Ready, and on occasions his own house, 'a minor hospital' for convalescing Canadian officers. As always he craved for both air and long walks. This summer the Amerys took a house on the high Surrey downs where during week-ends the two men often walked far and talked much. In London both 'Monday Night' and Moot dinners continued, though on a reduced scale. Hankey, commenting on the 'political congeries' he had met in war-time London, regarded the 'Round Table Group' as one of the most influential. Milner rarely attended evening parties such as those (often lavish) given by Lady Astor in St. James's Square. He dined alone, or with one or two friends in a club. Every weekday at least was a series of committees, interviews and visitors on official business. Yet, to quote Hankey again,

> . . . he sat up every night in his little house behind Westminster Abbey 'swotting' away at the vast documentation it was my duty to circulate . . . many a time I sat up with him giving him all the help I could for hours together . . . [his method] was to fine problems down by patient investigation and present them to the War Cabinet for decisions.

It seems fair to conclude that his contributions over shipping, the whole range of imports, manpower and food were the main ones in domestic affairs of his War Cabinet service. Lloyd George, who once said that he and Milner stood for much the same thing, since both were poor, independent of landlords and capitalists, and keen about social reform, was delighted with his vital achievements. Though co-ordination of home front departments and agencies still preoccupied Milner, for example manpower problems, much adjustment of boundaries and the substitution of weak by efficient civilian administrators had been made. Milner had, of course, been concerned since December at 10 Downing Street and elsewhere with problems of military strategy. Events and his personal interest and knowledge now gave him a more prominent role in this sphere.

Poincaré described 1917 as *l'année troublée*, the year of confusion. Nivelle's misjudged offensive proved catastrophic, though it was not until Wilson, now British liaison officer with Pétain, came home in June that the War Cabinet was aware that a poor state of discipline existed throughout the French Army. Milner, always keenly observant of Russian affairs, had been right to predict that Lvov's Liberal Government had shaky found-ations. Kerenski as War Minister soon proved its most forceful figure. But Lenin's arrival in April, as the leader of a number of Bolsheviks, further weakened the morale of the troops at the front. Next month the Provisional Government called for some form of general peace to be made. In July Kerenski launched a short-lived offensive, when a sweeping German counter-attack destroyed what was left of the Tsar's army.

Lloyd George had a strategy known as 'knocking away the props', meaning, of course, the props which supported the enemy. In the parlous condition now reached, and with no faith in Haig's costly, slogging battles in France, the props which he aimed at were Austria, Bulgaria and Turkey. On 8 June the War Cabinet, on Milner's suggestion, formed a War Policy Committee of four persons to concentrate on the military plans of the year. Besides Lloyd George this consisted of Curzon, Smuts and himself. Milner also proposed with success that

> . . . four or five people with the time and necessary qualifications should concentrate their minds upon the *military and political situation in the Balkans as a whole* . . . to be helped by the fresh and well-equipped mind of Smuts.[17]

Haig, supported by Robertson, had been planning a Flanders attack and begun its first round. Later this month Haig and Robertson came home and battled with this War Policy Committee for a week. Lloyd George gave in at last and authorized him to continue his plans for a major offensive subject to a conference he proposed to hold with the French. On 16 July Milner noted that the four-man Committee met for dinner and engaged in

> . . . interminable talk over the Western offensive and the alternative of support to Italians with no new arguments and no new conclusion.

Haig was authorized to begin the 3rd battle of Ypres, provided it was not too prolonged. He did so on 31 July, and it lasted for nearly four months.

The state of Russia had added new vigour to small sections in Britain who favoured a peace by negotiation. Henderson visited Russia for the War Cabinet in May, and came home convinced that the Labour Party in Britain should accept the Russian peace programme. His War Cabinet colleagues condemned his subsequent behaviour, asked him to resign and replaced him in August by George Barnes, a former Labour Party leader. In this further phase of Lloyd George's battle with 'the generals' he could count on firm support from Law: Curzon's position (as often) was uncertain while Milner, though by no means a Westerner by conviction, still felt reliance on the Army leaders' judgements. Spending a few days on holiday at Sturry he was 'greatly perturbed' to be summoned to Sir George Riddell's house in Surrey to discuss with Lloyd George the recurrent topic of Italian aid. Lloyd George, one of his staff recorded, was in 'a ferment of excitement' about Cadorna's victory on the Carso – 'he drafted about ten letters to President Wilson, but before we had finished one draft he would invariably get a "brainwave" and want a new one.'

Milner's view was expressed in a letter to Law a week later supporting the Haig–Robertson action,

> . . . it seems very important not to try to make naval or military commanders carry out operations of which they really disapprove. . . . That was the fundamental error in the Dardanelles proceedings. . . . in the face of the real disapproval of Lord Kitchener and Lord French it was bound to lead to disaster.[18]

In Egypt, General Allenby had taken command, but his forces were only sufficient to repel an attack on the frontier. Inadequate forces and shipping, and work needed on railways, postponed till November the prospect of his starting an all-out offensive against Turkey. At a conference with the French in September, Haig agreed to release heavy guns from his front to help the Italians. This move depressed Milner, and Lloyd George's hope that Italy's Army would knock down the Austrian prop had a serious setback. Cadorna's offensive petered out, and till the end of the year and beyond, Italy went on the defensive and was fighting for life. Though supplies were continuing under Milner's direction to Russia he recorded the War Cabinet as 'all greatly depressed' by the news from that country.

To add to these setbacks August proved the rainiest in Flanders for years. In the Passchendaele offensive men and guns sank in mud, tanks were useless, and slaughter continued for infinitesimal gains in more 'war of attrition'. Milner was writing more letters of sympathy as long casualty lists reappeared. To James Rendel, who lost a son, he wrote 'the scythe ... has not spared one household in which I am personally interested.' Among these two Grenfells, one of Selborne's sons, the gay Basil Blackwood, Bonar Law's elder sons and Asquith's son Raymond had been killed. Before this offensive had finished 250,000 names had been added to the casualties' total. Malcolm Muggeridge, still a schoolboy, wrote years later how this toll of death brought an all-pervading

> ... sense of hysteria, of life's agonizing brevity. There was something feverish in the very air one breathed.

The uniforms, marching feet, bands and railway stations of London all conveyed 'an artificial animation'.

Lloyd George, in a state of nervous tension, went to his home at Criccieth. On 17 September Milner joined him there for four days finding Riddell, Hankey and Kerr also present. He enjoyed the walks over lovely country, and much talk with his host on war problems at very irregular times. He wrote 'none of us are very hopeful of decisive results being achieved on present lines.' After over six weeks of Haig's effort in France Milner had reached greater agreement with Lloyd George's complaints. Hankey records a long walk with him on the banks of the Dwyfor which showed that he had

> ... completely come round to Lloyd George's view that the Western Front affords no opportunity for achieving complete success and that it is necessary to devote our main efforts against Turkey.[19]

But, as with the Dardanelles operation, he stressed that success in the Turkish theatre would depend on whole-hearted belief in it by the soldiers. On his last day he walked round the foot of Snowdon, then took a train for a day's work in London and a gardening Sunday at Sturry.

Besides the War Policy Committee's decisions the Cabinet was occupied in the following weeks with intensified air raids, fresh trouble in Ireland, a sub-committee concerned with Lord Edward's proposals on Egypt, the shortage of shipping, Zionism and domestic industrial unrest. Milner was associated closely with Smuts, in his famous report of October, recommending 'a real Air Ministry' to replace the existing Air Board and the creation of 'a united air service'. In early October he noted that the Policy Committee was making no progress in bridging 'the fundamental difference between the Prime Minister and Robertson, the C.I.G.S.', and later the Cabinet asked Lord French and General Wilson to report on future military policy.

Lloyd George was beginning to feel that no victory would be won before 1919 and to nourish the plan of a central body to control the Allies' military efforts. This was, of course, a way of outflanking the stubborn adherence of Robertson, Haig and Lord Derby to the Western offensives. It faced strong opposition from the fact that these generals enjoyed the confidence of the Army, of Balfour, Carson and other leaders, and of the country. French and Wilson reported critically of the current offensive, and in favour of central Allied control. Milner thought that Robertson should be shown this report at once, while forecasting that such action would probably break up the Government.

No account need be given in detail of Lloyd George's battle with Robertson which lasted for another four months, after which he retired as C.I.G.S. though Lord Derby continued in office.[20] Milner dined with John Buchan who, though a fervent imperialist, had never belonged to the Round Table group. When Buchan approached him he had helped to secure him a good post as Director of Information. The varied duties Milner performed in the War Cabinet recall Buchan's views on what formed his 'administrative genius'. He seemed, Buchan wrote, to possess

> . . . an instinct for what was possible, an extra sense which must have been due to nature and not to experience . . . next I should put the orderliness of his mind and his capacious memory. He could control any number of wires at once, for he had all the terminals in his hand . . . he could keep a score of matters steadily moving.[21]

The disastrous defeat of Italy at Caporetto caught both Britain and France by surprise and compelled them to send reinforcements. Some writers attribute it to Lloyd George's cunning that in Robertson's absence in Italy he secured the War Cabinet's final agreement on 2 November to creating a Supreme War Council composed of the Allied Prime Ministers advised by Allied civilian and military representatives, the latter independently of their Chiefs of Staff. Henry Wilson, Milner's high opinion of whom as a soldier both Churchill and Hankey, with their military knowledge, had now come to share, would be Britain's military representative. In a day which was desperately busy the Cabinet approved almost casually a letter to Lord Rothschild signed by Balfour which was destined to produce big results. This referred to a Cabinet minute drafted by Milner which stated that

> His Majesty's Government view with favour the establishment of a national home for the Jewish people.[22]

No doubt Milner's life-long friendship with the Montefiore family played a part in his sympathy with Zionism since the early years of the century.

On the next day Milner wrote a letter for Lloyd George to read on his journey with Wilson to an Allied Conference at Rapallo. This bound him still more firmly as Lloyd George's ally in opposing the Haig–Robertson view. Experience had made him more hostile to

> ... the idea of our tying ourselves up more than ever in France ... it is a waste to keep [our force there] stronger than is necessary for a lively defensive ... what we could afford to withdraw *should be the mobile force of the alliance* – the strategic reserve without which we can never win.

Hankey's arguments with him notwithstanding, Robertson at, Rapallo, was convinced that a Supreme War Council was a device of Lloyd George's to unseat him. His voice, however, proved the Conference's only really sour note. On the 7th it supported the plan of the Council, with a permanent military staff and with Hankey as its principal secretary. Back in Paris Lloyd George worked in private and public to gain sympathy for the Council, and later he achieved great success with a speech to a rather sceptical House of Commons. He asked Milner to go to Paris for two weeks or more to prepare for the institution to function. Milner's task was made easier now and for some years ahead by President Poincaré's request to Clemenceau ('*le Tigre*'), Lady Edward's close friend and therefore his own and now 76 years old, to lead a new government.

The day before Clemenceau took office, Kerenski had fallen as a consequence of the Bolshevik (October) revolution. The Bolsheviks asked Germany for an armistice, but their doings made no quick sensational impact in the West. News from Russia was hard to obtain, though the country was known to be in a chaotic condition and thought likely by Lloyd George, Pétain and others to drop out of the war. Milner was occupied at this date with talks with the American Mission and with Colonel House privately, with Air Operations and industrial unrest. At Churchill's suggestion he chaired a large committee inquiring into munition workers' wages, and, with Barnes, was performing a similar function with regard to the Clyde shipbuilders. The problem of supplying both Roumania and Russia was still his concern.

The day before he left for Versailles the death of Dr. Starr Jameson, who was one year his senior, was reported. Milner had called him this summer 'his great stand-by' in Rhodes Trust affairs, and was now the only trustee left of the seven Rhodes had named in his will. Both Rosebery and Michell had resigned in the early part of this year, Lord Grey had died and Otto Beit (the brother of Alfred), Lord Lovat and Kipling had been chosen to succeed them. Though the war, he told Lovat, had much reduced the Trust's work, they had had to 'go carefully' because Rhodes's estate, though enormous, was mainly in 'investments of an uncertain future'. The number of Scholars at Oxford earlier in this year was 97, of whom 76 were American. But questions such as electing Dominion soldiers discharged from the army as medically unfit, dealing with all kinds of demands for assistance in Oxford and elsewhere, and managing Rhodes's South African properties still had to be settled. In the meanwhile George Parkin was engaged once again in travelling all over North America. His first aim, as he put it, was 'to raise the standard of the men sent to us.' He had always been a good speaker and was, he wrote,

> ... bracing up American opinion ... [and] proving to Americans that England and her Colonies are fully more democratic than America itself.[23]

In France after costly stalemate at Ypres an attempt at a major offensive with far-reaching aims by the massed use of tanks in the Cambrai sector failed. Though initial surprise was achieved Allied lack of reserves gave the Germans the time to recover. So 'Passchendaele', sometimes used to describe the whole four months' campaign, had achieved a total advance of four miles at high cost. Milner called 'the position all round very grave' with only Allenby's progress in Palestine providing 'a much needed ray of light'. Allenby reached Jerusalem on 9 December, but the need to send reinforcements to Italy now excluded an all-out offensive against Turkey.

Amery, close to the heart of affairs, went a week before Milner to Versailes. Henry Wilson, already in Paris, saw Clemenceau and tried to convince him that the Council was worthwhile. He and Amery then requisitioned the Trianon Palace Hotel at Versailles as H.Q. for the Allies and obtained the Villa Romaine for the small British staff, both buildings with which Milner became very familiar. Milner crossed over to Paris to act under Lloyd George as Britain's second delegate. He called on Clemenceau whom he found 'very friendly'; though convinced that a united military command was required, he still needed persuasion to take the

Supreme War Council seriously. On 1 December the Council held its first formal meeting. A private session of the four heads, Lloyd George, Clemenceau, Orlando and Colonel House, President Wilson's personal representative, preceded the main meeting of some twenty-five persons. Clemenceau made an opening speech which Hankey, for some time very keen on the Council's success, had drafted on Lloyd George's instructions' This emphasized, besides military problems, the economic stamina of the Allies and such matters as manpower and shipping. Since he also drafted eight resolutions which the Council adopted it was not surprising that Hankey called the meeting 'a good send-off'.

While Lloyd George left for home Milner stayed on for a week to consolidate the Council's position through local visits and to work at the Villa Romaine or the Trianon Palace Hotel. Besides Henry Wilson, the chief Permanent Military Representatives were General Weygand, subordinate to the C.G.S., Cadorna, the former Italian C.-in-C., and the American General T. H. Bliss, all of whom had fair-sized staffs. The institution began to attract a growing number of visitors and Hankey, not given to romancing, saw it already as the 'germ of the real post-war League of Nations'. As its principal secretary he had been the chief architect of its staffing arrangements. Lord Derby, however, as well as Robertson felt very hostile towards it. On the day before Milner left Paris the War Office told Wilson he was to inform it of any advice he proposed to give to the Council.

Returning to England Milner shared in what appears the first serious War Cabinet discussion of the attitude to be taken with respect to the Bolshevik Government. The Germans had begun to transfer troops from the Russian front to the West in September, and on 14 December the Bolsheviks opened proceedings for a separate peace treaty. A day or two later Bruce Lockhart, reaching England before his official superiors, called on Milner. The Cabinet was also discussing familiar but still troublesome issues on the home front. In particular the production and distribution of food, a new Manpower Committee Report, and many fresh wage demands. Milner attended debates in the Lords on the Franchise Bill which the Commons had passed earlier in the month. As the Parliament Act, 1918, this increased the electorate by giving women of 30 or over the vote, and restricted plural voting to the University seats and a second vote for business premises. Milner had a very confidential talk with Lloyd George and Carson, which decided that Smuts should go on a mission to Switzerland to discuss with an emissary Austrian peace feelers made some months earlier by the new Emperor Karl. Though this had small concrete result Smuts later resumed the attempt to separate Austria from her allies.

More definite action resulted from the Cabinet's formation on 20 December of a Russian Information Committee over which Milner presided. Milner went with Lord Robert Cecil to Paris for four days of talks with Clemenceau, Pichon, the French Foreign Minister, and Foch at the Quai d'Orsay. They reached agreement in a secret convention to form 'zones of influence' in Russia, the French zone to be in the Ukraine and the British ones in the south. This, which lasted until 1920, disclaimed intention to interfere in the internal affairs of Russia, which at this date was hardly consistent since the Allies were wooing both the Bolsheviks and their 'White' enemies in the country. It meant, however, that Britain was now deeply involved in southern Russia.[24]

On his way home Milner spent a night at G.H.Q. having long talks with Haig and his staff in which manpower and railways were the main topics. A recent report of the Cabinet secretariat estimated that the Armed Forces needed 5–600,000 more men, and civil war work an eventual 400,000 more. Though shipping losses had fallen, demand still greatly exceeded the available tonnage. One need would be the transport of the American Expeditionary Force, only three to four untrained divisions of which had so far reached France.

1917 had been a year of defeats in every important theatre of war except Palestine and Mesopotamia. Hankey wrote in his diary on 29 December:

> Our prospects in the war are extremely rocky with Russia out, all the enemy's forces available for concentration against us . . . if we can get anything like a decent peace, we ought to do so.[25]

It happened that Milner had been dining with Curzon and discussing peace terms with him and Smuts on the previous night. Milner's aim had always been to conclude what he called a 'tolerable' peace with the Germans. But neither he nor anyone else could yet assess the political results, either inside or outside Russia, of the Bolshevik coup. What he seemed most to fear at this stage was the access the Germans might gain to Russia's large resources of foodstuffs and oil, and their means of obtaining these via the Black Sea.[26] There was, Lloyd George admitted in private, a good deal of feeling in the War Cabinet favouring peace, in which Milner shared. His 'tolerable' peace was a negotiable one which would exterminate Germany's militarism but retain her as an element of order and stability in Europe unable to be injurious to the Allies and Empire. Colonel House, who had formed a high opinion of Milner, had lately described him as ' . . . able enough and judicious enough to see where this war is leading Europe [with] a keen desire to bring it to an end in some way that will not make the sacrifice futile'.[27]

Before crossing to Paris Milner and Cecil had suggested that Britain and the Bolsheviks should exchange 'unofficial agents'. Due mainly to Milner, Bruce Lockhart was chosen to act in this capacity for Britain, while the Bolsheviks chose Maxim Litvinov. From early January 1918 before leaving for Russia Lockhart saw Milner almost daily. He records that at dinner at Brooks's Milner talked 'very frankly', was bitter regarding the Foreign Office where he wanted Robert Cecil, helped by Eyre Crowe, to replace Balfour, and was pessimistic over the war. Like so many of Milner's past young assistants he had come to regard him, he wrote later, with 'the greatest affection and hero-worship'. Though 'deeply concerned with the future of England' he was not a Tory reactionary. He supported in war

. . . . the highly organised state in which service, efficiency and hard work were more important than titles or money-bags . . . among all the so-called great men he had met none could hold a candle to Milner where *character* was concerned.[28]

Lockhart was convinced that the Bolsheviks' strength was far greater than most foreign onlookers thought, and was strongly against intervention without their consent. He refused to agree to 'forced' intervention until June; and the Allies put this into practice with the Archangel landings in August. The British Ambassador and Military Attaché did not reach London until later in January.

On 5 January Lloyd George made what Milner called 'a great speech' on War Aims to trade union leaders. In part this was meant as an answer to Landsdowne's famous letter of a month before which publicly advocated a compromise peace, and which Milner thought 'not very original or extreme' but presenting the pacifists with a handle. Lloyd George told his listeners they were not fighting a war of aggression against Germany's people, and did not intend to destroy Austria-Hungary or bleed Turkey white. But besides reparation to Belgium and France and independence for Poland, the Slav subjects of Austria-Hungary would be given self-government and some international body set up to settle disputes.[29] Three days later, without consulting the Allies, Woodrow Wilson made his famous 'Fourteen Points' speech.

Allied strategy of the main 1918 campaign was yet not firmly resolved. By mid-January Lloyd George had almost determined to replace

Robertson, and sent Smuts and Hankey touring France on a fruitless effort to find a replacement for Haig. Henry Wilson, designated by Lloyd George as the new C.I.G.S., preferred to be given more power at Versailles and thought up the plan, to which Lloyd George and Milner consented, of a General Reserve commanded by the four War Council Permanent Military Representatives. Clemenceau also liked the idea. After two days at Sturry for the first time for nine weeks and a week of 'great hustle' in the Cabinet, Milner went with Lloyd George and his 'circus' to Paris on 30 January for another session of the Supreme War Council.

The first meetings were stormy. Haig and Pershing disagreed about American battalions joining British brigades, and three sets of military advisers for each nation brought chaos. Lloyd George, though at his worst in the earlier meetings, was at his most skilful later. On 1 February the Council agreed to the Permanent Military Representatives' plan of a Western defensive campaign and offensive action against Turkey; and the generals were to submit their plans to Versailles. Foch (as the French C.G.S.) was as hostile as Robertson to Versailles control and they tried to gain the command of the General Reserve. Lloyd George got political colleagues to veto this plan; and then with Milner and Wilson he evolved the idea of a committee of the four Permanent Military Representations with Foch in the chair. According to Hankey's account his announcement about this brought tears of delight to Clemenceau and Foch.[30]

As, before, Milner stayed on for four days of talks with many people in Paris, including Smuts, being conducted by Amery to survey the Palestine campaign, Lord Esher, Izvolski the former Tsar's ambassador in Paris, various persons at the Russian Embassy, and Italian Ministers. He returned home in Clemenceau's very comfortable coach in a special train, and the Prince of Wales returning from Italy took him across the Channel on his destroyer. Reaching London he visited Lady Edward, finding her low and tired due to her mother's death that morning.

He had just lost one Cabinet colleague, Carson, who resigned partly over what seemed to him treachery by Lloyd George. While agreeing with Milner that Lloyd George was the only British politician capable of winning the war, he opposed the Supreme War Council, and supported the Haig–Robertson point of view. He was angered by the recent dismissal of his former First Sea Lord, Admiral Jellicoe; and worst of all, Lloyd George appeared to be going to accept the Plunkett Convention's plan for an Irish Parliament in the face of strong Ulster dissent.[31] Milner served Lloyd George well by again pouring oil on these waters, helping to make Carson's action appear publicly as primarily due to the last of these causes, and Carson was grateful. The problem of his propaganda responsibilities was resolved by creating a new Ministry of Information nominally in charge of Lord Northcliffe but actually run by Beaverbrook.

Lloyd George was always fertile with plans to reshuffle his Ministers. On his way back to London he spoke about Balfour joining the War Cabinet, expressing the possibility of becoming Foreign Secretary himself, and making Milner Secretary for War. Determined that Passchendaele should not be repeated his most pressing problem was the C.I.G.S. who refused several offers including Henry Wilson's post at Versailles. Milner drafted solutions to what he called 'a most embarrassing struggle over the War Office and Versailles' and 'an odious business'. Lloyd George was showing himself unable to face sacking Robertson, especially as Northcliffe had been agitating in his papers for this action. The King insisted upon one more offer being made to Robertson, which brought no result. Hankey, later joining Lloyd George, Milner and Henry Wilson at Walton Heath, said that though matters were 'very critical for the Government' the Prime Minister would eventually rise to the occasion full of fight.[32] On 16 February the War Cabinet announced that the C.I.G.S. had resigned and that Wilson was now in his seat. It appears that Milner had once again helped Lloyd George to overcome a phase of hesitation. Lord Derby, though often on the point of resigning, stayed on.

On the next day, a Saturday, Milner called on Bonar Law, whom he found very disgruntled. He then took Lady Edward for a walk on Esher Common, and visited Wilson who had seen both Lloyd George and Haig. Haig had not reciprocated 'Wully's' long support for him in the discussions just mentioned, and had made the Prime Minister aware that he had no high opinion of Derby. He also refused to give 'Wully' the command of an Army in France. For Milner there was satisfaction in the fact of the Government 'getting out of it pretty well' in a Lords' debate on the whole wrangle initiated by Lord Crewe. Though Press attacks had been violent the Government, he thought, had made out a good case for the changes. He himself made a public speech at Plymouth which he republished as a booklet under the title 'Fighting for our Lives'. The Russian collapse, he argued, had simplified the issue by making Germany's military party 'more than ever supreme'. The question now was 'whether Prussian militarism will destroy us'. He was certain greater efforts and 'far greater hardships' were before us but confident that 'the spirit of the nation will rise to grapple with them.' Two things above all were required: first, greater Allied co-ordination; and secondly the domestic unity of each Ally. He had no fear of a Russian-type revolution in Britain. But some people might unconsciously play into enemy hands as war caused 'frayed nerves and tempers'.[33]

The Cabinet's main topics were the Eastern campaigns, including Japanese intervention in Siberia, and the domestic food problem. Milner had long talks with Lloyd George about reconstructing the Government, and with E. F. Wise and Beveridge about food prices. Northcliffe was still friendly enough to ask him to act as supporter in the Lords on his elevation to Viscount. He was finding 'all days overloaded with business.' A bad cold which kept him a whole day indoors gave him time to catch up with reading official papers and to

> ... think a good bit. Not that I don't think hard all the time, tho' with increasingly disquieting conclusions.

The Supreme War Council met again on 14 March, this time in London. Haig had left the previous Session with every intention of disregarding its decision of forming an Allied General Reserve, an issue which continued the Council's chief topic. He had substituted a private agreement with Pétain amounting to no more than mutual support by extension, if necessary, of their lines. Unfortunately the two generals had won the approval of Clemenceau, who had now grown to mistrust Foch. Lloyd George, Milner and Wilson now realized with dismay that their plan had never been born; and Haig had just told the War Cabinet that a German attack on his front was impending. Clemenceau and Foch quarrelled bitterly, and the British were compelled to accept the Haig–Pétain scheme, though they seriously thought of dismissing Haig out of hand. So the soldiers, with the backing of France's Prime Minister, had won.

It was not, Hankey wrote in his diary,

> ... a sound or satisfactory conference. There was too much finessing and insufficient reality. L.G., in supporting Haig's refusal to co-operate, was dissimulating ... Clemenceau was dissimulating not to show the rift between himself and Foch.

The Council passed on to deal with political matters now overshadowed by the harsh Treaty of Brest-Litovsk imposed earlier in the month by Germany on the Russians. The chief topic was Japanese intervention in Siberia, and it was eventually agreed to send President Wilson a telegram encouraging Japan to do this. An instruction was issued to the Permanent Military Representatives to consider the question of sending a mission to Archangel to prevent seizure by the Germans.

The enemy's aim was the launching of massive offensives on a very wide front to smash Allied resistance before one of her own allies caved in, or American reinforcements could strengthen the Anglo-French line. The British army now consisted of wartime soldiers trained for trench warfare who, once driven from static positions, fell back in confusion. The weakness of Haig's pact with Pétain was revealed by the fact that the latter, convinced that the main attack would be in Champagne, kept his own main reserves far away in the south. Pétain even proposed to Clemenceau that his army should fall back on Paris, thus abandoning all contact with the British. With the Germans advancing forty miles in some sectors, Haig's position was desperate. He wired to London asking that the C.I.G.S. and Derby should come out to France at once.

A. J. P. Taylor writes:

Lloyd George rose undismayed to the height of the crisis. On 23 March he took over direction of the War Office from the helpless Derby

and quickly organized the transportation to France of the large number of men in Britain on leave. A few days later he ignored Balfour and successfully appealed to President Wilson for the use of American troops in the battle. Milner states that on the 23rd (his sixty-fourth birthday) Lloyd George rang him up from Walton Heath and asked him to go to Versailles on the next day (a Sunday). Milner did so, arriving in the early hours of the 25th. He saw Rawlinson, who had taken Wilson's place at Versailles and was considered by many the shrewdest and the ablest of Haig's generals, and later went with Clemenceau and Foch to Pétain's H.Q. at Compiègne. On the following day, the 26th, joined by Wilson, he drove to Doullens not far from the front, where these Frenchmen and Haig and his three Army Commanders foregathered.

The story of the following two hours has been told with variations in every account of Milner.[34] Haig, disillusioned with Pétain, had been persuaded by Wilson to agree that Foch should be empowered to co-ordinate operations. Foch made an attack, justified by much subsequent history, on Pétain for not fighting. Milner asked for a word with Clemenceau alone and then, to quote his own memo:

I told him quite frankly of my conviction . . . that Foch appeared to me to be the man who had the greatest grasp of the situation, and was most likely to deal with it with the intensest energy . . . Clemenceau at once agreed . . . and handed me a form of words

by which the two Governments charged Foch with directing a General Reserve and coordinating the actions of their armies in the West. Milner was in London by 11 p.m. reporting this decision to Lloyd George and adding that the Army Commanders were in great heart and matters behind the front in good order.

Milner's decisiveness, initiative and readiness to commit his own Government had contributed most to the outcome. He characteristically wrote to a journalist friend a year or two later playing down his own share and saying he hated the scramble for credit, in which some soldiers were prominent, then appearing in print. Most historians have found the phrase 'unified command' too extreme, and prefer to state that Foch obtained the 'strategic direction of military operations'. At further Allied conferences in April he was given the authority in this phrase and the title 'C.-in-C., Allied Armies', qualified by the right of Allied Commanders to appeal to their Governments if they thought their armies were in real danger.

With Wilson as C.I.G.S. the British section of the Versailles staff was brought into greater harmony with the War Office. The Allies decided at Doullens to make a supreme stand at Amiens. For a short time the German advance somewhat slackened, though anxiety in London was still great. The Cabinet was much occupied from late March with recruitment including the vexed question of conscription for Ireland. Oliver wrote to Milner urging him to press in Cabinet for this measure and not let President Wilson and House do it for them. The more balanced Steel-Maitland made a similar plea, adding that since Milner had 'very real influence' with Lloyd George he should urge him to get rid of five-sixths of the 'played out and irresolute' members of the Government who formed 'a source of indecision in others'.

The Government introduced a Military Service Bill on 9 April raising the age limit of compulsion to 50 with a possible further extension. Against Milner's wishes they compromised on Irish conscription, only taking the power to apply this by Order-in-Council. The assurance that this action would be accompanied by another Home Rule Bill failed to work as intended. Redmond had died and the Nationalists left West-minster in a body, most of them never to come back. Making common cause with Sinn Fein and acknowledging De Valera as their leader, they afforded the most massive demonstration of nationalist forces seen since

1914. Before long Lloyd George's Government supplied further fuel for Sinn Fein by replacing Lord Wimborne as Viceroy by Lord French, who introduced military rule.

In the meanwhile Milner had grown very anxious at news from France on 4 April suggesting that the German offensive was again under way. Though the Allies did not realize it at the time Ludendorff, checked in his effort to reach Amiens and divide them, had swung north. His initial success caused more informal discussion between Lloyd George, Law and Curzon on the topic of replacing Haig, and made Ludendorff decide on the aim of disrupting Britain's main front in Flanders and pushing us into the sea. On the 9th the Prime Minister had introduced the Irish proposals just mentioned in a rather flat speech to a sullen and unresponsive House of Commons. Hankey wrote in his diary:

I could not help noticing [from his seat in the gallery] how terribly L.G. has aged in the last twelve months. His hair has turned almost white.

The same day the Germans broke through the British front between La Bassée, near Béthune, and Armentières on the Belgian border. On the 10th, Milner wrote, there was bad news from France the whole day and the Cabinet almost decided to ask him to go over there; the next day was again 'very black'. He may have derived some distraction from the fact that the Cabinet was much occupied at this time with a further Air Ministry crisis, and still more from dining with Curtis to discuss India's constitution. They probably did not mention that Britain had had to recall troops from Italy, Palestine and Salonika as reinforcements for France, and that all except three divisions left in Egypt and Palestine contained far more Indian than white soldiers.

Although the British hung on to Béthune and Ypres the Germans continued their steady advance on a 25-mile front until their capture of the Channel ports seemed almost certain. On 13 April Haig issued to all ranks his memorable Order of the Day,

With our backs to the wall and believing in the justice of our cause each one of us must fight to the end.[35]

The same day Lloyd George asked Milner to go at the earliest moment to Paris to visit Clemenceau. Milner left with General Maurice, spent a night at Folkestone and crossed on Sunday the 14th in time to have breakfast with Haig at Montreuil. Then he spent six days in France in much the same fashion as those which had ended at Doullens. After a conference at

Abbeville with Haig and Foch he drove straight to Paris to talk to Clemenceau and sleep at Versailles. For three days, he travelled from Paris to conferences with the soldiers near the front about Foch and Haig's differences and reserves being sent in support of the British, and drove back to report the results to 'the Tiger'. On the 16th the news that the Germans had occupied Bailleul (on the road to Dunkirk) made the tone of his conference even graver. On his last day he found Clemenceau more cheerful and Haig at Montreuil seeming 'rather more hopeful, though regarding the situation as still intensely critical.' He reached London again late on the 19th and at once went to Downing Street.[36]

Lloyd George had held his hand about Derby from fear of political trouble which replacing him so soon after Robertson's exit might cause. Arthur Lee writes that Milner had been pressing him for some time to take action. Visiting him one day in Great College Street, he records that Milner suddenly shed his 'austere reserve', and drop-kicking a cushion across his room exclaimed,

> ... that's Derby ... he'll never keep shape or straight however much he's kicked.[37]

In early April Lloyd George made up his mind. Law told a colleague that the Prime Minister had been flirting with the plan of taking the War Office himself. It was certainly one of the posts which, curious though it seems, he thought might suit Hankey, who was highly competent in his own very specialized job. Milner had discussed the alternatives of Hankey and himself in a letter to the Prime Minister of 13 April, acknowledging the former's great qualifications but adding that he himself might be 'more generally acceptable to the Army' and so able to act in a crisis 'with greater resoluteness and authority'. He ended 'personally I have no feeling one way or the other.'[38]

Whatever Lloyd George thought of this argument he sent Milner a message and on the morning after returning from Paris, Milner was sworn in at Buckingham Palace as Secretary of State for War. Derby felt aggrieved, but was given the Embassy at Paris, and Hankey was only too glad to stay where he was.

Chapter 13

Secretary of State for War
(April 1918 – January 1919)

Backs to the Wall – The Turning Point – Armistice and Demobilization

When Milner was sworn in on 20 April Sir Almeric Fitzroy observed that his visit to Paris had

> ... so far lifted the cloud of his usual despondency that he permitted himself to speak with hopefulness.[1]

Talks with Clemenceau, whom he called 'the soul of the Alliance', had proved a tonic. He also always responded with zest to the grant of authority to deal with a crisis. At the outbreak of war, with no prospect of public office in sight, a friend wrote that 'the need for definite action seemed to give him a fresh lease of youthful energy.' In this April of 1918 his new office could be said to rank next in importance to that of the Prime Minister himself. With Ludendorff's second French offensive in progress the Allies lay in danger of final defeat, and 'much strain and uneasiness' and political uncertainty prevailed among Anglo-French leaders.[2] Milner wrote to Henry Gell that he felt 'an awful responsibility over being chucked in at the most critical moment of all our history.'[3]

His friend Austen Chamberlain replaced him in the War Cabinet and remarked 'the position at home and in France is so grave'; his main work for some months concerned Ireland, where ideas of Home Rule and conscription had both been abandoned and coercion was being tried again. An eccentric idea of Lloyd George's, two days after Milner's assumption of office, gives a further example of the turmoil prevailing. Hankey records a visit from Milner who told him the Prime Minister had pressed him hard to appoint him his Parliamentary Under-Secretary for War.

> I at once protested [Hankey wrote] that I was the last person in the world for such a post. My experience was entirely in the field of large questions of policy ... I had no liking for questions of administrative detail, and no desire to be a peer or to defend the War Office in either House.[4]

Milner knew of no one so well suited as Hankey for the difficult work he performed, and entirely agreed. He retained in the office in question its holder since 1916, a Liberal M.P. called Ian Macpherson. Amery, still attached to Hankey for Imperial War Cabinet work, joined Milner as a personal assistant secretary.

Though Lloyd George had introduced a new Military Service Bill on 9 April the German offensive gave fresh life to M.P.s and those in the Army who laid the chief blame at his door for inadequate reinforcements in France. Since Ludendorff's thrusts were still primarily aimed at Haig's armies in Flanders this question was linked with Haigh's promise to Pétain the autumn to extend his line southwards in which in fact he had done. In his diary of 22 April Henry Wilson, without guessing the rumpus to follow, called Lloyd George 'much upset' by some figures of comparative Army strengths compiled by General Maurice, until recently at the War Office. Of more urgent importance was his summons two days later to a Cabinet discussing the 'momentous decision' whether to fall back, join the French and abandon the near-sacrosanct Channel ports (Boulogne and Calais) or continue the effort to cover the ports. Wilson favoured the former and Haig, as Milner soon learnt, the latter. Lloyd George asked Geddes, the First Lord of the Admiralty, to send him a plan for evacuation of troops.[5]

Milner went off with Wilson again for three days at Montreuil for 'a very long and grave talk' with Haig, recording that 'news on the whole remained bad.' One more, conference with Clemenceau and his generals took place at Abbeville. It was after this visit that Haig wrote in his diary,

Milner has given me a very favourable impression as Secretary of State for War, and his one idea seems to be as helpful as possible.

He was impressed by his habit of retiring in the intervals of talks with his staff into 'purdah' to study the files bearing on some crucial problem.[6]

After two days in London Milner was back again on 1 May at the same two headquarters, only this time as part of what he so often called a 'dreadful circus'. Lloyd George, attended by members of his personal staff, the C.I.G.S. with a number of War Office colleagues and Admiral Wemyss, the First Sea Lord, left London at 7.30 a.m., crossed to Calais in the destroyer *Broke* and at 3 p.m. began a Supreme War Council meeting at Abbeville. With thirty two people present a session of four hours was summed up by Milner:

. . . atmosphere awful, discussion very time-wasting . . . so great loss of temper and very poor results.

A later private meeting of the 'Big Four', Clemenceau, Lloyd George, Orlando and himself proved 'much more satisfactory'.

The main topic of these meetings was again the one already mentioned of the two alternatives facing the British. On 2 May the procedure reversed that of the previous day. The four political leaders met first with only their chief generals and admirals. Pétain was characteristically gloomy, but Foch stoutly refused to believe that British abandonment of the ports, or retirement behind the Somme would be needed. Later full sessions of the Supreme War Council – described by Milner as 'dogfights' – were occupied with interminable discussion about the incorporation of U.S. battalions in British brigades. The Washington Government had in principle accepted British wishes for this, but left wide discretion to Pershing who not unnaturally opposed the whole scheme.

On 7 May a political bombshell exploded in the form of a letter by General Sir Frederick Maurice, waiting to leave the War Office, which appeared in most morning papers, impugning the statements of Lloyd George and Law in the previous month regarding the strength of the British Army in France at the opening of 1918. He wrote:

> . . . this letter is not the result of a military conspiracy [but written] in the hope that Parliament may see fit to order an investigation into the statements I have made.

He had been Sir William Robertson's protégé in France and when Sir William became C.I.G.S. he became director of Military Operations in the War Office. He had not, as stated by Taylor, been dismissed by Milner but, not thinking highly of Wilson, had gladly accepted an offer by Haig some time before Milner's appointment, to serve on the staff of the 5th Army in France.

Loyalty to the Army, not revenge, prompted his action. General Edward Spears, a young Brigadier who was head of the British Military Mission in Paris from 1917 to 1920, later described him as

> . . . imperturbable as a fish, always unruffled, the sort of man who would eat porridge by gaslight on a foggy morning in winter, looking as if he had enjoyed a cold bath . . . an admirable character, the soul of military honour, with a deep sense of civic duty which placed service to the country above all else, he suffered acutely from the tactics of the politicians and their too subtle methods.[7]

On a visit to France in April, when Haig was under strong pressure,

Maurice had found the Army indignant over what it considered Lloyd George's false statements in Parliament on the 9th about its strength. Comparison of the figure of 1 January 1918 with that of one year before, and confusion between total and 'combat' strength, both distorted the issue. On the 18th Macpherson, the War Office Under-Secretary, repeated this version to the Commons. Three days later, a day after Milner's appointment, Maurice (no longer D.M.O.) studied Lloyd George's speech in Hansard more carefully. What decided him to take public action was Law's false statement in the Commons on 23 April about the extension of Haig's front. The exact number of divisions not diverted to France, but kept in the Near East, had also now entered the argument.

What matters here is Milner's part, so far as it can be discovered, in the rumpus.[8] Lloyd George's annoyance on receiving new War Office figures on 22 April has already been mentioned, and he sent Milner, who had only held office two days, a brusque if not insolent memo.[9] It is ironic that Milner, with his unquestioned gift for dealing with figures, took office in mid-stream of a complex statistical current. He appears not to have answered Lloyd George's memo, but he supplied one or more additions to what an historian calls the War Office's 'many sets of confusing, and in some cases contradictory, statements of the Army's strength', emanating from different departments. He frankly admitted the misstatements of Macpherson in Parliament before he himself took office.

The importance of Maurice's action for history lies of course in the threat which it posed to the Government. In this fourth year of war people were tired and most nerves were on edge. In what proved an historic debate on 9 May the Asquithian Liberals saw their chance to bring down the Government with the probable help of Carson and some Unionist critics. But once more Lloyd George rose to a Parliamentary occasion in a speech which Milner called 'a complete personal triumph'. He had earlier admitted at lunch with Hankey that speeches dealing with figures were not his strong point, and Hankey described this speech later as

> . . . not the speech of a man who tells 'the truth; the whole truth; and nothing but the truth' . . . he had figures from the D.M.O.'s [Maurice's] Dept at the W.O. supporting [his own argument of a month earlier] and the Adjutant-General's figures saying the precise contrary, but was discreetly silent about them . . . M.P.s of all complexions kept coming to the official gallery to ask me what was the 'real truth'.[10]

Split openly in two, the Liberal Party, A. J. P. Taylor writes, committed suicide on this day, strangely enough on behalf of the Army. The debate, he continues, 'marked the beginning of Lloyd George's personal dictatorship.' The grim fact must be added that, in the four weeks which followed the start of the German offensive in late March, British casualties were 80,000 more than in the fourteen weeks of the Battle of Passchendaele.

Lord Blake, in some British Academy lectures, said that Lloyd George came closer to Presidential Government on the American model than any British Prime Minister before him or since.[11] He created his own group of hand-picked advisers (who worked in huts in No. 10's garden), apart from the Cabinet Secretariat under Hankey. He led no party, and relied much on the Unionist Law for attention to matters in Parliament. Though Lord Blake does not add this, his personal attendance in the Commons was unusually rare and confined for the most part to major occasions. When he went there he often, as on the occasion just mentioned, won an oratorical triumph. What reinforces the parallel, for the present writer at least, is the gap he maintained between himself as First Minister of the Crown and his colleagues, in and outside the War Cabinet. He was fertile in creating new informal machinery at the highest (i.e. his own) political level, and now did so in a form of close interest to Milner.

The secrecy of much information required for the Maurice affair had caused the methodical Hankey to begin a new series of especially secret 'X' files. In mid-May he recorded that the P.M. had

> . . . invented a new and most tiresome method of doing business. He puts the War Cabinet at noon and has a private meeting of his own with Lord Milner and the C.I.G.S. at 11 a.m.

He had to attend, and, assisted by Amery, kept a record of these (as he called them) 'X meetings'. Already hard-pressed in his job, he wrote: 'luckily Lloyd George is sure to tire of it soon.' This did not prove to be true, though Lloyd George later called in a larger variety of advisers. Amery surely pitches the matter too high when he writes that the triumvirate Hankey names, which met almost daily at 10 Downing Street, 'really ran the war during the critical spring and summer months of the German offensive.' Their discursive talk would wander from subject to subject with Lloyd George firing suggestions, 'shrewd or fanciful', at Wilson for some instant action. Milner intervened only occasionally, 'and yet somehow bringing them nearer to a definite conclusion, to which Hankey would pin them down if he could.'[12]

The Maurice affair increased the Prime Minister's inclination to grow more demanding and didactic to colleagues, more prepared to abandon old friends and supporters. In spite of X meetings he no longer gave Milner the man the esteem he had extended towards him in the previous year. It forms a surprise, in conflict with most of the evidence to find Riddell, a close friend of Lloyd George's, recording that

L.G. spoke very favourably of Milner's last speech as excellent and thinks he improves every day.

His own earlier impression of Milner had been that of 'a very pleasant courtly person'.[13] Milner took the rebuffs (most often arriving on paper) in a stoical spirit, at least until one public episode after the war. He knew Lloyd George's volatile nature, and his dependence on him in these critical months. In addition, he was absorbed in his job and knew he could do it.

Hankey, over twenty years younger than Milner, lived to succeed Fitzroy as Clerk of the Privy Council; then to accept a peerage and take office under two Prime Ministers in the Second World War. Later still he sent Wrench a summary of Lloyd George's relations with Milner which included the statements:

... for a long time [Milner] was Lloyd George's most trusted colleague ... Milner spent a good deal of time at the Supreme War Council in the last year of the war, and I am inclined to think that in 1918 Lloyd George relied on him more than on any other colleague; except, perhaps, Bonar Law – but he was more for political advice.[14]

When the X meetings started, a lull in the German offensive in France gave new impetus to top-level discussion about Allied intervention in Russia. Not long after the Brest-Litovsk Treaty Lloyd George told the War Cabinet they had talked in some detail about Archangel, Transcaucasia and elsewhere in Russia, but presented no concrete proposal to Trotsky or President Wilson. Like Milner (but unlike both the Foreign Office and the War Office before Milner got there) Lloyd George trusted Bruce Lockhart who had got on good terms with Trotsky and had received his invitation to the Allies to propose a scheme. Though Balfour disliked it, a preliminary telegram was sent to the President. At an early X meeting on 17 May Lloyd George thought up a plan to send Canadians to join the Czech Legion and deny to the Germans both minerals in the Urals and Siberia's grain. Some days later the War Office under Milner's direction, and with Lord Robert Cecil present, was discussing the more practical issue of saving the Murmansk and Archangel stores.

Milner went off again for four days in France, and was told by Clemenceau that a big new offensive had just started on the French front. This time it was against French troops with British reserves defending the Aisne and the city of Rheims. Back in London and preoccupied with this threat, Milner found a long Cabinet dealing again with Siberian action very tiresome. As June opened he was once more in Paris with Lloyd George and the 'circus' for long personal talks and another Supreme War Council session. Henry Wilson had for some time been pessimistic and wrote in his diary on 1 June that 'a possibility, perhaps a probability, [existed] of the French Army being beaten.'[15]

While crossing the Channel Lloyd George and his party again talked of abandoning Dunkirk for the purpose of shortening the line. At Versailles General Sir John Du Cane, who led Britain's mission to Foch's G.H.Q., thought decisive defeat of the French would hopelessly trap Britain's army, now grown to some $2\frac{1}{2}$ million men. He also told them that Haig and Foch were once more at odds, this time over cutting the size of divisions (Foch's preference) or reducing their number (in which Haig was engaged). Foch and Haig were both men who held firmly to their views and fierce wrangles between them were constant. It stands to their credit that these wrangles were usually resolved when they met, though this credit must be shared with their political masters and on the British side especially with Milner.

The P.M., General Spears wrote much later, had emerged with great power from his 9 May victory, but

. . . straightforwardness was not the most obvious weapon in his armoury. To him the soldiers who, it must be admitted, took little trouble to convince him, were stupid unimaginative blunderers [who] could conceive of no military concept beyond that of hurling men against barbed wire. On the other hand, the ideas Lloyd George put forward on military matters outraged all the teachings of military experience and history, concerning which he was as ignorant as he was about French poetry or the French language.[16]

The Supreme War Council meetings lasted two days and discussed the integration into Anglo-French forces of American troops, the appointment of a Mediterranean 'Admiralissimo', and a French plan for a Salonika offensive.[17] General Spears gives some vivid accounts of these meetings, especially of Clemenceau, their principal figure. With his 'diamond-hard stare' he was both the most cynical and most feared of men:

He distrusted Lloyd George, whom he regarded as little better than a clown . . . and who at times had to lash himself into a fury to face up to the formidable old Frenchman, whom he feared as most people did.

Taking twelve hours next day to travel from Versailles to London Milner lunched with the King on 5 June and told him the outlook was black. The Germans were again, as in 1914, on the Marne in the area of Château-Thierry, less than 60 miles from Paris. Twenty-four hours later Milner was again in Paris with Wilson, attempting to smooth out a new Foch–Haig wrangle. The effect in practice of the Doullens and Beauvais agreements was now becoming clearer. Foch, without consultation with Haig, had moved British troops in support of the French, which in Haig's view put his army in peril. After British talks, a meeting with the French chaired by Clemenceau was accounted by Milner 'very satisfactory' as removing much misunderstanding. The two statesmen agreed that Foch must retain full Generalissimo powers, but that his orders must pass through Haig's hands. Henry Wilson agreed that this meeting did 'a vast deal of good'.[18]

The Imperial War Cabinet resumed its meetings of the previous year on 11 June to hear a speech from Lloyd George which made Dominion Ministers well aware of the gravity of affairs. Many of them grew pessimistic about the French front. The Imperial War Conference of subordinate Ministers achieved useful work on the issues of Preference and the control of the Empire's raw materials, but returned to their homelands within a few weeks. The Imperial War Cabinets and fuller Dominion Prime Ministers' meetings met often again in this year and effectively merged, because of improved will to co-operate and better Imperial communications, into next year's British Empire Delegation in Paris.[19]

The writer cannot find evidence that in 1918, let alone in the previous year, Milner, as Gollin writes, had concluded that 'his great plan for a Council of Empire was invalid . . . and was not a measure of practical politics.' If creation of a more formal system had to wait, Milner was, in the writer's opinion, quite ready to accept this, using what persuasion he could combined with the principle of *solvitur ambulando*. The critical state of affairs in June 1918 had brought the Dominions' chief leaders into closer discussions with Lloyd George and his colleagues than ever before. Views on military strategy were interwoven with much discussion of peace *aims*. But the German collapse and the efforts at Paris to define peace *terms* still lay in the future.[20]

For the rest of the month the situation on the Western front remained grave. Foch, it is true, held fast to the axiom 'only he is vanquished who accepts defeat'; but he had, besides political critics, the tiredness of much of his army to contend with. Haig's optimism seemed, to close observers like Hankey, unwavering. But he also had to win the consent for important decisions from the politicians in Whitehall or – as Henry Wilson liked to call them – 'the Frocks'. Though the exercise would be worthless, a count of the times Lloyd George told some colleague (even long after Ludendorff's offensive was in progress) he was thinking of bringing Haig home would yield a high figure. Haig's favourable opinion of Milner, mentioned several times in this story, and the support Milner gave him, have tended to be overlooked by historians.[21] For this writer the reason is simply that Milner cared intensely for causes (or more precisely *some* causes) but hardly at all for the personal credits or debits which his work on these earned him. He lacked personal ambition except in so far as position (the 'status' of contemporary jargon) gave him power to advance some particular cause. The causes he felt deeply about in 1918 were, first, winning the war, and then making a peace which would bring to the Empire and Europe (in that order) stability and prosperity. Though what might be called a 'near-Easterner' (with a small 'n') his strong sense of loyalty and belief in the man's professional knowledge made him, with rare exceptions, back Haig. Gell had written truly to Jowett years before that Milner was

> a man who never does anything well until he is absorbed . . . the only barrier which would economize, accumulate and direct his energies is fixed work in which his heart can take hold.[22]

General Pershing now appointed Colonel Griscom as his personal liaison officer to Milner. Winston Churchill gave a demonstration for his benefit of new 'pill-boxes' in Kensington Gardens; and called on him several times at the War Office for long talks about tanks, mechanical traction and other devices. Milner's view in July that the most pressing need was for men not machines was, however, shared by the War Cabinet. As Churchill took over from Milner soon after the war it is convenient to add that since his appointment by Lloyd George as Minister of Munitions his political stock had been low. In the Government he stood almost alone, drawing mainly on his personal friendship with Balfour and F. E. Smith. He was hardly more than a protégé of Lloyd George's, who could afford to ignore his threats to resign.[23]

The Second Battle of the Marne, as it came to be called, still posed a grave threat to the Allies, with Ludendorff possessing the 'nose' (as the Army called it) of Château-Thierry. But for some weeks a lull intervened.

The 'X meeting', though much concerned with providing more troops for the West, was worried on June 19 by the advance of the Bolshevik forces towards the Caspian Sea and in Siberia. Roskill writes that Hankey's diary makes it clear 'how quickly intervention in Russia took on an overtly anti-Bolshevik hue in London,' and that Lloyd George told him to ask Balfour if he should meet Kerenski, who had turned up in London. Balfour was doubtful about the wisdom of this, yet Lloyd George met the exiled leader though it seems that no record was made of their talk. Kerenski later called one evening on Milner for a long talk.[24]

On 1 July Milner went over to Versailles again for a Supreme War Council meeting with Lloyd George and the 'circus'. Haig recorded the P.M. as 'very angry with the French' for taking too much credit in directing the war; while Wilson wrote that Foch was very angry with Lloyd George for threatening to reduce British forces to reinforce the Near East. Lloyd George had a violent altercation with Tardieu, and Milner tried to close the discussions as likely to exacerbate the differences of the Allies. With superb understatement Hankey said 'Versailles does not work smoothly.' As the angriest Supreme War Council meeting yet held it must have blurred Lord Robert Cecil's vision, shared by Hankey, of this body as the dress-rehearsal of some post-war League to bring peace on earth.[25]

About two weeks later Foch, confident that a new German offensive on the Marne was impending, ordered Haig to send four divisions to the south. Haig complied without fuss; but fuss and ill temper soon prevailed at a mansion called Danny at Hassocks lent by Riddell to Lloyd George. Hankey relates how, glad to escape for a time from Lloyd George's now frequent ill temper, he obeyed his command to fetch Milner who (the day being Sunday) was relaxing eighty two miles away at Sturry. He found this 'a quaint bachelor house', and sensed a romance since Milner was occupied 'carrying a basket of roses to a lovely neighbour.' Milner, hardly pleased, motored with him the eighty two miles back. At a conference after dinner Smuts and Borden (though not Milner) shared Lloyd George's suspicion that Clemenceau and Foch might sacrifice Haig. A telegram was then sent to Haig reminding him (quite unnecessarily) of his right to appeal to his Government.[26]

The following day, the 15th, the Germans attacked, and Foch had correctly forecast both the time and the place. At the X meeting and the Cabinet the next day, the situation in France was obscure; and Hankey considered Lloyd George 'very rude to Milner about Borden's [adverse] criticisms of the Higher Command.' On the 18th, General Charles Mangin's 10th Army, with four British divisions and U.S. support and massed tanks, struck back with success between Château-Thierry and Soissons. General Callwell, an experienced military historian, calls this 'the turning-point of the conflict on the French front', but his former chief, Wilson, was convinced that the Rheims attack was a feint and that a big German offensive would be aimed once again at the British.[27] Some days later Milner took the chair at the War Office of the Imperial War Graves Commission which had received a royal charter in the previous year. This body is interesting as a practical example of Imperial effort and of much work, helped by Milner, by his friend Fabian Ware who was now its Vice-Chairman and remained so (while War Secretaries came and went) until after the Second World War.

Milner was pleased with an 'excellent speech' Lloyd George made in the Imperial War Cabinet on Empire relations. He wrote that though the news from France remained good the process of pushing the Germans out of the Marne salient was proving a slow one.[28] Wilson, who was perhaps stressing his own views more than Milner's, claimed that on 31 July both Milner and Smuts were gloomy in speeches to the Dominion Prime Ministers over the prospects of the Allies ever thrashing the Germans in France.

On 3 August, just short of the start of the fifth year of war, Milner took young Helen Cecil to watch King George and Queen Mary open Australia House in the Strand. That evening he called the news of the Allied capture of Soissons 'very good'. His faith in Foch seemed well grounded. The war's anniversary was marked the next day by a big service attended by the King and Queen at St. Margaret's, Westminster. On 8 August General Rawlinson, one of Haig's best commanders and known as 'Rawly', successfully attacked east of Amiens, an occasion called by Ludendorff in his memoirs much later, 'the black day [in the war] of the German Army'.

Cyril Falls later called Rawly's attack the start of effective Allied offensives; with Napoleon's decline in his mind he calculated that the span from 8 August to 11 November was 96 days and not 100. He, of course, was a military expert looking backwards. In the minds of the Allied civil and military leaders most concerned at the time the direction and pace of the tide were by no means so clear. Many still held the view that the war would last well into 1919 if not longer, and were occupied in planning with this view in mind.

This watershed, as it in fact proved to be, gives opportunity for the mention of some features of Milner's private life unconnected with Whitehall. It seems that in 1918 he enjoyed less life of this kind than at any time since he had come home from Africa twelve years or so earlier. World wars, we now know, are periods of growing contraction, death, separation from friends and austerity. Few people in Britain were now following, as they had in 1914, their 'business as usual'. Milner, on the evidence of his papers, much reduced his large private correspondence. His week-end visits to Sturry, Great Wigsell and elsewhere outside London were now infrequent. When he met private friends, male and female, it was usually for dinner in London. Elinor Glyn, who always stayed at the Ritz, was perhaps the most advanced (or ahead of her day) of the bevy of ladies whose company he enjoyed. Most of these seem to have been either widows, like her and Loulie Dawkins, or effectively, if not legally, separated from their husbands, like Lady Edward and Mrs Gaskell.

If Mrs Glyn was ahead of her time she was not, to her sorrow, ahead of George Nathaniel, Marquess Curzon of Kedleston. It is tempting to imagine that Milner, having first lost his heart to Margot Tennant and been out-gunned by Asquith, then lost it again to Mrs Glyn, and was cut out by Curzon. But the evidence that he was really in love with, as distinct from attached to, this lady is flimsy. What is certain is that in 1908 she developed a passion for Curzon, whose wife had died some years before and came to believe this feeling was returned. In 1915 Mr Glyn, an obscure figure, conveniently retired to Richmond where he lived quietly. When Elinor opened *The Times* in December 1916 to see what appointment Curzon had been given by Lloyd George she read with surprise of his engagement to a rich South American widow, Mrs Duggan. She then burnt his 500 letters to her and never saw or wrote to him again. Besides possessing much attraction and vivacity she had made money; though not enough for this Marquess.

Milner had seen and written to her regularly for years and, her grandson Anthony Glyn writes, had 'a great regard for her judgement of people.'[29] She obtained some form of war work in Paris and stayed at The Ritz, where Milner often visited her, from the time when the Supreme War Council was founded until the end of the Peace Conference. She wrote in her memoirs, *Romantic Adventure*,

> ... he was still, as always, aloof and reserved, but this apparent stiffness merely threw into relief the great charm of his personality in those rare moments when he was able to unbend.

She thought both Milner and Curzon were in their different ways

> ... reserved, cold, exclusive, experienced and wise, but totally devoid

of the power of popular appeal . . . such men keep the feet of mankind within the orbit of civilisation while Lloyd George widened the orbit.[30]

Like many of his friends she used Milner's position to seek help for individuals (e.g. a young airman) connected with her work; and he always gave her this help in some form. One or two other acts to help friends may be mentioned. Somewhat earlier Charles Boyd, one-time secretary to the Rhodes Trust, had arrived at his London house after midnight 'in a state of great excitement amounting to dementia' and then dashed away, leaving Milner in the 'greatest anxiety'. Milner visited Boyd's doctor and his own, and thereafter at regular intervals an asylum in which he was confined; he died soon after the war.[31] A less painful incident concerned Stephen Hobhouse, eldest son of his Balliol friend Henry Hobhouse the Liberal M.P., and a young cousin of the Emily Hobhouse of South African fame. Perhaps through his marriage, Stephen had joined the Quakers and in the war was a conscientious objector to military service (or 'conchie'). People holding this view figured much more in this first World War than they did in the second. Stephen's mother campaigned stoutly for the 12,000 or so conscientious objectors and visited Milner several times at his office in her son's interest. He took practical action, though with results unknown to the writer.[32]

His Rhodes Trust responsibilities were light since the Oxford Scholarship system had now reached its lowest numerical ebb. In 1917–18 only eight scholars, six from the Colonies (mainly studying medicine) and two from the U.S.A., were in residence. Elections for 1918–19, though not the annual qualifying exams, had been postponed, and in May the Trustees decided to continue this postponement into 1919. Milner consulted A. L. Smith and others about electing another and younger Trustee; and in the following year Leo Amery, now aged 45, was chosen. Parkin, delayed by enemy submarines in the Atlantic, returned from his long North American tour, his last before his retirement two years later. In October he wrote to Milner suggesting that Smuts, who held strong views on the issue, should visit America to counter the widespread opinion prevailing there that Britain should restore Germany's colonies after the war. He added that the weight which Woodrow Wilson would bring to the Peace Conference was steadily growing. Events by this date had, however, outdistanced the Smuts project.[33]

Milner wrote in August that General Sir Hubert Gough, a leading figure in the Curragh affair, called at his home with the aim of enlisting his help. He was now what the French call *dégommé*, and the British

Army 'unstuck', since his 5th Army had allowed the line to break at the
opening of the German offensive in March. Sent home, he sought Milner's
help in obtaining an inquiry. The merits of the case lie outside the scope
of this story, though it seems that Henry Wilson was the main architect of
Gough's downfall and that Milner was not ready to doubt Wilson's
professional judgement. Gough found Milner's mind, not 'lost' in the
term which Lord Courtney had used years before, but firmly closed; and
he later described him in terms much less flattering than those used by
Elinor Glyn,

> . . . he was a distinguished-looking man who just missed being hand-
> some. He had a long face and a pale complexion and his grey eyes
> looked rather coldly at me. He gave me the impression of reserve, lack
> of sympathy, perhaps just a hint of callousness. . . . he straight away
> said that he was not prepared to do anything . . .[34]

A portrait of Milner not in ink but in paint must be mentioned, since
it hangs in a place of honour in Balliol. Over months in the previous
autumn he had sat for this purpose to a Miss Florence Upton, a friend of
both Mrs Alfred Lyttelton and Loulie Dawkins. Since he disliked sitting
to artists he probably did so to please his two friends. Miss Upton when
younger had invented the Golliwog, defined by the dictionary as a
'grotesque and usually black doll', and had written some 15 Golliwog
books; she had taken later to spiritualism. Soon after this date her portrait
of Milner was exhibited in the Grosvenor Gallery; she was disappointed
with it and wrote 'The Wind of the Spirit of God is not in that picture.'
A large number of subsequent members of Balliol would, one may guess,
agree with her judgement. It appears that Lady Dawkins presented the
portrait to Balliol. The College had made Milner an Honorary Fellow, a
much smaller company then, in 1916.[35]

To return to describe Milner's main business of this year is to re-enter
a tangle of argument and difference of views both in Whitehall and between Britain's leaders and her Allies. In a War Office paper on intervention in Russia the C.I.G.S. called July to September still 'critical
months' with the manpower resources of France and Great Britain
'nearing exhaustion', Italy proving a weak reed and the U.S. still unable
to contribute any quantity of trained men. Manpower was by this fifth
year of war more than ever a root cause of the problem. With a population of about 37 million Britain had to furnish an army, a navy, an air
force, and hordes of workers at home to keep these supplied. Foch was
created this August a Marshal of France. But in one of the many British

arguments with the French on the number of divisions Britain maintained (or intended to keep) in the West, Foch's well-deserved elevation did not deter General Wilson from reminding him that Britain now had boys of 18½ fighting.

Some of Milner's friends regretted in April that his new office had (since he held a portfolio) entailed his leaving the War Cabinet. They need not have done so, since he often attended this body, as well as the daily and most exclusive X meetings and had frequent informal talks with Lloyd George in Downing Street and the country. If Lloyd George was erratic and rude Milner did not suffer this treatment alone nor cease to be often consulted. Roskill quotes a letter from Lord Esher in Paris to Hankey relaying a rumour that Lloyd George was tiring of Henry Wilson, adding that the Prime Minister

> . . . like Henry VIII wants a new wife every six months . . . he has so many enemies that he should husband his resources of friendship. He must not get the reputation of a man who lets go of those who help him! Your influence is the only disinterested influence about the little man.[36]

Even the experienced, patient, efficient Hankey was before long expressing in his diary, and doubtless to friends, what in a later world war was called 'alarm and despondency'. A complaint by Lord Curzon caused him to write, '. . . my opinion is that the P.M. is assuming too much the role of a dictator and that he is heading for very serious trouble'. Leading figures like Curzon, Austen Chamberlain and Walter Long (the Colonial Secretary) were quick to take umbrage if they thought information which should reach them failed to do so.

After successful but limited offensives by both Haig and Foch, Milner wrote '. . . as I expected, the situation at the front has stabilized . . .' The top-level discussions of the following weeks, which much involved Milner, covered numerous topics. They mixed issues of an urgent strategical nature, for example the perennial one of West versus East, with discussion of Peace Aims on the assumption, not yet at all widely held, that the war might end soon. Besides operations on land in the Balkans, Syria and 'Mespot' (now Iraq), the 'East' had begun to be the focus for the War Office of various practical aims in the vast area of Russia. At the same time the 'far West', represented by the U.S.A. and its President, was a growing preoccupation of Lloyd George and his colleagues. One recalls Winston Churchill's saying to Parliament in the crucial year 1940 that

> . . . the British Empire and the United States will have to be somewhat

mixed up together in some of their affairs for mutual and general advantage . . .

The same 'mix-up' grew more intense in this summer of 1918. General Pershing, Colonel House and the leading Americans in Britain, with the help of the Anglophil Ambassador Walter H. Page, got on well enough with Britain's politicians and soldiers. The trouble lay further away with Woodrow Wilson, whom it was Lloyd George's little joke to describe to the C.I.G.S. as 'your cousin', and his peace aims. The President had enunciated his well-known Fourteen Points in January 1918 and saw himself, then and later, as a mediator between two sets of European belligerents. He was also, of course, under America's constitution Commander-in-Chief of her Army and Navy. British leaders felt it unreasonable when on entering the war he refused to call his nation an 'ally' or to speak of her as more than an 'associated' Power. In the discussions just mentioned the drafting of telegrams to the President on war aims now consumed much time.

Milner spent another week-end in August at Windsor having much talk with the King who, he wrote, 'expressed great anxiety' over the situation in Siberia. On the abdication of Tsar Nicholas, his first cousin, eighteen months earlier he had sent him a telegram of personal sympathy which for Russian political reasons never reached him. The King, with good judgement, doubted the wisdom of the Tsar and his family being granted asylum in England and the French Government agreed (though too late) to receive them. The Bolshevik Government had announced that they had shot the Tsar on 16 July, adding falsely they had sent the Tsarina and her children to a place of safety. King George then ordered four weeks' full mourning. It was not until late in the year that a report, which eventually proved true, that the whole of the family had been shot with the Tsar, reached England.[37]

On 21 August Milner noted a new advance by the British north of Albert, and next day he went again with Hankey and Amery for six nights at Criccieth where they found a huge party. The purposes of the gathering were, first, to prepare for a General Election which Lloyd George was anxious to risk while the tide in France seemed to be turning. Secondly, to discuss with Sir Bertrand Dawson (later Lord Dawson of Penn) and Dr. Addison what Milner found a very interesting scheme for a post-war national health service. The Prime Minister was in high spirits, there was plenty of music and Milner as usual was refreshed by the scenery and the walks, though occupied a good deal with work arriving in bags from London. Lloyd George, in spite of the music, showed a very hard attitude in their talks about peace terms.

When the party went back to London they were faced with a bolt from the blue in the serious form of a strike by the London police for recognition of their union. This summer had witnessed a wave of strikes by munition, cotton and other workers. A. J. P. Taylor writes that there was now an organized 'people', the factory workers, and that

> . . . the typical man of the people once a shopkeeper (preferably a cobbler) was now a shop steward.[38]

Not normally directly concerned with these strikes Milner was urgently called by the P.M. to a conference on this one which ended quite quickly. His Adjutant-General, Macready, was appointed Commissioner of the Metropolitan Police. He was concerned for much longer with the demand of the Coal Controller for the quicker release of miners from the Army.

He sat up till 3 a.m. one night reading what he called a 'contentious draft report of the [Dominion] Prime Ministers' Committee'. This was presumably the report which Hankey noted as raising 'most complicated constitutional difficulties for the unfortunate secretary' (i.e. himself) and taking him long hours to draft.[39] The Imperial War Cabinet and the larger body of Dominion Prime Ministers were having their last meetings of this series, though Smuts stayed in Britain, and so for a time did Hughes of Australia and Ward of New Zealand. These meetings achieved some advance towards Milner's aims. The critical military situation gave the views of the Dominion leaders more prominence and force; they had, it was obvious, a big stake in the human and other resources in battles now more widespread than ever. There was clear understanding that they would take a big part in a future Peace Conference. Perhaps as important, agreement was reached that all important War Cabinet papers should be sent to the Dominions 'for information' or (except the most secret) to their representatives in London.

On 3 September Milner, for the first time observed by this writer, used superlatives in calling the news from France 'extraordinarily good' and the previous days' fighting there 'very successful'. Yet the uncertainty still prevailing among Wilson's 'frocks' is shown by Haig, optimistic as ever, coming over from France a week later to tell Milner 'how greatly the situation in the field had changed to the Allies' advantage' and to state his view that the character of the war had now changed. Though Americans were now reaching France in great numbers, Haig still expressed urgent need for reserves, especially those mobile in nature, and Milner said he would do his best to acquire them. After time and effort he out-manoeuvred Lloyd George's eccentric attempt to appoint a civilian as Adjutant-General.[40] On the evidence of Amery and others both Wilson and Foch were still making their plans on the assumption that the best they could hope for was the start by the Allies of an effective offensive in France in the Spring of 1919.[41]

The day after Haig's visit Milner went on his own for a ten-day visit to a large area of the French front and to Paris. He included the Canadian H.Q. at Vimy Ridge and Foch's H.Q. near Breau. On a previous tour of this nature he had visited General Ellis at Tanks H.Q. Both in France and the Middle East Milner's friend Bendor had a vigorous four years' war service, much concerned with another mechanical weapon. His bio-grapher claims that he 'evolved the first practical armoured car which ever went into battle'.[42] In Paris Milner had talks with Clemenceau, Lord Derby and Spears, besides driving some distance to see General Sir John Monash, the Australian C.-in-C. at his H.Q.

Back in England he reported to King George; and then suffered a stomach upset for some days while a 'rather ugly' railway strike interfered with his undertaking over reinforcements to Haig, and the Cabinet was 'obliged to take strong action.' But late in September, as he was recover-ing, the startling news came in that Bulgaria had asked for an armistice, which was signed on the 29th; he wrote about this to Balfour and his letter was read by Law to the Cabinet. Two days later he noted 'most important news [was] pouring in from every quarter' including most of the Western front. The next day he motored at Lloyd George's request to Hassocks for a discussion with him of the possibility of some move to Constantinople to get Turkey out of the war; at breakfast he showed the P.M. a telegram about this he had drafted for him to Clemenceau.

On October 2 he attended a Cabinet engaged in very serious discussion of the political and military situation 'which, especially the former, is developing at a tremendous pace.' The C.I.G.S. went to Paris for talks about Eastern developments. Mention has earlier been made of the Anglo-French agreement of the previous December to create zones of influence in the Ukraine and South Russia.[43] For six months or more the Germans overran much of these regions, though later what the War Office called a 'very healthy pro-Ally anti-Bolshevik organization' prevailed in the south.[44] This June and July the Allies had been pressing Woodrow Wilson to agree to Japanese intervention in Siberia. In Henry Wilson's judgement, made early in 1919, there was

. . . neither a co-ordinated policy or whole-hearted co-operation between the Allied and Associated Governments.

The Allied anti-Bolshevik intervention was begun at Archangel by a small force under General F. C. Poole on 2 August. (The Bolsheviks had adopted the Western or Gregorian Calendar of the 16th century in January of this year.) The immediate purpose of intervention, ranking higher than denying Allied munitions and Russia's resources to the Germans, was to stop German transfers of troops to the West. The War Office reckoned (correctly for a time) that very small Allied forces in comparison with the German armies in Russia could help to do this. At quite an early stage the Czech Legion succeeded in reaching the Volga.

R. H. Ullman has fully recorded a story which much concerned Milner in 1918 but cannot be summarized here.[45] Over Russia's huge area the Allies helped the Czechs and White Russians with money, small pockets of troops and later with supplies. Bruce Lockhart came back from Russia in October now out of a job; and Ullman concludes that the serious attempt of his mission to make terms with Bolshevik leaders was based on the false assumption of a 'community of interest' between the Allies and the Soviet régime. To the Bolsheviks all that mattered was the consolidation as quickly as possible of their power; like the Allies this summer they were fighting for survival. In the last days of August the head of the Petrograd Cheka was shot dead, Lenin was gravely wounded in Moscow and the Terror began.

Milner, 'although overwhelmed with work', often invited Lockhart to the small house near the Abbey, and encouraged him to write memoranda for the Government on Russia.[46] Lockhart had an audience with King George and wrote,

. . . with the possible exception of Lord Milner he was better informed and better documented about Russia than any of his Ministers.

He concluded that neither Lloyd George nor any of his chief colleagues were much interested in the subject, a view which Hankey's diaries seem to confirm. Milner maintained his interest in Lockhart's career until his death some six and a half years from this date.

To turn from the subject of Russia, it had at last become clear that initiative in the West and the Near East had passed to the Allies. On 3 October Prince Max of Baden became Germany's Chancellor, dismissed Ludendorff and sued for an armistice and the opening of peace negotiations. On the 13th Milner called the day 'rather exciting [with] everybody in a twitter' over the German exchanges with Woodrow Wilson, and ten days later the Germans accepted the President's Fourteen Points. Just before this, on the 17th, an interview with Milner published in the *Evening Standard* about peace terms caused what he called 'a tremendous racket in the Press', especially by his old critics the *Manchester Guardian* and the *Daily News*, which included fresh allegations about his German origins. He had argued at length for reasonably 'generous peace terms' for Germany.

> There must be [he said] a German Government to negotiate an armistice with. . . . A complete transformation of the system . . . is already in progress. . . . It is in the interests of the Allies to see a stable government of some sort maintained in Germany . . . we do not wish to see Bolshevism and chaos rampant there.

Headed 'Killing Prussianism', by which Milner meant German militarism, the interview was distorted by some of the Press at the time and has been distorted by some historians since. Lord Northcliffe, hitherto Milner's ally but unlike him a strong advocate of Germany's unconditional surrender, joined in the attack with his powerful *Daily Mail* (published in London and Paris), and Carson counter-attacked in the Commons with cutting aspersions on Northcliffe. Milner clearly stated in a letter from Versailles to the War Office that, as he saw it, the main aim of Armistice Terms was to make Germany 'militarily impotent'. We should avoid any chance of her refusing the Terms by refraining from 'adding one unnecessary item' to punish her or gratify our feelings (however justified) of anger.[47]

Light on the mixed state of politico-military views prevailing among Britain's leaders is provided by a summons to Haig to come over from France for a top-level meeting on 19 October. Stout optimist though he was, Haig asserted that the Germans were not ready for unconditional surrender and were quite capable of retiring to their frontier and holding that line; so the war *might* continue well into 1919. If this did not happen he proposed certain moderate Armistice terms and Milner took a middle position between these and Foch's harder proposals.[48]

The Germans accepted the President's Fourteen Points on 23 October, and further American–German exchanges ended on 5 November. As Maynard Keynes later wrote, acceptance of the Points meant that 'the enemy had not surrendered unconditionally, but on agreed terms as to the general character of the Peace'.[49] On this day an X meeting in London was in 'a great ferment' over a telegram from Washington. The next day

Statesmen of World War I. Painting by J. Guthrie

Viscount Milner. Portrait by J. Guthrie

Hankey wrote in his diary: 'there is too much diplomacy and too little plain speaking with President Wilson.' He found himself, Roskill writes, 'almost overwhelmed by the pace at which events came to a climax.'

On 24 October Milner went with a large party to Versailles, soon joined by Lloyd George and Balfour, for a visit which lasted almost two weeks. Three days later Austria asked for an armistice which was granted on 4 November. Then an armistice with Turkey was signed. Lloyd George gave a private dinner one evening to Law, Balfour and Milner which finally fixed the plans for an early election and a continuing Coalition Government. On 4 November Milner wrote that the P.M.'s departure for London with his 'circus' meant that 'great peace reigned' in the Villa Romaine. He was left with Balfour and Geddes to attend the final wartime Supreme War Council, which accepted, with some Anglo-French reservations to be noticed later, Wilson's fourteen Points. Milner privately commented:

> ... we finally fixed the terms of the Armistice to be offered to Germany, which are in my opinion absurd.[50]

He then motored for four hours through the devastated areas of Flanders to see Haig near Bapaume, and returned via Montreuil to London.

He found wild but premature rumours all over London that the Germans had accepted the Armistice terms. At a meeting in Law's room at the Treasury the Unionist Ministers agreed to accept Lloyd George's proposals on the terms of a Coalition appeal to the country. At the Lord Mayor's Banquet at the Guildhall on 9 November the P.M. spoke for 45 minutes receiving a great ovation. Milner spoke for 10 minutes on behalf of the Army, first praising British fortitude in France in the past seven months and then stressing 'the grand omen for the future' of the big contribution made to victory by the Dominions, India and many small colonies.[51] The same day Kaiser William II abdicated and fled to Holland, and a republic was proclaimed in Berlin. On the following day Britain's Cabinet was engaged in grave talk about the Armistice negotiations in view of the revolutionary situation arising in Germany.

Milner was awakened at 7 a.m. on 11 November to be told by the War Office that German delegates had signed the Armistice two hours earlier in the forest of Compiègne. This was to come into force at 11 a.m. on this 100th day of the 5th year of war. After urging them at the Abbey to get on with their bell-ringing, he went with the Army Council to write names at Buckingham Palace and be received by King George and Queen Mary while a huge crowd was assembling outside the Palace. An afternoon's work at the War Office on demobilization preceded a brief call on Lloyd George, dinner with Lady Edward, and work at home until two the next morning.

The war's roll of honour for the Empire was nearly one million men, some three-quarters of whom came from the United Kingdom. The Frenchmen who died approached double this number. Since this attempt to describe Milner's part in the war began with a few lines by his friend Kipling it may suitably end with a few more. A friend sent him a printed copy of Julian Grenfell's poem 'Into Battle' with a parallel translation of this into Greek. He had headed Grenfell's poem with two lines of Kipling's:

> Life from the Earth and warmth from the Sun
>   is the warrior's portion:
> He is made free as the winds: he is reborn
>   as the trees.

There are several accounts, hardly varying at all, of answers to the game being played in some circles of who in Britain had accomplished the most towards winning the war by holding the office which he did. Amery records dining with Austen Chamberlain, Dawson and Oliver when each made a list (in descending order) on paper and each list proved the same – Lloyd George, Milner, Henry Wilson and Hankey.[52] In spite of critical passages in his memoirs, some of them written twenty years later, Lloyd George paid high tributes to Milner when in office. Haig wrote to Milner on 20 November that he and his Army Commanders all hoped that, whatever the outcome of the General Election, he would remain

> ... in supreme direction of the Army in the very critical period which must supervene between a state of war and the time when the Army assumes a peace footing.

Milner, though he had had some brusque treatment from Lloyd George and was due to have more, bore him no malice. Lionel Curtis records in his *Civitas Dei* that in personal talk after Lloyd George had fallen from power four years after the Armistice Milner expressed his opinion that the victory of the Allies was mainly due to Lloyd George's 'incomparable drive'.[53]

On the 16th, a big London meeting took place, at which Lloyd George,

Law and Barnes were the speakers; most Ministers supported a continued Coalition; this meeting opened the 'coupon' General Election. In a few days Dominion Prime Ministers began arriving, and Milner wrote that an Imperial War Cabinet on the 20th was engaged in a 'a long and futile discussion about "trying" or otherwise "punishing" the German Emperor and Crown Prince', and this performance was repeated a week later. As regards his main business Haig had not, in the letter just quoted, overdrawn the picture. Demobilization of the Army in a regular manner and at the right pace was now his principal War Office problem. This was mixed up with Industrial Demobilization and especially the question, which much exercised the Cabinet, of releasing the miners. At the end of the month Lady Edward sent a message to say that her husband was seriously ill. He had developed tuberculosis a year earlier and left Egypt for a sanatorium at Leysin in Switzerland. Milner saw off Lady Edward, accompanied by Lord Salisbury, on her journey to this place. The same day Geoffrey Dawson called to tell him that Northcliffe's vagaries were reducing his position as editor of *The Times* to a critical state.

December opened with a great gathering at Charing Cross station to meet Clemenceau, Foch, Orlando and Sonnino. They received a good public reception, and spent nearly all the next day at a Cabinet meeting. On the 4th Milner visited Lloyd George for what he called

> . . . an interview about election matters . . . [he was] rather upset over the prospects and the conversation was neither a satisfactory nor an agreeable one.[54]

This presumably concerned what he regarded as the P.M.'s extravagant public claims in the campaign for vengeance against Germany. He also kept on, he wrote, 'fussing' him about the War Office supplying newspapers (which eventually totalled 5,000,000 free of charge) for electoral reasons to all the troops serving abroad.

A more serious clash between the two men took place two days later. Summoned to a Cabinet, Milner found a crowded meeting, attended by Board of Trade and Railway officials, discussing demobilization in a somewhat heated atmosphere. Lloyd George was in his most explosive mood and, he considered, rather more than offensive in his complaints of the slowness with which the Army was releasing miners. His reason for concentration on this point was that coal supplies had now fallen off badly and gas and electricity companies were seriously short of fuel. This time Milner's hackles rose. He went home and wrote the P.M. a long and stiff letter asking for his 'discharge' as soon as the election was over.

Official life, he wrote, had lately become 'very irksome' to him, and he was 'extremely tired'. He was not willing to accept

> ... the position in which I am exposed to such vehement charges of dilatoriness and neglect ... in the presence of a large number of people, many of them not Ministers. ... To submit to that sort of public rebuke without protest ... is not consistent with self-respect.[55]

He told the C.I.G.S. he was going to resign; and Wilson felt unable to dissuade him, blaming the P.M.'s bad temper on 'this cursed General Election'. After Milner had spent two peaceful nights at Sturry the P.M. summoned him and a compromise was reached until after the election. Milner took no part in this, and on the 13th noted in his diary 'last day of electioneering. God be praised!'; though the results were not known until two weeks later when the votes of all the troops overseas had arrived. He received a Foreign Office message to say that Lord Edward Cecil had died on the 13th at Leysin. He had made quite a good recovery from T.B. but had succumbed, at the age of 51, to a 'flu epidemic in the sanatorium. His body was brought home for burial at Hatfield.

Lord Edward's life, private and public, had been a sad one, as Kenneth Rose has revealed.[56] He had fallen in love in his youth with Violet Maxse, but army service abroad had led to some years of physical separation between them. When, like so many others, he thought the Boer War was over he was seconded to the Egyptian Army to serve on the staff of the Sirdar, Milner's friend Reginald Wingate. Cromer smiled on him, and he left the Army to serve in Cairo first as Under-Secretary for War and then in the same office for Finance. But his wife, whose interests lay in art and the social world in Britain, declined to make a home for him and their children in Egypt; to quote Mr. Rose, 'he never quite concealed his sorrow ... [and] desperately missed a family life'. How much of his money contributed to the purchase of Great Wigsell is not recorded, but on his leaves he found the house 'too old, dark and damp'. In addition, work serving the Empire on the spot was not, as some pretend, all club whiskies and soda. Cromer's successor as Consul-General, Eldon Gorst, deprived Cecil of influence and promotion. Kitchener, who took Gorst's place in 1911, soon raised him to Milner's former high office of Financial Adviser. When war supervened he felt deeply the loss of his only son George, and fell out with his former commander, again Kitchener's successor, Reginald Wingate. In the Whitehall committee mentioned earlier of 1917, Milner proved an ally but could only record a minority memo.

Haig and his Army Commanders arrived soon in London to be met by the Duke of Connaught, the P.M. and an immense crowd, after which the King gave them lunch at Buckingham Palace. It is of interest to note that Milner attended a Zionist dinner given by Lord Rothschild, sitting next to Lawrence of Arabia who interpreted for him in a talk with King Feisal. The last V.I.P. to reach London, two days after Christmas, was Woodrow Wilson who at this date was the main character of the drama. To quote an American historian,

> ... the eyes of the world were turned on him. He was to be the saviour of men, the builder of a new civilization of peace and justice ... From across the sea there came to war-torn Europe his message of goodwill.[57]

On 28 December Milner attended a Mansion House luncheon to the President and developed a heavy cold. His secretary, Thornton, brought him the General Election results. A. J. P. Taylor writes that the contest had been 'fought around Lloyd George – his past record and his promises for the future.' The Coalition gained a big triumph in seats, with Coalition Unionists well to the fore and Asquithian Liberals and the Independent Labour Party almost wiped out. J. A. Spender, though sympathetic to Asquith and a fair-minded journalist, wrote that the fight was vindictive, and Lloyd George went to the Peace Conference 'loaded with chains of his own making.' This election brought to an end the longest British Parliament since the first one of Charles II's reign.

On what he called an 'intimate occasion' Milner gave a dinner to Haig, his Army Commanders and other senior officers. In his speech he said Haig had commanded for over three years 'incomparably the largest army Britain has ever put into the field ... in a struggle of continuous intensity.' Paying tribute to his tenacity, calm courage and moderation in victory he added that a nation's natural leaders were those who 'possess its best qualities in an exceptional degree.'[58]

Mention of these receptions and dinners must not give the impression that Lloyd George, Milner and other political leaders, domestic and Imperial, were engaged in six weeks of relaxed jollification. Sir Almeric Fitzroy wrote on the last day of the year that peace 'far from bringing rest and tranquillity' brought a widespread demand for people of vision who would infuse a new spirit into a 'perishing civilization'. It would be tedious to list the numerous topics which the Cabinets, 'ordinary' and Imperial and often attended by Milner, now discussed with the Peace Conference impending. But in view of misrepresentation by the Press at the time and by some later critics, further reference must be made to the campaign in Russia.

A letter from Milner's pen about this appeared in the Press on the 19th and was generally well received except by the *Manchester Guardian* and the *Daily News*, which distorted his views. He argued *inter alia* that Allied intervention had succeeded in denying resources to the enemy, saving the Czechoslovak Legion and securing the two northern ports. He soon after wrote a memo. for his colleagues setting out the true facts, adding that many letters he received showed complete ignorance of these, and misconceptions were doing great harm. With the Armistice the Germans had begun to withdraw all their troops from Russia, and the chief Bolshevik advance occurred in the Baltic States. Ullman's study concludes that Milner opposed 'a crusade against the Bolsheviks in countries where Bolshevism already prevailed.' For him the focus of British 'interests' was the borders where the British and Russian Empires marched together, and the War Cabinet accepted this principle. He also supported limited intervention from a feeling of moral obligation (as so markedly after the Boer War) to help those who had stayed loyal to the Allies.[59]

Attendance at a New Year's Eve party with Loulie Dawkins as hostess included the play *Charley's Aunt* and a bowl of toddy at midnight. The year 1919 opened with poor weather and his own cold still heavy. On the 4th his friend Birchenough called with some proposition of importance from the City. The same afternoon he was leaving for Sturry when the Adjutant-General reported very serious discontent among troops at Folkestone returning from leave. His last week or so at the War Office was indeed to prove troubled. Including those from the Dominions and India there were over one million British troops in France alone, apart from non-combatant 'labour units'. On the 5th Milner talked 'off the record' at the War Office to the Press beseeching that it should tell the public the exact state of affairs. Demobilization, he said, was bound to cause trouble for months, so the nation must treat the next six months as 'part of the war'. If public opinion, as it seemed, wanted 'very stiff Peace terms' it must be able to enforce them.

The Folkestone trouble was settled, but demonstrations of troops took place in the War Office quadrangle and on the Horse Guards Parade. The C.I.G.S., not given to restraining his language, blamed the trouble on Lloyd George's 'cursed campaign of election for vote-catching'. Milner told the P.M. there were minor disturbances outside London and much sporadic unrest; and asked him to issue a Government declaration which he sat up until 3 a.m. drafting himself. This, announced in the Press on 9 January, 'made things rather quieter all round.'[60]

While these troubles were occupying Milner and others Lloyd George was reshuffling his Government. Austen Chamberlain gives a picture of his unorthodox (one might say slapdash) methods. Lloyd George offered him the Chancellorship of the Exchequer though (to Austen's chagrin) without a seat in the Cabinet; Bonar Law was going to stay on but accompany him to the Peace Conference. When Austen went to Downing Street he found the P.M. very confused about the whole Cabinet situation; it was finally Bonar Law who suggested to Lloyd George he should keep the existing War Cabinet (including Austen) in being and Lloyd George replied he would 'try it'.[61] Milner, after talking to Law, agreed to become Colonial Secretary on condition that Amery should be appointed his Parliamentary Under-Secretary, about which the P.M. showed some reluctance. Churchill was going to succeed Milner at the War Office, and visited him for a long talk at Great College Street. On the 10th Milner formally accepted his new Office. The next day, a Saturday, Lloyd George left with Law, Wilson and others for Paris, and Milner went to Sturry for a part-time holiday of two weeks.

Chapter 14

Secretary of State for the Colonies

(January 1919 – February 1921)

Peacemaking and Imperial Matters – Egyptian Mission – Imperial Questions, and still Egypt

A part-time holiday is similar to a non-birthday present, though less pleasant. Milner had recently had a telephone installed at Sturry: and pouches from the Colonial Office were brought fairly often by messengers and had to be dealt with at once. But he had time for relaxation and a few visitors. On 18 January he noted that the Peace Conference in Paris held its first formal meeting. A week or so later he left to begin full-time work in his office. There was justice in the fact that his last public post was on the commanding heights of the Empire, the political institution he most valued. Fifteen years earlier he had refused this position, from a feeling of duty to complete South Africa's reconstruction. Now approaching his 65th birthday he was clearly, like many younger, less diligent men after four years of war, overtired.

The Colonial Office occupied the North-East wing of the great block of offices between Downing Street and King Charles Street which Palmerston had had built in the Italianate style in the 1860s and '70s. Lord Carnarvon had described the Secretary of State's room as 'vast', and it was this which Chamberlain and now Milner inherited. The Office now forms part of the Foreign and Commonwealth Office.

His former Imperial Secretary in South Africa, George Fiddes, a cautious and prickly civil servant, was Permanent Under-Secretary of the Colonial Office.[1] Milner took with him his chief private secretary since War Cabinet days, Major Hugh Thornton, now assisted by two younger men Lord Sandon (later Earl of Harrowby) and Harold Beckett. On his first evening he enjoyed a 'Monday Night' dinner with Carson, Oliver and Waldorf Astor. In the following days he attended several Cabinets over which Law presided, worked late on masses of Peace Conference Reports, attended a Moot to discuss *Round Table* finance and was given a full overhaul (producing a 'fairly satisfactory verdict') by his doctor. He continued to employ Miss Smith daily at his home as his private secretary.

February 3 proved agitating since Amery, who was in Paris, sent a message to say that Lloyd George required him over there at once. Two days later he went, to be told by Lloyd George that he wished him to act as Second British Representative at the Peace Conference in his absence, to which request he reluctantly consented. It was no longer a question of the relative calm of the Villa Romaine and the Trianon Palace Hotel at Versailles. The British Empire Delegation was housed at the Hotel Majestic which was staffed, Harold Nicolson tells us,

. . . from attic to cellar with bright British domestics from our own provincial hotels. The food, in consequence was of the Anglo-Swiss variety, whereas the coffee was British to the core.[2]

They worked at the adjoining Hotel Astoria which, somewhat illogically from a security aspect, was staffed by the French. The Delegation (B.E.D.) consisted of 207 people, 75 of whom were from the Dominions and a few from India. Milner called the Majestic

a vast caravanserai, not uncomfortable but much too full of all and sundry and too much of a 'circus' for my taste.

He later found himself a room in a house opposite the hotel occupied by Henry Wilson and others. Lloyd George and Balfour lived in flats further away.

He made five visits to Paris of varying lengths from this date until the Treaty with Germany was signed at the end of June. His movements depended entirely on the impulses and needs to attend to affairs at home of the P.M. The War Cabinet, as mentioned earlier, continued in existence; and Lloyd George's new Government consisted of much the same persons serving in different offices. Curzon became Acting Foreign Secretary until the autumn while Balfour, permanently in Paris, was at the centre of affairs, served by Lord Harindge of Penshurst, Permanent Head of the Foreign Office, Sir Eyre Crowe, Harold Nicolson and others of the cream of this Office. Philip Kerr continued, as Milner put it, to be Lloyd George's 'man Friday'.

The British Empire Delegation was a continuation of the wartime meetings, with their agreements and differences but general cooperation, of Dominion, Indian and British Ministers. These had, as Milner saw it, represented real achievement. Botha joined Smuts to represent South Africa. Of special importance was Hankey's familiar, if slightly changed, role as architect and leader of the Delegation's secretariat. The Supreme War Council became what, at his suggestion, was labelled 'The Council of Ten', composed of two representatives of each of the five principal

Powers. On 14 January he wrote to Milner that he wanted to include a member of a Dominion Prime Minister's staff at all B.E.D. meetings and to make this secretariat 'completely Imperial . . . a real Imperial Cabinet Office', as he had been trying to do for six years. His enthusiasm, complementing Milner's, stemmed in part from the fact that his father had settled in Australia, and married an Australian girl before returning to England.[3]

Roskill in his life of Hankey calls his chapter describing the first months of 1919 'The Hard Road to Peace'. Another British historian calls his account of the years 1919–23 'Into the Waste Land'. It is necessary to recall to the reader what can justly be called the world-wide turmoil of Milner's last years of office. The word can be used without hesitation of the condition of Germany, Bolshevist Russia and much of Europe. In the U.S.A. President Wilson faced hostility from Congress and the people; and Prohibition, which came into force this January, brought 'hooch' and much else, except peace or harmony, to the country.

It is not possible to describe in much detail Milner's work at the Paris Peace Conference. Two young Englishmen, both closely involved on the spot, wrote books which still rank as classic accounts. Maynard Keynes, a Treasury representative, published *The Economic Consequences of the Peace* at the end of this year. Harold Nicolson, a trained diplomat, gave in *Peacemaking, 1919* a wider (and later) account of the Conference. Both books are highly critical of the Conference's organization and achievements.[4]

President Wilson cared above all for the League of Nations and its embodiment with the Fourteen Points in the Treaty of Peace. He got the League Covenant adopted in time to visit America in mid-February, to find the Senate more hostile to this plan than he had expected, and to stay for a month. This project of world organization was naturally of much interest to Milner, particularly Article XXII of the Covenant dealing with Mandates, laying down clearly that the wishes of native communities and not the treaty claims of certain Powers were to be the criterion of their grant.

About the date Milner reached Paris, Haig visited the city and found many varieties of opinion as to how to coerce the Germans, with the French, he thought, marking time till Wilson went away. Clemenceau was Chairman of the Conference, and the central arrangements were organized by the French. The key-note of the assembly, Nicolson states, was 'appalling dispersal of energy', and its result a German Treaty which, as finally drafted, violated 19 out of Wilson's 23 'Terms of Peace'.[5] The reasons for this can only be listed. No previous agreement had been reached about aims, and no definite programme established. Nothing – least of all the Fourteen Points – was clear-cut; Balfour called the whole business 'a rough and tumble affair'. It had not been decided whether the Treaty was to be Preliminary or Final, negotiated with the Germans or imposed. No less than 27 states were represented. By allowing each of these to present its case, both in writing and orally, the error was made of introducing from the start the problems of the four lesser enemies including Turkey.

After undue delay 58 Committees (also called Commissions) of ten delegates, two from each of the Five Great Powers, were created. From a desire for secrecy only six Plenary Meetings, when the Press was admitted, were held. Mere congestion of business led to Councils of Five and then of Four – with Japan dropping out and Wilson, Clemenceau, Lloyd George and Orlando left in conclave – taking the ultimate major decisions.

After ten days in Paris Milner left to resume his business at the Colonial Office, being joined by Botha and Smuts at Boulogne. Driving to London, his car collided with another one in Lewisham, stunning him for a time and bruising him badly. The writer must try to record his chief Colonial Office preoccupations and personal life as interstices to his Conference visits. His two centres of business interlocked, though they certainly added to his burdens. In Amery he had, as his Colonial Office No. 2, a friend who, though often impulsive, shared most of his views. In Paris he had the advantage that the leading Dominion politicians were gathered together. But many Imperial matters which only he could decide got held up in his absence, or were sent to him in Paris for treatment.

On 19 February Geoffrey Dawson called to tell him he had finally tired of Northcliffe's behaviour and resigned from the editorship of *The Times*. He started work for the *Round Table* and soon married Cecilia, the daughter of Milner's former Lieutenant-Governor of the Transvaal, Sir Arthur Lawley. Mention has been made of Northcliffe's attack on Milner in the autumn for advocating what he thought a 'soft' peace. This was associated with his vendetta against Lloyd George for not taking his advice on his Government, or giving him an official position at the Peace Conference. The power he had acquired via Fleet Street was very large. By the Armistice, however, he was failing in health and showing symptoms of megalomania. He added throughout to the difficulties of the Conference by, in Nicolson's phrase, continuing to turn on Lloyd George 'a constant stream of boiling water'. The British public, Nicolson writes, recovered their nerve after the war very quickly, but were not allowed by large sections of their Press 'to convalesce in silence.'[6]

After a few days Milner went in February to Paris again for a stay of over three weeks. He dined on his first night with Henry Wilson who gave him the startling news that in the morning an anarchist had fired nine shots at Clemenceau in his car. The 'Tiger' was only wounded in the shoulder though put out of action for some days. The calendar must be shifted back slightly to mention that Hankey, in a letter of 11 February to his wife after lunching with Balfour and Milner, wrote 'the work is much less strenuous and exciting without the P.M.'. More important was Churchill's arrival at the Conference during Lloyd George's and Milner's absence, to press the Council of Ten for a meeting of the Allies and 'various Russian governments' at Prinkipo, and full military intervention in Russia. A report to Lloyd George from Kerr brought what Hankey called 'a very hot telegram' from the former repudiating Churchill's proposals; and the Conference henceforth made no serious effort to agree on an Allied policy towards Russia.[7]

Milner's attitude to this problem remained much what it had been in his letter to the Press of December. His concern for the Empire and special interest in Near Eastern matters made him support a policy of confinement of Bolshevism, or limited intervention in the south. But his other pre-occupations were many, and he seems to have left Churchill and the C.I.G.S. to fight their own battle with Lloyd George and the Cabinet.[8] His papers fully bear out Nicolson's view about faulty procedure, and he commented: 'masses of work but progress slow'. His own business and pleasure during this visit included chairing or attending meetings of the British Empire Delegation, starting to write a memorandum on Mandates, attending 'a long and unsatisfactory' discussion in the Council of Ten (with the Tiger now restored to the chair) of Disarmament proposals, talks with Keynes about Reparations, with T. E. Lawrence about Syria and Gertrude Bell about Mesopotamia, and meetings with Lady Edward who had taken what Sandon called 'a very jolly house' off the Avenue du Bois de Boulogne. Lloyd George arrived back on 5 March: a few days later Milner returned to London for what this time was to prove a stay, with one interruption, of a number of weeks.

On his first working day a meeting of Rhodes Trustees had so much business that it lasted 4½ hours. He had only been back a few days when Hankey sent him a message requesting his return to Paris, and he said he could not do this for three or four days. Dining with Astor and Garvin he found the latter 'very despondent about the kind of peace we are going to impose on Germany'. After heavy work at the Colonial Office he spent the week-end at Sturry with Lady Edward as his guest. He then went for 5 further days to Paris taking Lord Sandon as his secretary. Sandon was a temporary civil servant aged 26. After Oxford he had served from

August 1914 till the Armistice in the Royal Field Artillery in France. He had experienced much heavy fighting, been seriously wounded in the head and recovered. He wrote home that on the journey to Paris Milner told him much about his work in the War Cabinet and at the War Office, especially in the 'Great Retreat' of March. He found him 'intensely interesting [as] he doesn't in the least mind talking'. Milner, in the Kindergarten tradition, had picked another young associate in broad sympathy with his views, and well endowed with brains and discretion.

Long talks with Balfour, Allenby and David Hogarth, the Oxford scholar and Director of the Arab Bureau in Cairo from 1916 to 1918, about Syria, appear to have been the purpose of this visit. The French considered they had prescriptive rights to this country's mandate, but the Syrians did not welcome the prospect; and British pledges to the Arabs which conflicted with the later Sykes–Picot agreement had produced an embarrassing situation including one more breach in Wilson's somewhat metaphysical Fourteen Points. The dispute was shelved by the despatch to Syria of a Commission of Inquiry. Milner had a long talk on economic affairs with Bob Brand, now financial adviser to Lord Robert Cecil, a British representative with Smuts on the League of Nations Committee. Balfour records that in these months Milner was the only one of the Council of Ten who gave him strong support for pressing on with the Treaty's economic and territorial provisions.[9]

Sandon wrote that his Chief 'hates staying when not needed, as they make use of him on every sort of thing'. Back in London on 23 March Milner noted it was his sixty fifth birthday, adding he was not sure that

> . . . the outlook for this country and the world is not even blacker today than a year ago when they were in the middle of the great German Offensive.

On the major issue of German Reparations he wrote emphatically to Brand that the less we asked of her the more we were likely to get. German promises to pay in the future must be immediately marketable, i.e. guaranteed by the Allied and Associated Powers (or at least the former). The security behind bonds would be Germany, or in the last resort all Western Europe. When Keynes's critical *Economic Consequences of the Peace* appeared he agreed with it in substance.

As before, he was a fairly frequent speaker for the Government in the Lords, especially on economic topics. In a major debate he claimed that Britain's only way out of her difficulties was increased productivity, and that the country's greatest weakness was the wasteful system of production and distribution of some of her chief industries.[10] He had lately heard from Lord Stamfordham that Prince Arthur of Connaught was leaving the Army and wanted to acquire some experience at the Colonial Office with a view to future employment in the Empire. The Prince came to see him, and then went to the Colonial Office for training. Milner took the chair at the first meeting of a new Imperial Communications Committee, and spoke at a meeting of the Women's Emigration Societies. In early April he made important speeches at Manchester to the local branch of the Royal Colonial Institute and the Chamber of Commerce. By chance he met there a distant English cousin, James Milner, of whose existence he had been unaware, who took him home to tea. The next day he was taken down the Ship Canal and given a lunch by local notables in the Midland Hotel. Sandon wrote to his mother,

> The poor Chief is getting a terrible time . . . a dog's life, and rush isn't the word for it . . . he hardly gets time to eat, and carts boxes of 'bumph' away to read at night.

Lloyd George turned up from Paris for a few days, primarily for Cabinet discussion of the Budget; on his departure on 17 April Milner and Curzon breakfasted with him on the train to discuss the Egyptian situation. Milner had already had talks with Curzon over this problem, which was to occupy much of his time from this date and throughout the next year, 1920. Briefly stated, President Wilson's famous 'self-determination' had encouraged Egyptian nationalists, led by Zaghlul Pasha, to agitate for independence as the Turkish Empire crumbled. Wingate, the High Commissioner, had gone to Paris to plead for discussion of the topic but had been rebuffed, and the Nationalists were incensed by the fact that the Conference received an Arab deputation but denied this privilege to them. Wingate was scurvily treated, being superseded in March by Allenby as Special High Commissioner; and the leaders of the Egyptian independence party, the *Wafd* (meaning delegation) were arrested and deported.

Allenby acted with the speed and decision of some military commanders and telegraphed to Curzon for the immediate despatch of a Commission of Inquiry to Cairo. Milner was rightly regarded as an expert on Egypt and the natural leader of such a Commission. On 24 April he sent Curzon a letter which showed his usual habit of giving (time permitting) full thought to a problem before acting. Allenby's telegram struck him as proposing a 'hurried procedure'. He dissented from an early announcement of the Commission and its proposed form, and was not prepared to lead it under Allenby's conditions. What was needed was a 'Special

Mission' of Inquiry and Report with the aim of 'laying the foundations of a new system of Government' which could not usefully begin till the current crisis was over. Curzon in the main accepted these arguments.[11]

Milner had managed to snatch three week-ends at Sturry, and to invite guests there for a week or more while he was in London. At the opening of May he noted in his diary, as his habit was, the date of hearing the first nightingales. A day or two later Leo Amery was elected a Rhodes Trustee, a position he held till his death over thirty six years later, and Milner dined in London with Elinor Glyn. Feeling rather unwell, he postponed his visit to Paris, worked at the Colonial Office and went to Tite Street to sit to Sir James Guthrie for his picture of leading British War Statesmen which hangs in the National Portrait Gallery. On 10 May he went to Paris on his first flight accompanied by Sandon, landing after two and a half hours at Buc near Versailles; though they sat face to face in very cramped conditions, his only complaint was of deafness due to the 'terrific noise of the machine'.

His visit again lasted rather over three weeks. He at once met many colleagues, but soon commented that life was 'rather distracting. I can't make out clearly what I am supposed to be here for.' He found Lloyd George and officials engaged in a rather vague discussion about 'the attribution of Mandates for different parts of Asia Minor'; and after talking to Henry Wilson decided that 'the European "settlement" seems to be the most hopeless chaos.' The numerous Commissions were discussing *inter alia* the territorial claims of 27 states plus those of some gatecrashers. Nicolson calls the discussion of late March about Syria 'almost the last occasion on which President Wilson stood by his principles.' From then on, his state was one of 'collapse' as he saw the idealism of his Points, Principles and Particulars eroded by the Secret Treaties concluded by the Allies during the war. He consoled himself with Article XIX of the Covenant which allowed for the future revision of treaties. Lloyd George thought of his promises to Parliament and the public in Britain; and Clemenceau, though appearing to sleep through most meetings, thought of the Rhineland, Syria and the security of France.[12]

Milner's view of the Conference can be conveyed by noting his occasional comments. Slightly earlier he had written to the Duke of Devonshire, Governor-General of Canada, that the Conference was 'indescribable chaos'; though doing some good work it was not being 'pulled together, and no single guiding principle [was discernible] in the deliberations of the Big Five.'[13] Sandon credited him with making one of the best *mots* of the assembly: 'instead of it having been a war to end wars – it is a Peace to end Peace'.

In mid-May he called on the P.M. and finding him 'very anxious to settle up all outstanding Colonial Questions promptly' stayed in Paris longer than he had intended. He had in fact received one of Lloyd George's brusque letters hoping he would not leave Paris again without settling African questions, as no Colonial business pressed more for treatment. After this talk Milner wrote to Lloyd George that he probably did not realize the seriousness of giving up all that the Italians asked for in Africa.[14] There was in fact a new scramble for Africa going on. President Wilson had conceived that Mandates in Africa and elsewhere would be administered directly by the League. The Allies, including three British Dominions, took the opposite view that their conquests entitled them to outright annexation of these territories.

Milner found Smuts 'greatly perturbed about the terms to be imposed on Germany' which had been presented to them, with 15 days in which to reply, just before his arrival. A long pow-wow of British leaders about allotment of spheres of influence in the Turkish Empire revealed great differences of opinion, with a preponderant view that 'a remnant of Turkey, including Constantinople and most of Anatolia, should be kept alive under the supervision of America.' A talk with Lloyd George, President Wilson and Clemenceau about the awkward Syrian Question was 'not very friendly, with no agreement arrived at.' He dictated a memo. for three hours on the East African problem on Smuts's birthday, sitting later between Botha and Lloyd George at a dinner in his honour. The Germans had been granted an extra week to reply to the Terms; Milner wrote on the 26th that the British Empire Delegation had 'a very inconclusive discussion' about this. After he had flown home with Sandon on 2 June, Lloyd George did his best to tone down the German Terms, but with no support from Wilson or Clemenceau and attacks on him from Northcliffe's *Times* for 'weakening'.

A by-product of the Conference in May and June needs mention as a venture mainly by Milner's friends of a younger generation due in some degree to his inspiration. Nicolson's diary notes a dinner in Paris on 30 May 'to discuss the formation of an Anglo-American Institute of Foreign Affairs, with an annual register or year-book.' Lionel Curtis, the originator of the scheme, made an admirable speech. On 12 June, this Institute was formed and Lord Robert Cecil, Crowe and other supporters met to elect its Council. General disappointment with the Treaty, and a wish to keep in close touch with the future League of Nations, were feelings inspiring this group.[15]

Arnold J. Toynbee, the distinguished historian, the nephew of Milner's close friend and one of the experts at the Conference, later became the intellectual star of this Institute in London (better known as Chatham House) for 36 or so years. He told the present writer that so far as he knew, Milner's part in founding the body was nominal and added

> . . . Lionel Curtis was the sole true founder . . . the Institute would never have come into existence without his driving power and magnetic influence. His only real co-founder was Sir James Headlam-Morley, the Historical Adviser of the Foreign Office, who launched the Institute's intellectual work. But it was Curtis who won the necessary support and raised the money.[16]

The history of Chatham House has never been written, and many of Curtis's papers were later destroyed in a fire. But at another meeting in London in 1920 more concrete decisions were taken, and Curtis and Geoffrey Gathorne-Hardy were appointed Joint Honorary Secretaries. Years later Professor Eric Walker, the South African historian, sent an account of Curtis's aims to Dermot Morrah, then editor of *The Round Table*. These embraced the creation in each Dominion of an Institute which would stand in the same relation to the London body as autonomous Dominions stood to the British 'Commonwealth' (a word Curtis substituted for Empire). For the London Institute Curtis framed some important conditions. It would be, he wrote to Walker,

> . . . absolutely debarred from propaganda in any shape or form [with its] sole object to help individual members to get at the facts and think out conclusions together.

Great care would be needed in electing members, and in publications and meetings to 'get all parties and sections balanced.' They would especially welcome a South African Institute in view of that nation's crucial colour problem. Morrah relates that in 1922, having never heard of the Institute, he ran into Curtis in St. James's Square waving his arms at the home of the 1st Earl of Chatham (the conqueror of French Canada) and saying 'I've just bought that house!'[17]

Milner's detachment can be explained by the load of work which he bore, and the punctilio with which when in public office he refrained from office on voluntary bodies (except the Rhodes Trust and Toynbee Hall). Back in England as June opened, the end of the Conference on the German Treaty was in sight, though Milner was occupied for months to come as chairman of the Mandates Commission. He was also to be concerned to a growing degree with the problem of Egypt. Besides these two matters the major issues which faced him were the Empire's constitutional evolution and the continuation of Joseph Chamberlain's policy of 'developing our neglected estates.'

The strength of his views on the former was shown in a letter he wrote to Lloyd George at the end of May. The plan of an Anglo-American guarantee to France in the event of future German attack had been discussed at the Conference; and Botha had included in a letter to Lloyd George an assumption that in another European war one or more Dominions might be neutral as a result of the status of 'independent nationhood of the Dominions'. Milner told Lloyd George he was 'greatly staggered' by this statement, which seemed to embody a view of Imperial relations 'incompatible with the existence of the British Empire as a political unit.' It conflicted with constitutional theory which upheld the Crown as 'the bond which still holds,' even though the Dominions were now 'virtually independent'. He quoted a statement by Smuts at the Conference supporting this view.[18]

A few days later he received the first of several visits from the Prince of Wales to discuss his forthcoming tour of Canada. The Prince's father, when Duke of Cornwall, had begun the Monarchy's Empire tours and was most anxious that his son, now twenty five, should continue the practice. Milner's other official concerns included the formation of a committee to raise funds for a London School of Tropical Medicine, Cabinet meetings on the North Russian campaign, five hours with Miss Smith on a Sunday engaged in the 'wearisome job' of sorting official papers, and what he called 'the eternal question' of Nauru. This was a former German Pacific island north of Australia especially rich in phosphates, coveted both by Australia and New Zealand and much discussed at the Conference.

On 24 June Milner returned to Paris with Law, Sandon and others for the signing of the German Treaty. Two days or so later he commented:

. . . as the end of the Peace Conference approaches the number of unsettled questions which still call for a solution appears appalling.[19]

The day which preceded the signing was 'very racketing'. It was only the next day, the 28th, that he learnt he had been formally appointed by the Council of Four the Chairman of the Mandates Commission. After lunch with Sandon he motored to the ceremony in the Hall of Mirrors at Versailles. 'Never', Nicolson writes, 'had Versailles been more ostentatious and embossed', with much military grandeur and furniture imported from elsewhere. With Clemenceau presiding, two German civilian delegates, 'isolated and pitiable', entered the packed hall and signed first.

The Allied and Associated plenipotentiaries then signed, with Milner (who thought it all 'singularly unimpressive') signing, after Lloyd George and Law, third for the British. Guns fired a salute to tell Paris it was over. After dinner Milner walked about central Paris for a long time to see the crowds. Next day he accompanied his colleagues home, finding King George and a huge crowd at Victoria Station to meet them.

Though the shouting did not die for a time the captains of Dominion teams soon departed. Botha, and then Smuts, called at the Colonial Office to say goodbye; and one of Lloyd George's staff reported that all the other Dominion delegates in Paris had been much impressed by the great superiority of the South African delegation. Milner spoke at a farewell dinner to Hughes, the P.M. of Australia, having failed to persuade him to stay on as a member of the War Cabinet. In July, with the King's permission, General Pershing presented him, with Churchill and some others, with the American Distinguished Service Medal. The 19th was called 'Great Peace Celebration Day', when he went to the Palace with all the Ministers to watch a procession, which he called 'very impressive', and which took two and a half hours to march past the King. It being a Saturday, he went to Sturry and made a short speech at its Peace Fête. Lloyd George had already given a dinner to his seventy or so Ministers at No. 10, making 'a very short and very happy' speech.

These various celebrations did not lessen Milner's burden of work, and brief further reference must be made to Rhodes Trust affairs. He had written in March to Otto Beit, 'now that our finances are straightened out we shall be able to dispose of an ample income'.

He wrote of the 'enormous rise' of De Beers Deferred Stock. The Trustees made generous provision for Parkin, retiring at seventy-three after giving the Trust yeoman service since 1902. Gilmour, the secretary, was 'excellent' but unlikely to stay long. So Milner wrote in June to Colonel Ned Grigg offering him the combined jobs of Secretary of the Trust and Parkin's 'Organizer of Scholarships'. The report of Wylie, the Oxford Secretary, for 1918–19 showed that Scholars in residence had risen from 87 early in the academic year to something like 200 at its end, though stating that 'reconstruction' at Oxford had been proving no simpler than it was elsewhere.[20]

The Mandates Commission, now sitting in London, a Rhodesian Commission and legislation on the home front helped to consume Milner's time. He replied for the Government in a Lords' debate on nationalization of the coal mines, a proposal he favoured for limited areas. He recorded a Cabinet meeting on the 'very grave business' of a coal strike, which Lloyd George averted, as well as a dinner with Haldane at which he had a long and very interesting talk on this problem with Sankey, William Beveridge and the historian R. H. Tawney.[21] Henry Wilson and Allenby were both created Field-Marshals this month. Milner spent a week-end with Arthur Lee, created Lord Lee of Fareham in the previous year, at Chequers, describing the house as 'wonderfully interesting and beautiful, full of pictures and other art treasures'.

As a result of his Paris experiences Sandon was now advocating

> a really *advanced* policy [with regard to the Dominions] . . . wiping out *all* vestige of the old and predominant partner policy . . . [the Dominions would then probably realize] the colossal gain not only to their own special interests, but from the standpoint of world peace . . . [without some such drastic step] they would slip away.

He had often discussed the topic with Milner during their walks in the Versailles and St. Cloud woods; though whether Milner agreed with his view that the Dominions preferred the 'conference' and 'informal liaison' system to some new Empire Constitution is more doubtful. At any rate Milner had now moved, both in his thinking and practice, towards more emphasis on what was becoming known as the Dependent (i.e. non-white settler) Empire.

On 1 August he went to Oxford to give an important address on the Empire to the inaugural meeting of the Oxford University Extension Summer School in the Sheldonian Theatre. He said he regarded this word and 'Commonwealth' as synonymous. It was 45 years since as an undergraduate he was

> . . . first stirred by a new vision of the future of the British Empire . . . as a world-encircling group of related nations . . . united on a basis of equality and partnership.

Though he believed his vision was at last catching on, he had some anxiety about the immediate future; there was now a reaction everywhere against the trials of war. They had made big strides in Empire organization and co-operation during the war; but the institutions then created were in abeyance and the methods of future co-operation were undetermined. He could only point to 'one or two beacon lights': first, the relation between the Commonwealth and the League; secondly, the vast Dependent Empire in every stage of development in which Britain's role was

> . . . one of trusteeship for the advancement of their peoples not for our

own benefit . . . our present policy [whatever happened in the past] must be rigorously against exploitation . . . we must do all we could to encourage self-government;

third, in future the connection between the Dominions and the Dependent Empire was bound to be closer, though the importance of this was not yet generally recognized. This was a striking instance of the need for means of constant consultation, which he thought should take the form of 'a Council of Empire'.[22] A few days later he was among those who said good-bye to the Prince of Wales at Victoria Station as he left to join H.M.S. *Renown* for a three months' tour of Canada. He then wrote he was 'feeling extraordinarily tired' and left for a three weeks' holiday at Sturry. Sandon also relates that in his walks with him near Paris Milner had talked hard about flowers and forestry, and shown great keenness on his garden at Sturry.

John Buchan, in his sketch of Milner in *Memory-Hold-the-Door*, gives a false impression by stating that 'he seemed to read little, and had no taste for new books.' In the short time that Buchan was close to him after the Boer War this was doubtless true; but memory led Buchan astray in this generalization. On voyages and holidays Milner devoured books, old and new. This time his first choice was not, as with Elinor Glyn at Carlsbad, Plato's *Phaedo* but Matthew Arnold's *On Translating Homer*, the only one of Arnold's books he had not read. He often read a current book on economics or imperial problems, or a contemporary novel.

The Colonial Office rang him up with the news of Botha's sudden death at the early age of 57, which, he correctly forecast, portended the beginning of serious trouble in South Africa. The Office called him one day to attend a Cabinet under Law which engaged in what he thought a very unsatisfactory discussion of the Caucasus and Armenia. He spent time destroying and arranging old papers and letters, visited Loulie Dawkins and members of her family at Folkestone, had Lady Edward as a visitor, and presented £200 to his valet Axten who after some fourteen years was about to leave him. Though there is no scrap of evidence that Axten had a weakness for drink his name recalls Lord Curzon's valet Arketall who, as Harold Nicolson relates, borrowed his lordship's evening trousers for a dance at an international conference.[23]

On 9 September Milner went for a week to Paris to sign the Treaty of St. Germain with Austria. The Hotel Majestic he found 'very deserted and woe-begone' compared with its appearance earlier in the year. He spoke to Allenby who had 'no light to throw on the question of the Near East, which is all at sixes and sevens'; dinner with Balfour only produced 'a long and very inconclusive talk.' He did not doubt Balfour's brains or knowledge, but criticized his powers of decision and concentration; early in the year he had written to Lloyd George that he was quite excellent

> ... as a leader ... but he has strange lapses and ought not to be left too long without someone to prompt and *remind* him.[24]

On the 10th he signed the Treaty, with less senior Dominion Ministers signing for their countries. He had talks with Lloyd George, Law and other British Ministers in Paris; and with Sir Eric Drummond (later Lord Perth) just appointed first Secretary-General of the League of Nations about League procedures, especially over Mandates. On the 16th he returned home in Lloyd George's special train.

One feature of Milner's later years not so far mentioned is the constant trouble, recurring again at this time, he experienced with his teeth. Since he was able to afford the best doctors and dentists, it is surprising to read of the regular, long, and often painful sessions he was forced to undergo with the latter.

Talks with Curzon about his leading a mission to Egypt had been going on for months, although he had told Lord Stamfordham that he did not think deferring it would do any harm. Towards the end of September he was visited by Sir James Rennell Rodd, just retired after being Ambassador of Rome for 10 years, and who, it was proposed, would join his Mission in a month's time. He attended a Finance Committee of the Cabinet at No. 10 writing that he was

> ... much disgusted by the violent onslaught on Army Expenditure ... in an unnecessarily aggressive and rather reckless spirit.

It was the familiar British practice, with obvious bearings on the belief of Milner and others in National Service, neatly expressed by a historian in the phrase that within a year of the end of the war '... the Army again lay outside the mainstream of the nation's life and thought'.[25]

Though the War Cabinet still existed in theory, Milner found the 'ordinary' Cabinet overburdened with work. A great deal of the wartime machinery of government, often to his regret, had been abolished; but the coal-mines and the railways stayed until 1921 under Government control. This September a strike brought almost all the country's railways to a standstill and Milner attended emergency Cabinet meetings. The P.M. intervened and, in Taylor's words, gave railwaymen wages 'which showed a greater improvement on pre-war than in any other industry.' The T.U.C. established its modern, now powerful, General Council. But the Government took measures against a general strike by passing the important Emergency Powers Act, 1920.

Milner shared the anxiety of his colleagues about domestic industrial unrest. But the writer has found no good evidence for the view that he felt especially apprehensive over Bolshevist infiltration in Britain. For some time he had given support and helped to raise funds for a body called the British Workers' National League which made no secret of supporting the Empire and of Unionist inclinations. This published a magazine called *The Citizen*, which was naturally a target for the Radical Press. A feature of this League in which Milner was active was attempts to get Trade Union officials adopted as candidates for membership of Parliament. Ten had succeeded in being elected as Coalitionists in 1918.

He was now mainly absorbed in his work for the Empire, and the devious problems of the Near East. At a meeting with Curzon and Allenby (created a Viscount) in early October the decision was taken that the latter should go back to Egypt and that Milner's Mission should await his report on affairs there. A succession of British experts on Egypt, the Sudan and Arabia now called on him, including his old friend Sir Reginald Wingate, who had written to him asking for help over finding a job. Milner's talk with him was long and difficult, as he felt, with some justification, 'very sore about being displaced from the High Commissionership' in Egypt. He tried to help by writing an article about him in *The Times*.

A mention earlier of Wingate's attempts to get the Peace Conference to discuss Egypt must be slightly expanded. By the end of 1918 the situation in Cairo had been daily growing more strained. The Nationalists had increased their anti-British propaganda, with the Sultan showing no inclination to curb them and supporting the resignation of his Ministers. With Foreign Office approval Wingate had arrived in Paris to try to arrange for the reception in London of some Ministers and the grant of passports to the Nationalist Zaghlul and some of his followers to leave Malta. Balfour, though generally in agreement, had passed the buck to Curzon in London. There can be little doubt that Curzon, who was fully capable of such action, not only treated Wingate shabbily but by refusing his moderate proposals aggravated the situation. The confidence which the Sultan, Ministers and Nationalists had placed in Wingate's influence with his Government disappeared, and exactly what Wingate had foretold then occurred.

A murderous outbreak in Egypt was suppressed by the British General in charge, with inevitable results. Allenby, arriving as Special High Commissioner late in March, with Government approval carried out Wingate's policy, reissuing passports and releasing Zaghlul and his co-exiles from Malta. But, as so often, conciliation was too late. Zaghlul and his followers established headquarters in Paris, raised their demands and gained allies. Milner's mission was announced by Curzon in the Lords on 15 May. Wingate, not yet fifty eight, was then meanly treated over his pension.[27]

On 20 October Milner recorded that Lloyd George 'made an onslaught' on Churchill and Allenby over the strength they proposed for the Army in Palestine and Egypt; though in Milner's eyes he gained favour by propounding in Cabinet a good agricultural policy. A few days later the Government was defeated by ten votes in the Commons, and began suffering from general unpopularity. Milner wrote to Lloyd George reporting Australia's assent to ratifying the Versailles Treaty which meant that all the Dominions had now agreed about this, so 'the whole Empire can come in by a single act, which is rather a triumph.'[28] But agitation had arisen in Washington over the six votes proposed for the British Empire in the League of Nations Assembly. Hankey records that Lloyd George, Law, Churchill and he himself agreed that the War Cabinet should expire on the 27th to be replaced by a 'normal' body of twenty members, while the Cabinet Secretariat should continue. Milner's own comment on the first decision was 'awful mistake'.

He felt qualms of conscience about being unable to start his working day before 9.45 or 10 due to his habit of sitting up late at night. At the start of November he let Sturry for 4 months. He called the first meeting of the normal Cabinet

> ... a very unpromising beginning. A long and rambling discussion of our Russian policy, which left us as much at sea as ever.

Of greater interest was the Cabinet's approval next day of a 'Service of Silence' on Armistice Day, 11 November, and its appointment of him as Chairman of a Ministerial Committee to work out the details. After a meeting of this, Milner spent much time drafting a message for the King, took it to Buckingham Palace for approval and then embodied it in a telegram to the Dominions. When the day came he stayed in Great College Street for the Two Minutes' Silence, deterred by the large crowds from attending a Guildhall luncheon to President Poincaré.

Other events included chairing a dinner of the Empire Parliamentary

Association, attending a reception at Buckingham Palace for Basuto Chiefs, and voting (in vain) in the Lords for Peeresses in their own right to be allowed to sit in the House. Waldorf Astor had succeeded to his father's peerage and in this month Nancy, his wife, had been returned for his constituency of Plymouth, the first woman to sit in the Lower House. Harold Nicolson, himself an M.P. some years later, wrote in his *Diaries*:

> She has one of those minds that work from association to association, and therefore spread sideways with extreme rapidity.[29]

Milner talked with Law and Amery about Colonial Office work in his absence, was a guest at a luncheon of the King and Queen, heard Curzon speak in the Lords on his Mission, and made a new will. On 29 November he left with the five other members of his Mission for Marseilles whence he sailed via Malta to Port Said, reaching Cairo on 7 December. Sandon wrote that he was 'very glad to get away from here, and get more peace and quiet and . . . is looking forward to it'.

His colleagues were Rodd, Sir Cecil Hurst, a Foreign Office legal expert, J. A. Spender, the Liberal journalist often quoted in this story, General Sir John Maxwell, the Military Governor of Pretoria just after its capture and later C.-in-C., Ireland, and Brigadier-General Owen Thomas. This was a high-powered, all-party team. Milner was taken at once to see Allenby at the Residency, and then joined his colleagues at the Semiramis Hotel. Allenby took him for an audience with the Sultan, who, he had told him, was 'very much upset by the manifesto just issued by the Princes of the Khedivial family in support of the clamour for complete independence.'

It was a queer fate that Milner, who had started his overseas career in Egypt should end it with the same country as his major concern – or at least runner-up in what proved a close finish. His Mission stayed in Egypt three calendar months. Its departure, however, was far from the end of its labours. It continued throughout 1920 in London negotiating among others with Zaghlul and his friends in Paris, and did not present its report to Lord Curzon until a few days before Christmas. All this time Milner was responsible to the King-in-Parliament for developing and co-ordinating the affairs of the Empire in difficult post-war conditions.

Some critics are scornful of Milner's description of himself once as an 'emergency man', a trouble-shooter called in to deal with critical situations. If South Africa in April 1897, Britain at war in December 1916, the Allied front in France in March 1918, and now Egypt, were not emergencies one wonders how these critics define this word, which the dictionary calls 'a sudden juncture demanding immediate action'. There could hardly have been anywhere where the false definition of politics as a straight line between two fixed points was less appropriate than Egypt in the years now being discussed and later.

Spender has written a vivid picture of the Mission's sojourn in Egypt.[30] After welcoming it, Allenby tactfully went off to the Sudan. What followed was a boycott in an atmosphere of cloak and dagger. The Egyptian Ministers, he writes,

> were a gallant body of men . . . but they could give us very little help, and had all they could do to hold their offices and dodge the bombs that were being thrown at them . . . we were rigorously boycotted by all but a small minority of Egyptians.

Sentries surrounded the Semiramis hotel, the back windows were boarded up and the Mission was warned never to walk about without detectives, though some chose to ignore this irksome treatment. Spender himself, shadowed by young Egyptians from Cairo, went on an adventurous journey in the Provinces. After three weeks Milner telegraphed to the P.M. that the situation was much worse than he had imagined. The fellahin were better off than before, and the big landowners were immensely rich. But the middle and upper classes, officials, and others were

> . . . out to give us all the trouble they can [there was a countrywide agitation for] complete independence . . . moderates with backbone were very scarce, but we must have something to give them . . . British officials were all at sixes and sevens.[31]

He added that a Turkish Treaty transferring political rights to Britain would be an immense help to the Mission's task. The Treaty of Sèvres with Turkey was not in fact signed until 10 August of the following year.

The Mission's final Report includes an account of this 'on the spot' stage of its proceedings, and its provisional conclusions. A good judge of men, Spender writes that he cannot remember any occasion on which its members seriously differed, adding that if they had done so he doubts

> . . . if any of us would have succeeded in moving Milner from any position to which he was firmly anchored.

He thought that Milner was very conscious of the seriousness of ultimate failure to make a settlement; that he 'did not share the vulgar opinion that Egypt was part of the British Empire', but held that restoration of her independence, subject to safeguards, was the natural result of Britain's

1882 occupation. The Mission could only in the main obtain its material from official, or non-Egyptian, sources; though an exception must be made by mention of Adli Pasha, a moderate Nationalist and later Prime Minister. The faithful Ozzy Walrond, who lived in a native house, was active for the Mission throughout as an interpreter and go-between.[32]

Milner paid short visits to Alexandria, was flown to Helwan and spent 10 days on the Nile in the company of the famous Russell Pasha. Foreign friends visiting Cairo included such different personalities as Clemenceau and Elinor Glyn. He spent much time on his own or with colleagues drafting an interim report from the 'vast mass of material' they had gathered. This, briefly stated, proposed a Treaty granting Egypt independence, subject to safeguarding essential British rights. It insisted, however, on the approval of this by a genuine Legislative Assembly; and Zaghlul, regarded as certain to win a majority in such a body, had hitherto refused to leave Paris. Not long before leaving, Milner wrote informally to Lloyd George that the situation had deteriorated. Zaghlul, he said, was 'afraid of the Frankenstein he had created', so the extremists had it all their own way. They were getting fresh ammunition from the rise in food prices, and a false alarm which irrigation schemes had aroused in the peasants. The whole Mission, however, was pretty well in agreement over Britain's future policy.[33]

He was flown by an Air Commodore to Ramleh for a twelve days' sight-seeing tour of Palestine which was soon to be brought under civil administration as a British Mandate. On 25 March he was back in London.

While Milner was in Egypt, Amery, Fiddes and Thornton kept him well informed on Colonial Office business and sent him major problems for decision.[34] He had to warn Amery that letters from London to Cairo could easily take a fortnight. The chief problems perhaps were the Prince of Wales's Empire tours, the timing of the next Imperial Conference, and Mandates. The Prince had returned from his very successful but strenuous Canadian tour via Washington, D.C., and New York soon after Milner's departure. Ned Grigg, his political secretary for the tour, Amery wrote, had been 'tremendously impressed by the value [of the operation] from the Imperial point of view'. He added that Grigg had shown 'extraordinary skill in counselling the Prince and writing his speeches'. But, for what transpired to be mainly personal reasons, he was 'much perturbed' by pressure being exerted on him to accompany the Prince on his Australasian, South African and possibly Indian tours, though he felt 'it might be his duty to do so'. Milner, as already stated, had offered him the Secretaryship of the Rhodes Trust. He now with some reluctance agreed that Grigg ought to go with the Prince, but hoped he would take the Rhodes Trust job for a time before he did so.

Then two awkward problems arose. Hughes of Australia insisted that the Prince should put his country first on the tour, and only gave way after a struggle. The main actor, the Prince, was, as Lady Donaldson shows, developing a strong will of his own. She quotes a *Times* article of 1914 by Milner's friend Sir Herbert Warren, President of Magdalen, Oxford, written on the Prince's departure from the College after two years of residence:

> Bookish he will never be; not a 'Beauclerk', still less a 'British Solomon' . . . but he will not want for the power of ready and forcible presentation, either in speech or writing,

as well as an eagerness and capacity to learn about men.[35] The Prince then had the experience – which deeply affected those of his generation actively concerned – of over four years of war.

Quoting Frances Stevenson, Lady Donaldson writes that he felt 'very sick at having to go off on another tour', and believed Lloyd George bore chief responsibility for the plan. Also that the King and Queen were 'very sniffy' with Lloyd George for listening to the Prince's objection to an Indian tour following at once after those to Australasia. Milner, the Crown's chief adviser (after the P.M.) on the Empire, perhaps saw advantages (though he would never have said so) in sitting at this time in a hotel in Cairo with its windows boarded up. He felt concern over Grigg's perturbation as reported by Amery. It seems that the Prince had expressed a preference for his Chief of Staff, Admiral Sir Lionel Halsey, who complied with his wishes, as a political adviser; and that Grigg had tendered his resignation with some justice. Amery asked Milner to send a strong telegram (presumably to Lloyd George), which he did, stating that Australia would present many pitfalls and that Grigg, who had 'a quite unique knowledge of Dominion politics,' must be the Prince's chief *political* adviser. The battle was won in their favour. Grigg sailed with the Prince for New Zealand not long before Milner's return after having, it seems, spent some time at the Rhodes Trust. At Milner's invitation Dawson became the Secretary of the Trust in late June.

Amery also suggested that they should begin to plan an Imperial Conference, perhaps in Ottawa, in October 1920. But Milner was inclined to look upon this date as too early. The chief Imperial problem, of course, was still that of the association (now being called by some a Common-wealth) developing between the 'Mother Country' and her Dominions. Sir Kenneth Wheare has provided the classic account in *The Empire and the Peace Treaties, 1918–21* of what this story attempts to convey from the activities of one deeply interested and overworked Colonial Secretary burdened with duties extraneous to his office.[36] Sir Kenneth describes the achievement by Dominions at the Peace Conference of the 'double status' of sovereign states associated with the United Kingdom. The real significance of this evolution was made public when Britain conceded to the Dominions the right to individual signature of the Peace Treaties. Over ratification, he states that Milner

> clearly regarded the British Empire [not the United Kingdom] as one of the Principal Associated Powers ... [he also realized that] the Empire, though one Power, was a composite Power.

The signing and ratification processes 'had great political and constitu-tional significance' as establishing Dominion self-determination in foreign affairs. These two first epithets are important, since the situation reached in practice was not yet accepted by British Constitutional or International Law, which 'would one day be obliged to catch up'. [37]

Regarding the next Imperial Conference, Milner told Amery that one reason for his preference for 1921 was 'the extreme fatigue of all the leading men', especially Borden; another was the time required for ade-quate preparation. In January he wrote that he was all for asking individual Dominion Ministers to Britain but 'not very hopeful of success' since Dominion representatives had to be 'big men' and the P.M.s would not like sending away their important colleagues. Only pressure from Lloyd George, with Hankey as a channel, might manage to summon a real Imperial Cabinet. He referred to his speech at Oxford on the previous 1 August,[38] adding, 'we are in for a bad reaction in constructive Imperial politics, but if we can weather the next year or two' without letting the War achievement go quite to pieces it should be possible to rebuild on the foundations already laid.

Amery had suggested to Milner that he should go for a month to Constantinople leaving Rodd in charge of his Mission; he was sure we should not deprive the Turks of the city. Milner replied that it was impossible for him to leave Egypt. He agreed we should not turn the Turks out of Europe, and that settlement with them was the 'key to the whole Eastern Question', though he had failed time and again to convince the P.M. and Curzon of this. He was anxious about the rising tide of

Bolshevism in the Near East and thought our abandonment of the Caucasus line and command of the Caspian 'may cost us very dear'. He could not understand why Curzon, of all people, failed to realize this; or why Churchill and Kerr appeared to be giving little help over this issue.

The Mandates Commission, it has been seen, much preoccupied Milner after the Peace Conference. Canada had no territorial conquests to claim. But the three other Dominions, especially South Africa, had at the Paris Conference been less than enthusiastic over application of the Mandatory Principle to their conquests. A compromise was evolved by the creation of three classes of A, B and C Mandates, a descending scale of what today would be called stage of development. In due course Britain became Mandatory Power of Palestine and Mesopotamia (both Class A), and the latter soon became the kingdom of Iraq; as well as of parts of German East Africa and Togoland in the West (which were class B). Japan gained the mandate over certain islands north of the Equator, and Australia over ex-German territories south of this line. New Zealand won the mandate of ex-German Samoa; and the much-disputed phosphatic Nauru was shared between these two Dominions and Britain. France became mandatory of Syria (class A).

After his return late in March Milner had an audience with King George. Easter was early in April and he heard of the death of his stepmother Elise who had married his father in 1872. He spent a quiet holiday with Lady Edward and Helen at Great Wigsell. After that he was called frequently to 10 Downing Street for talks about foreign and Imperial questions; which hardly confirms Lloyd George's strictures in *Truth about the Peace Treaties*, published nearly twenty years later when he was about seventy five. Though a master of speech, Lloyd George is not often credited with a liking or aptitude for writing, and historians do well to remember that Duff Cooper (later Lord Norwich) wisely called his memoirs *Old Men Forget*.

Attention must turn to Milner's other duties this spring and summer of 1920. Amery calls the Colonial Office when he joined it 'very much a domain of its own'; though responsible, of course, to Parliament and the Cabinet, 'much of its most interesting and creative work raised no controversies outside.'[39] Milner set up a Colonial Development Council of experts to survey the economic prospects of the whole Dependent Empire and to formulate plans. Speaking to Crown Colony officials at the annual Corona Club dinner he said the demand for self-government was bound to grow since

the whole world is intoxicated with the new wine of self-determination . . . [there was] an immense amount of work to be done and [whatever can be done] is their due, and in the highest interest of the State.

He set up a Currency Board which took the first steps, against stout opposition from other Departments, in attempting to create effective currency unity throughout the Empire. He was much concerned with Colonial Africa, an important example being his appointment of Sir Gordon Guggisberg, a Canadian-born Royal Engineer introduced to him by Elinor Glyn, as Governor of the Gold Coast with the object of creating a first-class ocean port at Takoradi. W. A. S. Hewins, Amery's predecessor in his job, had created the nucleus of an Emigration Office, and this topic remained a prominent one in correspondence with the Dominions throughout the year.

Milner wrote an article on Egypt for *The Round Table* and spoke on the topic to a meeting of M.P.s, writing that these tasks 'put his regular work badly in arrears.' He had earlier sent Amery to inquire into difficult problems arising in Malta, and then sent him to Ottawa to advise West Indian delegations invited there by the Canadian Government to discuss economic relations. An important Colonial Office activity was obtaining and training a competent Colonial Service. This was in the capable hands of Major Sir Ralph Furse, who after leaving Balliol had joined the Colonial Office during Loulou Harcourt's rule in 1910, and returned there after distinguished war service. In answer to the present writer's request he gave him his impressions of Milner, of whom he did not see a great deal since he was always 'terribly busy'. Regarding Milner's appearance and nature he wrote:

> . . . he was always correctly, rather than well, dressed. I remember a certain air of formality, almost of stiffness, about him. . . . Apart from that I never could see anything 'Teutonic' in him. To me he was a very English Englishman, but with something of the retired General about him and I should have described him as a distinctly military civilian. That made him all the more attractive to me (though perhaps it put off some others) for he had many of the soldierly virtues.[40]

Lord Harrowby, the former Lord Sandon, told the writer that the story, still current, that he spoke with a pronounced German accent is totally untrue.

Correspondence with Governors-General and Governors, including their retirement and successors, formed a staple item of Milner's work. Since early 1919 he had engaged in correspondence of special interest with

Lord Buxton, Governor-General of South Africa, whose five-year term would expire in the autumn, though he had undertaken to stay on. Botha's death in August 1919 would, Buxton wrote, 'profoundly modify' the position in the country since he had exercised 'almost unlimited sway' over the Transvaal Dutch. He added there was 'still much provincial jealousy' existing, and made an interesting comparison of the influence and merits of Botha and Smuts, with both of whom he was on intimate terms. Smuts won the election in March 1920, but his South African Party obtained one seat fewer than Hertzog's Nationalists, and Sir Keith Hancock calls the result 'a catastrophic defeat.' Buxton wrote that Smuts was

> . . . very piano, and feels the election is a slap in the face for him – and this there is no denying. But he has plenty of courage . . .

Law made a speech in a Home Rule debate in the Commons which, appearing to give a Dominion the right to secede, provoked quick responses from Buxton and Milner. Smuts soldiered on till the end of the session. On Buxton's suggestion, and with Smuts's consent, Prince Arthur of Connaught became his successor and arrived in the country at the end of December.[41]

Late in July Milner wrote to the Prime Minister enclosing a letter from Sir Archibald Weigall, Governor of South Australia. This stated the hope that the Prince of Wales, who was 'weary in body and mind', would postpone his visit to India. Milner supported this plan, adding that only he (the P.M.) could ensure it since the King was 'very touchy' about this Indian visit, and resented any suggestion that the Prince should omit it. Harold Nicolson writes that since his first visit to India in 1905–6 the King had been 'under the spell' of that country and had followed its affairs 'with intense personal interest'. At the Durbar of 1911 he had 'to the surprise of all' himself risen and announced to the huge crowd 'two major boons'. Perhaps his desire that the Prince should proceed there at this date was connected with the Montagu–Chelmsford reforms. In any case Lloyd George did what Milner had asked. The Duke of Connaught went to India this autumn, and the Prince, after some rest at home, went there in 1921.[42]

In early May, meetings of Milner's Egyptian Mission were renewed in London and these, with negotiations with the *Wafd* under Zaghlul in Paris, continued to the end of the year. Walrond arrived to play his useful role of a go-between. The numerous meetings which took place consisted, it seems, mainly of unrecorded talks.[43] They formed for Milner a constant preoccupation. He attended on 12 May the unveiling, with an address by

Cartoon of Milner by Powys Evans

Curzon, of a plaque to Lord Cromer in the Henry VII chapel of the Abbey, not far from the beautiful effigy of Margaret, Countess of Beaufort. The architect of Britain's Late Victorian venture in Egypt and Milner's former chief had died in his 76th year over two years before. Unlike Curzon and Milner he had taken little part in British politics after his retirement; but had remained a staunch Liberal.

Milner, as the reader is aware, maintained a life-long and expert interest in foreign affairs apart from his special interest in the Empire. During this month he had lunch with a party which included Prince Yusupoff, one of those who had assassinated Rasputin, and attended a Ministers' conference at No. 10 to discuss impending negotiations with the Soviet delegate Leonid Krassin. He attended a Cabinet at which grave differences were again revealed about Persia and the Near East, and a night or two later worked up to 2 a.m. on a memo. for the Cabinet on Britain's military commitments in that area. His growth of interest in it was due not only to concern over India but to Britain's acquisition of the Palestine and Iraq mandates and his long Egyptian inquiry.

He spent the last two nights of May at New College, mainly to attend a Raleigh Club dinner. With Murray Wrong, a young Magdalen don, in the chair he replied to a speech on the Crown Colonies by another Canadian, Vincent Massey of Balliol. He later called on Reginald Coupland, a Trinity don, and on the Master of Balliol, had a long walk with Warden Spooner and attended another Raleigh Club dinner addressed by Bob Brand on the subject of 'Capitalism'. Oxford, he observed, was 'looking most beautiful'.

His Egyptian negotiations reached a new stage with the visit to London of Zaghlul Pasha. In May, Ozzy Walrond had been accompanied to London by the leading moderate nationalist Adli Pasha, and on 7 June Adli arranged Milner's first meeting with Zaghlul, followed by Zaghlul meeting the whole Mission at the Colonial Office in what Milner described as 'a social call to make one another's acquaintance'. His establishing direct relations with the Mission offered new hope for agreement.

Zaghlul has been described to the writer by Mohamed Abdel-Wahab, a young Egyptian historian and diplomat, as a 'charismatic leader' although basically an emotional one. The talks included both full meetings between him and his seven or so *Wafd* colleagues and the Mission, and private ones between one or more members of each side. They were always, the Mission later recorded, 'conducted in an amicable spirit'. Among the British, Rodd was regarded as Milner's No. 2 and was in general agreement with his views.

This topic must be interrupted to mention other matters simultaneously

M.—M

occupying Milner's time. He gave the first speech at a Mansion House meeting concerning a projected British Empire Exhibition. This, it seems, was the birth of the Wembley Exhibition of 1924, called by one historian 'Britain's greatest since the Great Exhibition of 1851'. Parkin, who had been created a K.C.M.G., died at the age of seventy three at Goring near Oxford; and his bust broods with a bust of Milner over the Parkin Vestibule of Rhodes House. For years Milner had jotted down in his diary the deaths of friends or eminent statesmen, British and foreign, and had been punctilious in attending memorial services. After Cromer in the Abbey it was the turn, somewhat late, and at the appropriately lower level of the Victoria Embankment, of the unveiling of a bust of the humane, gifted, and eccentric journalist W. T. Stead. As an elderly Ready cousin and then his Balliol tutor de Paravicini died, Milner noted, 'life is becoming an obituary'.

A dinner with the Overseas Bankers' Association, continuing business about Nauru island and a speech in the Lords on East African labour and Indian problems followed. In mid-July he was writing that he felt 'exhausted after many weeks of hard work, late hours and very little relief, physical or mental'.[44] On the 22nd he gave lunch to Zaghlul, noting that negotiations had reached a critical stage. While nationalist feeling was making progress in Egypt, similar feeling had been doing so in India. In the previous April, General Dyer had made the grave blunder of ordering troops to fire on an unarmed crowd in Amritsar, killing 379 persons and injuring many more. Though relieved of his command, the General received much support in long Parliamentary debates. Edwin Montagu was Secretary for India, and Milner was given the unpleasant task of replying to a vote of censure on the Government in a crowded House of Lords. Dyer's action, besides increasing Indian violence, caused the introduction of Ghandi's historic campaign for independence by *Satya-graha*, often defined as passive resistance or soul-force.

Milner spent Sunday 1 August 'swamped' by arrears of correspondence and official papers. He called the Cave Report on Trade Boards, a subject in which he had long had an interest, 'unsatisfactory and contrary to my advice and conviction'. The situation in Ireland had been more serious since January 1919 when the *Dáil*, the self-constituted Dublin Parliament, issued a declaration of independence. De Valera, an implacable nationalist leader, was the counterpart of Egypt's Zaghlul. Slowly the all too familiar war of an Irish Republican Army against Britain broke out, with Milner's former Adjutant-General, Macready, made C.-in-C. of the British forces; and I.R.A. outrage was met by the outrage of the Black and Tans. Professor Charles Mowat calls 1920 'the year of decision in Ireland'.[45]

Milner's concern, except as one member of the Cabinet, was now far more with the Near East. His Mission thought the *Wafd* delegates, especially Zaghlul, hampered by the uncompromising line they had hitherto taken. 'It was always difficult', the final report stated, to clothe agreement (often close) 'in words which did not conflict with formulae to which the Egyptians felt themselves committed'. It made what it viewed as large concessions, and drafted a settlement which more or less satisfied both sides called the 'Milner–Zaghlul Agreement' on 18 August. Its one condition was that Zaghlul and his colleagues should use all their influence to get a Treaty in these terms accepted in Egypt and approved by a genuine Popular Assembly. Then Zaghlul proposed the suspension of talks so that four of their number could go home at once to explain the proposals to their people. On 23 August *The Times* gave a fairly correct account of the substance of the talks.

The four delegates went to Egypt accompanied by Egyptian Press approval of the Agreement, and a rather inconclusive manifesto from Zaghlul. The reception they encountered, especially by members of the Legislative Assembly, was encouraging; they then rejoined Zaghlul and the others in Paris. In October the whole team, including Adli, came to London for two further meetings with the Mission. They reported good reception by their people of the settlement, but wanted some modifications of matters already discussed, which the Mission unanimously agreed it would be useless to reconsider. The Mission emphasized that the Agreement was still subject to official negotiations, and both Milner and Zaghlul made final speeches on 9 November.

Late in August Milner had taken three weeks off at Sturry, interspersed with nights at Great Wigsell. Elinor Glyn and her daughter came as his guests and were given a full tour over the Cathedral. On Garvin's behalf he made 'a great rummage' among his South African archives. Loulie came over from Folkestone, and Ozzy came to talk about Egypt, which, in spite of Zaghlul's departure, seemed never far from the thoughts of Milner and others, notably Winston Churchill. In September the American President had a paralytic stroke which eventually proved fatal; in March 1920 the Senate had voted down the German Treaty, and later the Harding administration made separate peace treaties with the Central Powers. Before this Congressional action Milner had told a friend he was doubtful of the League's success; though he was certain that any effectiveness it might have would only be due to the British Empire and the U.S., and that the influence of the Empire required its members, working together, forming 'a sort of sub-League among themselves'.[46] The first League Assembly meeting was due to take place at Geneva in November.

Milner's work in September included, as it had done since he took office, a good deal of discussion about Rhodesia. Dougal Malcolm, a Director of the British South Africa Company, wrote that a decision of Judicial Committee of the Privy Council in 1918 meant that 'the days of the Company as a governing authority were numbered'. Shareholders could not be expected to provide further funds, and the movement of settlers to end the Company's rule had gathered force. 'A long and un-edifying dispute' was in progress about the compensation the Company should receive. There was also a difference of opinion in Rhodesia, un-resolved until after Milner's departure, over whether to aim at self-government or at entering the South African Union.[47] In a referendum of 1922 the white inhabitants of Southern Rhodesia chose self-government.

On 1 October Lord Hardinge of Penshurst became Ambassador at Paris, and Sir Eyre Crowe replaced him as Permanent Head of the Foreign Office. Shortly after, Helen Cecil became engaged to the former's son Alec, now a private secretary to King George and later, under difficult conditions, to King Edward VIII. Hugh Thornton, doubtless tipped off by Milner about his retirement, left him to become the Second Crown Agent for the Colonies. Milner wrote an introduction to a new and last (13th) edition of his *England in Egypt*. With the King and Queen he received the Prince of Wales at Victoria Station on his return from Australasia. Chaim Weizmann visited him regarding the Palestine Mandate, already the scene of Arab–Jewish disturbances. As the con-sequence of crimes in Ireland he was one of the Ministers given police protection. He moved the second reading in the Lords of the important 1920 Emergency Powers Bill.

On 11 November he attended the unveiling of Lutyens's Cenotaph in front of the Home Office; and then joined a Ministerial procession to the Abbey for the ceremony of the Burial of the Unknown Warrior. The same afternoon he attended the opening by the Duke of York of his cherished London School of Tropical Medicine; he had made Sandon especially responsible for raising by personal appeals what was then regarded as 'the magic sum' of £100,000 for this venture. A little later he began with his habitual care to draft the Egyptian Mission Report. He dined at Toynbee Hall when the chair was taken by the new Warden, J. Mallon, who was to prove an outstanding success, and the guest of the evening was Major Clement Attlee, just elected Labour Mayor of Stepney and in due course Prime Minister. He attended the Lords' second reading of the Govern-ment of Ireland Bill which gave Ulster its own Parliament and became law just before Christmas.

On 27 November he wrote to Lloyd George to tell him he intended to resign at the end of the year, and two weeks later confirmed this with him in a talk at No. 10.[48] In the first half of December his Egyptian Mission (though without the Egyptians) held some half-dozen long meetings with him, engaged, in his phrase, in 'plodding away' on their Report. He relaxed in a week-end at Petworth, especially enjoying the pictures, and later much enjoyed a large gathering of the Moot. In a week-end at Sturry he read through the whole Egyptian Report in what he called its 'final revise', and wrote that on Monday, the 20th, he would have it delivered to Curzon.

It consisted of much that has already been outlined above, i.e. an account of the stages of negotiation. Since the fact gave a handle to its critics it should be emphasized that the Mission's short terms of reference asked specifically for proposals for a new form of Egyptian Constitution 'under the Protectorate'. It has been seen that before the Mission left Egypt in March it had nailed its flag to *independence* for the country, combined with a Treaty; and that negotiations which preceded and followed the 'Milner–Zaghlul Agreement' of August were concerned with the precise terms of the Treaty.

A brief summary of the terms the Report recommended, in the form it adopted, must be made: first, Egypt's foreign affairs, of a *political* nature only, should continue to be under British control, but the country should have the right to create its own diplomatic representation abroad; secondly, as an ally, Egypt should accord to Britain a military base on her territory. The Egyptians were prepared to accept such a force in a war; but in *peace* only provided this was not an 'Army of Occupation', and preferably if it was stationed on the eastern bank of the Suez Canal. The question of where the force would be stationed was left open, though further reference will be made to this problem; third, under safeguards, the Egyptian Government should be free to dispense with the services of British officials; fourth, certain reservations should be made for the protection of foreigners. The Sudan, with its status defined by the Anglo-Egyptian Convention of 1899, did not enter into the scheme.

The Report stressed that the War, among other factors, had broken continuity with the past. Martial Law and suspension of the Legislative Assembly had been necessary, at the price of almost universal Egyptian opposition. Since 'the word "Protectorate" had become a symbol of servitude . . . [they, the Mission] had [perforce] to get on new ground.' Britain had in the past often renewed her promise of self-government for Egypt. The Mission had no doubt that the Egyptians with whom it had negotiated so long were wholeheartedly in favour of the settlement's main features and anxious to secure its acceptance by their people.

This Report deserves to rank among classic State Papers. Milner, its main author, was driven (as so often) by what he conceived as a British moral obligation. He also perceived, as a realist, the clear necessity to move British troops outside the cities, where they constituted a visible affront to Egyptians, to some part of the Canal Zone.

The Report won Curzon's approval, but not that of the whole Foreign Office and still less of the War Office. The Cabinet was deeply divided, with Churchill a main objector. Milner noted in his diary of 29 December his deep dissatisfaction with the outcome of a Cabinet meeting on the matter. The Report was sent to Allenby, who approved it, and was published in February, receiving much attention, as Cmd. 1131 of 1921. It was in fact rejected, partly due to the Cabinet's simultaneous troubles over Ireland and India, and an opportunity for statesmanship was lost. Duff Cooper, then a young official in the Egyptian Department of the Foreign Office, describes the story and something of the disturbances which followed in 1921. It was not until 15 troubled years later that Milner's proposals were accepted in the Anglo-Egyptian Treaty, 1936.[49]

Milner spent New Year's Eve in London, stopping late work to hear the nearby Big Ben strike midnight. The first day of 1921, a Saturday, was devoted to his periodical task of clearing up papers, official and private. He had a heart-to-heart talk with Curzon a few days later about their relative positions in the Ministry and Egypt; and a hint of his forthcoming resignation appeared in *The Times*. The week-end of the 8th to the 10th was spent at Lord Lee's invitation at Chequers and proved historic. It was the formal handing over of the house with its art collection and furniture and estate by the Lees to the P.M. and the nation.[50] After dinner on Saturday with Lloyd George, the American Ambassador and his wife, and a few other guests, Lord Lee made a speech, was answered by Lloyd George and, after signing the deed of gift, left with Lady Lee for London. On Sunday Milner climbed Beacon Hill, and in a long talk with Lloyd George fixed the date of his retirement as 1 February. It was, perhaps, flattering that another guest, Lord Riddell, told him he would have made a first-class Viceroy of India, which office Lord Reading, also a guest, had just accepted. Milner replied, 'Yes, if I had been ten years younger.' On the Saturday before dinner the whole party had played the game of revealing their youthful careers, and Milner had said he thought he was born with a copper spoon in his mouth.

He spent a busy January on official and personal business. He consulted his solicitor about taking action over a libellous article on him in *Justice*; and for reasons which will soon be made clear had a distressing talk with Loulie Dawkins. It seems that Rio Tinto had already invited him to rejoin them. He went to join Claude Montefiore at Winchester for a meeting of big-wigs, including the Duke of Wellington and A. L. Smith, the Master of Balliol, to discuss the extension of University education in Wessex. Churchill, chosen by Lloyd George as his successor, was his guest at Great College Street for lunch, and had a very long talk about Colonial Office business. Another deputation came to him from the British South Africa Company to discuss their difficulties over Rhodesia resulting from Cave Commission's award to it of compensation. He spent a whole afternoon dictating letters of farewell to Colonial Governors.

Leo Amery's memoirs, often referred to in this story, were written at the end of his long and active life and are not always accurate in their details. He calls the opening of the Migration (which Milner called Overseas Settlement) Conference 'the last act of Milner's public life'; in fact this Conference took place in January before the engagements just mentioned. In addition, the deadline to which Lloyd George had agreed of 1 February for retirement somehow got postponed for nearly a week. Milner presided at a British Empire Club lunch to a Dominion Senator; and did the same thing next day at a meeting of the National Service League Council. This decided to close its career and to give what remained of the League's funds to the Boy Scouts Association. Milner was also interviewed before he left by what he called 'strings of journalists'.

On 7 February he handed back his Seals of Office to King George, who talked to him at length. What the writer prefers to record about his exit from office is, first, his generous letter to Sir Herbert Samuel to say that Churchill, who intended to visit Palestine soon, was

> . . . very keen, able and broadminded and I am sure, if he only gives himself time to thoroughly understand the situation, will take sound views and you will find him a powerful backer. His weakness is that he is too apt to make up his mind without sufficient knowledge.[51]

Secondly, his telegram to Smuts, his former foe and then his friend, replying to one of Smuts' regretting his resignation. This read in part

> . . . a great deal depends on your victory [in the South African Election] . . . though out of office I shall continue to do what lies in my power to promote development of Imperial relations on the lines which I think the right ones so I hope we may still be fellow-workers in the future.[52]

Part V

INDEPENDENCE

Chapter 15

Retirement

(February 1921 – May 1925)

Marriage, Provence, Homes and Work – Egypt, Ireland,
Palestine Visit, Many Activities – Questions of the Hour –
South African Tour – Oxford University Chancellor-Elect,
and the End

Sir Almeric Fitzroy states that in January Milner showed 'a curious
impatience to be quit of office', and that 'regret at his retirement was felt
by everyone' including the King. His detachment and restraint had

> ... placed him on a somewhat solitary level of public veneration ...
> [but] his very aloofness from public notice has bitten into the minds of
> many the great qualities of his work ... his mistakes never obscured
> the greatness of his aims.[1]

His impatience was due in part to Lloyd George's procrastination in
fixing the date of his retirement; and he wrote to his friend Matheson he
had been 'very near a physical breakdown for some time.' He had told
Stamfordham for the King's information on 3 January that his leaving the
Colonial Office was imminent, having pressed Lloyd George again on
that day to give him a final decision.

The day after his delivery of his seals of office he took a favourite
godchild, the grand-daughter of Goschen, Moira Somerville, to lunch and
then to the wedding of Helen Cecil to Alec Hardinge at St. Paul's,
Knightsbridge. This was, he wrote, 'a very grand affair' attended by the
King and Queen and other royal persons, any number of Cecils, Lord
Hardinge of Penshurst, Maxse relations and many friends. The reception,
which the King and Queen also attended, was held at Lord Salisbury's
London house, 21 Arlington Street. He dined alone with Lady Edward.
The next day, Ash Wednesday, he was seized with giddiness on rising and
could not stand. He feared heart trouble but his doctor diagnosed a gastric
attack and kept him in bed for the day.

He then went to Sturry for five nights, recovering rather slowly and
being visited by both Lady Edward and Loulie Dawkins. As he attended

church, answered his large post, received further visits and gardened he commented 'wonderful what a lot one always finds to do here. I have had a very busy day.' Several Ministerial changes were reported in the papers including the move of Lord Lee from the Ministry of Agriculture to the Admiralty and Churchill's replacement at the War Office by Sir Laming Worthington-Evans. On returning to his home in London he found a letter from 10 Downing Street telling him that the King had made him a Knight of the Garter. The next morning King George presented him 'in a very gracious way' with the Garter insignia. Some months later Countess Roberts, the Field-Marshal's daughter, offered him her father's robes which he gratefully accepted. Some adjustment by the tailor must have been needed.[2]

Milner lost no time re-creating his links with the City. He went first to Rio Tinto which re-elected him to its Board and then lunched in its familiar Board Room; before long the Rothschilds asked him to be Chairman. The next day he was re-elected to the Board of Indemnity Mutual Insurance. When his Egyptian Mission Report was published on the 19th he wrote that most of the newspapers commented on it 'without much intelligence or knowledge.' On the 22nd he attended the Cabinet for an hour's discussion of the situation in Egypt. The same day Sir Fabian Ware showed him *Punch* containing a Bernard Partridge cartoon of him in his Garter robes being addressed by Britannia. He commented (with justice) that this was hardly successful as a portrait, but he liked the quotation which read

> Long since we were resolved of your truth,
> Your faithful service, and your toil in war.

Lord Harrowby, Milner's former assistant private secretary at the Colonial Office Lord Sandon, has told the writer he remembers speculating with young colleagues about which of two ladies often mentioned in this story he might choose to be Lady Milner. He said that Lady Edward came constantly to the Colonial Office to see him, and in a small circle there Milner's intentions to marry were guessed at. Lady Edward was now 49 and Loulie Dawkins, who had married Clinton in 1888 and known Milner well much longer than her rival, was several years older. Irrespective of ages one cannot help wondering why Milner, almost 67 and frequently seeing both ladies among others, got married at all. He was far from helpless in practical matters, well supplied with doctors, London clubs and, it appears, domestic servants. As what follows will show, he remained active in the City and in various public and private causes. Perhaps the decisive factor was his lifelong, deep-felt desire for companionship. Lady Edward, it is certain, offered greater knowledge and liking than Loulie for the more strenuous intellectual and artistic pursuits, but Loulie had taken the news badly.

Milner was, it seems, unaware that Sandon and a few of his friends were engaged in the speculation just mentioned. For Geoffrey Dawson records that two days before the wedding 'Milner rather shyly imparted to me as a dead secret his arrangements for being married on Saturday.'[3] The marriage took place on 26 February, and it would be untrue to add that wedding bells rang out. Milner drove to the house of Ouvry, his solicitor, who introduced him to his brother, a parson. This brother and the Vicar, Prebendary Sharpe, married Milner and Violet (as Lady Edward will now be called) at St. James's Church, Paddington. The only guest Milner mentions, besides Ouvry, was Violet's unmarried sister Olive. The bridal pair then drove to Bryanston Square to sign their wills and Milner, as a trustee, also signed young Helen Hardinge's Settlement.

Milner went to Great College Street to say good-byes and collect his luggage, and sent an official announcement of his marriage to the Press Association. He had also, Sir Ralph Furse of the Colonial Office relates, taken the precaution of asking him to organize their evasion of Press photographers by getting their car stationed at the front door while Violet and he stepped out to a taxi at the back.[4] They arrived at Charing Cross quite unobserved, spent the night at Dover and the following evening were in Paris. The next day, a Monday, Milner noted that the Sunday papers had all given 'a more or less sensational account of our "Secret Wedding" '; and they left Paris for Avignon and a honeymoon of over six weeks.

In the train to Avignon for a stay there of two weeks Milner broke a tooth, but dentists' visits only slightly marred the enjoyment he always felt holidaying abroad. With cheap commercial flying and mass holidays still far distant, they varied local sightseeing at leisure with day trips by motor, further afield. They went on to Nîmes for a week with visits to the Camargue and the sea. With well-organized plans to receive letters and papers from home they learnt of Bonar Law's resignation due to ill-health and Milner wrote to him expressing regret. Proceeding to Carcassonne their days were upset by Violet suffering some indisposition which compelled them to postpone their departure. Turning north they took a motor to Albi and through the Dordogne before catching an express train to Paris for a stay of a week.

Violet went at once to visit Clemenceau. A year or so earlier the Tiger had been shelved by an ungrateful public in the Presidential elections in favour of a far lesser man. 'How,' he had asked of Lloyd George (an appropriate expert)) with his usual good humour, 'can I go to the Elysée without a wife?' With Milner she visited François Sicard the sculptor, who took them to a mason's yard to see the cast of the monument she had commissioned for erection at Villers Cotterêts on the spot where her son George had been killed. They reached Sturry in time for dinner on 12 April.

It seems best temporarily to abandon the chronological method and to summarize briefly some features of Milner's life with Violet in the four years ahead. Independence has never been known as a guaranteed feature of marriage. The label was chosen, of course, for this final phase to express Milner's liberation from his Whitehall office with its grind of continuous interviews, correspondence, files, memoranda to write or to master, and requests to attend on Lloyd George immediately if not sooner. The willing horse had at long last stepped out of the shafts.

In his altered (one avoids the word 'new') existence his marriage was clearly the principal feature. The devotion he felt for, and received from, Violet is unquestioned. Their tastes and their friends, their shared interest in political and economic questions, in art and travel, houses and gardens gave firm foundations for lasting companionship. Now they were home again there were two housing problems to be solved. Great College Street was too small, and they started on a search for a larger London home. The problem of their two country homes, with each devoted to his or her property, was less urgent and was resolved for the time by compromise.

There was, unhappily, a larger fly in the ointment than a difference about the attractions of Sturry and Wigsell. It has been seen that Violet became indisposed at Carcassonne; and this indisposition recurred on frequent occasions for the rest of their married life. It is usually described by Milner as 'headaches', or simply as Violet's being unwell or depressed and spending a day in bed. A year or so from this date he took her for examination to Lord Dawson of Penn, who gave a generally favourable report, laying emphasis only on digestive trouble. The writer is loath, without further evidence, to suggest any explanation. One has, however, been put to him which seems plausible. Violet was far from a shrinking or diffident specimen of her sex. For almost twenty years she had been a grass widow making her own home with two children, ordering her life in the way she saw fit. A masterful character, she was now subject to the constraints of union with an equally masterful one, however kind and considerate. While Milner left the shafts of office behind him she re-entered those involved in marriage.

The second feature of Milner's altered life was more freedom to take holidays abroad. These were in part directly linked with efforts to benefit Violet's health. A third, more important, feature was Milner's quick reinvolvement with business in the City. Already in the interval between leaving Whitehall and marriage he had been re-elected to the Boards of Rio Tinto and one or more Insurance Companies. He did not need to solicit the City; it was rather the City, especially the companies he had served in the past, which solicited him. Rio Tinto was again the front runner, and its complex affairs pursued him literally to his death-bed. Perhaps equally well known to the reader was the familiar but continuously expanding London Joint Stock Bank; after a Board meeting in 1923 he wrote they had decided the 'much vexed question' of changing its cumbrous name in favour of 'Midland'. Other Insurance Companies and a company called Road Rails, of which in a year or two he grew tired, were added to the list. He then began refusing offers since he had no time for more.

It is sometimes hard to accept Milner's description of himself to Gell in his heart-to-heart talk before sailing for Cape Town in early 1897. He was not, he had said, 'one of the brilliant men' and did not work rapidly, but was industrious and laborious, and had gifts of expression.[5] One has seen the truth of this in some of his work, but has doubts how far it applies to his City and financial activities. Violet, after his death, claimed he had an almost miraculous memory for figures; and it is hard to see how, lacking speed, he could have accomplished such a large, continuous, burden in the City. He was driven far less by acquisitiveness than by the normal needs of his class at this time, and by pure interest. He continued to be generous to those who were hard-up, many of whom had no claims on him, and to numerous societies. He now had a wife to support with ideas which had always verged on grandeur. Lord Edward Cecil had only left a limited estate; and his good-natured brothers and sisters had regarded him as more skilled in spending money than acquiring it.

The fourth general feature of these years is more easily dealt with. Milner had received many letters regretting his leaving public office, and congratulating him on his Garter and marriage.[6] A large number of these expressed the hope and belief that after a rest he would return to public office. Curzon wrote he would 'deeply deplore' Milner's absence from the Cabinet and the Lords. Smuts cabled that his gifts were 'indispensable' for the coming discussion of Imperial relations. Parkin thought he should be the next Governor-General of his country, Canada; and Ben Tillett, the Trade Union leader, wanted him back in office. His friend Henry Birchenough wrote,

I never consider you have withdrawn from public life – you are in reserve for great occasions and great national needs – that is all.

Birchenough knew his man, and that Milner was incapable of withdrawing from public service (as distinct from office) in one form or another. It could be said of him in the words of the seventeenth-century poet:

> Youth, what man's age is like to be doth show;
> We may our ends by our beginnings know.

Milner wrote to a friend in late April from Sturry that he was 'back again and fit for anything.'

Before long he and Violet were house-hunting in London. By a coincidence one of the first houses they saw was 14 Manchester Square, the home of Milner's long-standing friend Sir Algernon West, who had recently died at the age of 88. West had known and esteemed Milner when he was private secretary to Goschen and, as the reader will recall, worked actively for him to succeed him as Chairman of the Inland Revenue Board.[7] Such careful and demanding house-owners as the Milners were not going to make up their minds until after further visits of inspection. In mid-August Milner signed a cheque for the purchase of this house which they occupied for the first time on 8 November.

Milner wrote to Birchenough in May that he felt 'wonderfully rejuvenated.' They were having a lazy time at Sturry (though he often went to London) in perfect weather. Though the sensible thing to do would be to give up one of their country houses, '. . . we can neither of us make up our minds to give up either of them. A rather comical quandary!' Characteristically he added he was 'much out of sympathy with all the latest developments of policy.'

Ned Grigg, having decided not to accompany the Prince of Wales on his Indian tour, wished to succeed Philip Kerr as private secretary to Lloyd George, for whom he had much admiration. While more hitches on timing took place at No. 10, Grigg acted as Secretary of the Rhodes Trust. Milner wrote in May that the P.M. was anxious to get him as his private secretary (in the continuing 'Garden Suburb') for the Dominion Prime Ministers' Conference and for at least a year, and Grigg seems to have taken this position soon after this date. At Milner's invitation Geoffrey Dawson succeeded him in June as permanent Secretary to the Rhodes Trust.

J. L. Garvin paid visits to Sturry to work on Milner's archives for his life of Joseph Chamberlain, and Milner was much struck by the breadth of his knowledge and his memory. His own evenings at home were often spent in reading to Violet, or she to him, from English classics including Meredith and Dickens. It must be inserted here that the post-war British boom had ended abruptly in the previous winter, with over-production of primary products a dominant evil. The Government had handed the coal-mines back to their owners in March, but exports had fallen, unemployment had risen and a lock-out had followed. Partly due to Sturry's proximity to Kent coal-mines Milner expressed strong disquiet on the state of this industry. The railwaymen and transport workers failed to support the miners' desire for a fight to the finish, so that the coal strike ended on 1 July. A. J. P. Taylor asserts that this defeat 'set a general pattern. Wages fell heavily in every industry during 1921 . . . Lloyd George lost his last shadow of hold over the working class.'

Milner and Violet spent a week-end in Oxford in mid-June as guests of the Warden of All Souls. His main object was his usual occupation of the chair and proposal of the 'Memory of the Founder' at the annual Rhodes Scholars' dinner. The occasion was memorable for the presence of W. F. Massey, Prime Minister of New Zealand, Smuts and Sir Thomas Smartt in England to attend the Prime Ministers' Conference. Not much earlier the Moot had held a dinner and long talk to decide on its policy regarding what Milner called the forthcoming 'Imperial Cabinet'. His misgivings of eighteen months earlier in discussions from Egypt with Amery about the timing of this Conference seem to have persisted.[8]

The Conference lasted from 20 June to 5 August. Lloyd George was elected chairman, and in addition to thirty four Plenary Sessions met the Dominion Prime Ministers at eleven smaller sessions. The proceedings were even more confidential than on previous occasions and few speeches were published. They were less important than those of the Imperial Conference in 1923. Hankey, like Milner, believed that the Empire would best be served at this stage by a policy of *festina lente*. He battled manfully, but in vain, for a truly Imperial Secretariat; and opposed on practical grounds direct communication, short-circuiting the Colonial Office, between Dominion Prime Ministers and Britain's Prime Minister. No special constitutional discussions were included; but the right reached in 1918 for Dominions to nominate Cabinet Ministers to represent them at Imperial War Cabinet meetings, and some commercial decisions, were reaffirmed.[9] On two occasions Grigg gave Moot gatherings an inside account of the Conference proceedings.

An additional reason for Milner's detachment was the seemingly large-scale operation of moving in early July what he liked to call his 'summer headquarters' from Sturry to Wigsell. Violet had made large improvements in the rooms at Wigsell; but accident-prone as he was, Milner had a bad fall on the stairs there late at night and cut his head, which caused him discomfort for some time. They lent Sturry to Alec and Helen for their holidays. They attended various Imperial gatherings in London, including a Court Ball at Buckingham Palace, a big Guildhall meeting of the Victoria League and one of Abe Bailey's immense parties. Milner wrote to thank Darling for a copy of his address to the Empire Agricultural Congress, adding he had not been able to get hold of Arthur Meighen, the Canadian Prime Minister, and gathered that the P.M.s were so overwhelmed with a mass of questions that it was 'of little use trying to open their minds to anything more.' Smuts, in a farewell message, told Milner the Conference had 'avoided making mistakes even where no positive work was done.'[10]

In bitter Parliamentary debates the Corn Production Acts (Repeal) Bill was carried. In his role as a radical, or, if the reader prefers, a State Capitalist, Milner spoke out in vain against this particular and 'disastrous' dismantling of controls. His two former agricultural colleagues, Edward Strutt and Turnor, both wrote praising his action and called the outcome disheartening. He spent a quiet August, being ordered by his doctor a rest of some days due to a leg being swollen by a bite. Later he walked the few miles from Wigsell to the parish church at Salehurst where Violet's mother was buried.

Milner's views about foreign affairs continued to rate high in official and unofficial circles. This July Adli Pasha, now Egypt's Prime Minister, came to London and resumed negotiations directly with Curzon, who reported: 'the Cabinet all much stiffer than I am in the matter.' With Curzon's approval, Adli had many talks with Milner. Curzon was supported by Allenby, and would have been by most liberal opinion, had he not had the public image of what Nicolson, in a sympathetic study, calls 'the type of encased aristocrat'.[11] By November Adli told Milner he thought the Government's draft Treaty unacceptable. A note despatched by the Government through Allenby to the Sudan, drafted in Lloyd George's own secretariat, gave offence, caused Adli's resignation and a new round of repression. Curzon, to quote Nicolson, by a strong note to foreign powers

> . . . arrested the process of liquefaction which threatened to dissolve the remaining vestiges of our position in Egypt.

There were not wanting people to compare the alternation of conciliation and coercion in Egypt with the much longer application of these opposing methods to Ireland. Milner wrote this autumn that Henry Wilson was 'furious' over Ireland. A truce in the war with Britain took effect in July, but division among the Irish leaders began to grow. Complex negotiations began in London in October, with Lionel Curtis as the secretary of the British delegation. They ended in early December with the Irish delegation, headed by Michael Collins, accepting a Treaty giving the 'Irish Free State' dominion status within the Empire similar to that of Canada in return for Lloyd George's promise of a Boundary Commission. Milner, in spite of his action before 1914, remained detached from the problem. He read of the Settlement on a train returning from Spain and found Violet, like Henry Wilson, furious about it. Lord Dawson had again made a thorough diagnosis of Violet's case and reported 'serious digestive troubles [and the] need of great care.' Milner felt very anxious about this.[12]

In October he stayed again with Spooner to attend the New College Gaudy, propose the toast *stet fortuna domus* and visit the War Memorial in the chapel. He chaired a lecture at King's College, London, by Professor Hugh Newton on Mandated Territories. Not long after, they left Wigsell for one week at Sturry. Violet telephoned to say she had had her first grandchild, a boy to be called George. On 8 November they spent their first night in 14 Manchester Square, which Milner called 'just habitable, though most of the rooms were still in chaos', and for some weeks Violet was very busy getting the house into order.

Milner, who liked working in harness with friends, had been fortified by Steel-Maitland joining the Rio Tinto board. The affairs of this company grew more complex, involving negotiation with foreign rivals and a subsidiary body in London called the Pyrites Producers' Association. Milner went for three weeks to the mines, which always involved diplomatic discussions with the British Ambassador and high Spanish authorities en route in Madrid. Back at home he spent two weeks with Violet who was 'pretty unwell', at Sturry over Christmas. To the sound of church bells ringing in 1922 he noted:

> ... in my private life 1921 has brought me much happiness, but it has been a year of reaction in public affairs, and the outlook is not encouraging.

He gave a Presidential Address to the Classical Association at the City of London School, with Asquith moving the vote of thanks. He had agreed to be honorary secretary to Lord Roberts's Memorial Committee and on their behalf saw Blomfield to discuss the design of a bust on a site chosen in St. Paul's. A little time previously, at the instigation of Violet,

Lord Edward Cecil's *Leisure of an Egyptian Official* had been published. The writer agrees with Kenneth Rose's view that it was insensitive of her to publish so poor a memorial to her husband, who had stated that he wrote the essays 'for family consumption only'; and strange that Milner had failed to dissuade her from action which he must have known would offend Egyptian pride.[13]

Violet celebrated her 50th birthday and Milner gave her a silver-fox tippet. He held a meeting of what he called 'my Egyptian Committee', some members of his Mission and others. When Parliament opened he voted against the Government in a vigorous Lords debate on the problem of Ulster's Boundaries. An activity he had now started was an effort to fulfil his long-expressed wish to write a book on economics; this February 1922 he dictated a full analysis of the book for the scrutiny of his literary agent. The first anniversary of their wedding day came and went as they made preparations for a trip of two months to Palestine. Milner told the Road-Rails concern he would retire from their board. In early March they left with a servant called Hillman via Paris, paying visits to Clemenceau and to George's grave at Villers Cotterêts. From Marseilles they sailed via Cairo to Palestine.

It was Milner's habit to keep special diaries during trips abroad.[14] Herbert Samuel was convalescing in Jericho, so his Civil Secretary, Wyndham Deedes, and Ronald Storrs showed them Jerusalem. Samuel had clearly defined his programme, with the country to be treated much like a Crown Colony. His conciliatory policy appeared to be working quite well, with a Jewish National Home of some 80,000 Jews, mainly from Eastern Europe, in being. Unfortunately seeds of tension lay in the fact that the country had for long been the focus of rival strategic interests. Emir Faisal lost control of Damascus, and the problem of Trans-Jordan was unsolved. The Milners travelled over much of the country and revelled in its sages and thyme, cornflowers and anchusas. Milner could not avoid receiving deputations, for example from the Moslem–Christian League, an anti-Zionist organization. After one day of interviews he wrote, 'I feel thoroughly "fed up" with the Jewish question.' When they reached home he told a friend he was 'more in love than ever with the Holy Land' despite the political squabbles only caused by extremists on both sides and encouraged by a rotten Press.

They spent much of a hot May at Sturry, with Violet much better for their Palestine tour. His guests in London included Arthur Glazebrook from Toronto; and Milner began 'picking up his economic studies.' Henry Wilson relinquished his position as C.I.G.S., and on the day he left the War Office wrote a word of thanks to Milner for 'his many kindnesses to him.' Ten years younger than Milner, he at once entered the Commons as M.P. for North Down and became a trenchant critic of the Government's Irish Agreement. He found Belfast in a highly disturbed state, and was outspokenly critical of the military and police arrangements in both parts of Ireland.[15] Sir Herbert Samuel was visiting London and drew up with Churchill an important White Paper in June which made no proposal to create either a Jewish or an Arab State, but left to the future what the future would bring. He asked Milner to dine with the Arab delegation, and with Lady Samuel was asked back to Manchester Square to meet the Selbornes and others. Milner could not afford time to comply with Chaim Weizmann's request to help to form an Anglo-Palestine Society, or Claude Montefiore's to lead a movement for raising Universities' funds, or the Chancellor of the Exchequer's to chair a committee to examine the percentage grant system.

About the end of Oxford's Trinity term he spent another week-end with the Spooners to address first the British-American Club and on the next night the annual Rhodes Scholars' dinner. He then suffered from inflammation of his face which turned out to be shingles. On 21 June he wrote that the Prince of Wales returning from India had a great reception. But the following day was tragic. Henry Wilson, returning in uniform from unveiling a war memorial, was shot dead on the steps of his home in Eaton Place by two Irish gunmen. It is sad to have to add that a murder of this nature caused a far greater public sensation at this date than it would do in the mid-1970s. Milner went at once to visit Lady Wilson, to find her in the room where her husband's body was lying. Wilson was given a full military funeral and buried in the crypt of St. Paul's between two other Irishmen, Lords Wolseley and Roberts.

Milner and Violet spent a good deal of July and August at Wigsell. He wrote that he was making real progress with his book on economics 'tho' I compose slowly and with difficulty.' It becomes easier to understand his analysis of himself as not brilliant but 'laborious and industrious' when one reads of the time he often took to write articles and prepare speeches. This book was Milner in his aspect of a don intent on a thorough treatment of his subject, and it took much time in the making. He employed for a short period an assistant recommended by William Beveridge. He attended the inaugural meeting at Toynbee Hall of the 'International Conference of Settlements', unveiled a memorial to another friend, Mrs Humphry Ward, and attended a meeting at Lord Salisbury's to raise money for Irish Loyalists.

After some weeks, for some unknown reason he told his literary agent that since his work had been unproductive he could not fulfil his contract. Violet's ill-health, still a problem, may have contributed to this action. He called late August and early September, the anniversary of George's death, 'a bad time of the year for her.' On the last day of the month they went over to Compiègne and attended the inauguration of the monument by Sicard on the spot at Villers Cotterêts where George had fallen. The Mayor and local school-children added a flavour of French ceremonial. Violet put flowers on the grave in a permanent cemetery nearby, where George and other Guards officers were now buried. It may be added that a casting of Sicard's bronze bust of Milner was unveiled after his death by Lord Rosebery in the Oxford Examination Schools.

Milner lunched with Lloyd George at No. 10 for a talk about agriculture and before long was writing to the Minister about the threatening agricultural crisis, which, as he had foreseen, the repeal of the Act in the previous year would produce. He and Violet took two weeks' holiday, visiting a number of friends including F. S. Oliver in the North of England and Scotland. In early October Leo Maxse's wife Kitty was killed in an accident, causing Violet in particular great distress. Soon afterwards Amery called to talk about the political crisis and report that everyone was discussing a general election. Lloyd George, to the neglect of some serious problems at home, had been organizing or attending a long series of conferences abroad and met diplomatic defeat when the Turkish army reached Chanak. On the 10th the Cabinet decided to fight an election at once on a Coalition ticket. Milner had written in the summer that he didn't think the 'Goat' had lost his power of springing though 'where the devil he'll spring next is more unpredictable than ever', adding,

> I still love him for what he did in 1916–18. I have hated almost everything he has done since except his masterly handling of last year's Dominion Prime Ministers' Conference.

He wished for his own sake he could retire for a time before he got into 'any more muddles.'[16]

On the 19th, Steel-Maitland called to tell him about the famous Carlton Club meeting when Austen Chamberlain and his fellow Coalition Unionists were routed. Bonar Law, urged on by Beaverbrook, saved the unity of the Unionist Party. Lloyd George resigned at once and the King asked Law to form a Government. Two days later Milner was at Wigsell when Law rang up inviting him to join his Government, which on grounds of age and tiredness he declined to do. An enigmatic message arrived from Curzon, which in London the day after Curzon disclosed as a plan that he should succeed Lord Hardinge of Penshurst as Ambassador in Paris, for which he thought his abilities and Violet's gifts were most suited. Though Milner asked for time to think it over, they both agreed to refuse this proposal.

Milner had now resumed steady work on his economic notes or, alternatively, essays. He was elected an Honorary Governor of the London School of Economics. As an example of the weight attached to his influence Herbert Samuel had written in the summer asking him to help in persuading Churchill to obtain funds for Trans-Jordan, where Abdullah, Britain's most valuable asset, had to maintain his prestige by hospitality and gifts. Milner did what he could. Churchill fully recognized Abdullah, to the bitter resentment of the Zionists; although when the Palestine Mandate was at last formally approved by the League his régime was made internally independent. A small force was formed in Trans-Jordan which eventually evolved into the Arab Legion. Abdullah visited Britain in October and was entertained by Milner with his large party which included St. John Philby, the father of the traitor Kim Philby.

They soon began shutting up Wigsell and opening Manchester Square as their 'winter headquarters'. Following Northcliffe's death, John Walter and the Hon. J. J. Astor, younger brother of Waldorf Astor, became joint proprietors of *The Times*. The latter sent his 'man of business' to consult Milner about a new editor for the paper, and inevitably Geoffrey Dawson was among those considered. Milner advised Dawson to accept this job only if the conditions of appointment were entirely satisfactory. The proviso was a wise one, since Northcliffe had appointed a Managing Director with large powers, and in various ways left the business of the paper obscure. Dawson insisted on complete editorial authority; and it was early December before he replaced Wickham Steed in the chair he was destined to occupy until 1941.[17]

In the meantime, on 16 November, the results of the polling on the previous day came tumbling in fast. The Milners' Canterbury member Ronald McNeill (later Lord Cushendun), renowned for having thrown a Blue book at Churchill in the Commons, was an Ulsterman of impulsive temper who later achieved minor offices. The Conservatives, with 347 seats, had a majority of 88 over the other parties combined, Labour winning 142 seats and the Liberals only 117, fairly evenly divided between Lloyd Georgites and Asquithians. Ned Grigg wrote to say that if Dawson rejoined *The Times* he would be glad to become permanent Secretary of the Rhodes Trust, and he did so in the New Year until 1925. At the end of the year Otto Beit offered Milner the chairmanship of De Beers, which he declined.

Milner had been making faster progress with his book, which was now to take the form of essays, four of which he had completed and read to Violet. Abe Bailey had commissioned Sir William Orpen to paint his portrait and early in 1923 his sittings began. General Swinton, who was helping Lloyd George to write his memoirs, sought Milner's advice; two years later Swinton was elected to the Chichele Professorship of Military History at Oxford. At this date and for some time to come Milner paid periodical visits to the solicitors of Leo Maxse whose finances, it seems, were decidedly in the red.[18]

On four successive Sundays in January 1923 articles appeared in *The Observer* which were later to form the second essay, called 'Towards Peace in Industry', in his book. This shows the extent to which, influenced by the war, his views on domestic affairs had taken more radical form.

Violet had left for Paris where he soon joined her with other directors and officials for two weeks at Rio Tinto, as usual also doing business in Madrid. They stayed at the mines with the general manager, Walter Browning, a colourful character whose strong will, superb horsemanship and skill with a gun had earned him the title 'King of Huelva province'. His kingdom spread along the wine-red river was, Avery writes, 'a tumultuous one, with frequent and violent labour disputes, political turmoil and threats of assassination'.[19] On their journey home the Milners visited Cordoba, had an audience with the Queen in Madrid, and took the train via San Sebastian to Paris.

They had barely reached home when Colonel Ralph Verney, Acting Secretary to the Speaker, asked them if they would let Great Wigsell for a number of years. Perhaps Violet's spells of ill-health were a factor in their joint agreement to this plan. She offered to let the house furnished for three years from March, with an option on both sides of renewal, and Verney agreed to these terms. Milner attended a big Toynbee Hall dinner of members and local employers, undertook the chairmanship of an Imperial Forestry Institute into which Furse had lured him, and presided at a meeting of the Oxford University Endowment Fund. Attending an 'enormous party' given by the Astors to meet the King and Queen was presumably relaxation. On 21 March he at last finished the fifth and final essay of *Questions of the Hour*. It was curious, and certainly not due to serious ill-health, that he should write just after his 69th birthday to Jim Rendel that he looked upon any years of vigour which might remain to him

. . . as a sort of bonus, something to be grateful for but not to be counted on.

Another form of public service he now undertook made one more claim on his time. The Ministry of Health set up a Committee to inquire into the East Kent coalfields and he consented to act as its chairman. He and Violet went to Sturry for some time, in her case to endure more bad headaches and in his to pay regular visits to London. He presided at the dinner given by Rio Tinto directors to their English staff on the company's 50th anniversary. At Sturry he had still another accident, this time wrenching his knee picking bluebells. With Violet he attended the Duke of York's wedding in the Abbey. In mid-May he took Violet for a cure to Aix-les-Bains for nearly four weeks. These were followed by days at Fontainebleau, with the inevitable visit to Clemenceau, whose talk was as usual 'witty, vivid and compact'; he had no bitterness or resentment, only resolution to keep clear of public affairs for the future.

They had not been long at Aix when Bonar Law resigned for reasons of ill-health. The famous incident followed of Curzon, summoned from Somerset by Lord Stamfordham, assuming he had won the succession but finding that honest Stanley Baldwin, whom he called a man of 'the utmost insignificance', had been chosen. Baldwin made few changes in the Government, remaining Chancellor of the Exchequer until appointing Neville Chamberlain to this office in August.

Reaching home Milner found that *Questions of the Hour* had been published (by Hodder & Stoughton) a few days before. In his preface he wrote that these essays were written 'from an impulse of protest against some of the "stunts" of these distracting years.' Though topical in subject matter he hoped they would not be found 'altogether topical in spirit' since he had been trying to grope his way 'through the mist of current controversy to some firm resting ground of principle.' He was writing in what in one essay he called the 'great reaction', the change in a few years from the unity, co-operation between management and labour, and positive role of Government in over four years of war back to old pre-war methods.

In the essay published earlier in *The Observer* he was especially concerned with industrial relations. The previous essay deplored the wholesale dismantling, particularly in Agriculture, of official controls and emphasized that our annual output had increased hugely in the war, but that dissolution and lethargy had now taken over. We were back, he wrote, in the old pre-war feud between Capital and Labour – the pendulum had swung all the wrong way. The mass of people were worse off than before 1914, and industrial relations were 'greatly embittered'. Labour, however, had 'abandoned none of its aspirations' and with the franchise and advance of education now aspired to a higher status, while four-fifths of top industrial direction was still controlled by the 'moneyed class' and not by producers. The area of public ownership was sure to extend, but only slowly. He deplored the casual reception of the careful scheme of the Sankey Coal Commission.

He correctly forecast that 'an unmixed Labour Government was probably a long way off.' What was needed was the gift to wage-earners of more share in the conduct and policy of their business. Whitley Councils set up in the war had led to a number of Joint Councils, mainly in small industries. It was development of these, not chiefly for settling disputes but to associate masters and men in the conduct of their business, giving birth in due course to National Councils, that he saw as the best hope for the future.

He thought the Labour Party had taken over some of the worst as well as the best of the Liberal traditions. Approving of its enthusiasm for education, he deplored its indifference, if not hostility to, the Empire, and its lukewarm attitude to Defence. It failed to appreciate that, whatever the mistakes of the past, Britain now saw herself as the trustee of her subject races, responsible for their much-needed economic development. He now saw the growth of the Commonwealth–Empire as due more to outstanding individuals than to any 'settled national purpose or even sustained interest in our heritage' – a generalization which probably few modern historians would dispute.[20]

The book represented his mature views, his concrete – and in some respects radical – proposals for the welfare of all classes and larger understanding of the assets of Empire. He sent copies to various friends including Warden Spooner, writing that he ought to have put 'a great deal more work into it' but was impatient to protest against current and mischievous clichés. Violet later wrote that, dissatisfied with his treatment of economic problems, he at once began reading on modern currency and banking, which he had to fit in with his varied round of activities.

They soon made their annual move to Sturry, where they gave a fête in the garden to some 1,500 persons for McNeill and the Tory Association. Milner corresponded with Leonard Hobhouse about their mutual interest in the Trade Boards Bill, created in 1909 to fix wages in sweated industries but now languishing. Herbert Samuel implored him to speak in the Lords on a Palestine issue. He chaired a meeting of the West Indies Agricultural College. In mid-July he went with Violet to Le Quesnoy, north of Cambrai, to unveil a New Zealand Memorial at the place where their troops, with French help, had plugged a gap in the German break-through of March 1918.

They had weeks of perfect summer weather, with Helen and Alec and the Somervilles for long visits. Parkin died this year, and Milner met Dr. Frank Aydelotte, President of Swarthmore University, who as United States Secretary was to give long and eminent service to Rhodes Scholars from his country. In September he and Violet paid a visit to Clemenceau at his home near the sea in La Vendée; now eighty two his physical and mental activity was still marvellous. In early October they moved their household back to London. Before long the Duke of Connaught unveiled Lord Roberts's memorial at St. Paul's.

The Imperial Conference of 1923 opened on 1 October with Baldwin presiding. Broad agreement was reached on the Singapore base, but later sessions did not go smoothly. Baldwin contributed little, and much argument followed on foreign affairs. Hankey considered that the 'one absolutely clear outcome was the insistence of the Dominions on full consultation. No longer were they content to allow Downing Street to speak for them.'[21] A modern historian concludes that the Dominions' reluctance to involve themselves in Britain's diplomacy meant that the Conferences were now back to their looser pre-war form. Milner had previously written an article on the Conference for the *Empire Review*, and during the sessions he saw a good deal of Mackenzie King, now Canadian Prime Minister, and the other Dominion leaders. In this book he had written he was

... in revolt against the present all too pervading spirit of pessimism ... at last Britain seems to be awakening to the supreme importance of Imperial development to her economic salvation.

Not long after dispersal of the Conference Bonar Law died of cancer. A day or two earlier, partly stimulated by the Imperial Economic Conference held concurrently with the main Conference, Baldwin spoke at Plymouth in favour of a Protectionist policy, taking his party and the country by surprise. On 1 November he asked Milner to be chairman of a Tariff Advisory Committee, reporting to Neville Chamberlain, to work out the details, and Milner wrote: 'I think I shall have to do it.' In the following weeks he gave much time to this committee.[22] On the 16th Parliament was dissolved and the election was fixed for 6 December. In the evening of this day Violet went out to Selfridges to learn the first results, and by the 7th it was evident that Baldwin's plunge had miscarried. Defence of free trade had inspired Lloyd George and Asquith to fight together, and 159 Liberal members were elected. Ned Grigg had won Oldham as a Lloyd George Liberal, persuading his followers to accept Imperial Preference. Tories remained the largest party, but declined to 258 members. The chief gainers, especially in Greater London, were the Labour Party who won 191 seats. It was not clear what Government would materialize from this situation and Baldwin decided to face Parliament in the New Year.

About this date the Warden of All Souls enlisted Milner's help in forming an 'Oxford Trust', to appeal for money to buy and preserve as an open space the 'Scholar Gipsy country' on Cumnor and Boar's hills. Also, thanks to Amery's initiative, the Compatriots Club was revived.

Parliament met on 8 January 1924, and on the 13th Milner motored with Violet to Chequers to have a long talk with Baldwin on political matters. On the 21st the Labour Party's vote of no confidence in the Government was carried; next day Baldwin resigned, and the King asked Ramsay MacDonald to form the first Labour Government. MacDonald's final list of Ministers, Mowat writes, was 'anything but revolutionary . . . it was a cabinet of moderates, more representative of the upper and middle classes and of new recruits to the party than of the trade-union side and the old-timers'.[23] It confirmed Milner's forecast that an 'unmixed Labour Government' was far distant. Haldane became Lord Chancellor, Philip Snowden the Chancellor of the Exchequer and J. H. Thomas the Colonial Secretary, while the P.M. was also Foreign Secretary.

On 1 February the Milners left once more for Rio Tinto, spending two weeks at the mines and another two doing business in Madrid and sight-seeing at Seville, Toledo and Burgos. Back in England in March Violet's ill-health, especially her headaches, persisted. They dined in a fairly small party at Buckingham Palace when, as usual, Milner had talks with the King and Queen. He chaired a meeting of the Oxford University Endowment Fund. They went to Sturry, and when *The Times* announced that the next day was his 70th birthday Violet very successfully fended off all the reporters. They spent a week-end, now a rare occurrence, with the Desboroughs at Taplow Court. He chaired the Rio Tinto annual general meeting; and then a lecture, linking him with his early boyhood, by his friend Reginald Blunt on 'Old Chelsea'.

Something more must be said of his chairmanship of the East Kent Coalfield (also called Development) Committee, since this work had obvious links with the views about labour and management and the emphasis on production set out in his book. It seems that a few years before the war borings had suggested the possibility of a large coalfield in the area east of Canterbury. The first four sites included Chislet, not far from Sturry, and Betteshanger; in spite of setbacks due to the war forty companies to develop these mines had been registered by 1919 and the prospect was opened up of large local demands for houses and shipping facilities.

In April Milner was told by F. Urquhart ('Sligger') of Balliol of the death of his old friend A. L. Smith, the Master, who had dominated history teaching in the College for 37 years.[24] He himself contracted lumbago and spent a long Easter holiday at Sturry. He then went to Oxford to open a meeting to gain support for Toynbee Hall, short of money as usual, and also Mansfield House; he was re-elected chairman of Rio Tinto for the year ahead, but declined Arthur Greenwood's offer of the chairmanship of the Royal Commission on Insurance. On 31 May he went with Violet to Winchester for the opening by the Duke of Connaught of the College War Memorial and to visit her gift in her son's memory of a Cecil firing range and tablet. Milner soon went to Oxford again for the annual Rhodes Scholars' dinner and his round of visits which included Mrs. Arnold Toynbee, now very feeble in body, and her great friend and contemporary Mrs. T. H. Green. He spent a night at Cuddesdon with Bishop Burge of Oxford who enlisted his help in the Lords with his forthcoming Liquor (Popular Control) Bill. Back in London he spent four or five hours with Violet at the Wembley Empire Exhibition, a project he had helped to launch as Colonial Secretary and which he thought very impressive.[25]

The 19th of June he called 'a black day' as Smuts suffered what Sir Keith Hancock describes as 'a smashing political and personal defeat' in elections in which Hertzog replaced him with a Nationalist-Labour 27 majority. The defeat on the same day of Baldwin's preference resolutions was, under the circumstances, not unexpected. He found Rio Tinto board meetings, as often in this period, long and trying due to differences between certain directors. He visited the company's works at Port Talbot, and made many visits from Sturry to London on its business. He had moved with Violet for another summer semi-holiday at Sturry. Besides another Tory Garden Party they entertained fifteen South African cricketers who were playing Kent at Canterbury; and laid plans, perhaps initiated by Violet, to employ Blomfield to reconstruct the house's garden front. Milner had his 'digestive apparatus' X-rayed in Harley Street, and though nothing much appeared to be wrong, thought he might be feeling some symptoms of his appendicitis trouble in South Africa twenty years before. Together they paid their annual pilgrimage to Paris and Villers Cotterêts.

Milner wrote an article for the *Round Table* on Egypt and the Sudan, and supplied notes for a *DNB* article on Lord Edward Cecil. At the persistent Ralph Furse's request he undertook to preside over still another committee, this time a Colonial Office one on Recruitment of Agricultural Experts for the Crown Colonies. Through his literary agent he received an offer (which he did not take up) of £5,000 from Macmillans for his Reminiscences. On 9 October the Labour Government was defeated and MacDonald announced dissolution and an election on the 29th, the unusual event of three general elections in three successive years. When the day came Milner and Violet issued forth again after dinner to Selfridges to learn the early results. On the next day it was clear that the Conservatives had won handsomely, with a final total of 415 seats compared with Labour's 152 and a mere 42 for the Liberals.[26] Baldwin formed his second Government, destined to last until 1929.

Milner and Violet had decided in the summer to make a long (English) winter tour of South Africa. Being persons who prepared affairs well in advance they had arranged to let Manchester Square to the Selbornes, and prepared a careful itinerary. Sturry was organized for their absence, and Milner began to read up his South African diaries. They sailed on the 31st in the *Walmer Castle* for Cape Town. On the ship's radio they heard the changes which Baldwin had made in his Government. Milner was glad to learn that Amery had become Secretary for the Colonies, though less glad that Churchill was Chancellor of the Exchequer and (for different reasons) Steel-Maitland Minister of Labour. Curzon suffered what Nicolson calls his 'second humiliation', being superseded as Foreign Secretary by Austen Chamberlain and given the post of Lord President of the Council. The Milners also learnt that Calvin Coolidge had succeeded Harding as President of the U.S.A.

Reaching Cape Town, they went to the Mount Nelson hotel and were given a welcoming dinner by some 70 persons with Sir Thomas Smartt presiding. The next day they were shown the Rhodes monument at Groote Schuur, driven down the lovely eastern shore to Muizenberg and dined with the Rose-Inneses at Newlands. They went north for a week's stay at Kimberley in a train the Government had provided. As guests of De Beers they were shown the diamond-washing machinery, the native compound, Baker's War Memorial and much else. Violet suffered from the heat, and partly for this reason they had to abandon their intention to visit Rhodesia. Milner was still re-reading his South African diaries, often aloud to Violet. Proceeding to Johannesburg they were met by their friend Patrick Duncan and had full days meeting other friends, and sight-seeing. Milner's home for years, Sunnyside, was a hostel for girls, and next to the South African Roedean School. They motored via Vereeniging to see the Vaal River Barrage, and toured a large northern area visiting British land settlers.

Going to Pretoria they stayed with the Governor-General, the Earl of Athlone, who showed them Herbert Baker's imposing new Union Buildings. Lunching with the Prime Minister Hertzog, Milner wrote that 'though rather embarrassed at first meeting me he was quite civil.' A pleasanter occasion was lunching with Smuts in a family party at his large farm at Irene; he lived, Milner wrote, 'like a yeoman farmer, in a very simple style, tho' in perfect comfort.' Another visit to 'Milner Settlers' in the north was followed by a gathering of his 'old Civil Service' at the Pretoria Club. More days of visits to friends at Johannesburg preceded their turning south for two nights at Bloemfontein. Sir John Fraser at 84 was still wonderfully vigorous. A long train journey took them to West-minster, named after Bendor, and the 'manor house', or central farm of the estate built by Baker. Major A. K. Apthorpe, conspicuous in land settlement work since Milner's day, arrived to greet him. Settlers dating back to his time as Governor, in most cases prosperous due, in his view, to the help of the Land Settlement Board, came from long distances to two centres to greet him. His opinion was confirmed that only group as distinct from individual settlement by the British had a chance of success.

Their days had been so full that it was not until reaching Ladysmith on Boxing Day that he began to compose his fuller record.[27] He climbed to the top of Spion Kop and Wagon Hill and visited other Natal battle-fields. In Natal, the Transkei, and eastern Cape Colony the warmth of their reception increased as they travelled. The Mayor, Town Council and notables of Durban gave them a large formal luncheon, and the city seemed to Milner to be developing fast. In the Transkeian Territories, of special importance in South Africa's history and also today, they found native agricultural methods very primitive. As they went westwards Milner was impressed by the difference which motor cars had made to the country, though also by the precipices, boulders and pot-holes they encountered. Joined by his friend, Sir Charles Crewe, he had much talk about South African politics.

For Milner, education equalled land settlement as a means of maintain-ing British influence in South Africa. He had long since realized that large-scale British immigration was no longer possible, and that the quality of the settlers was the goal to be aimed at. Hence his keen support for the 1820 Memorial Settlers' Association, his interest in the local Rhodes

Scholars and subventions when possible from the Rhodes Trust to educational bodies in the country. He took much interest in Grahamstown's famous high school and the future of Rhodes University College. Late in January they reached Cape Town for their last fortnight, making their headquarters at Abe Bailey's house on the sea at Muizenberg, next door to the cottage in which Rhodes had died. 'The pace grew if possible', Milner wrote, 'more fast and furious as we neared the end.' They made an excursion to Cape Point and climbed a good distance up Table Mountain delighting, as they had both done throughout, in the flowers. Meeting many more people, on their last day they attended the opening by the Earl of Athlone of the Union Parliament, visiting both Houses. It was a point of honour, Milner noticed, for every Government supporter who could do so to speak Afrikaans, though the Speaker was careful to hold an even balance between the two languages.

They left Table Bay in the *Saxon* on a most lovely afternoon. Milner's leaving closed as it had done almost twenty years earlier with a farewell message from Smuts,

> Bon voyage to you and Lady Milner. I trust your visit has been as agreeable to you as it has been helpful and encouraging to your friends.

This may serve as an epitaph to a career of eight years which must be seen as success as well as failure.

They had a quiet voyage, keeping largely to themselves, and doing much varied reading. On the 26th they landed at Madeira to find the usual pile of English letters and copies of *The Times* awaiting them.

They docked at Southampton early on 2 March and were driven by Olive from Victoria Station to Manchester Square. Both of them felt pretty tired; but for Milner the round of City and public engagements was resumed at once. Calling at the Rhodes Trust office and talking to Grigg he found, as he may have been told, that the Trustees had accepted the Warden of Wadham's offer to sell part of his garden at £10,000 per acre to build a Rhodes House. Milner was not destined to see the building, designed by Sir Herbert Baker and opened in 1929 with its large main Hall bearing his name.[28] The next day he went to the City and spent a long afternoon at Rio Tinto where he found 'a lot of important work lay ahead of us.' He wrote his name at Buckingham Palace, and lunched with Astor at *The Times* to meet the Prince of Wales. He dined with Amery to meet the five Dominion High Commissioners, went to Sturry for a day to look round and presided again at the Oxford University Endowment

Fund annual meeting. On the 20th he learnt that George Curzon, some five years his junior, had died. Nicolson writes that Curzon spent the last year of his life in a spirit of genial humour which triumphed over personal mortification and physical suffering. After a service at Westminster Abbey his scarlet coffin, studded with golden nails, was carried down the steps of Kedleston to burial in the village church.

Milner spent a quiet 71st birthday with an afternoon at home on Rio Tinto accounts and a visit to Loulie. A few days later he was thoroughly overhauled by his London doctor Sir Humphry Rolleston who appears to have found nothing particularly wrong.[29] Swinton again came to consult him about Lloyd George's memoirs.

Several persons had approached him asking him to agree to be nominated to succeed Curzon as Chancellor of Oxford. To one of these, Sir John Marriott, he had written that though 'physically quite strong and well' he was 71, and

> . . . clearly conscious that I cannot do as much work as I could till the
> last few years. My mind is as sound as ever, but more easily tirable. I
> have a lot of private business to attend to . . . and a number of public
> duties to discharge.

It was strange if he did not realize that the duties of the office were normally not onerous; and that Curzon's intention to reside at Oxford for long periods and take a large share in administering the University would not have commended itself to most members of the Hebdomadal Council.

In early April either pressure in this matter from others, or feelings of ill-health, caused him to have a further long talk with Dr. Rolleston. He spent working days in London and Sturry until Dr. Reid of Canterbury advised him on the 5th to rest and lead a quiet life for a few weeks since, though in good physical health, he was suffering from mental fatigue. He did not at once take this advice, since two days later he worked in the City and received a visit at Manchester Square from Sir Herbert Warren, one of his keenest supporters for the Chancellorship of Oxford. He told Warren that he had just had his doctor's advice to go slow, and asked for time to think it over.[30] Next day he chaired a Rio Tinto annual general meeting, and the day after obeyed his doctor by joining Violet for eleven lazy days of gardening, walks and reading for pleasure; for once he did not even engage in much correspondence. Colonel Ralph Verney wrote to say he had just read in the papers of Milner's agreement to stand for the Chancellorship, and Violet agreed to renew his lease of Great Wigsell for a further year. Milner told a friend that he thought that the choice at Oxford lay between Asquith, Lord Grey of Fallodon and himself, and he favoured the second.

He returned to London alone to resume his duties, but after one day saw another doctor who advised him to return to Sturry as soon as possible. On the 22nd he did some business in Manchester Square and was then seen off by the faithful Miss Smith on the train to his wife and home. He spent a few lazy days; but on the 28th he felt too unwell to get up; one side was partly paralysed and his speech was difficult to understand. Violet suggested to Miss Smith that he might have got *encephalitis lethargica* (sleeping sickness) and Dr. Reid agreed that this was possible.

As May began, both Violet and the doctor thought he was showing definite signs of improvement. The Press had begun commenting on his illness, and was now writing about his maintaining his strength and making progress. The Rhodes Trustees, Matheson of New College and others wrote to congratulate him on his recovery. A number of others, for example Sir Michael Sadler and Lord Crawford, wrote through Violet to tell him that his support by Oxford Convocation was overwhelming.[31] On 5 May a meeting of his supporters in New College, where the historian H. A. L. Fisher had just succeeded Spooner as Warden, nominated him for the office. The *University Gazette* a week later announced that in default of other candidates he was duly elected Chancellor as from 25 May. Though Dr. Farquhar Buzzard came down from London and confirmed that the illness was *encephalitis*, the public bulletin of the 6th still spoke of good progress.[32]

The dawn unhappily proved a false one. On the 7th Milner was drowsy, and asked for his Rio Tinto papers. Next day he was moved downstairs to his sitting room from where he could see the garden which delighted him so much. Several days of unconsciousness or semi-consciousness followed. He died in lovely weather about noon on 13 May.

Three days later his coffin, draped with the Union Jack and with one wreath from Violet of iris, wild hyacinth, tulips and violas, left for Canterbury Cathedral. The Archbishop, Dr. Davidson, officiated, and the Cathedral, flooded in May sunlight, and with both the King and the Prince of Wales represented, was full. The service was simple, with the lesson read by the Vicar of Sturry, and Parry's setting of 'Crossing the Bar'. After the Archbishop's blessing the family mourners and the coffin left to the music of Chopin's funeral march. They drove with a motor-hearse the 40-odd miles to Great Wigsell, lent to them for the day by the Verneys, where they met Milner's cousin Basil Ready. The service at the parish church of Salehurst was private, attended only by Violet, Helen and Alec, Olive and Leo, Basil and Oliver Ready, Moira Somerville, Miss Smith, the Kiplings and a few other intimate friends. Milner's 'twin', Bishop Hamilton Baynes, conducted the service with the village choir singing 'Lead, Kindly Light'. Milner was buried close to Violet's mother in a corner of the simple churchyard near the open fields.

Two days later a memorial service, attended by Baldwin and the Cabinet, was held at Westminster Abbey. Carlyle's translation of Luther's hymn *Ein Feste Burg*, Sullivan's setting of the 23rd Psalm and Kipling's 'Recessional' were included. On the same day memorial services were held at New College and, six thousand miles away, at Cape Town Cathedral.[33]

Epilogue

Violet Milner outlived Milner by 33 years, dying at the age of 86 in 1958 when Great Wigsell was sold. For years she was inconsolable over her loss. It seems true to say that she devoted her life to keeping public memory of him alive, and in particular to correcting what she saw as the unjust assessment made in some quarters of his work in South Africa. Strong-willed, she had the further advantages of knowledge and literary talent. On her brother Leo's death in 1932 she took over the editorship of the *National Review*. Though her mind remained lively and incisive into old age, she wrote only one book, *My Picture Gallery, 1886–1901*, her memoirs as a girl and young woman. This title was derived from one of the books Milner had always hoped to write, not of memoirs but sketches of outstanding men he had known.

Milner left a gross estate of nearly £46,000, appointing Violet and Ouvry, his solicitor, his executors. He left Loulie Dawkins books and pictures at Sturry which had once belonged to Clinton and some articles of plate or jewellery she could choose; also legacies to his cousins Sybil and Josephine Ready, his secretary Miss Smith and several of his Sturry employees. The residue of his property and effects he bequeathed absolutely to Violet, only asking her to give some token of his affection to a number of friends on a list he had left her. By some previous arrangement he had given an annuity of £200 to Cecile, now Mrs. James of Alberta; Violet exchanged letters with her and she died in 1930.

Milner's death had been too unexpected and sudden to allow him to put certain minor financial matters in order. Violet wrote that he had 'helped many people, both with money and great kindness' and in their short married life he 'gave lavishly'. She was overwhelmed with tributes from people writing about what he had done for them. Since his generosity had for years included loans and guarantees besides gifts, she had also to deal with false claimants and debtors. Henry Birchenough, especially helpful over Milner's affairs, advised her to 'turn a deaf ear to all black-mailers and even piteous beggars.'[1]

Lady Milner conceived a plan to erect a tomb for Alfred with effigies of them both carved from one block (her own to be covered until her death) in a small 'Wigsell chapel' in Salehurst church. For mainly structural reasons the vicar was unenthusiastic, and skilled at stonewalling. An argument followed which four years later reached a Consistory Court; but by this time Lady Milner was tired of the struggle. She had a large white table-tomb, designed by Lutyens, built in the graveyard. Besides Milner's remains and those of her mother it eventually contained her own and those of her sister Olive. It bears no cross or religious inscription or allusion to Lord Edward Cecil, but simply the names of the four persons mentioned in clear royal blue lettering.[2]

A memorial committee of Milner's close friends was set up under Amery to raise funds and plan private and public memorials.[3] In time these took a variety of forms. Lady Milner gave some land she wanted known as the Milner Memorial Ground, close to Sturry Church, which was only a stone's throw from his house. Though she was not enthusiastic about this, the Committee, with the help of Dean Bell (later an eminent Bishop of Chichester) had the apsidal chapel of St. Martin of Tours in the Cathedral restored under Herbert Baker's direction and Milner's services commemorated on its walls. An authority calls St. Martin, a fourth-century bishop,

. . . in character strong and independent, of unassuming simplicity, noble benevolence and an incorruptible sense of justice.

A contrast is afforded by the Westminster Abbey memorial which Lady Milner inspecting the site, called, with some justice, 'very hole and corner'. This is a small rather dark recess off Henry VII's chapel in which five years before Milner had seen Cromer's memorial unveiled. A portrait plaque of Curzon had been added; and a similar plaque of Milner, bearing the simple, most appropriate, inscription suggested by Kipling, 'a servant of the State', joined it in 1930. On the centenary of Rhodes's birth in 1953 a simple tablet bearing his name joined the memorials of the three pro-consuls. The author of a chapter in the 900th anniversary history of the Abbey takes the discouraging, though presumably realistic, view that these names convey little or nothing to the crowds visiting the Abbey, and 'the sentiment of the Empire only haunts the place as a ghost.'[4]

Lady Milner's intention to live at Great Wigsell led to the most useful memorial to Milner and the one which he would probably have valued most highly. For a time she wrote about letting or selling Sturry. She then decided to present the house with its Tudor tithe barn, cottage and about 6 acres of land to King's School, Canterbury, for its Junior School, then housed in cramped quarters in the Cathedral precincts. She sold further land to the Governors, and the memorial committee seems to have made up her gift to a total of some 70 acres. It also bought land to endow for the main school five Milner Scholarships (one awarded each year) for the sons of men engaged in the Colonial Service.

Sturry Court, which she left in 1927, thenceforth became Milner Court. New buildings were needed for the boys, for which Lady Milner laid the foundation stone and which were well designed in red brick. In 1929 these were opened in the presence of the Archbishop and a large gathering by Kipling, and Lady Milner formally handed the property over. A quarter of a century later on the centenary of Milner's birth, when she was over 80, she spoke to the boys on Milner's career saying: 'he would have liked you to be here.'[5] She presumably had a hand in arranging the memorial outside the house in Doullens where Milner and Clemenceau had agreed over Foch's appointment in March 1918; also in placing a cast of Sicard's bronze of Milner, unveiled by Lord Rosebery, in Oxford's Examination Schools.

Milner, as stated earlier, had not wanted his official biography to be written, but only that his papers should be published. Violet at once began writing for information from his many friends, especially those who had known him since his youth. She began the considerable task of combing through his large collection of papers, private and public.[6] Presumably she knew that one day a biography, official or otherwise, would be written. She consulted F. S. Oliver, who advised her to employ a qualified person to produce several volumes of Milner's papers which some future biographer could use as a quarry. This presumably caused her to engage Cecil Headlam, whose two stout volumes of Milner's selected *South African Papers* appeared in the 1930s. Soon after Milner's death *The Times* printed a short document called 'Credo, or key to my Position' which she had found in his papers and re-issued as a 1*d.* pamphlet. John Buchan persuaded her to allow his publishing firm to issue a cheap edition of Milner's *Questions of the Hour.*

Milner's close interest in the Rhodes Trust requires mention that on his recommendation Ned Grigg (later Lord Altrincham) had been appointed by Baldwin Governor of Kenya. He was succeeded as Secretary to the Trust by Philip Kerr. In the year Milner died Kipling resigned as a Trustee, and four new Trustees were appointed, Baldwin, H. A. L. Fisher, Dawson and Lord Hailsham. Lady Milner's interest in South Africa remained unabated, especially in its educational problems and work for the 1820 Memorial Settlers' Association.[7] When she spent a week-end at Chequers

Baldwin wrote an extract from Milner's diary of January 1921, presumably his remarks on Lord Lee's farewell party, in the Chequers book.[8]

In 1931 she wrote to Warden H. A. L. Fisher offering to give New College Milner's papers, some of his furniture and other items, and he replied that the offer was gratefully accepted. Much further correspondence with the Warden and Librarian took place about the conditions she wished to attach to her gift. Three years later she signed a Deed of Gift with the College; this included a clause that if the College ever wanted to part with the papers it must hand all of them over to the Public Record Office 'and not to any other body'. Owing to Headlam's activities the large mass of papers arrived in the course of the following years in instalments. At her wish the College created a 'Milner Room' near the Founder's Library in the Front Quad where his books, his settee, and the 31 volumes of signatures to the Address regarding his South African work presented to him in 1906 are preserved. In early 1935 Lady Milner spent a week-end with the Warden, when the College held a ceremony in gratitude for her gifts.[9]

Lady Milner also presented an unfinished portrait by Sir James Guthrie and a few other items to Rhodes House. A bust of him by Lady Kennet stands with one of Parkin in the Parkin vestibule.

Soon after his death an anonymous 'Appreciation' of him was substituted for a formal obituary notice in the *Oxford Magazine*, a comprehensive journal for senior members. This called him, which historians must surely confirm, 'always something of an enigma'. His exceptional frankness has enabled many instances to be quoted in this story of his failures as well as successes, of both personal attacks and unusual popularity with many who worked with him and knew him. An attempt must, however, be made to frame some conclusions on his character and very varied career.

Lady Milner told the Canterbury schoolboys that his mother

. . . remained his ideal woman. Brave, cheerful, deeply religious, perfectly unselfish . . . with a splendid gaiety . . . he lived all his life by the torch she lit.

In a reticent age he was more reticent than most over matters about which he felt deeply. This makes it hard to judge whether he was, like his mother, religious; though Beatrice Webb's *mot* quoted earlier is hardly adequate evidence, other facts make this seem unlikely.[10] What cannot, however, be disputed is his decidedly moral outlook on practical, including political, affairs reinforced at Oxford by the influence of Arnold

Toynbee. This did not make him a prig or censorious of his friends and colleagues with different approaches. But it sometimes influenced to excess his views; for example, of the British race and Empire as beneficent, of party politics as an exercise which evaded real issues, of Gladstone as a humbug and all politically-minded Boers as deceivers. In politics, which he made it his life ambition to serve, his insistence on 'principle' (a word which he constantly used) was perhaps his main handicap.

He had a marked addiction to, and capacity to absorb himself in, certain causes – the British Empire in general, Britain's ameliorating role in Egypt and attainment of supremacy in South Africa, the retention of Union with Ireland, National Service as essential to defence, and victory against heavy odds in the 1914–1918 World War. His loyalty to these knew no limits in terms of exertion, and sometimes of prudence. He extended a similar loyalty to his family – conspicuously to Marianne Malcolm – to the many persons who had served him and to those, such as British colonial officials and other loyalists in South Africa, to whom he felt a personal obligation.

A second main ingredient of his outlook was ingrained belief in logic, and in the powers of persuasion to secure the agreement of others with his views. Imperialism was, after all, as an historian has written, 'a faith and an emotion before it became a political programme'. But the same writer holds it against Milner that he was too 'buttoned up' and too engaged in stifling his emotions. There is truth in this, but it fails to take account of the real strength of Milner's passions. Sir Edward Grigg, who knew him well, wrote that underneath his external calm, controlled features, and constant readiness to hear the views of others 'there burned intense convictions and the decisive spirit of a born leader of men'. His temper was not easily kindled. But against any real challenge to his faith or resolve 'he would collect his forces inwards like a strong place calling a garrison to arms'. Under a challenge of this kind he did not display heat; his resolution 'froze rather than flared', and a vizor of steel would fall across his normally quiet face.

Perhaps his German uncle, quoted earlier, was right in suggesting he had inherited his share of the 'wild von Rappard blood' of his German–Dutch grandmother's family. It seems that from his undergraduate days he had made great, and usually successful, efforts of will to control his passions. Occasionally in later life these broke loose, to his detriment, in pungent public phrases like 'damn the consequences', which stuck in the minds of strangers. It is surprising how many who associated him with this phrase were astonished when they met the 'real Milner'. But in his private letters and diaries strong disagreement with some course of action is usually conveyed in facetious language; and disgust with a decision by the Cabinet or some other body of importance is expressed in the mild term 'unsatisfactory'. Service under Lloyd George during 1916–20 made great demands on those near him; but Milner showed much patience since he believed that the P.M. was the indispensable war leader.

Before he left for South Africa at the age of 43 he told Gell both that he had learnt with difficulty the need for limitation, and that he was quite indifferent to 'being out of the swim' or not conforming to the current tides of opinion. He had already experimented with the different careers of the Bar, private secretary to a statesman, daily journalism, Treasury official, official in Egypt, and tax-gatherer at the Inland Revenue Board. But in each one of these, after a time, he grew restless and anxious to achieve what he called his 'independence'. Presumably his reference to limitations meant his realization that he was not cut out for what one of his friends called 'normal pot-and-kettle politics and for trimming compromises'. Other considerations apart, the Liberal Party did not share his enthusiasm for the Empire nor the Tory Party his genuine interest in social reform. He testified that the methods of his Imperialist friend A. L. Bruce, who died in 1893, had made a lasting impression on him and wrote,

I see that a man can do any amount of good public work, and be of greater service, without joining in the fray – can, in fact, be of greater service because he keeps himself in the background.[11]

Like Bruce he was essentially, with all his gifts and liking for social life, self-effacing. One recalls the tribute of a fellow member of the Toynbee Society, that though his political knowledge 'gave him great authority among us, he was far from showing any consciousness of this'. But he later went to great lengths in the indirect political techniques of influence, exerting his powers of persuasion upon his numerous acquaintances and friends in high places, and establishing close relations with persons in key positions in the Press. The ruling class of Late Victorian and Edwardian Britain was still small, and the fruits of the Franchise Acts and Education Act of the late nineteenth century had still barely developed. What would now be called the 'quality' papers, and (now mainly extinct) monthly and quarterly journals played a large part in forming opinion.

Milner's career in the first forty-odd years of his life have been labelled in this story 'Apprenticeship' to suggest that the job in which he felt he could make a real contribution to the Empire had not yet come his way. When Chamberlain offered him what he knew to be the 'cliff-hanging' post of High Commissioner in South Africa he did not hesitate to answer

'I'll do it'. Undoubtedly the power he hoped to exercise was one attraction. But as usual the moral aspect was uppermost. He emphasized to friends the big responsibility he was facing, and wrote to Parkin of 'his solemn sense of the great national interests at stake'.

Established in Cape Town he was well aware of the obstacles facing British supremacy in South Africa. It is untrue to say that he wanted war, or until late in 1899 thought it inevitable. He wanted troop reinforcements as a deterrent, but believed that the various pressures would compel Kruger to put his house in order and that if he did not do so it would collapse. When neither of these happened he could not prevent war without sacrificing British to Boer aims (or British democracy to Dutch oligarchical rule) throughout the whole country. As Chamberlain knew, he was the last man to do this.

Milner had written to Goschen from Egypt eight or nine years before:

the true Jingo is for limited expansion but unlimited *tenacity*.

He shared much of Goschen's moderation, and like him was no rabid expansionist. He limited his views to the safeguarding and efficient organization of the existing sphere of British interests.[12] But absorbed in his job in South Africa he sometimes forgot Britain's other obligations, and the difficulties of bringing public opinion at home to contemplate war. Tenacity was a leading feature of his character, as well as of his Imperialist views; and as 'the man on the spot' he grew convinced that he understood the situation better than anyone in London. So occasions arose before war broke out when he virtually forced Chamberlain to exert pressure on Kruger with a strength and at a pace greater than he wished.

His eight years in South Africa had exacted a heavy mental and physical strain. The historian Arnold J. Toynbee, though he never knew him well, describes him on his return to Britain as 'out of action at the height of his powers', and this was especially painful to him as he was

ambitious for opportunities of exercising his great abilities in an adequate field. The stoicism that was a prominent trait in his character now came out strong. He took his eclipse with patience and dignity.

As a Liberal Government inherited power, what was always, perhaps, his major dilemma – intense desire to contribute to politics, especially consolidation of the Empire, with uncertainty about how to do this effectively in practice – was naturally aggravated.

He added to proconsul the new career of a business man in the City, campaigned for National Service, was very active in Rhodes Trust affairs and worked for the Empire through 'Moots' and *The Round Table*. He showed ambivalence towards the Unionist party, often standing aloof but fighting with zest against what he saw as highly unconstitutional measures – Lloyd George's 1909 Budget, reduction in the House of Lords' powers and attempts to abolish the Union with Ireland.

Lady Milner wrote after his death that his mild manners covered

> a strength of mind that nothing could shake. Slow to come to a decision . . . once he had made up his mind he persisted in the course of policy dictated by what he conceived to be the situation.

Many of his well-wishers would have agreed with Lloyd George's remark to Lord Riddell that he was 'an obstinate man when it comes to a decision.'

Some years before 1914 he had said to his future wife, 'the old patriotic Germany has gone war mad. The English have left everything to chance, and we shall suffer fearfully.' When the war started his impulse for action at once quickened, and grew stronger as the gap between needs and Asquith's Government's neglect grew more obvious. He became the leader of a ginger group to bring all the pressure it could to force on more vigorous action. When Lloyd George asked him to join his War Cabinet at the end of 1916 he began to accomplish his life's greatest official achievement, which occupied over five years. His exceptional administrative gifts could be harnessed to a wide scope of functions, civil and military, and his strong vein of radicalism to improving the lot of the working classes. More mellow than in his days in South Africa, he became a co-ordinator of many national activities, and an essential mediator between the P.M. and his officials and soldiers.

At his suggestion, Dominion Ministers were invited to join an Imperial War Cabinet. That body, as it worked in the last two years of the war and at the Peace Conference of 1919, represented the high-water mark of effective Imperial unity yet achieved. Milner's conception, Lloyd George's ready approval, and Smuts's considerable contribution, were the main forces behind this achievement.

Milner's well-known phrase embodied in his 'Credo' – 'I am an Imperialist and not a Little Englander, because I am a British Race Patriot' – requires, due to subsequent history, brief comment. For him race was no crude and reactionary thing, no Hitlerite wish to exclude or exterminate the best in other strains. The mission of Empire he conceived as one of service not dominance; he was aware of other races and growing national sentiment in the Dominions. But he believed that these national strains would be richer and stronger in some single political systems formed on British principles of government and cemented by its British elements. Partnership, not domination, was his dream. In the last years of his life he saw the centripetal forces of the war years growing weaker. But he remained hopeful that co-operation and self-interest would in time restore some more formal unity.

A high British official with long experience of the country's leading politicians wrote on his death,

> . . . his mistakes had never obscured the greatness of his aims . . . he possessed an almost sublime honesty of purpose. He has never run away from the consequences of his acts.

Sources and References

SOURCES

1 Milner's Published Writings
1892 *England in Egypt* (13th and last edition, 1920).
1895 *Arnold Toynbee: a reminiscence.*
1913 *The Nation and the Empire* (a selection of his speeches during 1897–1912 edited by Charles Boyd, with an introduction by Milner). N & E
1914 essay on 'Mr Chamberlain and Imperial Policy' in a popular *Life of Joseph Chamberlain.*
1923 *Questions of the Hour* (2nd posthumous edition with a preface by Lady Milner and the addition of some of his notes and of his 'Key to My Position' statement, 1925).

In the habit of his times Milner issued many speeches, apart from those in the collection mentioned above, in the form of cheap pamphlets. These can be found in a variety of boxes in the Milner Papers.

He also wrote a considerable number of articles, many of which are mentioned in this book, and some introductions. Because he occupied an official position at the time, or from the policy of the journal or his dislike of personal publicity nearly all of these are anonymous. The earliest were written as an occasional contributor or member of the staff of the *Pall Mall Gazette*. Later, and especially in the years 1906–25, he contributed introductions and articles to *The Scotsman, the Observer*, the *National Review, The Times, The Round Table* and other newspapers and journals.

He wrote a number of biographies, usually of close friends, for the *Dictionary of National Biography* under the initial M.

2 Manuscript Sources
Milner papers (Bodleian Library) MP
Milner additional papers I. (Bodleian Library) MAP
Milner additional papers (property of Bodleian Library) MSS. ENG. HIST.
Milner Court papers (Milner Court, Sturry, Canterbury) M.COURT
Milner papers: South Africa, 1897–1905. A selection edited by Cecil Headlam and published in 2 vols, 1931–3 H. I, II
Asquith papers (property of Bodleian Library) ASQ
Brand papers (Sir Edward Ford, Eydon Hall, Northants) BRAND
Curtis (Lionel) papers (property of Bodleian Library) CURT
Gell papers (Mrs Gell, Hopton Hall, Derbyshire) GELL

Hamilton (Sir Edward) diaries (Add.MSS. 48658–72, British Museum) E.H.
Harcourt papers (Bodleian Library) HARCOURT
Lee of Fareham papers (Courtauld Institute, London) LEE
Lloyd George papers (House of Lords Record Office) L.G.
Roberts papers (National Army Museum, London) ROB
Selborne papers (property of Bodleian Library) SELB
Strachey (St. Loe) papers (House of Lords Record Office) STR

3 Published sources

AMERY, LEOPOLD. *My Political Life*, 3 vols. 1953–5 AME.
CALLWELL, SIR C. E. *Field-Marshal Sir Henry Wilson, his life and diaries*, 2 vols.
     1927 CALL.
CHURCHILL, RANDOLPH S. *Winston S. Churchill*, vols I, II. 1966–7 WSC.
GILBERT, MARTIN, *Winston S. Churchill*, vols III and IV 1971, 1975
GOLLIN, ALFRED M. '*The Observer*' & *J. L. Garvin 1908–1914*, 1960 GOLL.
HANKEY LORD. *The Supreme Command, 1914–1918*, 2 vols., 1961 HANK I, II.
ROSKILL, STEPHEN. *Hankey, Man of Secrets*, 3 vols. 1970–4 ROSK I, II.
WRENCH, JOHN EVELYN. *Alfred, Lord Milner: The Man of no Illusions*. 1958
     WRE

REFERENCES

The page numbers refer to the first edition, unless otherwise stated

PART I: APPRENTICESHIP

Chapter 1 Youth (1854–1872)

1. M.P. 217
2. Warburton, A. B., *History of Prince Edward Island*, 362–82
3. M.P. 217.
4. Wrench, John Evelyn, *Alfred, Lord Milner*, 21.
5. Davitt, M., *Fall of Feudalism in Ireland*, 144–5
6. A. Günther (1830–1914) later settled in London becoming Keeper of the Zoological Department of the British Museum. His eldest son Robert (1869–1940) became a prominent scientist and University Reader at Oxford.
7. In his *DNB* article on Alfred Milner.
8. Blunt, Reginald, *Memoirs of Gerald Blunt of Chelsea, his family and forbears*. This contains a photograph of Milner's father at Tübingen of unknown date. The Rev. Gerald was Rector of St. Luke's, Chelsea, for 42 years.
9. M.P. 178.
10. It seemed that if the University made Charles's post permanent he might eventually become a German subject. Perhaps Mary was thinking of the complication that Charles, afterwards pleading 'ignorance' for his neglect, failed until 1872 to register Alfred's birth at a British Consulate.
11. Charles Ready (1813–83) had commanded a regiment in the Crimean

War and married a Canadian. Soon after this date they settled in Canada.

12. Hearnshaw, F. J. C., *Centenary History of King's College, London*, ch. 9.
13. King's College School moved in 1897 to its present site at Wimbledon. The writer is indebted to its Headmaster for information.
14. John Cromie, Alfred's elder half-brother, died in India at about this date. After his mother's death he had expressed willingness to contribute to the cost of Alfred's education.
15. Hearnshaw, op. cit., 304.
16. In 1874 Abbott became Fellow and Classical Tutor at Balliol, remaining so until his death in 1901. He was joint author with Prof. L. Campbell of the *Life and Letters of Benjamin Jowett*.
17. A house in St. Giles called Balliol Hall, founded in 1867 to accommodate poor exhibitioners and presided over by T. H. Green; now demolished.

Chapter 2 Oxford (1873–1879)

1. Faber, Sir Geoffrey. *Jowett* (2nd ed.), 358–9.
2. M.P. 180, 185. Most of Milner's earlier letters are undated and often difficult to place with precision.
3. Warren became a Fellow of Magdalen in 1877 and was President from 1885 to 1928. He was Milner's life-long friend and admirer.
4. pp. 22–26.
5. Sir Thomas Raleigh (1850–1920) became a Fellow of All Souls, a barrister and Legal Member of the Viceroy of India's Council in the early years of the twentieth century.
6. p. 29.
7. Grenfell's athletic feats included winning the Thames punting championship for three successive years, stroking an eight across the Channel, swimming Niagara twice and climbing the Matterhorn by three different routes.
8. Sir Isaac Goldsmid, financier and philanthropist, had been created by Melbourne in 1841 the first Jewish baronet.
9. pp. 46–47.
10. George Brodrick, Warden of Merton, and uncle of Milner's Balliol friend, the successful politician St. John Brodrick.
11. Wrench, op. cit., p. 40 for a long extract of this and a letter about his failure in the previous year.
12. Montague, F. C., *Arnold Toynbee*, and Milner's lectures and article on him in the *DNB*.
13. Milner, A., *Arnold Toynbee: a reminiscence*, reprinted in 1908 edition of Toynbee's *Lectures on the Industrial Revolution*.
14. Green became White's Professor of Moral Philosophy in 1878 and died just before his 46th birthday four years later.
15. Collingwood, R. G., *An autobiography*, 17.
16. As there was then no Senior Treasurer this office, usually held for three terms, could involve much administrative work.

17. Morrah, A. H., *The Oxford Union, 1823–1923,* 220; see also Hollis, Christopher, *The Oxford Union,* ch. 6.
18. *Memories & Reflections,* I, 20.
19. *Minutes of Oxford Union Society,* Vols. X, XI form a valuable record but do not summarize public debates.
20. One of the early seventeenth-century houses demolished in 1937 and replaced by the New Bodleian building.
21. Jowett, whose responsibility for raising the large sum required for this building has been mentioned, firmly believed, H. W. C. Davis writes (ed. of 1899, ch. 11), 'in good living as an ingredient of good fellowship'.
22. i.e. his election just anticipated new Statutes following the University Commission of 1877; see George, H. B., *New College.*
23. The present Hall for which, the foundation stone was laid in 1878 and which came into use the next year.

Chapter 3 Journalism and Politics (1879–1886)

1. *Questions of the Hour* (1923).
2. *English Social History,* 568.
3. pp. 37, 41.
4. *Arnold Toynbee: a reminiscence,* 14–15.
5. Ashley, Sir W., 'A Notebook of Arnold Toynbee', *Econ. Hist. Review* (1927).
6. op. cit., 36. Its membership of about 9 also included Gell, D. Ritchie, J. D. Rogers, W. Bruce (all Balliol), E. T. Cook (New) and the Australian B. R. Wise (Queen's).
7. M.P. 183.
8. *Canon Barnett,* I, 302–3.
9. Campbell, L., *On the Nationalisation of the Old English Universities,* 229.
10. Rogers, F., *Labour, Life & Literature,* 78–85.
11. His half-brother John Cromie, who had died in India in 1871.
12. Privately printed, London, 1881.
13. Hart-Davis, Rupert, *Letters of Oscar Wilde,* 49, 59–60.
14. Morrah, op cit., 261.
15. p. 41.
16. M.P. 250–2.
17. *Jowett,* 362–5.
18. Rogers, F., op. cit., 139; M.P. 240–5.
19. Whyte, F., *Life of Stead,* I, 95.
20. John Tobin Ready, Col. of 2nd Berks Regt, was the son of Milner's maternal grandfather's second marriage.
21. M.P. 183.
22. Rogers, F., op. cit., 139. These Lectures were published after Milner's death in the *National Review,* Jan.–June, 1931.
23. They were published, with a note by Milner, later this year for one shilling.

As Toynbee spoke *ex tempore* and made no notes they had, with some difficulty, to be written from the shorthand writer's notes.

24. *Memoir*, printed in the 1884 and some later editions of Toynbee's *Lectures on the Industrial Revolution in England*.
25. The letter is printed almost in full in WRE, 57–8.
26. Goschen, born in 1831, had become a Liberal M.P. for the City of London in 1863 and held office since 1865. He was thought a very successful 1st Lord of the Admiralty in the latter part of Gladstone's 1st Ministry.
27. *Life of G. J. Goschen*, I, 277.
28. In St. James's St. Founded as a 3rd Oxford and Cambridge London Club in 1863. Milner became a Trustee in 1911; it was absorbed by the United University Club in 1938.
29. *England, 1870–1914*, 71.
30. This lady, wife of the 9th Earl of Carlisle, was prominent in the Women's Rights and Temperance Movements; M.P. 252
31. *Nineteenth Century*, May 1887.
32. *Review of Reviews*, May 1912, 477–8.
33. Whyte, F., op. cit., I, 99.
34. Pimlott, J. A. R., *Toynbee Hall*.
35. Clark, G., *The Idea of the Industrial Revolution*, a lecture delivered and printed in 1952–3.
36. p. 50.
37. WRE, 73–4.
38. The rather drab porticoed house survived the last war's bombing in the neighbourhood and still stands.
39. Mills, J. Saxon, *Sir Edward Cook*, 65–7.
40. Luke, W. B., *Lord Milner* (1901), chs. 3, 4.
41. Goschen, G. J., *Political Speeches during the General Election, 1885*.
42. Though Milner had often criticized Gladstone's policies, as a Liberal candidate he felt it his duty to defend those elements of his foreign and imperial policy favouring limitation of commitments. It is alleged, however, that he never once mentioned Gladstone's name.
43. *Gladstone and the Irish Nation*, 500–5.
44. Elliot, op. cit., II, 35–6.
45. Later 4th Earl Grey, and associated with Milner in South Africa.
46. 13th Earl, a Balliol contemporary, a friend of Jowett's and a naval officer.
47. Elliot, op. cit., II, 82, 87.
48. M.P. 254.
49. See his letter to Davitt in the latter's *Fall of Feudalism in Ireland*, 382.
50. *Great Contemporaries* (1938 ed.), 347–8.
51. Elliot, op. cit., II, 99.
52. James, R. R., *Lord Randolph Churchill*, ch. 10, which includes an analysis of the 'I forgot Goschen' story.

Chapter 4 Her Majesty's Treasury (1887–1889)

1. See Colson, P., *Lord Goschen and his Friends* for letters to him from many Victorian personages.
2. St. Helier, Lady (Mary Jeune), *Memories of 50 years*, 247–8.
3. Moses, R., *Civil Service of Gt. Britain*, chs. 7, 8.
4. Luke, op. cit., 109–15
5. Hutchinson, H. G., *Private Diaries of Sir Algernon West*, 5.
6. Mallet, B., *British Budgets, 1887/8 to 1912/13*, 8.
7. Young, Kenneth, *A. J. Balfour*, 124.
8. *Memoirs of an Old Parliamentarian*, II, 117.
9. M.P. 184.
10. Hancock, W. K., *Smuts, The Sanguine Years, 1870–1919.*
11. pp. 2, 10; M.P. 179, 217. Milner's father, the eldest of this generation, would now have been 58.
12. M.P. 183
13. West, Sir A., *Recollections* and *Contemporary Portraits*; Hirst, F. W., in *DNB*.
14. Curtis, L.P., *Coercion and Conciliation in Ireland*, 239–58.
15. Abbott, E. and Campbell, L., *Life and Letters of B. Jowett*, II, 336.
16. Gell, Hon. Mrs. E., *Under Three Reigns, 1860–1920* which contains much reference to Milner.
17. Hobson, J., *Imperialism*, 3rd ed. (1938), 17–24.
18. Egerton, H. E., *British Colonial Policy* 2nd ed. (1908), ch. 7.
19. Robinson, R. and Gallagher, J., *Africa and the Victorians*, 9–21.
20. See pp. 56, 67, 71–2.
21. M.P. 187.
22. M.P. 184.
23. The raffish Royalist agent of Scott's *Woodstock*.
24. His family banking firm had pioneered promoting Egyptian securities on the London market, and he had been joint leader of an Anglo-French mission to the country before the collapse of 1879.
25. M.P. 183.

Chapter 5 Egypt (1889–1892)

1. Landes, D. S., *Bankers and Pashas: international finance and economic imperialism in Egypt*, 80, 90.
2. Lutfi, op. cit., p. 38.
3. Of 120 superior British Officials at this date, thirty-nine were in the Chief Civil Departments, seventy officers in the Egyptian Army and eleven in the Mixed Administration.
4. Parliamentary Papers, 1890, vol. 83.
5. Marlowe, J., *Anglo-Egyptian Relations, 1800–1953*, 129.
6. GELL Mil. I, 261.
7. Garvin, J. L., *Chamberlain*, III, 447–56.

8. Magnus, P., *Edward VII*, 219ff.

9. M.P. 182–3; WRE, ch. 8.

10. Cecil, Lady G., *Salisbury*, IV, 171–2.

11. GELL, Mil. I, 261

12. *England in Egypt*, 64–9.

13. M.P. 182–3. In her *Egypt and Cromer*, 75, Dr. Lutfi also assesses Riaz unfavourably.

14. P.R.O., F.O. 141.

15. M.P. 252.

16. M.P. 187.

17. Parliamentary Papers, 1890–1, vol. 97.

18. M.P. 183.

19. M.P. 182.

20. Lutfi, op. cit., 77–8.

21. pp. 115, 243–4, 389.

22. Jenkins, Roy, *Asquith* (Fontana edition), 58–9. Asquith's wife, Helen Melland, died in September of this year.

23. 'Eight Years of Egyptian Progress', *P.M.G.*, 15 June 1891.

24. II, 481.

25. M.P. 252.

26. Magnus, P., *Kitchener* (Penguin edition), 104.

27. M.P. 182–3; WRE, 120–2 gives a long extract.

28. WRE, 124–7 gives much of this lengthy correspondence.

29. M.P. 182.

30. ibid. Smith had died on 6 October 1891, the same day as Parnell.

31. M.P. 231.

32. *England in Egypt*, 315–22.

33. He called the Egyptian Army 'an excellent school, not only in military respects'. It then consisted of 13 infantry battalions, a camel corps and other arms.

34. 'Britain's Work in Egypt', 18 and 19 December 1891.

35. M.P. 182.

36. Blunt, W. S., *My Diaries*, I, 44–5.

37. GELL, Mil. I, 290.

38. The Gells were electioneering for the Unionist candidates in Woodstock and North Oxon.

39. M.P. 187.

Chapter 6 Somerset House (1892–1897)

1. Abbott, E. and Campbell, L., op cit. II, 462; M.P. 187.

2. Magnus, P., *Kitchener*, 81–2.

3. see chs. 12 and 14.

4. Johnston, Sir A., *The Inland Revenue*, 20–1.

5. Lewis, later 1st Visct. Harcourt (1863–1922), was widely known in social and political circles by this sobriquet.

6. Parliamentary Papers, 1893–4, vol. III.

7. Cook had left the *P.M.G.* in January when it was sold over his head to the Tory millionaire William Waldorf Astor, an exile from the U.S.A. and founder of the English branch of his family.

8. M.P. 187–8.

9. M.P. 188.

10. ibid, p. 42.

11. M.P. 188.

12. M.P. 212 contains a list of contributors.

13. M.P. 188, letter of 15 December 1893.

14. M.P. 183. W. N. Bruce, later a senior civil servant in the Board of Education, to Lady Milner.

15. pp. 245–6.

16. pp. 115, 243–4, 389. No letters from Cecile exist. Milner or his wife would certainly have destroyed them.

17. Cromer, Lord, *Abbas II*, 64.

18. Welby had retired, had been created a baron, and succeeded as Permanent Head of the Treasury by Sir Francis Mowatt.

19. HARCOURT, L.H's Journal, 390–1

20. Diary in Add.MS. 48663, vol. 34, 21 March.

21. James, R. R., *Rosebery*, 340–4.

22. Mallet, Bernard, op. cit., 69–101; MS. ENG. HIST. c. 694.

23. *Diary of Home Rule Parliament, 1892–5*, 340–74.

24. HARCOURT, L.H's Journal, 408.

25. Lord Hartington, for long conspicuous in the Commons, succeeded his father as 8th Duke of Devonshire in 1891.

26. M.P. 188.

27. Ensor, R. C. K. op. cit., 217–18

28. M.P. 183, 188. The book had a 2nd impression in 1901 and was also reprinted in the 1908 edition of Toynbee's *Lectures*.

29. M.P. 189.

30. Robinson had been High Commissioner during 1880–9, was under Rhodes's influence, and now over 70, was reluctant to return.

31. M.P. 189.

32. GELL Mil. I, 328.

33. A character in Anthony Hope's successful romantic novel published in the previous year, *The Prisoner of Zenda*.

34. Slatin became a British public hero, was received by the Queen and then served in Egypt as an Intelligence Officer under Wingate.

35. M.P. 183.

36. Diary in Add.MS. 48668, vol. 39.

37. M.P. 190. Published soon after Cromer's retirement in 1908.

38. July, 1896, pp. 237–68.
39. M.P. 190.
40. Lutfi, op. cit., chs. 6, 7. Dr Lutfi's father was an eminent moderate nationalist.
41. Diary in Add.MS. 48670, vol. 41.
42. M.P. 183.
43. *Annual Register*, 1896–7; Murray, A. E.'s standard *History of Commercial and Financial Relations between England and Ireland* supports Milner's views.
44. Garvin, J. L., op. cit., III, 142–5 gives a full account.
45. M.P. 183.
46. A Commons Select Committee which sat for five months; see Van de Poel, *Jameson Raid*, and Pakenham, E., *Jameson's Raid* for opposing views of the event.
47. Robinson, R. and Gallagher, J., *Africa and the Victorians*, 425–6.
48. Walker, E. A., *Lord Milner & South Africa*, 6.
49. Knowles, L. C. and C. M., *Economic Development of the British Overseas Empire*, III, 258.
50. Robinson and Gallagher, op. cit., 427.
51. Walrond had left Balliol without a degree, occupied a junior official post in Egypt and was in his late twenties.
52. M.P. 183.
53. N & E, 1–6.

PART II: OPPORTUNITY

Chapter 7 South Africa – Peace or War? (1897–1899)

1. GELL Mil. 1./346.
2. M.P. 8; pp. 160–1.
3. H. I, 40–1.
4. Rose-Innes, *Autobiography* (ed. Tindall, B. A.), 165.
5. M.P. 2.
6. M.P. 8.
7. H. I, 72.
8. M.P. 31.
9. H. I, 63–4.
10. Davenport, T. R. H., *The Afrikaner Bond*, 324. During Milner's years in the country the form 'Afrikander' was used; it was later replaced by the form 'Afrikaner'.
11. M.P. 36, letter to Eugene Marais of 22 May 1903.
12. Walker, E., *Lord Milner in S. Africa*, 4–6.
13. Adrian Hofmeyr was a cousin of the Bond leader, and a Minister at the Dutch Reformed Church in Wynberg.
14. H. I, 38, 40, 119.

15. Mansergh, N., *Commonwealth Experience*, 81.

16. H. I, 118.

17. This had been granted in 1887 to a German friend of Kruger's named Lippert; see Marais, J. S., op. cit., 27–33. The Netherlands Railway Company was another of Kruger's main concessions to foreign interests.

18. M.P. 235.

19. Lockhart, J. G. & Woodhouse, C. M., *Rhodes*, ch. 23; H. I, chs. 4–5.

20. H. I, 88–9; Kruger had been President since 1883.

21. Marais, op. cit., 205.

22. H. I, 218–24.

23. Lockhart and Woodhouse, op. cit., 408.

24. Published respectively in 1906 and 1901. Professor Eric Walker in his standard books gives the most balanced accounts.

25. H. I, 156–76.

26. H. I, 177–80.

27. Judd, D., *Balfour & the British Empire*, 196–7.

28. Kitchener tried to obstruct Churchill's journalistic activities, and by withholding information delayed publication of his *River War* until late 1899.

29. Walker, E., *W. P. Schreiner*, 122.

30. Garvin, J. L., op. cit., III, 378–9, derived from the author's later talk with Milner.

31. Butler, Sen. Sir W., *Autobiography*, 389–90.

32. McCourt, E., *Remember Butler*, 218.

33. H. I, 292–7, 313–17.

34. Greville, J. A. S., *Lord Salisbury & Foreign Policy at the Close of the 19th Century*, 236–7.

35. Chapin, Adèle, *Their Trackless Way*.

36. Marais, op. cit., 243–5.

37. H. I, ch. 13; Marais, op. cit., 257ff.

38. H. II, 501, speech of 1904 to Bloemfontein Town Council.

39. H. I, 349–55.

40. H. I, 400.

41. Harris, Frank, *My Life and Loves*, 763. Marais, op. cit., 6–10.

42. On the Conference see M.P. 11; H. I, ch. 15; Marais op. cit., ch. 10; Cmd. 9404 of 1899. On Milner's dislike of Boer bargaining, pp. 140–1, 196.

43. op. cit., 247.

44. op. cit., III, 408–11

45. Gell succeeded Jameson as President in 1920 and remained on the board until 1925.

46. *Imperial Sunset*, I (1969), 19.

47. Newton, Lord, *Lord Lansdowne*, 156–8.

48. p. 137.

49. Symons, J., *Buller's Campaign*, 125.

50. Milner, Lady, *My Picture Gallery*, 125.

51. Markham, V., *Return Passage*, 54–6.
52. AME, I, 100–1.
53. M.P. 16, 17.

Chapter 8 The Second Boer War (1899–1902)

1. AME, I, 107–8.
2. Wyndham, G., *Letters of George Wyndham*, I, 459–504.
3. Nevinson, H. W., *Changes & Chances*, 130.
4. Walker, E. A., *W. P. Schreiner*, 197.
5. H. II, 18.
6. Cecil, Lady Edward, op. cit., 132ff.
7. Kruger, R., *Good-bye Dolly Gray*, 101.
8. WSC. I. Companion Vol. Pt 2, 1057–8.
9. Hancock, Sir K., *Smuts, Study for a portrait*, 26.
10. M.P. 32.
11. H. II, 55.
12. Kruger, Rayne, op. cit., 248.
13. M.P. 47; see also Le May, op. cit., 57, who concludes, unlike Milner at the time, that the Cape rebellion now 'withered away'.
14. Churchill, Winston, *My Early Life* (Fontana edition), 337–8.
15. Thornton, A. P., *For the File on Empire*, 28–30.
16. *Times History of War in South Africa*, III, IV.
17. M.P. 47 contains the main Roberts–Milner correspondence.
18. *Ian Hamilton's March;* also Hamilton's *Listening for the Drums.*
19. Wilson, Lady Sarah, *South African Memories*, 241.
20. M.P. 57.
21. p. 171.
22. M.P. 29.
23. H. II, 56–7.
24. ibid., 62–4.
25. Davenport, T., op. cit., 211–14.
26. Pyrah, G. B., *Imperial Policy & South Africa*, chs. 2, 3.
27. Spender, J. A., *Life of Sir H. Campbell-Bannerman*, I, 264. The author was another Balliol man, eight years Milner's junior.
28. H. II, 143.
29. ibid., 145–7.
30. Juta, M., *The Pace of the Ox: the Life of Paul Kruger*, 300.
31. Lyttelton, Gen. Sir N., *Eighty Years*, 246.
32. pp. 175–9.
33. H. II, 112.
34. ibid., 101–3.
35. ibid., 115–17.
36. Lyttelton, E., *Alfred Lyttelton*, 240–2.
37. Cd. 623–5, 1901.

38. M.P. 29.
39 Curtis had served earlier in the war as a bicyclist in the City Imperial Volunteers and been introduced to Milner by Lord Welby, now Chairman of the L.C.C. CURT, 167.
40. Rose-Innes, *Autobiography*, 189.
41. M.P. 49.
42. See speech in H. II, 176–8.
43. H. II, 185, 193–202.
44. Fry, A. R., *Emily Hobhouse*, 93–6.
45. Vol. 5 (1907) edited by Erskine Childers, who served in the H.A.C. in the Boer War and was later the prominent Irish nationalist.
46. H. II, 207–15.
47. Saki, *The Westminster Alice*.
48. Rose, K., *Superior Person*, Ch. 13.
49. M.P. 47.
50. H. II, 80–1.
51. *Margaret Hobhouse and her Family*, 152.
52. C.B. I, ch. 18; Wilson, J., *C.B.*, 349–52.
53. Magnus, op. cit., 226.
54. H. II, 273.
55. Wedgwood, Josiah, *Essays and Adventures of a Labour M.P.*, ch. 3.
56. M.P. 43; Pyrah, op. cit., app. 246–9.
57. See CURT, 140; *Round Table* papers; Nimocks, W., *Milner's Young Men*.
58. Roberts, B., op. cit., 221.
59. Millin, Sarah Gertrude, *Rhodes*, 352.
60. See H. II, ch. 9 and for the Peace terms 350–1, 359.

Chapter 9 South Africa, Reconstruction (1902–1905)
1. Hancock, *Smuts*, I, 171.
2. Amery, Julian, *J. Chamberlain*, IV, 108–12.
3. M.P. 40.
4. H. II, 416–22.
5. Curtis, Lionel, *With Milner in South Africa*, 216, 324.
6. Buchan, John, *Memory Hold The Door*, 102.
7. Wedgwood, Josiah, *Memoirs of a Fighting Life*, ch. 4.
8. He then became Governor of Madras, commanded the British Red Cross in France, 1915–19 and in 1931 succeeded his brother as 6th Baron Wenlock.
9. H. II, 388.
10. Buchan, John, *The African Colony: Studies in reconstruction*, 69–75.
11. Gretton, R. H., *A Modern History of the English People*, 594.
12. Cmd. 1552 of 1902.
13. M.P. 20.
14. H. II, 398.
15. Wilson, Lady S., *South African Memories*, 241.

16. M.P. 38.
17. M.P. 48.
18. for extracts see Worsfold, W.B., *Reconstruction of the New Colonies under Lord Milner*, I, chs. 8, 9.
19. Hancock, *Smuts*, I, 192.
20. H. II, 380.
21. Amery, J., *J. Chamberlain*, IV, 341; p. 196.
22. H. II, 442.
23. Hofmeyr, J. and Reitz, F., op. cit., 582.
24. M.P. 41.
25. *Times History of War*, VI, 154.
26. M.P. 38.
27. Markham, V., op. cit., 37–40.
28. Cmd. 1163, 1902.
29. e.g. Kruger's Industrial Commission of 1897 had discussed it as an urgent problem.
30. Speech of March to Inter-Colonial Council, H. II, 491.
31. H. II, 461–2.
32. Godfrey Lagden was nominated by Milner as its chairman and the Commission issued a valuable report in January 1905.
33. M.P. 22.
34. See Maud, J. P. R., *City Government: the Johannesburg Experiment.*
35. Amery, J., *J. Chamberlain*, IV, 529–33.
36. Cmd. 1895, of 1904.
37. Fry, Anna, op. cit., 185–219; M.P. 70 contains an account of her previous unsuccessful attempt to return to South Africa in October 1901.
38. H. II, 465.
39. Walker, E., *Lord Milner in South Africa*, 21ff.
40. Glyn, E., *Romantic Adventure*, 128.
41. Glyn, Anthony, *Elinor Glyn, A Biography*, 103–5.
42. Hardinge of Penshurst, Helen Lady, *Loyal to Three Kings*, 38.
43. M.P. 41, 48, 183.
44. H. II, 472–5.
45. Walker, op. cit., 20.
46. H. II, 482.
47. Cmd. 1895, of 1904.
48. Pyrah, op. cit., 80
49. M.P. 41.
50. M.P. 44.
51. Engelenburg, F. V., *General Louis Botha*, 1909, 117.
52. see *DNB* article by Dougal Malcolm, private secretary to Milner's successor Lord Selborne.
53. M.P. 23, 44; H. II, 507–8.
54. Cmd. 2103, 1904. Before the war, due to Kruger's objection on Biblical

grounds, only one partial census (of Johannesburg and its suburbs) had been held in the Transvaal.

55. Le May, G. H., *British Supremacy in South Africa, 1899–1907,* esp. ch. 7.
56. M.P. 41.
57. H. II, 543–7.

PART III: OPPOSITION

Chapter 10 The City and Political Bouts (1905–1914)

1. M.P. 44; H. II, 550–8.
2. H. II, 541–2 gives Smuts's letter almost in full.
3. Cromer's first wife had died after Omdurman and he had since married Lady Katherine Thynne with whom years before Milner's name had been linked.
4. M.P. 44.
5. Essay in Goldman, C., *Empire and the Century,* 520.
6. Egerton (1855–1927) retained this Chair (now History of the British Commonwealth) until 1920.
7. Samuel, Visct., *Memoirs,* 43ff.
8. N. & E., 93–108.
9. WSC, II, 165–93.
10. Webb, Beatrice, *Our Partnership,* 312, 351–2.
11. Grigg, E. (Lord Altrincham), essay in *The Post Victorians.*
12. M.P. 74.
13. *Round Table* MSS.; Brand, Lord., *Union of South Africa.*
14. Vol. II, 343.
15. ROB, 45
16. N. & E., 302–65; M.P. 169, 170.
17. M.P. 72, 74–7, 82.
18. For Milner's speeches see N. & E., 388–413.
19. M.P. 72–7.
20. Newton, Lord, *Retrospections,* 171.
21. M.P. 93–4. Rosebery was often absent and other Trustees often in South Africa.
22. p. 115.
23. Chamberlain, A., *Politics from the Inside,* 368–9.
24 Blake, Robert, *The Unknown Prime Minister,* 125.
25. See Avery, D., *Not on Queen Victoria's Birthday: the story of the Rio Tinto Mines.*
26. M.P. 294.
27. AME I, 391–3.
28. M.P. 101.
29. M.P. 211.
30. SELB 12.

31. See especially Fergusson, Sir J., *The Curragh Incident*.
32. Lyons, F. S. L., *Ireland since the Famine*, 307.
33. GOLL, 214–18; M.P. 100.
34. M.P. 99, 100.
35. Hyde, H. Montgomery, *Carson*, 366–75; SELB, 12.
36. *Asquith* (Fontana edition), 355–61.
37. M.P. 99.
38. Macready, Gen. Sir C. N., *Annals of an Active Life*, I, 193–4.
39. Spender, J. A., *Life, Journalism and Politics*, II, 1–4.

Chapter 11 War Service (1914–1916)
1. M.P. 139.
2. Spender, J. A., op. cit., II, chs. 21–4.
3. M.P. 218.
4. ASQ, 41.
5. M.P. 139
6. Taylor, A. J. P., *English History 1914–1945*, 12.
7. M.P. 191.
8. Gretton, R. H., *Modern History of the English People*, 935.
9. M.P. 94.
10. Brett, M. V., *Journals & Letters of Reginald, Viscount Esher*, III, 207.
11. SELB. 12.
12. M.P. 135, 137.
13. Shanks, E., *Rudyard Kipling*, ch. 7.
14. For extracts from these speeches see GOLL, 305, 311.
15. M.P. 217.
16. GOLL, ch. 13.
17. AME, II, 81.
18. M.P. 137.
19. M.P. 167.
20. M.P. 102, 222. Sir R. Redmayne, author of *The British Coal Mining Industry during the War*, wrote 'to work with Milner was both to admire and to love him'.
21. Article on War in Elton, Ld., (ed.), *First 50 Years of the Rhodes Trust and Scholarships*, 103–10.
22. M.P. 95.
23. Beaverbrook, Ld., *Politicians and the War*, 308ff.
24. Fitzroy, Sir Almeric, *Memoirs*, II, 641.

PART IV: OFFICE

Chapter 12 War Cabinet (1916–1918)
1. HANK II, 578, 594.
2. Katkov, G., *Russia 1917, the February Revolution*, 237–40.
3. Lockhart, R. B., *Memoirs of a British Agent*, 160–5.
4. Katkov, op. cit., 226–8.
5. Hanbury-Williams, Gen. Sir J., *Emperor Nicholas II as I knew him*, 152–5.
6. CALL I, 322–3. Gen. Callwell, the posthumous editor of Wilson's diary, had won distinction both as a soldier and a military historian.
7. Vol. I, 942–3.
8. Addison, Dr. C., *Politics from Within*, II, 57–8.
9. p. 227.
10. Markham, V., *Return Passage*, 150–4.
11. GOLL, 412–13.
12. HANK II, 650. Hankey accompanied L.G. and describes the episode as a very friendly one.
13. See Beaverbrook, Lord, *Men and Power*, ch. 5; Colvin, III, *Lord Carson*, chs. 28–9; L.G. F/38/2/10 and 12.
14. Gretton, R. H., op. cit., 1025–6.
15. M.P. 104–6.
16. MS ENG. HIST., c. 692. The Act was passed in 1917 but came into force in January 1921; p. 358.
17. ROSK I, 399.
18. M.P. 144.
19. HANK II, 697. The Dwyfor was the river from which Lloyd George took his title and on the bank of which he was buried in March 1945.
20. See GOLL, chs. 17–18; Churchill, R., *Lord Derby*, chs. 12–14; Robertson, F. M. Sir W., *From Private to Field Marshal*, chs. 15–16.
21. Buchan, op. cit., 101.
22. M.P. 118.
23. M.P. 95–6; p. 269.
24. Ullman, R., *Anglo-Soviet Relations, 1917–21*, I, 53–7.
25. ROSK I, 474.
26. L.G., F/38/2; ROSK I, 471.
27. House, Colonel, *Intimate Papers*, III, 232.
28. Bruce Lockhart, Robert, *Memoirs of a British Agent*, 198–200; M.P. 109, 110.
29. For what Lloyd George omitted to say see Taylor, A. J. P., op. cit., 116.
30. HANK II, 769–73.
31. Hyde, H. Montgomery, op. cit., 427–9.
32. HANK II, 778.
33. M.P. 135.

34. Milner's account of the Doullens conference written the next day is in M.P. 146. Haig's *Diary* is inaccurate in some of its details.
35. Cornwall, Gen. M., *Haig*, 266, 271.
36. M.P. 281.
37. Lee, Lord, *A Good Innings*, II, 734.
38. L.G. F/38/3/23.

Chapter 13 Secretary of State for War (1918–1919)
1. Fitzroy, Sir Almeric, op. cit., II, 673.
2. Falls, Cyril, *First World War*, 325.
3. GELL Mil. I, 676.
4. HANK, II, 794.
5. CALL, II, 94.
6. Blake, R. (ed.), *Private Papers of Douglas Haig, 1914–19*, 306.
7. Maurice, N., *The Maurice Case*, 4. Written from the General's papers, the most recent and probably most accurate account of the affair: M.P. 147.
8. Milner's Papers shed little light upon this.
9. Since 22 April was a Monday two days is perhaps an exaggeration. He had visited Lloyd George at Walton Heath on Saturday and spent a 'very busy and trying' working Sunday.
10. ROSK I, 545; ch. 17 contains a detailed account of the whole Maurice affair as conducted by Lloyd George with much help from Hankey.
11. *Sunday Times*, 30.11.75.
12. AME II, 157–8. Though a methodical man, Amery published these memoirs in old age.
13. Riddell, Lord, *War Diary*, 334, 275 [*sic*].
14. WRE, 343–4.
15. CALL II, 103.
16. pp. 4–5 of an 'appreciation' by General Spears in *The Maurice Case* (see 7 above).
17. M.P. 124.
18. Blake, R. (ed.), op. cit., 314–18; CALL II, 107.
19. AME II, 158ff.
20. GOLL, 396–400.
21. pp. 302, 322.
22. p. 49.
23. WSC IV, chs. 1–11.
24. ROSK II, 565; after the October revolution Kerenski had fled to the U.S.A.
25. HANK II, 820; ROSK I, 569–70.
26. HANK II, 827.
27. The military historian Liddell Hart does not go beyond viewing it as 'a first taste of victory'.

28. M.P. 281.

29. Glyn, Anthony, *Elinor Glyn*, 169ff; see pp. 211–12 of present work. Curzon married again in 1917. His stepson, Alfred Duggan, went to Balliol after the war. Later, he became a successful historical novelist.

30. ibid., pp. 245, 273. The book was not published until over ten years after both men were dead.

31. M.P. 279–81.

32. Hobhouse, Stephen, *Margaret Hobhouse and her Family*, 232–9.

33. M.P. 96; Willison, Sir J., *Parkin*, chs. 12, 13.

34. Gough, Gen. Sir H., *Soldiering On*, 179–80. Farrar-Hockley, A. H., *Goughie*, 317, 320–1. Lord Roberts's widow proposed to Gough that he should try to enlist Milner's help.

35. Lyttelton, Edith, *Florence Upton: painter*, 47–9 with a reproduction of the portrait. The *College Register* incorrectly gives 1918 as the date of his Hon. Fellowship.

36. ROSK I, 602.

37. See Nicolson, Harold, *King George V*, 299–302. The author writes that Nicholas 'fatalistically blind to the coming danger', would probably have refused to go into exile.

38. Taylor, A. J. P., op. cit., 106.

39. HANK II, 831–5.

40. Blake, R., op. cit., 326–7; M.P. 121, 132.

41. Even Smuts, the one soldier in the War Cabinet, told this body in August that the war was likely to last until 1920 and agreed with Milner in advocating a compromise peace.

42. Harrison, M., *Lord of London: a biography of the 2nd Duke of Westminster*, 163; WSC IV, 61, 78, 86–8. Churchill, a close friend, saw much of the Duke in France in 1918.

43. p. 292.

44. M.P. 117 contains a secret War Office. *Short History of Events in Russia, Nov. 1917–Feb. 1919.*

45. Ullman, R., *Anglo-Soviet Relations, I. Intervention and the War.*

46. Lockhart, R. B, *Retreat from Glory*; also Young, K. (ed.), *Diaries of Sir R. Bruce Lockhart, I.*

47. MS. ENG. HIST., c. 692.

48. M.P. 281; Blake, R., op. cit., 332–3.

49. Keynes, J. M., *Economic Consequences of the Peace*, 51–60.

50. WRE, 349 quoting Mordacq, Gen., *Clemenceau*. This officer was Clemenceau's *Chef de Cabinet*.

51. M.P. 147, 281.

52. AME II, 172.

53. AME II, 375.

54. M.P. 281

55. L.G. F/38/4/31.

56. Rose, K., *The Later Cecils*, ch. 7; Cecil, Lord D., *The Cecils of Hatfield House*; Wingate, Sir R., op. cit., 207–9.

57. Woodward, W., *A New American History*, 656.

58. M.P. 147.

59. M.P. 111, 117, 118; Ullman, R., op. cit., II, 13–15, 80, 297.

60. M.P. 146, 282.

61. Petrie, Sir C., op. cit., II, 135–6.

Chapter 14 Secretary of State for the Colonies (1919–1921)

1. Sir G. Fiddes wrote a standard account of *The Dominions & Colonial Offices* in 1926. A separate Dominions Office was created in 1925, and Amery became its Secretary of State while holding the same office for the Colonial Office.

2. Nicolson, Harold, *Peacemaking*, 35–7.

3. Hankey, Lord, *Supreme Control at the Paris Peace Conference, 1919: a commentary*, 23–4.

4. The standard British history is Temperley, H. W. V. (ed.), *History of the Peace Conference* in six volumes. The first three deal with the German Treaty, and the others with the Treaties with the lesser Powers.

5. Nicolson, Harold, *Peacemaking* 5, 13. The Fourteen Points had been expanded by Four Principles and Five Particulars.

6. Ryan, A. P., *Lord Northcliffe*; and an objective sketch by Geoffrey Dawson in the *DNB*.

7. Hankey, Lord, *Supreme Control*, 66–73.

8. pp. 319, 325–6; Ullman, R., op. cit., II 171–2, 295–6.

9. Dugdale, B., *Arthur James Balfour*, II, 270.

10. M.P. 222.

11. MS. ENG. HIST. c. 699.

12. Nicolson, Harold, *Peacemaking*, 143.

13. M.P. 170.

14. L.G. F/39/1/18, 21.

15. Nicolson, Harold, *Peacemaking*, 289, 296.

16. Letter to the writer of 13 Sept. 1973. Toynbee died at the age of eighty six in 1975.

17. D. Morrah MSS.

18. L.G. F/39/1/23.

19. MS. ENG.HIST., c. 705.

20. M.P. 95.

21. Sankey was a High Court judge and Lord Chancellor in the Labour Government of 1929. Lord Haldane held this office in the first Labour Government of 1924.

22. M.P. 168.

23. Nicolson, Harold, *Some People*.

24. L.G. F/39/1/18.

25. Barnett, Correlli, *Britain and her Army, 1509–1970*. Conscription was not re-introduced until late April 1939 against Labour and Liberal opposition. National Service, introduced by the Attlee Government in 1947, was abolished in 1960.

26. MS. ENG. HIST. c. 704–5.

27. Wingate, Sir R., *Wingate of the Sudan*, 228–46.

28. L.G. F/39/1/41.

29. Nicolson, Harold, *Diaries & Letters, 1939–1945*, 285, 451.

30. Spender, J. A., op. cit., ch. 26.

31. L.G. F/39/1/52.

32. Walrond had returned, once again ill, to England in the summer. Due doubtless to Milner's influence the Foreign Office had agreed to prolong his job in the Arab Bureau for the Milner Mission's visit to Egypt; MSS. ENG. HIST. c. 705.

33. L.G. F/39/2/7; also M.P. 161–3.

34. Most of this correspondence is in MS. ENG. HIST. c. 703.

35. Donaldson, F., *Edward VIII*, 47, and see Magnus, L., *Herbert Warren of Magdalen*. The former contains good summaries of this series of royal tours in chs. 6, 7 and 8.

36. *Camb. Hist. of British Empire*, III, ch. 17.

37. ibid., 664–5.

38. p. 340.

39. see AME, II, ch. 6 for period of Milner's office.

40. see Furse, Sir R., *Aucuparius*, 55–7. The writer calls Milner easily the greatest of the 17 Colonial Secretaries he served between 1910 and 1948.

41. M.P. 80, 81 for important Buxton correspondence. M.P. 168–71 for that with other Governors-General and Australian State Governors; Hancock, W. K., *Smuts, The Fields of Force 1919–1950*, II, 28–31.

42. L.G. F/39/2/16; Nicolson, H., *King George V*, 165ff, 170–2, 363–4.

43. M.P. 161–3 offer some documentation.

44. M.P. 283.

45. Mowat, C. L., *Britain Between the Wars, 1918–40*, 57–78.

46. M. P.221.

47. MS. ENG. HIST. c. 699, 705; Malcom, Sir D., *British South Africa Company*; Long, B. Drummond Chaplin, 254–8.

48. L.G. F/39/2/34.

49. M.P. 163, 283; Duff Cooper, *Old Men Forget*, ch. 6; ROSK II, 209, 214.

50 Lord Lee began a second art collection, part of which he bequeathed on his death in 1947 to the Courtauld Institute of Art in London, which was originally his conception

51. WSC IV, 520. The administration of Palestine and Iraq had lately been transferred from the F.O. and other Departments to the Colonial Office.

52. MS. ENG. HIST., c. 702.

PART V: INDEPENDENCE

Chapter 15 Retirement (1921–1925)

1. Fitzroy, Sir A., op. cit., 743–5.
2. ROB 45, 7 June 1921. Lord Roberts's widow had died at the end of 1920.
3. Wrench, Sir E., *Geoffrey Dawson*, 201.
4. Furse, Sir R., *Aucuparius*, 81. The title meant 'bird-snarer'. But after exhaustive inquiry among Oxford scholars the author of this book had to admit he had failed to establish whether the individual was mythological or mythical.
5. p. 137.
6. M.P. 174.
7. pp. 102, 106.
8. pp. 348.
9. ROSK II, 230–3; Fiddes, Sir G., op. cit. 266–8.
10. M.P. 174. The Conference had not formally ranked as one of the Imperial series.
11. Nicolson, Harold, *Curzon: the Last Phase*, 176–82.
12. M.P. 284.
13. Rose, K., op. cit., 217–18. It aggravates the gaffe that the book was a success, achieving 8 editions.
14. M.P. 231–3; see also Bowle, J., *Viscount Samuel*, chs. 13, 14.
15. CALL II, chs. 34–5.
16. M.P. 174–5.
17. *History of The Times*, II, ch. 20.
18. The Leo Maxse papers are deposited in the West Sussex Record Office, Chichester.
19. Avery, D., op. cit., 270–9, 283–95.
20. M.P. 156–9, 246–9.
21. ROSK II, 347–51.
22. M.P. 160.
23. Mowat, op. cit., 171–4.
24. Davis, H. W. C., *History of Balliol College* (1963 edn.).
25. pp. 353–4.
26. This election had been disfigured by the 'Red Scare' of the so-called Zinoviev letter.
27. M.P. 295, also 287–8.
28. M.P. 95.
29. Rolleston was appointed this year Regius Professor of Physic at Cambridge.
30. Magnus, L., *Herbert Warren of Magdalen*, 33–5.
31. For correspondence from his supporters see M.P. 214. Lord Cave, the Lord Chancellor, was elected to fill Milner's place; after his death three years later, Lord Grey of Fallodon did so.

32. Sir Farquhar Buzzard was Regius Professor of Medicine at Oxford, 1928–43.
33. M.P. 215.

EPILOGUE

1. M.P. 216.
2. M.P. 219.
3. GELL Mil. 2; MS. ENG. HIST. c. 708.
4. Fox, Canon Adam, chapter on 'Abbey's Overseas Visitors' in Carpenter, E. (ed.), *A House of Kings*.
5. MS. ENG. HIST. c. 708; M. COURT 81ff. and *Milner Court Chronicle*.
6. M.P. 183.
7. M.P. 220.
8. MS. ENG. HIST. c. 708.
9. 21 May 1935.
10. p. 232.
11. M.P. 188.
12. Stokes, E., 'Milnerism', *Historical Journal*, V, i, 47–60 (1962).

Select Bibliography

ABBOTT, E. & CAMPBELL, L. *Life & Letters of Benjamin Jowett.* 2 vols 1897.

AMERY, JULIAN. *Joseph Chamberlain.* vols. 4, 5, 6. 1951, 1969. (see also Garvin, J. L.).

AMERY, LEOPOLD C. *My Political Life.* 3 vols. 1953–5.

— (ed) *Times History of War in S. Africa.* 7 vols. 1899–1909.

ASQUITH, HERBERT H. *Memories & Reflections, 1852–1927.* 2 vols. 1928.

ASQUITH, MARGOT. *Autobiography of Margot Asquith.* 2 vols. 1920, 1922.

ASTOR, MICHAEL. *Tribal Feeling.* 1963.

BARNETT, HENRIETTA O. B. *Canon Barnett: his life, work & friends.* 1918.

BEAVERBROOK, LORD. *Decline & Fall of Lloyd George.* 1963.

BELL, E. MOBERLY. *Flora Shaw (Lady Lugard).* 1947.

BELOFF, MAX. *Imperial Sunset,* vol. I. 1969.

BLAKE, ROBERT. *Private Papers of Douglas Haig, 1914–1919.* 1952.

— *The Unknown Prime Minister: the Life & Times of Bonar Law.* 1955.

BLUNT, W. SCAWEN. *My Diaries, I, 1880–1890.* 1922.

BOYD, CHARLES W. (ed.) *Joseph Chamberlain's Speeches.* 2 vols. 1914.

BRAND, ROBERT H. *Union of S. Africa.* 1909.

— *War and Finance,* 1920.

BRODRICK ST. J. *Records & Reactions, 1856–1939.* 1939.

BUCHAN, JOHN. *The African Colony: Studies in Reconstruction.* 1903.

— *Memory Hold the Door.* 1940.

BUTLER, J. R. M. *Lord Lothian, 1882–1940.* 1960.

CALLWELL, SIR C. E. *Field-Marshal Sir Henry Wilson, his life & diaries.* 2 vols. 1927.

Cambridge Hist. of British Empire, Vol. III. Empire – Commonwealth, 1870–1919. 1959. Vol. VIII. S. Africa, Rhodesia & High Commission Territories. 2nd ed. 1963.

CARRINGTON, CHARLES. *Rudyard Kipling.* 1955.

CECIL, LORD DAVID. *The Cecils of Hatfield House.* 1973.

CECIL, LORD EDWARD. *Leisure of an Egyptian Official.* 8th ed. 1941.

CECIL, LADY GWENDOLEN. *Life of Robert, Marquis of Salisbury.* 4 vols. 1921–32

CHAPIN, ADÈLE. *Their Trackless Way.* 1931.

CHAPMAN-HUSTON, DESMOND. *The Lost Historian: memoir of Sir Sidney Low.* 1936.

CHILDERS, ERSKINE (ed.). *Times Hist. of War in S. Africa*, Vol. V, 1907.

CHURCHILL, RANDOLPH S. *Lord Derby, 17th Earl*. 1959.

— *Winston S. Churchill*, Vols. I, II. 1966–7. (See also Gilbert, Martin).

CHURCHILL, WINSTON S. *My Early Life*. 1930.

— *The River War*. 3rd ed. 1933.

COLVIN, IAN. *Life of Jameson*. 2 vols. 1922.

COOK, SIR E. T. *Edmund Garrett, a memoir*. 1909.

— *Rights and Wrongs of the Transvaal War*. 2nd ed. 1902.

CRANKSHAW, EDWARD. *The Forsaken Idea: a study of Viscount Milner*. 1952.

CROMER, EARL OF. *Modern Egypt*. 2 vols. 1908.

— *Abbas II*. 1915.

CURTIS, LIONEL. *Problem of Commonwealth*. 1916.

— *With Milner in S. Africa*. 1951.

CURTIS, L. P., JR. *Coercion & Conciliation in Ireland*. Princeton, U.S.A., 1963.

DAVENPORT, T. R. H. *The Afrikaner Bond*. Cape Town, 1966.

DE KIEWIET, C. W. *Hist. of S. Africa, Social & Economic*. 2nd ed. 1941.

DE WET, CHRISTIAN R. *Three Years War*. 1902.

ELIOT, T. S. *Choice of Kipling's Verse*. 1941.

ELLIOT, ARTHUR R. *Life of G. J. Goschen*. 2 vols. 1911.

ELTON, LORD. (ed.) *First 50 Years of the Rhodes Trust & the Rhodes Scholarships, 1903–1953*. 1955.

EMDEN, PAUL H. *Randlords*. 1935.

FABER, GEOFFREY. *Jowett*. 1957.

FAWCETT, MILLICENT., Concentration Camps Commission Report. Cmd. 893. 1902.

FITZPATRICK, SIR PERCY. *Transvaal From Within*. 1899.

FITZROY, SIR ALMERIC. *Memoirs*. 2 vols. 1925.

FRY, ANNA R. *Emily Hobhouse*. 1929.

GANN, L. H. *Hist. of Southern Rhodesia*. 1965.

GARDINER, A. G. *Sir William Harcourt*. 2 vols. 1923.

GARVIN, J. L. *Life of Joseph Chamberlain*. vols. 1–3. 1932–4.

GELL, EDITH M. (Hon. Mrs). *Under Three Reigns*. 1927.

GELL, PHILIP L. (ed.) Jowett, B. *Essays on Men & Manners*. 1895.

GILBERT, MARTIN. *Winston S. Churchill*. vols. III and IV. 1971, 1975.

GOLDMAN, CHARLES S. (ed.) *The Empire & the Century*. 1905.

GOLLIN, ALFRED M. *'The Observer' & J. L. Garvin, 1908–1914*. 1960.

— *Proconsul in Politics*. 1964.

GOOCH, G. P. *Life of Lord Courtney*. 1920.

GOSCHEN, GEORGE J. *Life & times of G.J.G., Publisher & Printer of Leipzig*. 2 vols. 1903.

— *Political Speeches delivered during general election of 1885*. 1886.

GRENVILLE, J. A. S. *Lord Salisbury & Foreign Policy: the close of the 19th Century*. 1964.

GRIGG, EDWARD W. M. essay on Lord Milner in *The Post-Victorians*. 1933.

HALPÉRIN, VLADIMIR. *Lord Milner & the Empire.* 1952.

HAMILTON, SIR IAN. *Listening for the Drums.* 1944.

HAMMOND, J. L. *Gladstone & the Irish Nation.* 1938.

HANBURY-WILLIAMS, SIR J. *Emperor Nicholas II as I knew him.* 1922.

HANCOCK, SIR W. K. *Smuts, I, The Sanguine Years, 1870–1919.* 1962.

— *II, The Fields of Force, 1919–1950.* 1968.

— *Smuts, study for a portrait.* 1965.

HANKEY, LORD. *The Supreme Command, 1914–1918.* 2 vols. 1961.

— *The Supreme Control at the Paris Peace Conference, 1919, a commentary.* 1963.

HARDINGE OF PENSHURT, HELEN, LADY. *Loyal to Three Kings.* 1967.

HEARNSHAW. F. J. C. *Centenary Hist. of King's College, London.* 1929.

HEWINS, W. A. S. *Apologia of an Imperialist.* 2 vols. 1929.

HICKS BEACH, LADY VICTORIA. *Life of Sir Michael Hicks Beach.* 2 vols. 1932.

HILL, RICHARD. *Slatin Pasha.* 1965.

HILLCOURT, W. *Baden-Powell.* 1964.

HOFMEYR J. H., & REITZ, F. W. *Life of Jan Hendrik Hofmeyr.* Cape Town. 1913.

HOLLAND, BERNARD. *The Eighth Duke of Devonshire.* 2 vols. 1911.

HUTCHINSON, H. G. (ed.). *Private Diaries of Rt. Hon. Sir Algernon West.* 1922.

HYDE, MONTGOMERY. *Carson.* 1953.

IWAN-MÜLLER, E. B. *Lord Milner in S. Africa.* 1902.

JAMES, DAVID. *Lord Roberts.* 1954.

JAMES, R. RHODES. *Rosebery.* 1963.

JONES, THOMAS. *Lloyd George.* 1951.

JUDD, DENIS. *Balfour & the British Empire: a study in Imperial Evolution, 1874–1932.* 1968.

JUTA, M. *The Pace of the Ox: the Life of Paul Kruger.* 1937.

KATKOV, GEORGE. *Russia 1917, the February Revolution.* 1967.

KRUGER, RAYNE. *Good-bye Dolly Gray: the story of the Boer War.* 5th ed. 1964.

LANDES, DAVID S. *Bankers & Pashas: international finance & economic imperialism in Egypt.* 1958.

LANGHORNE, E. *Nancy Astor & her Friends.* 1974.

LAURENCE, SIR PERCIVAL. *Life of John X. Merriman.* 1930.

LEE OF FAREHAM, VISCT. *A Good Innings.* 3 vols. 1939–1940. *ibid.* edited by Clark, A. I vol. 1974.

LIDDELL HART, B. H. *Hist. of 1st World War.* new ed. 1970.

LLOYD GEORGE, DAVID. *War Memoirs.* 6 vols. 1933–6.

— *Truth About the Peace Treaties.* 2 vols. 1938.

LLOYD GEORGE, FRANCES. *The Years That Are Past.* 1967.

LOCKHART, J. G. & WOODHOUSE, C. M. *Rhodes.* 1963.

LOCKHART, ROBERT BRUCE. *Memoirs of a British Agent.* 1932.

LUCAS, SIR CHARLES. *Historical Geography of the British Colonies.* Vol. 4. South & East Africa. 1897.

LUKE, W. B. *Lord Milner.* 1901.

LUTFI AL-SAYYID, A. *Egypt & Cromer: a study in Anglo-Egyptian relations.* 1968.

LYONS, F. S. L. *Ireland since the Famine.* 1971.

LYTTELTON, EDITH. *Alfred Lyttelton.* 1917.

MCCOURT, EDWARD. *Remember Butler: the story of Sir William Butler.* 1967.

MCDOWELL, R. B. *The Irish Administration, 1801–1914.* 1964.

MACKAIL, J. W. & WYNDHAM, GUY. *Life and Letters of George Wyndham.* 2 vols. 1924.

MAGNUS, PHILIP. *Kitchener: portrait of an imperialist.* 1958.

MALCOLM, SIR DOUGAL. *British South Africa Company, 1899–1939.* 1939.

MANSBRIDGE, ALBERT. *Arnold Toynbee.* 1906.

MANSERGH, N. *The Commonwealth Experience.* 1969.

MARAIS, J. S. *Fall of Kruger's Republic.* 1961.

MARJORIBANKS, E. & COLVIN, IAN. *Life of Lord Carson.* 3 vols. 1932–6.

MARKHAM, VIOLET R. *The New Era in South Africa.* 1904.

— *Return Passage.* 1953.

MARLOWE, JOHN. *Anglo-Egyptian Relations, 1800–1953.* 1954.

MARSHALL-CORNWALL, GEN. SIR J. *Haig as Military Commander.* 1973.

MAY, G. H. LE. *British Supremacy in S. Africa, 1899–1907.* 1965.

MAY, H. J. & HAMILTON, I. *The Foster Gang.* 1966.

MILLIN, SARAH GERTRUDE. *Rhodes.* 2nd ed. 1952.

— *The South Africans.* 2nd ed. 1934.

MILLS, J. SAXON. *Life of Sir E. T. Cook.* 1921.

MILNER, VISCOUNTESS. *My Picture Gallery, 1886–1901.* 1951.

MONROE, ELIZABETH. *Britain's Moment in the Middle East, 1914–1956.* 1963.

MONTAGUE, F. C. *Arnold Toynbee.* Baltimore, U.S.A. 1889.

MONTEFIORE, CLAUDE J. *Outlines of Liberal Judaism.* 2nd ed. 1923.

MONTEFIORE, LEONARD. *Essays & Letters.* Privately printed, with memoir, 1881.

NEVINSON, H. W. *Changes & Chances.* 1923.

NEWTON, LORD. *Lord Lansdowne.* 1929.

— *Retrospection.* 1941.

NICOLSON, HAROLD. *Curzon: the Last Phase, 1919–1925.* 1934.

— *Peacemaking, 1919.* new ed. 1944.

NIMOCKS, WALTER. *Milner's Young Men.* 1970.

OLIVER, FREDERIC SCOTT. *Alexander Hamilton.* 1906.

— *What Federalism is not.* 1914.

— *Ordeal by Battle.* 1915.

PAKENHAM, ELIZABETH. *Jameson's Raid.* 1960.

PETRIE, SIR CHARLES. *Life & Letters of Sir Austen Chamberlain.* 2 vols. 1940.

— *Life & Times of Walter Long.* 1936.

PIMLOTT, J. A. R. *Toynbee Hall.* 1935.

PORTER, BERNARD. *Critics of Empire: British Radical Attitudes to Colonialism in Africa, 1895–1914.* 1968.

POUND, R. & HARMSWORTH, G. *Northcliffe.* 1959.

PYRAH, G. B. *Imperial Policy & South Africa, 1902–1910.* 1955.

REITZ, DENEYS. *Commando: a Boer Journal of the Boer War.* 1929.

RIDDELL, LORD. *Lord Riddell's War Diary, 1914–1918.* 1933.

— *Lord Riddell's Intimate Diary of the Peace Conference & After, 1918–1923.* 1934.

ROBERTS, BRIAN. *Cecil Rhodes & the Princess.* 1969.

ROBERTSON, FIELD-MARSHAL SIR W., BT. *From Private to Field-Marshal.* 1921.

ROBINSON, R. & GALLAGHER, J. *Africa & the Victorians: the Official Mind of Imperialism.* 1961.

ROGERS, FREDERICK. *Labour, Life & Literature.* 1913.

ROSE, KENNETH. *Superior Person: a portrait of Curzon & his Circle in Late Victorian England.* 1969.

— *The Later Cecils.* 1975.

ROSE-INNES, SIR JAMES. (ed. Tindell, B.). *An Autobiography.* 1949.

ROSKILL, STEPHEN. *Hankey, Man of Secrets.* 3 vols. 1970–4.

RYAN, A. P. *Lord Northcliffe.* 1953.

SCOTT, J. W. ROBERTSON. *Life & Death of a Newspaper.* 1952.

Selborne Memorandum contained in Cmd. 3564, 1907.

SMITH, COLIN L. *The Embassy of Sir William White at Constantinople, 1886–1891.* 1957.

SMITH, JANET ADAM. *John Buchan.* 1965.

South African Native Affairs Commission, 1903–1905 Report. 5 vols. 1905.

SPENDER, J. A. *Life of Rt. Hon. Sir H. Campbell-Bannerman.* 2 vols. 1923. C.B.

— *Life, Journalism & Politics.* 2 vols. 1927.

SYKES, CHRISTOPHER. *Life of Lady Astor.* 1972.

SYMONS, JULIAN. *Buller's Campaign.* 1963.

SYNGE, BERTHA. *Story of the World at War.* 1926.

TERRAINE, JOHN. *Douglas Haig: The Educated Soldier.* 1963.

THOMPSON, L. M. *Unification of S. Africa, 1902–1910.* 1960.

THORNTON, A. P. *Doctrines of Imperialism.* 1965.

TOYNBEE, ARNOLD. *Progress & Poverty: a criticism of Henry George.* 1883.

— *Lectures on the Industrial Revolution.* 1884, also 1908 ed.

ULLMAN, RICHARD H. *Anglo-Soviet Relations, 1917–1921.* Vol. I. Intervention and the War. Princeton, U.S.A.

VAN DER POEL, JEAN. *Jameson Raid.* 1951.

WALKER, ERIC ANDERSON. *History of Southern Africa.* 3rd ed. 1957.

— *Lord Milner and S. Africa.* 1942.

— *Lord De Villiers & his Times.* 1924.

— *W. P. Schreiner – A South African.* 1937.

War in South Africa, Report of Royal Commission, Cmd. 1789, 1792, 1903.

WARBURTON, A. B. *History of Prince Edward Island.* New Brunswick, 1923.

WHYTE, F. *Life of W. T. Stead.* 2 vols. 1925.

WILKINSON, SPENSER. *Thirty-Five Years, 1874–1909.* 1933.

WILLIAMS, BASIL. biography of Lord Milner in *DNB.*

— *Cecil Rhodes.* 1921.

WILLISON, SIR JOHN. *Sir George Parkin.* 1929.

WILSON, JOHN. *C.B.: a Life of Sir Henry Campbell-Bannerman.* 1973.

WILSON, MONICA & THOMPSON, L. (ed.) *Oxford History of South Africa.* 2 vols. 1969–71.

WILSON, LADY SARAH. *South African Memories.* 1909.

WINGATE, SIR RONALD, BT. *Wingate of the Sudan.* 1955.

WINTERTON, EARL. *Orders of the Day.* 1953.

WORSFOLD, W. BASIL. *Lord Milner's Work in S. Africa from 1897 to 1902.* 1906.

— *The Reconstruction of the New Colonies under Lord Milner.* 2 vols. 1913.

WRENCH, JOHN EVELYN. *Alfred, Lord Milner: the Man of No Illusions.* 1958.

— *Geoffrey Dawson & Our Times.* 1955.

YOUNG, KENNETH. *Arthur James Balfour.* 1963.

Index

McNeill, Ronald (later Lord Cushendun), 375, 378
Macpherson, Ian (later Baron Strathcarron), 302, 304
Macready, General Sir Nevil, 254, 317, 354
Madrid, 250, 376, 380
Mafeking, 144, 203; siege of, 167; relief of, 174
Magersfontein, battle of (1889), 169
Magnus, Sir Philip, 90, 101, 189; on Milner's *England in Egypt*, 108
Majuba Hill, 202
Malcolm, Dougal, 356
Malcolm, John (second cousin), 22, 24, 28; Milner shares London home of, 26, 27; death, 29
Malcolm, Marianne, 22, 23, 24, 31, 42, 44, 53; warm friendship with Milner, 24–5, 26, 33–4, 59; their correspondence, 25, 27, 28, 29, 30, 31, 32, 33, 34, 36, 38, 39, 40, 41, 42, 54, 67; ill-health, 28, 29, 35, 39, 48; money worries, 29, 35–6; shares London lodgings with Milner, 32, 43, 44, 54; as 'very loving sister-cousin', 33; holidays with Milner, 36, 39; failure of stay in Oxford, 41, 48; drink problem, 48; Milner ceases to share home with, 54; death, 59; memorial window to, 120
Mallon, J., 356
Malvern College, 23, 24
Man, Isle of, 20, 25
Manchester, 334
Manchester Guardian, 320, 325
Manchester Square (No. 14), Marylebone, Milner's London home after marriage, 368, 371, 373, 375, 382, 385, 386
mandates, 336, 347, 350, 375
Mandates Commission, 350; Milner as chairman, 337, 338, 339
Mangin, General Charles, 310
Manning, Henry Edward, Cardinal, 36
manpower problem, 263–4, 266, 279, 282, 291, 292, 302, 303–4, 309, 314–15
Mansergh, N., 143
Marais, J. S., 143, 146, 153, 154
Marathon, 96
Maritzburg, 169
Markham, Violet, 161, 228, 279
Marlow, 115
Marne battles: (1914) 258; (1918) 309, 310–11
Marriott, Sir John, 253, 260, 385
Mary, Queen, 249, 311, 321, 345, 356, 363, 376, 380
Massey, Vincent, 249, 353
Massey, W. F., 369
Matheson, Percy, 75, 94, 107, 112, 228, 363, 386

Maude, F., 63
Maurice, General Sir Frederick, 299; and figures of Army strength, 302, 303–4
Max of Baden, Prince, 319
Maxse, Cecilia (mother of Lady Milner), 295, 370, 390
Maxse, Katharine (Kitty), 374
Maxse, Leo, 374, 376, 387, 389
Maxse, Olive, 365, 384, 387, 390
Maxwell, General Sir John, 345
Mayor, Rev. J. B., Professor of Classics at King's College, London, 26, 27, 29, 30, 46
Meighen, Arthur, 370
Memory-Hold-the-Door (Buchan), 341
Merriman, John Xavier, 151, 156
Methuen, Lord, 169, 193
Michell, Sir Lewis, 269, 290
Middleburg Peace Talks (1901), 184
Midland Bank, 367
Migration Conference (1921), 359
Military Service Act: (1916) 266; (1918), 298, 302
Millin, Sarah Gertrude, 192
Milner, Alfred, Viscount: birth and ancestry, 19–21; boyhood in Germany, 21–2; in London, 22–3; education, 23–4, 26–43; return to Germany, 23–6; death of mother, 25; at King's College, London, 26–9; holidays in Germany, 27–8, 34, 37, 40, 43, 46, 77, 96, 213, 244; at Oxford, 30, 31–43; and gospel of hard work, 31, 33, 35, 36, 49, 74, 112; takes pupils, 34, 37, 43, 48; help for friends and relatives, 35–6, 39, 47, 48, 59, 75–7, 112, 115, 120, 242, 247, 313, 389; Liberalism, 40, 51, 58; devotion to Empire, 40, 51, 52, 56, 81, 83, 114, 393, 395; reads for Bar, 42, 43, 44; in Toynbee circle, 44–6, 52; interest in social questions, 46, 47, 50, 51, 53, 56–7, 112; called to Bar, 48; freelance journalism, 48; gives up Bar, 49–50; absorption and concentration, 49, 72, 73; lectures on 'Socialism', 50, 53; journalistic career, 50–1, 53, 54, 55–6, 60; death of father, 52; Normandy visits, 52–3, 84; unsuccessful bid for Parliament, 54, 58, 59, 60–2; social and political progress, 55, 63–9, 74–80, 112–15; opposes Home Rule, 62, 64–5, 78, 113; and creation of Liberal Unionist Association, 63–5; Irish holiday, 66–7; at Treasury, 70–86; refuses Private Secretaryship to Viceroy of India, 73–4, 75; social diversions, 74–8, 80, 98–9, 112–15, 119, 120; decides on celibacy, 80, 102; plan to visit South Africa, 81, 82–4; his view of Imperialism, 83, 92–3, 393, 396;